HENRY DAN PIPER

F. Scott Fitzgerald
A Critical Portrait

FₛF

Carbondale and Edwardsville

SOUTHERN ILLINOIS UNIVERSITY PRESS

FEFFER & SIMONS, INC.

London and Amsterdam

09671

Excerpts from the following works by F. Scott Fitzgerald and others are used by permission of
Charles Scribner's Sons:
FITZGERALD, F. SCOTT *Afternoon of An Author* (Copyright © 1957 Frances Scott Fitzgerald
Lanahan), *The Beautiful and Damned* (Copyright 1922 Charles Scribner's Sons; renewal
copyright 1950 Frances Scott Fitzgerald Lanahan), *The Great Gatsby* (Copyright 1925
Charles Scribner's Sons; renewal copyright 1953 Frances Scott Fitzgerald Lanahan), *The
Last Tycoon* (Copyright 1941 Charles Scribner's Sons), *The Stories of F. Scott Fitzgerald,*
edited by Malcolm Cowley (Copyright 1951 Charles Scribner's Sons), *This Side of Paradise*
(Copyright 1920 Charles Scribner's Sons; renewal copyright 1948 Zelda Fitzgerald), *Tender Is
the Night* (Copyright 1934 Charles Scribner's Sons; renewal copyright © 1962 Frances Scott
Fitzgerald Lanahan) and "The Vegetable" (Copyright 1923 Charles Scribner's Sons; renewal
copyright 1951 Frances Scott Fitzgerald Lanahan).
FITZGERALD, ZELDA *Save Me The Waltz* (Copyright 1932 Charles Scribner's Sons; renewal
copyright © 1960 Frances Scott Fitzgerald Lanahan).
HEMINGWAY, ERNEST "The Snows of Kilimanjaro" (Copyright 1936 Ernest Hemingway; re-
newal copyright © 1964 Mary Hemingway)
JAMES, HENRY Prefaces to *The American, The Reverberator, A Passionate Pilgrim and Other
Tales* (Copyright 1907, 1908 Charles Scribner's Sons; renewal copyright 1935, 1936 Henry
James), from *The Art of The Novel,* The Critical Prefaces of Henry James.
WHEELOCK, JOHN HALL, (Ed.) *Editor to Author The Letters of Maxwell E. Perkins* (Copy-
right 1950 Charles Scribner's Sons).

Acknowledgment is also made to Charles Scribner's Sons for permission to quote from unpublished letters written by Maxwell E. Perkins to F. Scott Fitzgerald and Ring Lardner, and
to New Directions for permission to quote from *The Crack-Up* by F. Scott Fitzgerald, edited
by Edmund Wilson (copyright 1945 by New Directions).

Designer: Ernst Reichl

Printed in the United States of America

This book
is for
my mother

Foreword

In recent years such perceptive critics as Edmund Wilson and Cyril Connolly have expressed alarm over the way Scott Fitzgerald, during the quarter century since his death, has been transformed into a kind of twentieth-century culture hero—"a martyr, a sacrificial victim," according to Mr. Wilson, "a semi-divine personality." Actually this process of mythicizing began long before Fitzgerald died. As far back as 1922, at the start of his public career, we find him complaining to Robert Bridges, the editor of Scribner's, "Any strange happening in the new literary generation is at once attributed to me—when we returned from Europe last summer there were legends enough current to supply three biographers."[1]

By 1927 Gilbert Seldes, writing in *The Saturday Evening Post*, could refer casually to "the epic of Fitzgerald," confident that most of his readers needed no further explanation. According to Seldes, the Fitzgeralds—Scott and Zelda—were not only an established part of the national folklore but "authentic legends in the life of France" as well.[2]

It was typical of the Twenties that it exaggerated. Still, Scott Fitzgerald's life had indeed a legendary quality—for which he himself was in part responsible. It was characteristic that, as a small boy, he should decide he was not the son of his parents. Instead, as he went around earnestly telling the neighbors, he had been found on the Fitzgerald doorstep one morning wrapped up in a blanket, to which was pinned a piece of paper emblazoned with the name of the royal House of Stuart!

Yet the legends that grew up around him were not always of his own contriving. As some people are accident-prone, he was "legend-prone." When the lighting system accidentally short-circuited during a performance of his play, "Assorted Spirits," at the White Bear Yacht Club near St. Paul, Minnesota, the seventeen-year-old author, director, and starring actor, characteristically leaped to the front of the stage and entertained the audience with an improvised comic monologue until the damage was repaired. Next morning Fitzgerald's feat was headlined on the society pages of the St. Paul newspapers.[3]

From the boyhood dream that he was a lost prince to his undergraduate resolution to become one of the richest and most famous American authors, Fitzgerald was committed to a romantic destiny. For a while he succeeded in living up to that destiny so spectacularly that the myth of his early success overshadowed his more solid and mature literary achievement. Many admirers of his later work, impatient with the legend, have tried to come to terms with his fiction without taking sufficient account of the way in which the facts of his life continually illuminate the nature of his craft. Fitzgerald's art was so personal that it cannot safely be divorced from his life. He himself was unwilling to make such a separation. As he once wrote Max Perkins, his editor at Scribner's, "I cannot dissociate a man from his work."[4]

The purpose of this book is to separate myth from fact and to tell the story of Fitzgerald's life as a writer more fully than it has been told before. There are, as Arthur Mizener pointed out in his excellent biography of Fitzgerald, three legitimate centers of interest for the study of an author: the man, his writings, and his relation to his time. One of the several virtues of Mr. Mizener's book is the balanced treatment he has given all three. More recently, in another well-drawn biographical portrait, Andrew Turnbull has centered his attention almost exclusively on Fitzgerald the man. By focussing instead on Fitzgerald's career as a writer and artist, I have deliberately narrowed my scope. I have not attempted to write another biography. I have chosen instead to tell how he became a writer—how, especially, he went about writing those two or three novels and the dozen or so short stories that, more than anything else, justify the continuing passionate interest in his career.

In telling it I have tried not only to shed new light on his work but also to add significantly to our knowledge of the situation of the young professional writer of fiction in this country during the years between the two world wars. Fitzgerald was one of the few writers of his generation who believed—seriously believed—that he could combine a career as a high-priced magazine author with one as an experimental artist. He chose to do so deliberately in 1920 at the age of twenty-three, and for a while he succeeded. What that success cost him is another of the things I have tried to make clear.

Writing this book would have been impossible without the help of a great many people. I am especially grateful for the encouragement of four individuals: the late Maxwell E. Perkins, Fitzgerald's editor at Scribner's and his greatest friend, and the first person with whom I discussed my plans; Fitzgerald's daughter, Mrs. Samuel J. Lanahan, who generously gave me access to her parents' papers and allowed me to quote from them, and who read my manuscript; the late Harold Ober, Fitzgerald's literary agent and long-time friend, who opened his files to me and read and criticized my manuscript; and Arthur Mizener, Fitzgerald's biographer.

I am indebted to Mr. Charles Scribner, president of Charles Scribner's Sons, for his kindness in giving me access to his firm's correspondence files and for permission to quote from those works by Scott and Zelda Fitzgerald for which his firm retains the copyrights; to his assistant, Miss Elizabeth Youngstrom, and the editorial staff of Scribner's, for many courtesies; and to Miss Anne Louise Davis of Harold Ober Associates who, after Mr. Ober's death, helped me in innumerable ways and arranged for permission to quote from the Ober correspondence as well as from the portion of Fitzgerald's work which Ober Associates control as agent for the Fitzgerald estate.

I am also indebted to the following individuals: Fitzgerald's widow, the late Zelda Sayre Fitzgerald; her mother, the late Mrs. Anthony Dickinson Sayre; Judge John Biggs, Jr., Fitzgerald's college roommate and literary executor; the late Mr. C.N.B. Wheeler, former headmaster of St. Paul Academy, St. Paul, Minnesota; his successor, Mr. John De Q. Briggs; and especially Mr. Edward Read, the school's present headmaster; Mr. Edmund Wilson, for permission to quote from his letters and published writings; the late Mr. John Lardner, for permission to quote from the unpublished letters of his father, Ring Lardner; Mrs. Maxwell E. Perkins, for permission to quote from her husband's unpublished correspondence (with the permission, also, of the Scribner firm); Mrs. Richardson Bronson, for permission to quote from John Peale Bishop's letters to Fitzgerald.

For permission to quote from their letters to Fitzgerald, or to myself, I am also indebted to Mrs. Gordon R. Jameson, Mrs. Herbert Lewis, Mr.

Charles Donahoe, Sir Shane Leslie, Mr. Charles M. Warren, Mr. Kenneth
Littauer, and certain others who prefer to remain anonymous.

For interviews, replies to queries, and other courtesies I am also
indebted to the late Mr. H.L. Mencken, the late Mr. Joseph Herge-
sheimer, the late Mrs. Maurice Flynn, the late Reverend Thomas
Delihant, S.J., the late Professors Frank MacDonald and Gordon Hall
Gerould of the English Department, Princeton University; Mr. John
O'Hara; Mrs. Margaret Culkin Banning; Mr. Thornton Wilder; Mr.
Edward Everett Horton; Professor Gregg Dougherty of the Chemistry
Department, Princeton University; Mr. C. Lawton Campbell; Mrs. W.
Blair Flandrau; Mr. Devereux Josephs; Mrs. William K. Pirie; Mr.
Arnold Gingrich, editor of *Esquire* Magazine; Mr. Day Edgar, of *The
Saturday Evening Post;* Mr. Michael Fisher; Miss Sheilah Graham; Mr.
Philip Fitzpatrick; Miss Adelaide Rogers, Montgomery, Alabama; the
late Mr. Van Wyck Brooks; and Mr. Thoburn Snyder, M.D., for his con-
versations with me about the psychiatric background of *Tender Is the
Night.*

I owe a particular debt of gratitude to Mr. Alexander Clark, Curator
of Special Collections in the Firestone Library, Princeton University, and
to his associates, Mr. Alexander Wainwright and Miss Julie Hudson. I am
indebted to Miss Marion Green, of the Montgomery (Alabama) Public
Library; Mrs. Marie Bankhead Owen, Director of the Alabama State
Department of Archives and History; Miss Mary Isabel Fry and the
staff of the Henry E. Huntington Memorial Library and Art Gallery,
San Marino, California; and to Harry T. Moore, Matthew J. Bruccoli,
and my wife, Roberta, who read my book in manuscript, caught numerous errors, and made many helpful suggestions.

For personal encouragement and advice I am grateful to Professors
Sculley Bradley and Robert Spiller of the University of Pennsylvania
and Professor Willard Thorp of Princeton. I am indebted to the University of Pennsylvania for the Harrison Fellowship that made it possible
for me to begin this book, and to the John Simon Guggenheim Memorial
Foundation for the Guggenheim Fellowship, and the California Institute
of Technology for the concurrent leave of absence that enabled me to
finish it. I am also indebted to the students of the *section d'anglais* at
the University of Lille for the privilege of discussing with them many
of the ideas I have presented here, when we read and studied Fitzgerald's fiction together during a Fulbright year teaching in France.

Portions of this book, in somewhat different form, have appeared in
the *American Quarterly,* the *Huntington Library Quarterly,* the *Prince-*

ton University Library Chronicle, and *The Great Gatsby: A Study,*
edited by Frederick J. Hoffman, Charles Scribner's Sons, New York,
1962.

Carbondale, Illinois   H.D.P.
January 1, 1965

Contents

Errata

PAGE 87, LINE 31: *For* that new he felt *read* that now he felt

PAGE 116, LINES 16–17: *For* the jurors. For this Fallon was subsequently convicted and imprisoned, disgraced for life. *read* the jurors—an allegation which resulted in Fallon's subsequent indictment and imprisonment.

PAGE 218, LINE 11: *For* "raised his hand *read* "raised his right hand

PAGE 249, LINE 10: *For* only thirty-six years old *read* thirty-seven years old

PAGE 264, LINE 36: *For* and the cohorts *read* and the minions

PAGE 292, LINES 13–14: *For* "The 42nd Parallel. *read* "The 42nd Parallel."

PAGE 299, LINES 29–30: *For* Absolom! Absolom! *read* Absalom, Absalom!

PAGE 299, LINE 31: *For* 1939 *read* 1940

F. SCOTT FITZGERALD
A Critical Portrait

Alone

From childhood's hour I have not been
As others were—I have not seen
As others saw—I could not bring
My passions from a common spring—
From the same source I have not taken
My sorrow—I could not awaken
My heart to joy at the same tone—
And all I lov'd—*I* lov'd alone—
Thou—in my childhood—in the dawn
Of a most stormy life—was drawn
From ev'ry depth of good & ill
The mystery which binds me still—
From the torrent, or the fountain—
From the red cliff of the mountain—
From the sun that round me roll'd
In its autumn tint of gold—
From the lightning in the sky
As it pass'd me flying by—
From the thunder & the storm—
And the cloud that took the form
(When the rest of Heaven was blue)
Of a demon in my view—

Edgar Allan Poe

I
Demon in
View

Late one January evening in the year 1910, a slender, yellow-haired boy of thirteen, who should have been asleep hours ago, was busily writing on the blue-lined pages of his school composition book. Outside, a wintry wind stormed along the streets of St. Paul, Minnesota, and past the unpretentious Fitzgerald residence at 514 Holly Avenue. But to Scott Fitzgerald, immersed in writing "Reade, Substitute Right Half" for his school magazine, the windy clamor sounded more like the distant roar of a football crowd on a sunny autumn afternoon.[1]

"Hold! Hold! Hold!" The slogan thundered up the field to where the battered, crimson warriors trotted wearily into their places again. The blues' attack this time came straight at center and was good for a gain of seven yards. "Second down, three," yelled the referee, and again the attack came straight at center. This time there was no withstanding the rush and the huge Hilton full-back crushed through the crimson line again and again and shaking off his many tacklers, staggered on toward the Warrentown goal.

Finally, in desperation, the Warrentown coach sent in young Reade, the smallest and greenest halfback on the bench. At once the tide turned. Time and time again Reade slipped through the Hilton line, racing seventy yards in the final minute of play to score the winning touchdown. The story ended with the cheers of the admiring crowd ringing in his ears: "Reade! Reade! Reade!"

Several months earlier the story's thirteen-year-old author had tried out for a place on his class football team. "A light haired stripling," much like his hero, Fitzgerald had been too light and fragile to make any kind of a showing. In one practice scrimmage his fumble had resulted in a touchdown for the other side; another time he had cracked a rib and was carried off the field. But out of such defeated dreams of success he wove "Reade, Substitute Right Half," the best of the seven short stories that he published in various school magazines before he was seventeen years old. "Reade" stands apart from these other schoolboy pieces because Fitzgerald had lived it so intensely that every word mattered. Here, at the age of thirteen, his work was already stamped with the mark that would continue to distinguish it for the rest of his life. To write well, he was obliged to come to terms with some rankling injury or disappointment to which he could reconcile himself in no other way. "You especially have to be hurt like hell before you can write seriously," Ernest Hemingway would later tell him. ". . . When you get the damned hurt [,] use it—don't cheat with it. Be as faithful to it as a scientist. . . ."[2]

Even at thirteen, Fitzgerald was already so accustomed to sublimating his troubles in stories that he regarded himself as an "inveterate author." Instead of doing his homework, he sat up till all hours of the night, secretly reading or writing, with the result that his record at St. Paul Academy, the private country day school where he was enrolled in the third form (ninth grade), was a shambles. During classes he scribbled in the backs of his "geography and first year Latin [books] and on the margins of themes and declensions and mathematics problems." Later, looking back at his childhood, he felt that there had never been a time when he had not wanted to write more than any other thing. ". . . Three months before I was born," he said, "my mother lost her other two children. . . . I think I started then to be a writer."[3]

It was characteristic that he associated his literary beginnings with his parents, Edward and Molly Fitzgerald. At the age of nine Scott had gone around telling the neighborhood that he had been found on the Fitzgerald doorstep wrapped in a blanket to which was pinned a note bearing the regal name of "Stuart." Like Goethe, Byron, and many another gifted son of undistinguished parents, he believed he was of royal descent and that in some mysterious way he had been dispossessed of his rightful heritage. "That is where I buried my first childish love of myself," he would later say, "my belief that I would never die like other people, and that I wasn't the son of my parents but a son of a king, a king who ruled the whole world."[4]

His relationship with his parents was to become a recurrent theme in his fiction. From Molly McQuillan he inherited his energy and his single-minded pursuit of success. His father, on the other hand, was a failure—the sensitive, cultivated offspring of a genteel Maryland family who married into the wealthy McQuillan family and then retired on his laurels. Between them, Fitzgerald's mother and father represented two contrary points of view; and their son's fiction can be seen as an effort to resolve the conflict implicit in his ambivalent McQuillan-Fitzgerald heritage.

The McQuillan point of view was dramatically illustrated by the career of Grandfather Philip F. McQuillan—a shining example of the American success story. Born in County Fermanagh, Ireland, he came to this country with his parents in 1842, when he was eight. The family eventually settled in Galena, Illinois. When he was twenty-three, young McQuillan left home for the frontier settlement of St. Paul, Minnesota. It was not the best time to strike out on one's own; in 1857 the nation was suffering one of the worst depressions in its history. But McQuillan, with characteristic vigor, found a job in a grocery store and two years later was running a store of his own.

Thereafter, his star rose like a rocket. In 1860, he returned to Galena to marry Louisa Allen, his childhood sweetheart. His business prospered so that in 1862, and again in 1869, he moved to larger premises. In 1872 he merged with a former employer to form the wholesale grocery firm of McQuillan, Beaupré and Co. Several years later the firm moved again, this time to an imposing new building on the corner of Third and Wabash streets. The largest building in the city, dominating the skyline, it belonged to Mr. McQuillan and was known locally as "The McQuillan Block."[5]

By this time Grandfather McQuillan was respected as one of the most up-and-coming young businessmen in St. Paul. He owned an ornate Victorian mansion, kept a stable of blooded horses and a prize pack of hounds; and McQuillan, Beaupré and Co. was reportedly grossing over a million dollars a year. Among his friends was James J. Hill, who was to become the greatest railroad tycoon in the Middle West, a millionaire many times over.

But not Grandfather McQuillan, who died suddenly in April, 1877, at the age of forty-three. His sudden death only underscored the legendary quality of his success. He was the perfect exemplar of the self-made businessman—a fact recognized by one newspaper obituary which praised him especially for his "clear head, sound judgment, good habits, strict honesty and willing hands." (His grandson, Scott, preserved this yellowed clipping in his scrapbook.)[6]

After deductions had been made for Philip McQuillan's many bequests to his church and various charities, his estate, much of it in real estate, amounted to almost a half-million dollars—more than enough to provide comfortably for his widow and five children. Although she continued to regard St. Paul as her home, Mrs. McQuillan traveled extensively, often wintering in Washington, D.C., where she had many acquaintances. It was here, in her residence at 1315 N Street, that her youngest daughter Mary—"Molly" as she was usually called—married Edward Fitzgerald in February, 1890. Although he was employed in St. Paul at the time of his marriage, Edward Fitzgerald was even more at home in Washington than were the McQuillans, having been born in 1853 in what he called his "grandfather's great-grandfather's house" in Montgomery County, Maryland, just across the District of Columbia line.[7]

It is difficult to think of two more contrasting personalities than those of Molly McQuillan and Edward Fitzgerald. Although his youngest daughter had not inherited Philip McQuillan's good looks, she had his zest and vitality. Molly was the only McQuillan who got any fun out of life, according to her brother Edward. But where she and her father lived in the present and the beckoning future, her husband, like Miniver Cheevy, preferred the more romantic past. The Fitzgeralds could trace their distinguished lineage back through Irish history to the ancient Geraldini clan of Tuscan Italy. In the fifteenth century, an Earl Fitzgerald had ruled all of Ireland. Two centuries later, a Fitzgerald migrated to the Catholic colony of Maryland where his descendants remained for several generations. Edward Fitzgerald liked to say that he was the first of his family to reside outside the borders of his native state. His father, Captain Michael Fitzgerald, had married Cecilia Ashton Scott, the daughter of Judge John Scott of Baltimore and Eliza Key of the distinguished Maryland Key family. One of his mother's second cousins had been Francis Scott Key, author of "The Star Spangled Banner"; and an aunt, Key's sister, was the wife of Roger Brooke Taney, Secretary of the Treasury under Andrew Jackson and, later, Chief Justice of the Supreme Court. (Justice Taney's pro-slavery decision in the Dred Scott case, in 1857, is often cited as one of the causes of the Civil War.)[8]

Another of Edward Fitzgerald's relatives, Mrs. Mary Surratt, was hanged after the Civil War (unjustly, according to some historians) as an alleged accomplice of John Wilkes Booth in the assassination of President Lincoln. Although Edward Fitzgerald was a child when the war broke out, he was a loyal rebel, and later remembered excitedly watching Early's Confederate guerrillas gather on the banks of the

Potomac for their ill-fated raid on the city of Washington. The defeat of the South was a blow from which he never fully recovered. "When he was twelve," his son later wrote, "he felt that life was finished for him." So, some years later, after a short stint at Georgetown University, he went west in search of his fortune.[9]

He found it in St. Paul, in the person of Molly McQuillan. For several years their marriage went serenely. After a leisurely honeymoon tour of Europe, they returned to Minnesota where Edward managed a furniture factory. But the business failed in the depression of 1893, and he was obliged to take a job as a traveling salesman for Procter & Gamble. For the next fifteen years, the Fitzgeralds moved from one sales district to another—from Syracuse to Buffalo and back to Syracuse again. Molly was in St. Paul visiting her mother in the mansion Grandmother McQuillan had just built on fashionable Summit Avenue, when her third child and only son, Francis Scott Key Fitzgerald, was born on September 24, 1896. Two baby daughters had died previously and a third girl, born in 1900, died soon after birth. The fourth girl, Annabel, born in 1901, survived.[10]

Fitzgerald's memories of early childhood were haunted by a series of dreary hotels, flats, and semidetached houses. Inevitably, he contrasted them with the solid grandeur of the Summit Avenue mansion, where he frequently visited. Finally, in 1908, Mr. Fitzgerald was fired from his job as a soap salesman, and the family packed up and moved back to St. Paul for good. Here they lived in a succession of modest houses in the neighborhood of Summit Avenue, on McQuillan money, until Grandmother McQuillan's death in 1913 provided them with a small independent income.[11]

So far as Summit Avenue was concerned, Molly McQuillan's marriage had been a mistake. The McQuillans generously paid for the Fitzgerald children's private school education, but made no secret of their opinion of a husband unable to support his wife and children. Furthermore, everyone knew that Edward Fitzgerald drank more than was good for him. The result was a continuing family quarrel that puzzled and finally exasperated their small observant son. "I am half black Irish and half old American stock with the usual exaggerated ancestral pretensions," Fitzgerald later wrote John O'Hara. "The black Irish half of the family had the money and looked down upon the Maryland side of the family who had, and really had, that certain series of reticences and obligations that go under the poor old shattered word 'breeding' (modern form 'inhibitions'). So being born in that atmosphere of crack, wisecrack and countercrack I developed a two-cylinder inferiority complex."[12]

The death of three children, and her husband's failure to earn a respectable living, combined to center Molly's dreams more and more on her talented, handsome son. As she grew older, she became increasingly eccentric and possessive, and so never really succeeded in winning Scott's friendship or respect. She perennially worried that he would succumb to a chronic family weakness toward tuberculosis, a fear that was justified, as things turned out. He was so bundled up in hats, coats, and overshoes that he developed a lifelong hatred of protective clothing of any kind. And, on the pretext of his delicate health, Molly let him stay home from school whenever he felt like it—which was often. She also encouraged his tendency to show off in public. Nothing pleased her better than to have her five-year-old son perform for the neighbors in the front parlor, reciting poems he had memorized or singing popular ballads. "God!" he would one day write in the margin of his autobiographical account of his childhood, jabbing his pen angrily through the page at this humiliating memory.[13]

Because she taught him no self-discipline or routine study habits, young Scott was often in trouble at school with his teachers and his classmates. "At 11 and 12 and thereabouts," according to one contemporary, "Scott was handsome but we thought him a sissy; he was afraid of a dead cat in the alley . . . [and] just didn't fit at all into the 'gang' one way or another." Later, he not only resented his mother but felt embarrassed by her. "Dressed like the devil, always coming apart," one of his schoolteachers has described her. A neighbor's child remembered her as "a pathetic, wispy little woman. People were cruel to her and Scott was ashamed of her."[14]

Molly, on her side, was unsympathetic toward her son's literary ambitions. She lined up with the rest of the McQuillans in trying to discourage his writing and, until her death in 1936, took very little interest in his career as an author. She burned most of his schoolboy manuscripts, and in 1933 Fitzgerald noted in a characteristic letter, after having let her read the manuscript of *Tender Is the Night,* "My mother wasn't interested, so it must have *some* merit." Her ambitions for him were for a successful career in business, like her father's, or in a profession like that of the regular army. Nevertheless, Scott inherited her vitality and her stubborn determination to succeed. Like her, too, he was greatly influenced by the example of Grandfather McQuillan, whom he had never known, but whom he strikingly resembled in looks and natural charm. There is a portrait of Philip McQuillan as a young man that could almost pass for his famous grandson. There were also remarkable similarities between their two careers. Both were remarkably successful as young men, and both died in their early forties.[15]

Fitzgerald's relationship with his father was more complicated than that with his mother, and it changed more as he grew older. On the one hand, he was embarrassed by his father's drinking and his failure to hold his own in St. Paul. Scott never forgot the afternoon in Buffalo when Mr. Fitzgerald came into the back yard drunk and insisted on joining his son and some other children in a baseball game. Soon after this Mr. Fitzgerald was fired from his job—another memory that haunted his son for the rest of his life. "That morning he had gone out a comparatively young man, a man full of strength, full of confidence. He came home that evening an old man, a completely broken man. He had lost his essential drive, his immaculateness of purpose. He was a failure the rest of his days."[16]

On the other hand, it was father who taught him to love literature, who introduced him to poetry, and who read aloud Poe's "The Raven" and "The Bells," and Byron's "The Prisoner of Chillon." It was his father, too, who backed him against the McQuillans in his desire to become an author. Once, after Scott played badly during a football game, he sought to right himself with his classmates by writing a poem in praise of football which was published in the school paper. To his son's great delight, Mr. Fitzgerald told him he was more pleased by the poem than if Scott had won the game.[17]

Fitzgerald owed to his father his romantic love of the past as well as a lifelong fascination with lost causes. Edward Fitzgerald was proud of his family traditions. His great-grandfather, Philip Barton Key, was one of the most romantic figures in Maryland history. The son of a prosperous eighteenth-century Maryland planter, Key had been sent off to England as a young man in the 1770's to acquire a gentleman's education. After studying at the University of Edinburgh and reading law in the Middle Temple, he had volunteered as a loyalist in His Majesty's army when the Colonies rebelled. Although the rest of his family supported the American cause, Philip Key fought with the British troops, was wounded and finally discharged with a commission and pension. He had been outlawed by the Maryland legislature, but at the war's end he petitioned for and received a pardon, returned to his native state, married a daughter of the governor, set up a prosperous law practice, and was elected to Congress! A haughty Tory and one of the most eminent members of the Maryland bar, he became a power in the Federal Party, and, after retiring from Congress, opened a law office in Washington, where he successfully specialized in cases before the Supreme Court. He had few equals as an attorney; it was said that he once held an Annapolis court-room spellbound while he extemporaneously declaimed his plea in rhymed couplets—and won the case. His nephew, the more celebrated Francis Scott Key, was also an accomplished rhymster and a prosperous member of his uncle's law firm. "Woodley," Philip Barton Key's hand-some home near Washington, served for many summers as the vacation home of a succession of American Presidents and until recently was the residence of the late Henry L. Stimson, former Secretary of State and of War.[18]

Edward Fitzgerald loved to tell his son stories of the Fitzgerald and Key families, and of his own adventures as a boy rowing Confederate spies across the Potomac at night. One of these yarns his son later made into the magazine story, "End of Hate." No wonder that young Scott also associated himself with lost causes and the "Stuart" tradition, or that he would one day say, "There has never been an American tragedy. There have only been great failures. That is why the story of Aaron Burr—let alone that of Jefferson Davis—opens up things that we who accept the United States as an established unit hardly dare think about." Although Fitzgerald himself was determined to be a success, his imagi-nation responded more sympathetically to a tale of failure. As a child, one of his most moving experiences had been listening to a story read from a nursery book that filled him with "the saddest and most yearning emotion. I have never been able to trace it since. It was about a fight that the large animals, like the elephant, had with the small animals, like the fox. The small animals won the first battle, but the elephants and lions and tigers finally overcame them. The author was prejudiced in favor of the large animals, but my sentiment was all with the small ones. I wonder if even then I had a sense of the wearing-down power of big, respectable people. I can almost weep now when I think of that poor fox, the leader—the fox has somehow typified innocence to me ever since."[19]

The differing attitudes of Molly and Edward Fitzgerald toward their only son are seen in an exchange of letters during the summer of 1907, when ten-year-old Scott went away to camp for the first time. After a few days he was homesick and, as he wrote home, "desperately unpopular." Mrs. Fitzgerald's characteristic response was to volunteer to come out to a hotel at a resort near the camp, where she would be close to him. In his reply, however, Scott firmly and tactfully discouraged this sugges-tion. His father, on the other hand, sent him a copy of St. Nicholas magazine and a dollar bill, together with the advice that he "spend it liberally, generously, carefully, judiciously, sensibly. Get from it pleasure, wisdom, health, experience." It is too bad that more letters from Mr. Fitzgerald to his son have not been preserved.[20]

As a child growing up in St. Paul, Scott accepted the prevailing judgment of his father as a failure. But gradually, as he began to think for himself, he questioned Summit Avenue's opinion of Mr. Fitzgerald. The first short story that he published after going away to college was an attempt to understand a hero who resembles his father. It was called "Shadow Laurels" and was published in the *Nassau Literary Magazine* at Princeton when Fitzgerald was eighteen. Like "Reade, Substitute Right Half," it stands apart from his other early work not only because of its autobiographical background, but also because of its force and vitality. It is the story of a young American, "his manner . . . that of a man accustomed only to success," who has come to Paris in search of his lost father. In a Left Bank café, he hears that his father is dead. Even worse, he learns that his father died disgracefully in a drunken brawl. But when the humiliated son angrily criticizes his father's conduct, he is reproved by a bystander, who says that he had been one of the father's drinking companions. "He was a wonderful talker," the stranger tells the unhappy son. ". . . He knew everything . . . he used to tell me poetry . . . [of] roses and the ivory towers of Babylon and . . . 'the silent chords that flow from the ocean to the moon.' That's why he made no money. He was bright and clever. . . . Don't you see, he stood for us as well as himself . . . how shall I say it?—he expressed us. . . . It was everything to me."[21]

Soon after Mr. Fitzgerald's death in 1931, his son tried to write an essay about him, "The Death of My Father." But he could not finish and tore it up in despair. Luckily, the scraps were saved, and in this fragmentary manuscript he said, "I loved my father—always deep in my subconscious I have referred judgments back to him, [to] what he would have thought or done. He loved me—and felt a deep responsibility for me—I was born several months after the sudden death of my two elder sisters and he felt what the effect of this would be on my mother, that he would be my only moral guide. He became that to the best of his ability. He came from tired old stock with very little left of vitality and mental energy but he managed to raise a little for me. We walked downtown in the summer to have our shoes shined, me in my sailor suit and father in his always beautifully cut clothes, and he told me the few things I ever learned about life until a few years later from a Catholic priest, Monsignor Fay."[22]

In both *The Great Gatsby* and *Tender Is the Night*, Fitzgerald turned to the image of Mr. Fitzgerald as a kind of moral touchstone. Nick Carraway, the narrator of *Gatsby*, is indebted to his father for his ability to sympathize with Jay Gatsby, the hero, as well as for the capacity for judgment that saves him from making almost as much of a fool of himself as Gatsby. "In my younger and more vulnerable years," Nick says at the start of his story, "my father gave me some advice that I've been turning over in my mind ever since. 'Whenever you feel like criticizing any one,' he told me, 'just remember that all the people in this world haven't had the advantages that you've had.' He didn't say any more, but we've always been unusually communicative in a reserved way, and I understood that he meant a great deal more than that. In consequence, I'm inclined to reserve all judgments. . . ."[23]

Tender Is the Night, Fitzgerald's next novel, was not completed until 1934, and by then Edward Fitzgerald had been dead three years. Yet his memory is even more pervasive than in *Gatsby*. He represents the moral touchstone, the "good instincts—honor, courtesy, courage," to which Dick Diver, the hero, returns time and again, until he finally realizes he has betrayed them through his irresponsibility.[24]

But we do not need to read "Shadow Laurels" or *The Great Gatsby* or *Tender Is the Night* as literal autobiography to see the crucial role Edward Fitzgerald played in his son's moral and creative life. After Scott became a successful author at twenty-three, he learned more and more to respect the older standards—"the good instincts"—which he identified with his father. He could not completely reject the McQuillan point of view; as a self-made American, he was too emotionally involved in his grandfather's dream of success to deny it unequivocally. Yet measuring that dream by his father's moral standards, he realized its limitations. He also recognized its undeniable virtues—its vitality and, above all, its insistence on each individual's moral responsibility to the possibilities of his own imagination. These virtues Edward Fitzgerald, for all his charm and breeding, clearly lacked.

Afterwards, looking back on his early years, Fitzgerald spoke of "that series of unmitigated mistakes that passes for one's childhood." But it would be inaccurate to think of his childhood as one of unrelieved unhappiness. He was a handsome, winning child, "a sunny light-haired boy," according to one of his teachers at St. Paul Academy. Yet the record of his boyhood that he set down afterwards both in his autobiographical Ledger and in his unpublished novel, "The Romantic Egotist," is chiefly a list of humiliations and disappointments: the birthday party to which nobody came; the summer camp where he was homesick and desperately unpopular; the McQuillan wisecracks about his father's failure to earn a decent living; the taunts of his Academy classmates—"Will someone poison Scotty or find some means to shut his mouth?"[25]

The truth lies somewhere between these melancholy pictures of his youth and the much more detached and humorous version that he made the basis for his "Basil Duke Lee" stories in 1928. His emotional life, like that of most children, consisted of alternating dips and upward swoops. During periods of frustration, he learned to escape into his imagination. Envying the possessions of the richer children along Summit Avenue, he pretended he had a pony and described it so convincingly that for the moment his grandmother believed him. Later, he was scolded for having told a "lie."[26]

Lies or not, such stories gave an order and beauty to his world that transcended everyday experience. He would continue to be troubled for the rest of his life by the discrepancy between the moral order represented by the resources of his own imagination and the more flat and conventional morality of society at large. One day when he was devoutly but rather tediously spinning off his weekly list of trivial sins in the confessional booth, the priest unexpectedly asked him if he ever told lies. Without thinking, he instinctively seized upon the opportunity to draw himself up proudly and reply, "Oh, no, Father, I never tell lies." For a few moments he savored the dramatic pleasure of his performance to the full, but afterwards he was terrified of God's punishment for lying at confession. Some days later, he forced himself to call on the priest, admit his error, and ask for absolution. But was it really a sin? If what he had done was wrong, why had he found such pleasure in it? It was a question that he would explore again in his short story "Absolution," and later in *The Great Gatsby*, which grew out of that story.[27]

Like other children's imaginations, his was readily stimulated by books. Soon after he learned to read, he began his lifelong habit of reading in bed. His favorite books were adventure romances—*Scottish Chiefs*, the novels of Scott and G.A. Henty, and Harry Castlemon's endless series of Civil War stories. After seeing his first play, he went home and wrote a version of his own which he persuaded some playmates to help him stage in his attic. By the time he was ten, he had begun a history of the United States as well as a long narrative poem about medieval chivalry. He also put the same enthusiastic imagination into inventing games for his friends. One was called "The White Handkerchief"; and another, which was played with croquet mallets, he called "Indians." A third, "The Boy's Secret Service," was especially ingenious, although Fitzgerald insisted that only he should play the role of the

"Chief Scout." But projects like this won him only a brief popularity in spite of their originality; his playmates were disturbed by his bossy, quicksilver temperament, as well as by his invariable insistence on always being Chief Scout.[28]

Mr. C.N.B. Wheeler, the headmaster of St. Paul Academy, which Fitzgerald entered in 1908 after his family moved permanently to St. Paul, was one of the first to recognize the boy's literary talent. Wheeler assisted him and several other students in starting a school literary magazine, *Now and Then,* for their stories. "Actually I helped him by encouraging his urge to write adventures," Mr. Wheeler said later. "It was also his best work. He did not shine in his other subjects. He was inventive in all playlets we had and marked his course by the choice and delivery of his pieces before the school. . . . It was his pride in his literary work that put him in his real bent."[29]

Often he used his English themes to revenge himself on the classmates. "He wasn't popular with his schoolmates," Mr. Wheeler recalled. "He saw through them too much and wrote about it. His descriptions of characters were mostly St. Paul people thinly disguised. This did not make him popular at home. But his stories were unmistakably 'Fitzgerald.' " Before long, he also began to see his talent as a means of acquiring popularity. Instead of lampooning his neighbors, he began to study and to copy the conventions of popular magazine stories. Except for "Reade . . ." all the other stories he published before he went off to college were increasingly proficient imitations of stories he read in magazines like *Cosmopolitan* and *The Saturday Evening Post.*

Yet, although writing provided an occasional emotional release and aroused the admiration of his classmates, it was at first only a substitute for the success he had failed to win socially or on the football field. "It was in my mind," he later said of these early years, "that if you weren't able to function in action you might at least be able to tell about it[,] because you felt the same intensity—it was a back door way out of facing reality." So long as he thought of his writing only as a "back door," he would have difficulty distinguishing between a really original piece of work like "Reade . . ." and a smart imitation of some other writer which won him ready popularity. He was still quite willing to publish a hasty, poorly written story, so long as someone else admired and wanted it. "The trouble is," his hero in *This Side of Paradise* would say, a few years later, "I get distracted when I start to write stories, get afraid I'm doing it instead of living—get thinking maybe life's waiting for me in the Japanese Garden at the Ritz or on the lower East Side."[30]

At St. Paul Academy he dreamed of becoming a famous and successful author like Booth Tarkington or Rupert Hughes or E. Phillips Oppenheim, whose names he saw featured on the covers of his favorite magazines. In his singleness of purpose he let his homework slide, while he wrote stories for *Now and Then,* and kept a daily diary. After three years at the Academy, his scholastic record was so poor and his study habits were so undeveloped that some drastic step had to be taken. At a family conference in June, 1911, it was decided that he should be sent away to the Newman School, a Catholic boarding school in New Jersey where he would be "forced" (as he later said) to study.[31]

Fitzgerald received the news enthusiastically. He was glad to be leaving the scene of so many mistakes; now he would start all over again. He boarded the New York-bound train in September with high expectations—still several days short of his fifteenth birthday. He was going East at last—to that "faraway East that he had loved with a vast nostalgia since he first read about great cities. Beyond the dreary railroad stations of Chicago and the night fires of Pittsburgh, back in the old states, something went on that made his heart beat fast with excitement. He was attuned to the vast, breathless bustle of New York, to the metropolitan days and nights that were tense as singing wires. Nothing need be imagined there, for it was all the very stuff of romance—life was as vivid and satisfying as in books and dreams."[32]

II
Literary
Apprenticeship

Newman School in 1911 was a small Roman Catholic boarding school for boys at Hackensack, New Jersey, not far from New York City. Started by Dr. Jesse Albert Locke eleven years earlier, it was modeled after the famous Oratory School founded by Cardinal Newman in England in 1859. Both schools differed from the usual parochial school in that they were run by laymen and permitted their teaching staffs to marry. Like the Oratory, Newman was to rival the older and better known Protestant preparatory schools, and its purpose was to prepare the sons of wealthy American Catholic families for admission to Yale, Princeton, and other leading colleges. When Fitzgerald arrived, it had a good academic reputation, and after World War I it moved from Hackensack to a handsome new campus at Lakewood, New Jersey. But during the 1920's wealthy Catholics increasingly prepared to send their sons to the more famous Eastern prep schools, notably those with High Church Episcopal traditions. This trend, combined with the depression of the 1930's, brought about the closing of Newman permanently at the beginning of World War II.[1]

Within a few weeks of his arrival Fitzgerald was just as unpopular with his Newman classmates as he had been at St. Paul Academy. Only now there was no bedroom of his own to which he could escape when the other boys made life unpleasant for him. Mornings were spent in classes, afternoons at sports in the gym or on the playing fields, and evenings in the study hall under the eye of the proctor. In his Ledger, he described this first year away from home as one of "real unhappiness." "I didn't know until [I was] fifteen that there was anyone except me and it cost me plenty." Boys who liked to write, his scornful class-mates told him, were "morbid." "When I wrote stories, I wrote them secretly and felt like a criminal. If I gave birth to any idea that did not appeal to . . . [their] pleasant, vacant mind[s] I discarded the idea at once and felt like apologizing."[2]

His efforts to make the football team were no more successful than before. In one game he missed a pass and was plunged into gloom for days. Once again he tried to atone for this humiliation by writing some-thing—this time a thirty-six-line poem in praise of football, in rollicking Kiplingesque meter, which was published in the Newman newspaper and earned him some distinction.[3]

One advantage of Newman was its proximity to New York. On Satur-day afternoons groups of boys, chaperoned by masters from the school, were allowed to attend theater matinees. Fitzgerald saw Ina Claire in *The Quaker Girl* and Gertrude Bryan in *Little Boy Blue*, and he was especially impressed by H. B. Warner's stirring performance in the title role of the mystery thriller, *Alias Jimmy Valentine*. The following June, on the train going back to St. Paul for summer vacation, he decided to write a two-act play of his own. "The Captured Shadow" had as its hero a "society crook" based on Jimmy Valentine and on the famous Arsène Lupin invented by Maurice Leblanc, another of his favorite authors. Like most of Fitzgerald's youthful short stories, it was a slick, competent copy of the conventional mystery plays and stories he had been seeing or reading. The characters are all familiar types: a fluttery heroine and a suave hero "from the highest circles of New York society," who, in the last act, turns out not to have been a thief at all, but a mastermind from Scotland Yard. There were also the standard comic roles: an Irish police-man, a French detective ("the cleverest gen d'arme [sic] in Paris"), a comic spinster governess, and a stage drunk. None of it is very original, but it has action and humor and shows that Fitzgerald was learning from his models.[4]

The Elizabethan Dramatic Club of St. Paul, a group of young people organized and directed by Miss Elizabeth Magoffin, produced "The Captured Shadow" in August, with its fifteen-year-old author starred as "The Shadow." This one-night performance was a great success, netting $60 for a local charity and giving Fitzgerald considerable newspaper publicity. That summer he also had the satisfaction of receiving a $2 check from *Smart Set* magazine for a poem he had written the year before.[5]

His second year at Newman was a modest triumph. As he gained self-confidence, he learned to control his more unpopular traits, his bossiness and eagerness to dominate every situation. He went out for football again. And during the annual game with Kingsley School, when the captain of the Newman team sprained his shoulder, Fitzgerald was sent in at left halfback to replace him. Left halfback! It was as if the old "Reade" dream had come true at last. During the final quarter, with the score tied 0-0, Havens and Donahoe and Fitzgerald, in a brilliant triple play, carried the ball up the field to Kingsley's three-yard line. Then, while the spectators waited expectantly, Fitzgerald and Havens each gained an extra yard on the next two downs. And, finally, on the fourth and last down, Donahoe crashed through center to score the winning touchdown. Fitzgerald's "fine running with the ball" received special praise in the account of the game that appeared in the *Newman News*—an account that reads suspiciously as though it had been written by Fitzgerald himself, who had just been made associate editor.[6]

At last, he was accepted by his classmates. At the end of the season he was awarded a coveted varsity letter for football. And Charles Dona-hoe, his teammate, became his intimate friend and, later on, a Princeton roommate. Besides his editorship of the *News,* he also won his letter in track the following spring and starred in the senior-class play. Motivated by mixed feelings of pride and generosity, he made himself popular with several classmates by writing their weekly English compositions. They were impressed by his ability to turn out a theme for each of them in a different style. He also published three short stories and several articles in the *News* during this second year at Newman. And at Commencement in June, when every member of the class received some sort of award in that Alice-in-Wonderland fashion so peculiar to prep schools, Fitzgerald was given prizes for excellence in elocution and debating.[7]

Several weeks later his family's financial situation was stabilized by the death of Grandmother McQuillan. Now there was money for Fitz-gerald to attend the university of his choice. And his first choice was Princeton. It was close to Newman School and to New York City; New-man customarily sent up a small contingent to Princeton each year; and, most important of all, it was the home of the Princeton Triangle Club. This was a student organization which annually wrote and staged its own original musical show, taking it on tour to most of the larger Eastern cities during the Christmas holidays. Members were responsible for practically every aspect of the production, and Triangle had become a well-known training ground for aspiring young actors and authors. One of the club's founders was Booth Tarkington, who then represented Fitz-gerald's ideal of the successful popular writer.

Because his grades were so poor and he did so miserably in his college boards, he had to take special admissions examinations in September. And he barely passed them. Perhaps another year of prep school would have made his academic career at Princeton easier, for he was still not quite seventeen when he entered in September, 1913. But he was in no mood for that. Later, writing of Newman, he would say, "My two years there were wasted, were years of utter and profitless unhappiness."[8]

It is not surprising that he barely squeezed into Princeton. Instead of preparing for the September entrance exams, he spent the summer of 1913 writing, rehearsing, directing, and starring in a new play—a Civil War melodrama called "The Coward." Miss Magoffin and the Elizabethan Dramatic Club assisted him in the production, which was given two performances: one in St. Paul and a second at the Yacht Club out at White Bear Lake. Once more the youthful author and impresario was the subject of front-page stories in the local newspapers which he carefully clipped out and pasted into his already well-filled scrapbook.[9]

Fitzgerald's four years at Princeton, from 1913 to 1917, break into two parts. The first extended from his admission as a freshman to his withdrawal, for reasons of health and poor scholarship, in December, 1915. After nine months at home, he returned in September, 1916, to begin his junior year all over again, leaving Princeton for good in October, 1917, to report to officers' training school.

In many ways, those first two and a half years at Princeton were the happiest in Fitzgerald's life. To most of his friends, he seemed well on the way toward some kind of fame, although they expected him to wind up on Broadway as an entertainer or showman rather than to be remembered as a serious novelist. Handsome, endowed with the McQuillan vitality as well as with his father's charm and careful manners, he cultivated an air of romantic mystery. The St. Paul girls who had known him as a sissy scared of dead cats now viewed him differently. "He had a 'line' and flattered you and that began to be fun." He had a reputation for drinking, too, and for being "fast."[10]

During freshman and sophomore years, his chief interest at Princeton remained the Triangle Club. As soon as he was settled in his off-campus rooming house, he signed up for the club's freshman tryouts. For ten weeks each competitor was expected to make himself available, twenty-four hours a day, for whatever menial tasks were necessary to get the annual Christmas show into production. Fitzgerald's classic profile and slender figure, as well as his previous acting experience, won him a place in the "all-girl" chorus line. No member of the cast worked harder nor watched the complex operation of putting a musical show on the road more intently than did Fitzgerald. And no one enjoyed more the cocktail parties and debutante balls that accompanied the Christmas holiday tour. At the end of the tour, Fitzgerald was elected to full membership in the club, and, as soon as he returned to Princeton in January, he set to work writing an original script for the following year's show. In March he had the satisfaction of learning that his entry, "Fie! Fie! Fi-Fi!," had won the competition. Most of the following spring and summer was spent polishing his script and writing words for the songs.

During that summer of 1914 he also found time to write a third play for the Elizabethan Dramatic Club—a farce called "Assorted Spirits," about spiritualism and hard liquor. It was performed early in September, with Fitzgerald once more featured as author, director, and star, and was so successful that this time over $300 in profits were donated by the club to local charity.[11]

He spent the autumn of his sophomore year getting "Fie! Fie! Fi-Fi!" into rehearsal. As Triangle shows go, it was one of the most original and entertaining in the club's history. Unlike most undergraduate musical comedy scripts, it still makes lively reading. The prevailing influences were Gilbert and Sullivan, Victor Herbert, and Rudolf Friml. Fitzgerald had profited from studying these masters carefully; but his dialogue was written in a distinctively contemporary idiom. He not only introduced Triangle audiences to a new comic stage character, "The Flapper," but he incorporated several new jazzy ragtime rhythms into his lyrics.

In March, 1915, he was elected secretary of Triangle. Barring something unexpected, this meant that he would automatically succeed to the prestigious office of club presidency the following year. That spring he was also invited to collaborate with a talented upperclassman, Edmund Wilson, Jr., in writing the next season's show, "The Evil Eye." Wilson was editor-in-chief of the campus literary magazine and a student in the Department of Romance Languages, and he had written an unusually literate script (some said "too literate" for Triangle's holiday audiences). Fitzgerald's task was to furnish lyrics for the songs and also to do what he could to add luster to Wilson's book. "Infuse into it some of the fresh effervescence for which you are so justly famous," Wilson wrote when he sent his manuscript to Fitzgerald that summer.[12]

When Fitzgerald came back to Princeton at summer's end to begin junior year, it seemed as though he had finally reached the summit of that popularity toward which he had struggled so long and with such determination. Never again would he be quite so sure of himself. He had just turned nineteen and was well on the road to becoming one of the Big Men on Campus. The front-ranking candidate for the presidency of Triangle, he was also an editor of the popular campus humor magazine, the *Tiger*, and a recently elected member of the Cottage Club, one of Princeton's most exclusive and reputedly hardest-drinking clubs. As co-author of the forthcoming Triangle show, he also reserved for himself one of the juiciest roles—that of the seductive "Show Girl." Advance photographs of Fitzgerald in a blonde wig and a glamorous picture hat went out to all newspapers on the route of the projected Christmas tour. For the first time in its history, St. Paul, Minnesota, was included in Triangle's Christmas itinerary. Throughout the late autumn of 1915, the drama and society columns in the St. Paul newspapers repeatedly discussed the approaching holiday visit of "The Evil Eye" and the city's talented native son.[13]

Most important of all, Fitzgerald was head over heels in love with a pretty, popular, seventeen-year-old girl, Ginevra King, of Lake Forest, Illinois. She had everything that he had been taught to admire in a girl: money, good looks, vitality, and social prestige. In Chicago society, she was known as one of "The Big Four"—one of the city's four most beautiful and popular debutantes. Fitzgerald met her in his sophomore year at a Christmas dance in St. Paul, and deluged her with twenty-page letters of entertaining prose and passionate verse. She attended a girl's boarding school in New England, from which she occasionally ventured—properly chaperoned—to New York, where Fitzgerald escorted her to the theater, and danced with her afterward at the Plaza or the Midnight Frolic. In August, he visited her in Lake Forest, and the following autumn she was his date for several of the big football weekends. She promised also to be in the audience when "The Evil Eye" arrived for its holiday performance in Chicago.

Then, one by one, each of his hard-won triumphs was abruptly taken from him. Six weeks after he began his junior year, the administration took official notice of his sorry scholastic record and ruled him "ineligible for extra-curricular activities." A committee of classmates and Triangle associates called on the dean, and on some professors in the English department, in hopes of obtaining special dispensation. After all, his Triangle photograph had by now appeared in newspapers from New York to Minnesota. But their pleas were in vain. Fitzgerald had run up a total of 138 unexcused absences from class. He had flunked freshman math and hygiene, one term of sophomore Latin, and both terms of sophomore chemistry. At the end of his second year, his grade average was below the minimum permitted for admission to an upper-class departmental field of study. The English department, in which he planned to major, had accepted him only on the understanding that he would raise his grades during the first term of junior year. Instead, he had spent the autumn rehearsing "The Evil Eye" and writing letters to Ginevra King. When he inevitably botched his midterm exams in November, there was nothing for the dean's office to do but insist that he devote the rest of the semester to his academic studies.[14]

Besides, none of his English professors made any effort to come to his rescue—though this is understandable in view of Fitzgerald's ill-concealed contempt for their literary abilities. It was "a surprisingly pallid English department," he later said, "top-heavy, undistinguished, and with an uncanny knack of making literature distasteful to young men." One of its livelier members was Jesse Lynch Williams, who had attained a modest fame as the author of short stories, and whose play, *Why Marry?*, was a Broadway hit. Fitzgerald made it a point to see the play; then, with characteristic tactlessness, introduced himself to Professor Williams and pointed out to him some of the play's more obvious structural deficiencies. Williams was not amused.[15]

When another of his English professors, Frank Macdonald, warned him in class one day that if he didn't get down to work he would fail the course, Fitzgerald drew himself up to his full height and answered haughtily, "Sir, you can't flunk me. I'm a writer." "And he was right, damn it," Macdonald would chuckle ruefully when he told this story many years afterwards. "He was the best damn writer that ever came out of Princeton." But Macdonald's view was exceptional—possibly because he never earned a doctor's degree and so had remained all his life a lowly assistant professor. Another of Fitzgerald's professors, who later wrote several minor novels and a textbook history of the modern novel, and who eventually served as chairman of the English department, went to his death maintaining that Fitzgerald had not written *The Great Gatsby*. Fitzgerald couldn't have written it, this gentleman claimed, because his English grades were never good enough.[16]

Following the collapse of his Triangle career, Fitzgerald took to the Princeton infirmary with a fever. Whether his illness was malaria, as the university physician thought at the time, or a slight attack of tuberculosis, as Fitzgerald later came to believe, remains a mystery. In any event, he was in no condition to make up his academic deficiencies in time to take part in Triangle's Christmas tour. Early in December he went home to convalesce, and he was in bed the night that Triangle arrived in St. Paul to give its long-awaited performance of "The Evil Eye."[17]

In January, he was advised that, if he wished to stay on at Princeton, he would have to drop back a class and begin his junior year again the following September. At this point he might have quit college altogether and gone on the stage. His lyrics for "Fie! Fie! Fi-Fi!" and "The Evil Eye" had already caught the attention of several newspaper critics. "He could take his place right now with the brightest writers of witty lyrics in America," was the opinion of one admiring reviewer for the Louisville, Kentucky, *Post*. His acting brought him mash notes from men as well as women that might have turned the head of a less purposeful young man. He also received several offers from New York agents and producers who wanted him to leave college and embark on a Broadway theatrical career.[18]

Instead of going on the stage, Fitzgerald chose to return to Princeton, even though he knew that he had forfeited forever his dream of becoming a campus leader. He was no longer a serious contender for the presidency of Triangle. And later in the spring he was informed that his idea for next year's show had been turned down. This was an especially bitter disappointment.[19]

Then, hardest blow of all, he lost his girl. Finally he was obliged to face the fact that he had very little to offer her compared with her older, wealthier, and more experienced suitors. When he saw her that summer in Lake Forest, he finally realized how things stood. "She ended up by throwing me over with the most supreme boredom and indifference," he philosophically wrote to his daughter in later years. But his real bitterness can be seen in the laconic sentence he set down in his autobiographical Ledger opposite that fateful August of 1916. "Poor boys shouldn't think of marrying rich girls."[20]

He began his junior year again in a radically different state of mind from that of the previous autumn. Instead of writing only for Triangle or the *Tiger*, he started to contribute more serious pieces to the campus literary magazine. As a freshman he had felt, like Amory Blaine in *This Side of Paradise*, "that writing for the *Nassau Literary Magazine* would get him nothing," and so put his energies into the more socially prestigious Triangle Club and *Tiger*. But now, beginning with the *Nassau Lit's* autumn issue, he would have something—a story, book review, poem, or essay—in almost every number for the next two years, submitting pieces even after he had left for the army.[21]

Indeed, his experiences writing for the "Lit," and as a member of its editorial board, probably did more for his development as an author than any other single feature of his Princeton education. It encouraged him to try literary forms other than *Tiger* jokes and musical comedy patter. It also introduced him to a fresher and more provocative realm of ideas than he had encountered elsewhere on the campus. This is not to say that Triangle, *Tiger,* and the *Nassau Literary Magazine* were mutually exclusive worlds. But the John Peale Bishop with whom he caroused and danced as a fellow member of the Triangle chorus was not the same John Bishop, the serious student of Mallarmé and Rimbaud, with whom he helped edit the "Lit." Nor was "Bunny" Wilson, his witty collaborator on "The Evil Eye," the scholarly, serious Edmund Wilson, Jr., who served as editor-in-chief of the nation's oldest college magazine.

Fitzgerald was at Princeton during the liveliest intellectual renascence that university had known since the generation of James Madison, Hugh Henry Brackenridge, and Philip Freneau in the 1770's. "Everything around us seemed to be breaking up," he described it several years later in *This Side of Paradise.* "These were great days; battle was on the horizon; nothing was ever going to be the same again. . . ."[22]

One of the major forces contributing to this intellectual revolution was the *Nassau Literary Magazine.* Over the years the "Lit" (founded in 1842) had printed the work of such gifted undergraduates as Woodrow Wilson, Booth Tarkington, and David Graham Phillips. But the "Lit" reached its golden age from about 1910 until 1918 under the successive editorships of T.K. Whipple, '12; Edmund Wilson, '16; John Peale Bishop, '17; and John Biggs, Jr., '18. In addition to publishing the work of a number of talented undergraduates, these editors built up a camaraderie and a spirit of loyalty, apparent from the many solicitous references to the "Lit" and to its future in the correspondence of Wilson, Biggs, Bishop, and Fitzgerald, that is rare in the history of college magazines.

These years from 1910 to 1918 also marked Princeton's academic transition from a genteel, rural Presbyterian college to a university with genuine intellectual aspirations. The deeply entrenched provincialism that blocked Woodrow Wilson's reforms a few years earlier still prevailed in many quarters—nowhere more conspicuously than in the English Department, headed by the old-fashioned Dr. Henry Van Dyke, a Presbyterian minister. But Wilson's "New Freedom," emanating from the White House itself, began to permeate Princeton's cloistered walls. Young Edmund Wilson (no relation to the President), entering Princeton in 1912, was chagrined to discover that the most recent authors approved for study by the English Department were those two *fin de siècle* dilettantes, Oscar Wilde and Ernest Dowson. Under Edmund Wilson's aggressive leadership, the *Nassau Lit* promptly set about introducing the campus to the works of such recent, provocative writers as

Shaw, Whitman, Tolstoy, and William and Henry James. Soon unfamiliar words like "sex," "socialism," "neurosis" were appearing in its pages, and even in the conversation of its readers.[23]

During his first two years, while he had been preoccupied with Triangle and Ginevra King, Fitzgerald had had little time to spare for the investigation of these new ideas. But after his return in 1915, as he began to write regularly for the "Lit" and to spend more time with its editors, Wilson, Bishop, and Biggs (with whom he roomed during his last year), he was caught up in their lively spirit of skeptical inquiry. "It is the last two years in college that count," he would later write of this period of intellectual ferment. "I got nothing out of my first two years—in the last I got my passionate love for poetry and historical perspective and ideas in general (however superficially) that carried me full swing into my career."[24]

Intellectually, he was no match for these friends. He never achieved those analytical habits of mind that characterize the typical intellectual. Indeed, his inability to discuss ideas rationally was to be the lifelong despair of his friends. His genius lay, rather, in his gift for communicating in his fiction the emotions that ideas can generate in people—in itself no mean achievement. Wilson and Bishop especially should be credited with having inspired him with a genuine and lasting respect for ideas. Perhaps even more important was his discovery of the craft of poetry. Previously, his talent had been restricted almost entirely to writing plays and musical shows. He had a good ear and a nimble wit, but he had little mastery of the resources of imagery and rhythm, and so far no formal understanding of art at all. It was John Bishop who first introduced him to the study of poetry as a complex art. Bishop not only taught him to read Keats and Swinburne critically but encouraged him to write serious poems of his own. "It isn't something easy to get started on by yourself," Fitzgerald afterwards wrote his daughter about those first undergraduate efforts to become a poet. "You need, at the beginning, some enthusiast who also knows his way around—John Peale Bishop performed that office for me at Princeton. I had always dabbled in 'verse,' but he made me see, in the course of a couple of months, the difference between poetry and non-poetry."[25]

For the next year or so Fitzgerald devoted himself whole-heartedly to becoming a poet. He read and studied Bishop's models—Keats, Swinburne, Wilde, Rupert Brooke, and Verlaine, whose poetry he translated into English—and he published ten poems of his own in the *Nassau Literary Magazine* (half a dozen of which he incorporated into *This Side of Paradise*). Most of them are undistinguished but competent and rather sentimental echoes of his favorite models, with nostalgic titles like "Rain Before Dawn," "City Dust," "My First Love." Although he was obviously not cut out to be a poet, these exercises were valuable. They helped him objectify and control his disappointment over his unhappy love affair with Ginevra King. And even more important, they made him conscious in a brand new way of imagery, rhyme, rhythm, alliteration, assonance, and the other technical elements of verse. "Years later I realized that my failure as a big shot in college was all right—instead of serving on committees, I took a beating in English poetry; when I got the idea of what it was all about, I set about learning to write. On Shaw's principle that 'If you don't get what you like, you better like what you get,' it was a lucky break—at the moment it was a harsh and bitter business to know that my career as a leader of men was over."[26]

How much chance had there ever really been of his emerging as a "leader of men"? Was this, perhaps, one more illusion to be put away along with the dream of making a last-minute touchdown and saving the day for his school? There is no question about his classmates' admiration for his skill as an entertainer, but was he ever seriously regarded as a potential campus leader? So far as the evidence of the Class of 1917 "Senior Poll" goes, it seems unlikely. He received fifteen votes as the member of the class who "Thinks He Is Wittiest," eight for "Thinks He Is Biggest Politician," and two for "Thinks He Is Best Dressed," but none at all as the "Wittiest," "Biggest Politician," or "Best Dressed" member of his class. Instead, he got five votes as "Prettiest," two as "Handsomest," and two as "Most Brilliant."[27]

The United States declared war on Germany in April, 1917, and two months later most of the Class of 1917 went from June commencement ceremonies directly to military training camps. Fitzgerald still had another year of college ahead of him, after which, according to the Class of 1917 yearbook, he expected to "pursue graduate work in English at Harvard and then engage in newspaper work." In any event, he could not be commissioned as an officer in the army until he was twenty-one, and this meant marking time at Princeton at least until September twenty-fourth. He spent a lazy month visiting John Peale Bishop at his home in Charleston, West Viriginia, and writing more verse. Bishop, who had finished Princeton in June and was awaiting orders to report to army training camp, was busy correcting the proofs of his first volume of published poetry, *Green Fruit*. Fitzgerald looked on enviously and worried about his own future. "I had read somewhere," he later recalled, "that every great poet had written poetry before he was twenty-one. War was impending and I must publish a book of startling verse before

I was engulfed." His twenty-first birthday found him back at Princeton as a senior. Two days later, on the twenty-sixth, he was writing Edmund Wilson, "I sent twelve poems to magazines yesterday. If I get them all back I'm going to give up poetry and turn to prose."[28]

Within two weeks, all but one of the poems had been sent back. Fitzgerald gave up his career as a poet and turned to prose. He would write a novel, a fictionalized account of his life from childhood to Princeton. He was in the planning stages in October when he received his commission as a second lieutenant, and a few weeks later, manuscript under his arm, he left Princeton for good. His orders were to report to Fort Leavenworth, Kansas, for training with the 45th Infantry.[29]

Fitzgerald's departure from Princeton marked the end of his literary apprenticeship. Henceforth, his main object was to finish his novel, which he called at first "The Romantic Egotist." For the next two and a half years, in spite of war, army camps, a love affair, and several unhappy months working in an advertising office, the publication of this first novel was his consuming dream. And he stuck to it until it literally came true for him on the morning of March 27, 1920, when he awoke to find that the first edition, retitled *This Side of Paradise*, had sold out in twenty-four hours and made him a national celebrity. At twenty-three, he was a successful writer.

At this point several generalizations are in order about this early literary apprenticeship. The first thing that strikes the reader of his schoolboy and undergraduate writings is their extensiveness. Beginning with the first short story Fitzgerald published in 1909 when he was thirteen and ending with his last poem in the *Nassau Literary Magazine* (mailed from army camp in 1918), his list of published writings included sixteen short stories, ten poems, five book reviews, and a score or so of light comic pieces in the Princeton *Tiger*. During these nine years he also wrote, directed, and acted in three full-length plays, and wrote the books for two and the lyrics for three Triangle shows.[30]

Of the various forms which he tried, he was best in the medium of the short story. His poetry was important only for what it taught him about the resources of verse; its value is most evident in the steadily improving texture of his prose. His plays and Triangle books and lyrics were clever and amusing; they taught him a lot about the use of dialogue as a comic device as well as a means of portraying character. But they lack the variety as well as the emotional range of his short stories. The book reviews he wrote for the "Lit" (like those he later wrote for newspapers in the early 1920's) lacked both the detachment and erudition necessary for first-rate literary criticism. They tell much more about Fitzgerald than they do about the book he is reviewing.

But his short stories got better and better. Of the seven that were published in the St. Paul Academy *Now and Then* or the *Newman News,* only "Reade, Substitute Right Half" struck a distinctly personal note. All of them, however, demonstrated that he was rapidly learning the tricks of the professional magazinist. Each was a competent imitation of a popular form of magazine fiction: the detective mystery, the football action story, the historical romance, the ghost thriller, or the melodrama of high society. The three stories he wrote at Newman were less successful than the earlier St. Paul pieces because they were more ambitious and much harder to bring off. One attempted to dramatize the paradoxical idea that Americans, for all the emphasis they put on money-getting, are resentful if money is given to them out of charity. Another story ineptly satirized the doctrines of Christian Science. The third and best was a romance, complete with O. Henry surprise ending, based on Fitzgerald's naïve conception of life among the "Four Hundred" of New York society. The important thing about them all is the overwhelming evidence they offer of his conscientious study of the craft of writing commercial fiction.

During his first three years at Princeton, he submitted only two stories to the *Nassau Literary Magazine,* but in his last year the "Lit" published six more. All of these were more professional than his schoolboy work; the best were those in which he was writing about his personal problems. In "Shadow Laurels," his first Princeton story, he had tried to come to terms with his relationship to his father. In "The Ordeal" (later revised and published in *Smart Set* as "Benediction"), he dealt with his developing religious scepticism. Both stories were weakened, however, by his straining to make something clever of them. The first has an ornate, unconvincing Paris setting. The second is spoiled by a tricky surprise ending.

The scars of the previous year were still fresh when he came back to Princeton in 1916; and the best of the six stories that he published subsequently were written out of the need to reconcile himself to these disappointments. "Babes in the Woods" and "The Debutante" explore the implications of his unhappy affair with Ginevra King; in "The Spire and the Gargoyle" he tried to objectify his mixed feelings about Princeton, which he both loved and hated. Like "Reade . . . ," these three stories have an economy and force missing from his other early pieces. He had little difficulty later in incorporating all three into the text of *This Side of Paradise.*

Thus, by the time he was twenty, a distinctly personal note had already begun to emerge in his work ("the stamp that goes into my books so that people can read it blind like Braille"). "One's influences are largely literary," he said toward the end of his life, "but the point where the personal note emerges *can* come very young (*vide* Keats). I'll go further than that. I believe that with the natural prose writer it might very well come long before twenty, depending upon the amount of awareness with which it is looked for . . . my mother did me the disservice of throwing away all but two of my very young efforts—way back at twelve or thirteen, and later I found that the surviving fragments had more quality than some of the stuff written in the tightened-up days of seven or eight years later."[31]

The "fragments" Fitzgerald mentions were pages from his "Thoughtbook," a kind of journal dating back to 1910, when he was thirteen, and incorporating parts of an even earlier diary. The first thing that strikes the reader of these yellowed pages is thirteen-year-old Fitzgerald's already well-developed sense for the more dramatic aspects of life. He had a remarkably accurate ear, and he wrote first-rate dialogue. Here, for example, is his "Thoughtbook" record of a scene that occurred between himself and a girl named Violet Stockton:[32]

"Violet," I began, "Did you call me a brat."
"No."
"Did you say that you wanted your ring and your picture and your [lock of] hair back."
"No."
"Did you say that you hated me?"
"Of course not, is that what you went home for."
"No, but Archie Mudge told me those things yesterday evening."
"He's a little scamp," said Violet Indignantly.

Fitzgerald, apparently, always responded first to the dramatic aspects of life, and his early stories, at their best, consist mostly of dialogue. He seemed naturally to know how to begin a story *in medias res*. "Reade . . ." is an excellent example of this skill. Another story, "A Debt of Honor," which he wrote when he was fourteen, opened with this attention-arousing army roll call:[33]

"Prayle!"
"Here."
"Martin!"

"Absent."

"Sanderson!"

"Here!"

"Carlton, for sentry duty!"

"Sick."

"Any volunteers to take his place?"

"Me, me," said Jack Sanderson, eagerly.

His fascination for the stage and his experiments in play-writing did much to encourage these habits of style. Nothing marks the "personal note" in Fitzgerald's fiction more than his dramatic sense. He somehow managed to preserve the child's naturally dramatic and literal way of responding to experience.

Probably the most convincing proof that he began writing by ear is his spelling. He was a notoriously bad speller all his life. But it was not just a matter of ignorance. If you look carefully at his misspelled words, especially those in the manuscripts of his early work, like the early drafts of *This Side of Paradise,* you will see that his misspellings were consistent and followed simple phonetic principles. He spelled the way he heard words spoken. Here are some of his most frequent "blunders": conciet, siezed, Nieche (*i.e,* Nietzsche), niether, nessessary, essense, adress, disallusion, accute, phenomenum, exstatic, sandwitches, scientificly, dramaticly.[34]

He cared less for words themselves than for what they revealed about the people who used them. Since childhood he had learned to listen for those subtle differences in tone and pitch that disclosed distinctive traits of personality and character. Of Violet Stockton he wrote in his "Thoughtbook": "She spoke with a soft southern accent leaving out the 'r's." And of another girl: "I think it is charming to hear her say 'Give it to me as a com-pliment!' " But a good story consists of more than a dramatic situation and accurate dialogue. The author must also know how to handle straightforward exposition and the art of the simple declarative sentence. It was Fitzgerald's study and practice of the writing of verse under the tutelage of a much better poet, John Peale Bishop, that taught him how to put words together with care. At first, this new word-consciousness made him overwrite extravagantly. Of one pretentiously phrased Princeton story, "Tarquin of Cheapside," he later said, "At the time of its conception I had but one idea—to be a poet—and the fact that I was interested in the ring of every phrase, that I dreaded the obvious in prose if not in plot, shows throughout."[35]

Writing of this story in a review of the *Nassau Literary Magazine* for the *Daily Princetonian*, Katharine Fullerton Gerould, the critic, made a point of the fact that its author had successfully "learned the important lesson of making the verb do the work . . . [of] the over-burdened adjective." Mrs. Gerould's article was one of the first appraisals of Fitzgerald's fiction to appear in print, and he never forgot what she said. "About adjectives," he wrote twenty years later, in a letter to his daughter discussing her undergraduate prose style, "all fine prose is based on the verbs carrying the sentences. They make sentences move. Probably the finest technical poem in English is Keats' Eve of St. Agnes. A line like

'The hare limped trembling through the frozen grass'

is so alive that you race through it, scarcely noting it, yet it has colored the whole poem with its movement—the limping, trembling and freezing is going on before your own eyes."[36]

In another letter to his daughter, describing the service that his exercises in verse had done for his prose style, he said:[37]

The chief fault in your style is its lack of distinction—something which is inclined to grow with the years. You had distinction once— there's some in your diary—and the only way to increase it is to *cultivate your own garden*. And the only thing that will help you is poetry, which is the most concentrated form of style. . . .

Through poetry—especially the poetry of Keats and his disciples, Wilde, Dowson, Rupert Brooke, with their emphasis on concrete sensuous imagery—Fitzgerald found a way of conveying depths of feeling for which his early realistic dialogue had been entirely inadequate. Now, instead of writing clever patter for plays and musical shows, he began exploring the resources of imaginative prose fiction. Many years later, he said about himself, "Sometimes I wish I had gone along with that gang [*i.e.*, Cole Porter, Rodgers and Hart, and the other skillful entertainers of Fitzgerald's generation], but I guess I am too much of a moralist at heart, and really want to preach at people in some accepted form, rather than to entertain them."[38]

What poetry did for his prose can be seen by comparing two short stories and a poem that were published in 1917 in the *Nassau Lit*. All three had been inspired by his recent unhappy affair with Ginevra King. The first, "The Debutante," was a tongue-in-cheek skit written entirely in dialogue. It is the story of a spoiled rich girl who wants her handsome young boy friend to keep on loving her, even though she has decided to marry an older, duller but richer suitor. It is an amusing conversation piece, but nothing more.[39]

"Babes in the Woods," a much better story, makes use of the clever dialogue of "The Debutante," but also it goes beyond this and conveys the emotions implicit in the situation, which a literal transcription of a conversation will not convey. It is a truism that at moments of great emotional intensity "speech fails"—or conversation, at any rate, drops to inadequate understatement. Here the writer must rely on the poetic image as his "objective correlative." "The only way of expressing emotion in the form of art," T. S. Eliot has said, "is by finding an objective correlative: in other words, a set of objects, a chain of events, which shall be the formula of that *particular* emotion; such that when the external facts, which must terminate in sensory experience, are given, the emotion is immediately evoked."[40]

The dramatic writer, wishing to convey emotions by means of imagery, must make use of his images in either of two ways. He can incorporate the imagery into the dialogue itself, as a dramatic poet like Shakespeare does, and give up the illusion of realistic speech. Or he can keep the ordinary speech patterns, and introduce images into the text in some other place. Fitzgerald, who instinctively adopted the second method, supplemented the dialogue in "Babes in the Woods" by the introduction of background imagery at strategic moments. The more intense the emotional experience, the more one's senses are alerted, and the more one becomes aware of images of touch, smell, and taste, as well as the more usual ones of sight and hearing. Therefore, the writer must provide increasingly more evocative images as the situation he is describing approaches its climax. It is because of its images that the following passage from "Babes in the Woods" has a force and immediacy that is missing from "The Debutante." It begins with a commonplace dance-floor conversation, but builds up to a climax which mere representational dialogue alone could not convey:[41]

"Is Froggy a good friend of yours?" she asked.

"Rather—why?"

"He's a bum dancer."

Amory laughed.

"He dances as if the girl were on his back instead of in his arms."

She appreciated this. "You're awfully good at sizing people up."

Amory denied this painfully. However, he sized up several people for her. Then they talked about hands. . . .

"Isabelle," he said suddenly, "I want to tell you something." They had been talking lightly about "that funny look in her eyes," and Isabelle knew from the change in his manner what was coming—indeed, she had been wondering how soon it would come. Amory reached above their heads and turned out the electric light so that they were in the dark, except for the red glow that fell through the door from the reading-room lamps. Then he began:

"I don't know whether or not you know what you—what I'm going to say. Lordy, Isabelle—this sounds like a line, but it isn't."

"I know," said Isabelle softly.

"Maybe we'll never meet again like this—I have darned hard luck sometimes." He was leaning away from her on the other arm of the lounge, but she could see his eyes plainly in the dark. . . . Silence for a moment. Isabelle was quite stirred; she wound her handkerchief into a tight ball, and by the faint light that streamed over her, dropped it deliberately on the floor. Their hands touched for an instant, but neither spoke. Silences were becoming more frequent and delicious. Outside another stray couple had come up and were experimenting on the piano in the next room. After the usual preliminary of "chopsticks," one of them started "Babes in the Woods" and a light tenor carried the words into the den:

> "Give me your hand—
> I'll understand
> We're off to slumberland."

Isabelle hummed softly and trembled as she felt Amory's hands close over hers.

"Isabelle," he whispered. "You know I'm mad about you. You *do* give a darn about me."

"Yes."

"How much do you care—do you like any one better?"

"No." He could scarcely hear her, although he bent so near that he felt her breath against his cheek.

"Isabelle, I'm going back to college for six long months, and why shouldn't we—if I could only just have one thing to remember you by—"

"Close the door. . . ." Her voice had just stirred so that he half-wondered whether she had spoken at all. As he swung the door softly shut, the music seemed quivering just outside.

> "Moonlight is bright,
> Kiss me goodnight."

What a wonderful song she thought—everything was wonderful tonight, most of all this romantic scene in the den, with their hands clinging and the inevitable looming charmingly close. The future vista of her life seemed an unending succession of scenes like this: under moonlight and pale starlight, and in the backs of warm limousines and in low cosy roadsters stopped under sheltering trees—only the boy might change, and this one was *so* nice. . . .

Even though today this passage is somewhat hackneyed, it did not seem so when Fitzgerald published it in the "Lit" in 1917; nor in 1919 when H.L. Mencken bought it for *Smart Set* magazine and wrote its author enthusiastically asking for more fiction in the same vein; nor a year later when it was published as part of *This Side of Paradise*. The sentiment of "Babes in the Woods" does not differ very much from "The Debutante" or a 1918 poem like "My First Love":[42]

> All my ways she wove of light,
>   Wove them all alive,
> Made them warm and beauty bright . . .
>   So the trembling ambient air
>   Clothes the golden waters where
> The pearl fishers dive.
>
> When she wept and begged a kiss
>   Very close I'd hold her,
> And I know so well in this
>   Fine fierce joy of memory
>   She was very young like me
> Though half an aeon older.
>
> Once she kissed me very long,
>   Tiptoed out the door,
> Left me, took her light along,
>   Faded as a music fades . . .
> Then I saw the changing shades,
>   Color-blind no more.

The difference lies mainly in the fact that the feelings which inspired "My First Love" are conveyed in tired Edwardian meters and conventional clichés, so that the poem lacks that freshness and immediacy of dialogue and imagery which Fitzgerald wove more skillfully into his prose.

This technique of combining the elements of literal dialogue and carefully timed images was destined to become one of the most distinctive features of American prose style during the next decade. It did not originate with Fitzgerald; earlier examples can be found in the fiction of Mark Twain, Stephen Crane, Flaubert and Conrad. Nor did Fitzgerald develop it as elaborately in his stories as Ernest Hemingway later would in "Hills Like White Elephants"—probably the finest example of this technique in the English language.

Nonetheless, it continued to be one of Fitzgerald's most useful stylistic devices. The high art of which it was capable can be seen in the climactic scene toward the close of *The Great Gatsby* in which Nick Carraway takes leave of Gatsby for the last time. Here, in a passage written seven years after "Babes in the Woods," Fitzgerald has fleshed out the bare bones of dialogue and imagery with rhythm, assonance, rhyme, recurring symbols, and many other subtle poetic effects. The result is one of the most memorable passages in the novel. On the surface Nick seems merely to be saying good-by once more to the mysterious neighbor of whom he disapproved "from beginning to end." But this judgment of Gatsby is now complicated by the fact that Nick has discovered that all of Gatsby's more fashionable neighbors—including Nick's own cousins, the Buchanans—are no more admirable. In fact, for all his faults, Nick realizes that Gatsby is "worth the whole damned bunch put together." The scene is thus an important turning point in Nick's moral life as well as in the narrative of the book. Although Nick does not realize yet that this is his final parting from Gatsby, the forthcoming denouement is implied in Fitzgerald's imagery: Gatsby in his "pink rag of a suit" beside the garish swimming pool that will soon be stained pink by his blood; the aimless, casual talk of clocks and watches and missed trains, and beneath it Nick's prophetic sense of time ticking relentlessly on toward some fateful end; even the change in the weather —moral as well as meteorological.[43]

But all this still lay some years in the future. The important thing about the stories and poems Fitzgerald wrote as an undergraduate is that they taught him to overcome the limitations of a spontaneous natural talent that had begun dramatically and was dependent chiefly on his accurate ear. Gradually, he forged a fresh and original technique for describing both the literal surface as well as the emotional depths of adolescent experience—experience which, for obvious reasons, was still restricted pretty much to his feelings about Ginevra King, Princeton, his father, and his own still unfulfilled dreams. Still, a personal style was already beginning to emerge, though it would be several years before he would recognize this fact confidently enough to make consistent use of it. His fiction was still a mixture of his own personal technique and the aping of authors like Tarkington and O. Henry. And as late as *The Beautiful and Damned* he was still trying to write some scenes in the spare form of dramatic dialogue.

It is not surprising that well-known critics like William Rose Benét and Katharine Fullerton Gerould, in the reviews of the "Lit" they wrote for the *Daily Princetonian*, singled out Fitzgerald's fiction for special praise. But most striking of all was the attention his *Nassau Lit* stories elicited from his own youthful contemporaries. Editors of literary magazines on other college campuses discovered his stories with a shock of recognition and took admiring notice of them in their own editorial columns. Here, as early as 1917, is ample evidence of Fitzgerald's special talent for voicing the feelings and viewpoint of his own generation, then just coming of age. *This Side of Paradise,* in other words, did not owe its overnight success or its tremendous influence on popular techniques in fiction merely to a lucky historical accident. Behind that success lay at least nine or ten years of serious apprenticeship in the complex craft of writing prose fiction.[44]

III
This Side of Paradise

It never occurred to Fitzgerald that summer of 1917 that there was anything particularly unusual about a twenty-year-old college student's undertaking to write a full-length novel. On the contrary, it seemed as though everyone he knew and admired was working on some sort of book. John Bishop's *Green Fruit* would be published any day; "Peevie" Parrott, a Newman classmate now studying architecture at Massachusetts Institute of Technology, was busy on a novel; Edmund Wilson, now a volunteer member of the American Ambulance Corps "somewhere in France," wrote that he planned to make a book from his overseas adventures and had been gathering lots of "material." Shane Leslie, a young Anglo-Irishman whom Fitzgerald had met recently during a visit to Newman School, had published his first volume of verse at the age of twenty-one and was currently at work on his fourth book.

Most important of all, Father Sigourney Fay, Fitzgerald's closest older friend, was planning a book and had encouraged Fitzgerald to begin one, too. Fitzgerald had become acquainted with Fay at Newman School in 1912, when he was sixteen and the latter thirty-seven. During the next seven years, until his death in 1919, Fay became one of the major formative influences on Fitzgerald's life. In 1917 he was commissioned a major in the U.S. Army and assigned to organize an American Red Cross mission to Russia, our wartime ally. It was his intention to have Fitzgerald commissioned as an army officer and appointed to accompany him as his aide-de-camp. "I think the best thing you and I can do is to write a book while we are away," he had written Fitzgerald

37

on August twenty-second. "I am going to take a Corona typewriter. I am so glad you know how to work one."[1]

A telegram from Fay instructed Fitzgerald to be ready to sail with him from Vancouver for Vladivostok on September twenty-seventh. Herman Hagedorn, in his biography of one of the leaders of this mission, Colonel William Boyce Thompson of Chicago, says that it was undertaken because "powerful elements outside the Wilson administration but high in its confidence were uneasy about the Eastern Front." Fay, a member of the official family of Cardinal Gibbons of Baltimore and an experienced diplomat of the Roman Catholic Church, presumably represented one of these "powerful elements." According to Sir Shane Leslie, it was Fay who, several months earlier, had single-handedly "originated the policy early in the war of making Redmond premier of Ireland . . . and then using a pacified Irish-America to prop up Wilson's wobbly war policy." In any event, Fay's personal reasons for accompanying the mission seem to have had little to do with its stated official objectives. On August twenty-second he wrote Fitzgerald that he intended to convert as many Russians as possible to the Church of Rome.[2]

Yet, for some reason, Fay's plans were canceled at the last minute; instead, he was sent to London and Rome by Cardinal Gibbons (at the request of President Wilson, according to Sir Shane Leslie) to consult with the British Foreign Secretary, Lord Balfour, and the Pope on American foreign policy. Following this mysterious errand, during which (also according to Leslie) Fay was "followed by the secret service of three nations," the Pope rewarded him with the rank of Monsignor and the title of Bishop of the Uniat Churches in America.

Meanwhile, after receiving Fay's wire that the Russian trip had fallen through, Fitzgerald returned to Princeton in September to begin his senior year and to start work on his proposed novel. And in spite of his other duties, Fay followed the book's progress with intense interest. He was writing about it enthusiastically as early as October fourth, and he even provided Fitzgerald with the title. "Your book [he wrote on October tenth] should be called 'The Romance of an Egotist' or 'A Child of the Last Days.'" Fitzgerald adopted "The Romantic Egotist" and retained it until, on his third revision, he decided on *This Side of Paradise*. Even then, he kept "The Romantic Egotist" as the title of the first part of his now greatly expanded novel. Fay, indeed, was more responsible than any other person for Fitzgerald's having begun the book in the first place, and Fay having died in the interim, the final version was appropriately dedicated to his memory.[3]

By mid-November, 1917, Fay was getting ready to go abroad, and

Fitzgerald was en route from Princeton to Fort Leavenworth for officer's training. There, during the next ten weeks, he put his leisure time into finishing the first draft of "The Romantic Egotist." "There was no time for revising," he later recalled. "I would begin work at it every Saturday afternoon at one and work like mad until midnight. Then I would work at it from six Sunday morning until six Sunday night, when I had to report back to Barracks. I was thoroughly enjoying myself."[4]

Before sailing for Europe, Father Fay had entrusted his protégé's literary career to their mutual friend, Shane Leslie, who was then living in Washington, D.C. When he heard of "The Romantic Egotist," however, Leslie at first threw cold water on the project. He had already read and been impressed by several of Fitzgerald's poems, which were rather like his own, and he advised Fitzgerald to devote himself to verse rather than to prose. "Leslie thinks of you as the Rupert Brooke of America," Fay had confided to Fitzgerald. And Leslie himself wrote Fitzgerald after hearing about the novel, "I wish you would stick to your idea of a book of poems. I was much interested in those you read me at Newman School." This was high praise. Leslie had once edited an Oxford literary magazine in which he had published the undergraduate verse of Rupert Brooke. Even so, Fitzgerald decided instead to stick to his novel, sending Leslie carbon copies of each chapter after they had come back from a professional typist at Princeton. Once Leslie had a chance to read them, he quickly changed his tune. "I like the idea of your book," we find him writing encouragingly on January 1, 1918. "Conceit is the soul or germ of literature and of course 'egotism' is the long sought synonym for 'style.' . . . Put your utmost into your writing while the furor of youth, its cynicism and indignation is upon you."

"Is it all like that? I think you have hit on something," he wrote even more warmly on February twenty-eighth, after reading several more chapters. "You must come and talk it over with me." Fitzgerald was by then on furlough at Princeton, where he spent a busy holiday polishing his completed manuscript. His orders were to report next to Camp Taylor, near Louisville, Kentucky, and en route he stopped off in Washington to talk about his novel with Leslie. After spending a week editing the manuscript and correcting the author's frequent mistakes in spelling and grammar, Leslie sent it off to his friend, Mr. Charles Scribner, head of the publishing house, with a warm letter of recommendation. The novel's talented young author had gone off to fight in the trenches, he said inaccurately, and would probably be killed. Leslie, however, had been duly authorized to make whatever changes Scribner felt were necessary for publication. There was, of course, no question of the author's genius. "I knew the poetic Rupert Brooke," Leslie wrote, "and this is a prose one ... though Scott Fitzgerald is still alive it has a literary value. Of course when he is killed it will also have a commercial value."[5]

But in spite of Leslie's endorsement, Scribner's sent Fitzgerald a polite letter in August declining the manuscript. At that time he was stationed at Camp Sheridan, near Montgomery, Alabama, where he was attached to the 67th Infantry. He was now a first lieutenant, and he had been transferred from Camp Taylor earlier in July. After spending most of the late summer and early fall revising "The Romantic Egotist," he submitted it to Scribner's a second time in October, shortly before being ordered to Camp Mills, Long Island, from which he expected to be sent immediately overseas. The armistice on November eleventh canceled these orders, however, and Fitzgerald remained at Camp Mills until he was finally discharged from the army the following February, 1919. Meanwhile, he received word that Scribner's was rejecting his manuscript once more.[6]

It was discouraging news. But by now Fitzgerald was in no state of mind to begin a third revision of "The Romantic Egotist." For several months he had been deeply in love with a pretty eighteen-year-old Alabama girl, Zelda Sayre of Montgomery. He had met her at a country club dance while he had been stationed at Camp Sheridan the preceding summer. Zelda was attractive and vivacious and reminded him in many ways of Ginevra King, who had announced her engagement to a wealthy young Chicagoan the same month that Fitzgerald met Zelda. At their first meeting, he impressed Zelda by telling her that she reminded him of "Isabelle," the heroine of "The Romantic Egotist" (and a portrait of Ginevra King), and a few days later he mailed her his "Babes In the Wood" chapter as evidence. Zelda, who had never been wooed in this manner before, was swept off her feet. Within a few days they were passionately in love, and they were secretly engaged when Fitzgerald went north to Camp Mills in October.[7]

Much as she loved him, however, Zelda was determined not to rush into marriage until Fitzgerald had demonstrated his talents as a money-maker. She admitted quite frankly that she had expensive tastes and that she did not intend to settle down to dreary middle-class domesticity. She possessed all the charm and social assurance of a Southern belle whose father was a Justice of the Supreme Court of Alabama and whose grand-father and great-uncle, respectively, had been distinguished United States Senators from Kentucky and Alabama. Unfortunately, Judge Sayre's eminent position carried with it an annual salary of only four thousand dollars—hardly enough to permit his wife and five children to live in luxury; but Zelda was well aware of her attractions and she was also as impatient of genteel poverty as Fitzgerald. Ever since graduating from high school the previous June, she had been surrounded by suitors, and her high-school classmates had voted her the "prettiest and most attractive girl" in the graduating class.[8]

In short, if Fitzgerald wanted Zelda, he must prove that he could earn enough money to satisfy a restless craving much like his own for possessions and adventure. So the manuscript of "The Romantic Egotist" was put aside while he took a job in New York in February, 1919, as a copywriter in the advertising firm of Barron J. Collier, Inc., at $35 a week. He found a bedroom in a seedy rooming house at 200 Claremont Avenue near Columbia University and spent his evenings revising his old *Nassau Lit* stories and writing new ones, which he submitted to editors of popular magazines, but without much success. All but two came back. While H.L. Mencken enthusiastically bought two for *Smart Set,* he was unable to pay more than $40 each. And this was not even enough to cover the cost of Fitzgerald's frequent train trips to Montgomery, where he unsuccessfully tried to talk Zelda into marrying him. Finally, in June, after four unhappy months, he threw up his job, went on an epic three-day drunk, borrowed some money from a Princeton classmate, and bought a train ticket home to St. Paul.

The rest of the summer he spent holed up in the attic of the Fitzgerald house, rewriting "The Romantic Egotist" for the third and last time. He reduced his manuscript to half its size, added an equal length of new material based mainly on his recent adventures in New York, re-titled it *This Side of Paradise,* and mailed it off to Scribner's on September 3, 1919. Maxwell Perkins, the editor who had rejected it a year earlier, liked the new version enough to wire his acceptance two weeks later, just a few days short of Fitzgerald's twenty-third birthday. "The book is so different that it is hard to prophesy how it will sell," Perkins wrote several days later, "but we are all for taking a chance and supporting it with vigor."[9]

Fitzgerald naïvely supposed that Scribner's would publish *This Side of Paradise* immediately, and he was disappointed to learn that it had been accepted too late for the Christmas season and would have to wait over until spring. It was published at the end of March, 1920, and to Scribner's amazement the first printing sold out within twenty-four hours. Less than two weeks later, on the morning of April eleventh Heywood Broun attacked it in his nationally syndicated newspaper column, calling both the book and its author callow, silly, and uninteresting. But this attack merely increased its sale. By July, it had appeared on the

Bookman's monthly list of national best sellers, and by the year's end it had sold close to fifty thousand copies—more than any other Scribner novel that season.[10]

More important than this commercial success was the impact of Fitzgerald's new book on the younger generation of writers. John O'Hara, a teen-age reporter on his school newspaper in Pottsville, Pennsylvania, would literally never recover from his first reading of *This Side of Paradise.* "He was the first novelist," according to O'Hara, "to make me say, 'Hot Dog, some novelist, I'll say.' The people were right, the talk was right, the clothes, the cars were real." For the next twenty years he would reread *Paradise* religiously every twelve months. And Katharine Brush, poised on the threshold of her career as a popular magazine writer, read it that same spring and "wasn't the same again for years." "There was a Thing to Be Done in the fiction world," she later wrote, "and Mr. Fitzgerald knew how to do it." Magazine editors to whom she sent the manuscripts of her first stories wrote back advising her to "study Fitzgerald"—"quite needlessly," according to Miss Brush.

One way of indicating the revolution in taste that Fitzgerald's book produced is to list the ten best-selling novels of 1920: Zane Grey's *The Man of the Forest,* Peter B. Kyne's *Kindred of the Dust,* Harold Bell Wright's *The Re-creation of Brian Kent,* James Oliver Curwood's *River's End,* Irving Bacheller's *A Man for the Ages,* Eleanor H. Porter's *May-Marie,* Joseph C. Lincoln's *The Portygee,* and Kathleen Norris' *Harriet and the Piper. This Side of Paradise* was too unconventional to sell more copies than the fiction of these well-established favorites. But within a very few years American taste would swing in a new direction. By 1924, Percy Mark's novel of jazz-age college life, *The Plastic Age,* was among the year's top best sellers, followed in subsequent years by Anita Loos' *Gentlemen Prefer Blondes* (1926), Vina Delmar's *Bad Girl* (1928), and dozens of imitations. But by then Fitzgerald had changed radically and was no longer writing best-selling novels.[11]

For all its commercial success and literary influence, *This Side of Paradise* was not an especially good novel. Its interest today lies chiefly in what it reveals about Fitzgerald's development as a serious writer of fiction. Twenty years after he wrote it, and shortly before his death, he would describe it as "one of the funniest books since 'Dorian Gray' in its utter spuriousness." Yet, he went on to say, ". . . here and there, I find a page that is very real and living."[12]

This Side of Paradise was the first popular example to be published in this country of that already well-established European literary form, the *Entwicklungsroman*—the novel of youth's coming of age. Although its historical roots ran back deep into the culture of northern Europe, the *Entwicklungsroman* reached its first popular flowering at the close of the eighteenth century, in that romantic impulse which inspired such works as Rousseau's *Confessions,* Wordsworth's long autobiographical account of his youth, *The Prelude,* and Goethe's widely read *Wilhelm Meister.* Implicit in the *Entwicklungsroman* was the assumption borrowed from contemporary science that human nature, like physical nature, was an organic process best understood through study of its origins and development. To know what man is, therefore, one must begin by examining his childhood and adolescence. Following the tremendous success of *Wilhelm Meister,* the *Entwicklungsroman* became not only the dominant form in the nineteenth-century German novel but found its English counterpart in such works as Dickens' *David Copperfield* and Thackeray's *Pendennis.*

At the beginning of the twentieth century, the novel of youth's coming of age had a second flowering, with the publication of such works as Samuel Butler's *The Way of All Flesh* (1903) and Romain Rolland's many-volumed *Jean-Christophe* (1906–1912). The form had been especially popular in England where, from 1903 until the end of World War I, it was tried at least once by practically every British novelist of any consequence: Arnold Bennett in *Clayhanger* (1910), H.G. Wells in *The New Machiavelli* (1911) and *The Research Magnificent* (1915), Hugh Walpole in *Fortitude* (1913), Compton Mackenzie in *Youth's Encounter* (1913) and its sequel, *Sinister Street* (1914), Somerset Maugham in *Of Human Bondage* (1915), D.H. Lawrence in *Sons and Lovers* (1913), and James Joyce in *A Portrait of the Artist as a Young Man* (1916). Joyce's *Portrait of the Artist* was not only one of the last but by all odds the best of the genre. By the end of the war, probably because the *Entwicklungsroman* was now so closely associated with a world that lay in ruins, it went quite out of fashion with British novelists. A new generation was asserting itself, and Aldous Huxley's impudent summary of the by-now-standardized plot in his own first novel, *Crome Yellow,* also served as its obituary:[13]

Little Percy, the hero, was never good at games, but he was always clever. He passes through the usual public school and the usual university and comes to London, where he lives among the artists. He is bowed down with melancholy thought; he carries the whole weight of the universe upon his shoulders. He writes a novel of dazzling brilliance; he dabbles delicately in Amour and disappears, at the end of the book, into the luminous Future.

As early as 1905, a passage in the privately printed edition of *The Education of Henry Adams* had lamented the absence in American literature of instructive and edifying novels modeled on the *Entwicklungsroman*. And, in view of the perennial American romantic interest in all matters relating to the training and education of youth, it does seem remarkable that this well-known European form of fiction did not find its first native exponent until *This Side of Paradise*. *Huckleberry Finn, Tom Sawyer*, and Thomas Bailey Aldrich's *The Story of a Bad Boy* hardly qualify under this category since their authors were more interested in recapturing their lost childhood than in describing the tribulations of late adolescence. Indeed, to the degree that it is a truly imaginative work of art, *The Education of Henry Adams* was probably the first (as well as the most successful) native attempt to make use of this literary genre, but it was not widely read until a popular edition appeared in 1918 after Adams's death.

Fitzgerald had read and studied *The Education of Henry Adams*, and he had also known the author, who was an intimate friend of Monsignor Fay. Henry Adams actually makes a brief appearance in *This Side of Paradise*. "Thornton Hancock is Henry Adams," Fitzgerald wrote Max Perkins in 1919, "—I didn't do him thoroughly of course—but I knew him when I was a boy." In spite of the great difference between the two books, they resemble each other in tone and in certain attitudes. There is no evidence, though, that Fitzgerald was consciously borrowing from *The Education;* more probably, *This Side of Paradise* reflects certain assumptions about human nature and human society that Fitzgerald at the time shared with both Adams and Fay.[14]

So far as his British models were concerned, Fitzgerald seems to have been unacquainted with the best novels of this genre—Lawrence's *Sons and Lovers* and Joyce's *A Portrait of the Artist as a Young Man*. Of the books that he had read the most influential were Compton Mackenzie's novels about English school and university life, *Youth's Encounter* and *Sinister Street*. The first, which described the childhood and adolescence of a sensitive, attractive boy named Michael Fane, Fitzgerald admired extravagantly. In fact, it was his idea of the "perfect book." Its sequel, *Sinister Street*, carried Michael safely past Oxford, the advances of several voluptuous women, a job in London, and into the bosom of the Church of Rome.[15]

Tastes have changed so radically in the past fifty years that it is hard to understand how these two books could ever have aroused the admiration they did among Fitzgerald's contemporaries. Yet T.K. Whipple, ecstatically reviewing *Youth's Encounter* for the *Nassau Literary Maga-*

zine in 1913, described Michael Fane as a paragon of "brains, imagination, passion of intellect, of feeling, and above all, charm." Whipple, who was to become a respected academic literary critic, was especially impressed by what he regarded as Mackenzie's "normal, healthy attitude toward sex." *Youth's Encounter,* he said at the end of his review, was one of the few novels that he wanted "to reread . . . again and again." Even Edmund Wilson, reviewing *Sinister Street* in the "Lit" two years later, spoke of the book's "brilliance" although he grumbled about Michael's sudden conversion to Rome in the last chapter. Nor was adulation of this kind confined to college undergraduates. Henry James, Edith Wharton, and Katharine Fullerton Gerould, three respected authors and critics, all effused over these examples of Mackenzie's art. More recently, Professor M.R. Proctor, after a study of hundreds of British novels dealing with aspects of university life, ends his monograph, *The English University Novel,* with the statement that *Sinister Street* is still the best of the lot.[16]

Present-day critical opinion, however, tends to side with Cyril Connolly, whose catalogue of the more conspicuous faults of *Youth's Encounter* applies equally to its sequel. It was, he says:[17]

> . . . a work of inflation, important because it is the first of a long line of bad books, the novels of adolescence, autobiographical, romantic, which squandered the vocabulary of love and literary appreciation, and played into the hands of the Luculluses and Literary Puritans. . . . It popularized schoolboy friendship, incense, Oxford and the English countryside, literature as the pool of Narcissus into which one gazes, the romance of prostitution, of priests, of murderers, and the ugliness of London and first love. It is a pastiche of the Pater of *Marius the Epicurean* and the Wilde of *Dorian Gray,* brought up to date and expanded; it is prose Rupert Brooke . . . the clever adjective and the classy noun.

Everything Connolly says here applies with equal force to "The Romantic Egotist," as well as to much of the final version of *This Side of Paradise.* The problem Fitzgerald faced in writing his first novel, and that he only partially solved during its subsequent revisions, was one of freeing himself from the hypnotic appeal of Mackenzie's Mandarin prose and returning to the natural, more dramatic, and more authentic style of his earlier schoolboy writing.

Much of Fitzgerald's admiration for *Youth's Encounter* and *Sinister Street* was due to the influence of Father Sigourney Fay. Like both

Compton Mackenzie, the author of *Youth's Encounter*, and the novel's hero, Michael Fane, Fay was also a recent convert to the Church of Rome. With all the new convert's characteristic enthusiasm, he encouraged Fitzgerald to read Mackenzie's novels as well as those of Robert Hugh Benson, another recent convert to the Church. Such books, he believed, would help shield the boy's faith against the winds of Princeton Presbyterianism. Fitzgerald began "The Romantic Egotist" during his senior year at Princeton as a highly self-conscious imitation of *Youth's Encounter*, chiefly to amuse himself and Father Fay. In the first version of his opening chapter, his hero was actually named "Michael Fane." When Fay objected to this plagiarism, Fitzgerald renamed the hero "Stephen Fitzfay," in honor of his friend and himself, and Stephen ("Peevie") Parrott, a Newman classmate and another of Fay's protégés. The surname "Fitzfay" indicated the filial affection Fitzgerald felt toward the older man. After further objections from Fay, the hero's name was changed to "Stephen Palms."[18]

Sigourney Cyril Webster Fay had been born on June 16, 1875 in Philadelphia, the son of an army officer, Brevet Lt. Col. Alfred Forbes Fay. After graduation from the University of Pennsylvania in the Class of 1897, he prepared for the ministry at the nearby Protestant Episcopal School of Divinity and was made a deacon of the Episcopal Church in 1904. For the next several years he served as canon of the cathedral church at Fond du Lac, Wisconsin, and taught courses in moral theology and church dogma at a neighboring seminary. Then, in 1908, he was converted to Roman Catholicism and went to Washington to study for the priesthood at The Catholic University of America. Following his ordination in 1910, he was made a member of the personal staff of Cardinal Gibbons in Baltimore.

Fay was a stout, nearsighted albino who owed his influence in the Church to a brilliant intellect and remarkable charm. He efficiently supervised the Cardinal's paper work and prepared many of his letters, sermons, and speeches—remarking half-jokingly on one occasion that his nom de plume was "James Cardinal Gibbons." He occasionally lectured at Catholic University and preached at the nearby Convent of the Perpetual Adoration, where he was a frequent guest. Probably his greatest interest, however, was Newman School, for whose educational aims he had strong sympathy. He recognized the need for better-educated leadership among Catholic laymen in America, and he hoped that Newman would play a major role toward this end. For a time he served as the school's director and, even after he moved on to other responsibilities, he continued to visit it often and to observe its progress. He was instrumental in helping to staff it, and among the many vital teachers he helped to attract was Shane Leslie, whom Fitzgerald at the time regarded as "the most romantic figure I had ever known."[19]

Leslie and Fay did not become permanent members of the Newman staff until after Fitzgerald was graduated in 1913. But the youth saw them frequently during his subsequent visits to the school while he was at Princeton. Meeting the scintillating young Shane Leslie was rather like meeting the fictitious "Michael Fane" in person. The son of a baronet and a cousin of Winston Churchill, Leslie had attended Eton and Cambridge, had known Tolstoy and Rupert Brooke, and had once studied at the Sorbonne with the talented and ill-fated young American poet Trumbull Stickney. Like Fay, he had recently forsaken the Church of England for the Roman Catholic faith.[20]

Fay's other friends, to whom he introduced the impressionable Fitzgerald, included Mrs. Winthrop Chanler, a woman of great wealth and beauty who appears briefly in *This Side of Paradise* as Mrs. Lawrence. She built a chapel on the grounds of her lovely Hudson River estate expressly for Father Fay's use, and there is an affectionate portrait of him in her memoirs. There was also Henry Adams who, during his twilight years in Washington, enjoyed nothing better than a visit with Father Fay—". . . round, jolly, worldly to a degree that only an ordained priest can attain without loss of spirituality," as R.P. Blackmur once described him in an essay on Adams. "Father Fay is no bore far from it . . . bless the genial old sinner," Adams wrote Elizabeth Cameron not long before his own death.[21]

It is easy to understand the huge, eunuch-like priest's fatherly affection for the handsome, blond boy and Fitzgerald's admiration for Fay, who introduced him to his first glass of wine and to a more sophisticated world than he had ever known. A brilliant raconteur of after-dinner stories, the jolly priest conversed with equal facility on Celtic music, American politics, Thomist philosophy, or Irish literature. His favorite poets were Wilde and Swinburne; his favorite philosopher was Bergson, whom he had known in Paris; and he took particular pride in what he described as his own "*fin-de-siècle* intelligence." Characteristically, he obtained special dispensation to celebrate the Roman mass according to the more exotic rites of the Greek Church, which he found more aesthetically satisfying. In short, he opened up to Fitzgerald a world as romantic and exotic as that described in *Youth's Encounter*. And, even more than Edward Fitzgerald, the celibate priest became the boy's aesthetic, as well as his spiritual father. Fitzgerald was visiting Zelda Sayre in Montgomery on January 10, 1919, when Fay died of pneumonia

in New York. It was during the famous flu epidemic, soon after Fay had
returned from one of his mysterious diplomatic missions abroad. Zelda
and Scott were sitting together on the couch when an inexplicable feeling of foreboding suddenly seized Fitzgerald. Next morning he received
a telegram saying that Fay had died the previous night. "I'll think of the
days when I came back to school to join his circle before the fire," he
wrote about Fay soon after, "as the happiest of my life."[22]

This Side of Paradise was thus, among other things, an idealization
of Fitzgerald's friendship with Fay; and "Father Darcy," the priest
whom he modeled on Fay, was in the author's opinion the "most sympathetic character" in his book. It had been Fay's hope (so he told Shane
Leslie) that Fitzgerald would find his ultimate vocation in the Roman
Catholic priesthood and would put his literary talent at the service of
American Catholicism much as Thomas Merton was to do a generation
later. By this time, however, Fitzgerald was becoming increasingly more
skeptical of religion, and in his Ledger opposite his twenty-first year,
he wrote, "last year as a Catholic." Twenty-one years of religious ob-
servance are not to be dismissed lightly, however; like James Joyce, Fitzgerald continued to be influenced by Catholic values long after he had
left the Church itself. Nor can we ignore, in judging Fitzgerald's later
fiction, the continuing influence of the image of Father Fay, the priest
who brought into Fitzgerald's life a spaciousness he had not hitherto
known.[23]

Unfortunately, nothing remains of the manuscript of that first version
of "The Romantic Egotist" which Shane Leslie submitted to Scribner's
for Fitzgerald in the spring of 1918. It consisted of "twenty-three chapters, all but five [of which] are written," Fitzgerald had told Edmund
Wilson earlier, in January "and it is poetry, prose, *vers libre* and every
mood of a temperamental temperature. It purports to be the picaresque
ramble of one Stephen Palms from the San Francisco fire thru school,
Princeton, to the end where at twenty-one he writes his autobiography
at the Princeton aviation school. It shows traces of Tarkington, Chester-
ton, Chambers, Wells, Benson (Robert Hugh), Rupert Brooke and includes Compton Mackenzie-like love-affairs and three psychic adventures including an encounter with the devil in a harlot's apartment.

"It rather damns much of Princeton but it's nothing to what it thinks
of men and human nature in general. I can most nearly describe it by
calling it a prose, modernistic *Childe Harold* and really if Scribner takes
it I know I'll wake some morning and find that the debutantes have
made me famous over night."[24]

But even though this first version of "The Romantic Egotist" has disappeared, we are fortunate in having five chapters from the second version (which Scribner's also rejected). These are all heavily revised and appear to be the drafts from which Fitzgerald prepared the clean typescript of his novel which he submitted to Scribner's in the autumn of 1918. After sending in this second version, he mailed these five representative chapters (still in their rough state) to Charles W. ("Sap") Donahoe, a former Princeton roommate, for comment. In his covering letter he asked Donahoe to return them, but luckily Donahoe saved them; and from them we can deduce quite a bit about the successive stages of "The Romantic Egotist." Chapter II, for example, which described Stephen Palms's prep-school career, was at one time marked "Chapter IV." This indicates that, in the earlier versions of the novel, Fitzgerald had given much more attention to his hero's childhood and early youth. Not only did he have to condense a great deal of autobiographical material in the revision of "The Romantic Egotist," but in the final version of *This Side of Paradise,* Amory Blaine's prep-school experiences were further condensed and squeezed into the first chapter.

The chapters that have been preserved from "The Romantic Egotist" are especially valuable as biographical material. Much more than *This Side of Paradise,* these earlier versions were straightforward first-person autobiography. Stephen Palms's childhood parallels the more concise month-by-month record of his own childhood which Fitzgerald has left us in his Ledger. "The Romantic Egotist" spelled out in considerable detail such experiences as the lie Fitzgerald told in the confessional when he was ten, and the humiliations he suffered at school from his unpopularity with his classmates. Although he omitted many of these in *This Side of Paradise,* he afterwards used them in such short stories as "Absolution" and the Basil Duke Lee series.

The portrait of himself as Stephen Palms that he painted in "The Romantic Egotist" is qualitatively very different from the Basil Duke Lee version he wrote ten years later. Basil, in spite of his amusing difficulties, is a more typical boy in every way than Stephen Palms, and he corresponds to the impression Fitzgerald himself made on his friends at the age of fifteen. Stephen, however, portrays more faithfully Fitzgerald's own turbulent state of mind during adolescence. And even though "The Romantic Egotist" is less skillfully written than the Basil stories, Stephen Palms is a more original and better-conceived literary character. Basil is too indebted to Penrod and the other tiresomely normal teen-age heroes of Booth Tarkington.

The greatest artistic flaw in "The Romantic Egotist" was that Fitzgerald had made the mistake of writing his novel in the first person. He was so close to his material that he failed to dramatize it sufficiently. Most of it is a dull, garrulous monologue. "I am informed that the time has come for a long rambling picaresque novel," he announced grandly in his first paragraph. "I shall ramble and be picaresque. I shall be intellectual and echo H.G. Wells, and improper like Compton Mackenzie. . . . My form will be very original for it will mingle verse and prose and not be vers libre; and this interests the new poets. . . . Anyway, this is an autobiography which begins in vagueness, passes slowly through clarity and ends up in the filmy mist of an aviation school. . . . I'd better proceed or I'll be giving away my climax in the beginning like H.G. Wells." And so on for most of the opening chapter. "I can't rewrite," he admitted candidly at one point, "and all I do is from vague notes for chapters that I have here beside me, and the uneven channels of an uneven memory. . . . I'm trying to set down the story part of my generation in America and put myself down as a conscious factor. . . . I've got to write now for when the war's over I wont be able to see all these things as important—even now they are fading out against the map of Europe."[25]

The third and last version of *This Side of Paradise*, which he wrote a year later in the summer of 1919, necessitated a complete overhauling of "The Romantic Egotist." He switched from his first-person narrator to the more objective third-person point of view. He renamed his hero Amory Blaine and gave him two amusing parents. He cut out a great deal of autobiographical material and, most important of all, replaced his monotonous monologue with dramatic scenes that he knew how to write more naturally and effectively.

The result was a two-part novel: Book I, "The Romantic Egotist," which consisted entirely of material salvaged from his two previous attempts; and Book II, "The Education of a Personage," consisting of two heavily revised chapters ("The Debutante" and "Young Irony") from "The Romantic Egotist" and three brand-new chapters based on his unhappy months working in New York. The Mackenzie influence was still evident, but less so than in "The Romantic Egotist." During the intervening two years, Fitzgerald had grown increasingly aware of the limitations of the *Entwicklungsroman*. On the train ride home from New York in 1919, he had come across a copy of Hugh Walpole's recent novel, *Fortitude*—another popular example of the genre. "If this fellow can get away with it as an author," he said, "I can too." Then and there he determined to rewrite once again his twice-rejected novel. "His [Walpole's] book seemed to me to be as bad as possible," he explained, "but I knew they sold like hot-cakes. The principal thing he did was to make the unessentials seem important. I dug in after that and wrote my first novel."[26]

The last third of *This Side of Paradise,* most of which was new material that Fitzgerald added during his final revision in the summer of 1919, differs from the preceding chapters both in style and content. During the year that elapsed between the second and third versions, Fitzgerald had become enamored of the novels of H.G. Wells—notably *Tono-Bungay, The Research Magnificent,* and *The New Machiavelli,* which, he now agreed with Edmund Wilson, was "the greatest novel of the century." Just as the inflated prose and romantic characters of *Youth's Encounter* had inspired the early chapters of *This Side of Paradise,* so H. G. Wells' flat journalistic prose and his interest in controversial social ideas found echoes in the later section. The incident where Amory Blaine chivalrously sacrifices his social reputation to save a friend from being arrested for fornication, as well as the concluding chapter in which Amory defends his half-baked socialism against the arguments of a wealthy captain of industry, came straight out of Wells. In defense of this last chapter, it should be noted that it was at least a considerable improvement over Fitzgerald's two earlier attempts to end his novel. In the first version of "The Romantic Egotist," he rid himself of Stephen Palms by sending him off to join the Army Air Corps. But, according to Fitzgerald, Scribner's objected that "the hero failed in the end to find himself and that this defection would so certainly disappoint the reader as to predestine the book to fail." So, in the second version, he "callously slew" Stephen in battle. When this also displeased his publisher, he decided to make his hero, now renamed Amory Blaine, a convert to Fabianism. In this final chapter, however, Fitzgerald is more successful at evoking Amory's spiritual disillusion than in explaining his newfangled social philosophy. Edmund Wilson, with typical insight, spotted his friend's literary debts as soon as he read his copy of the manuscript. "It sounds like an exquisite burlesque of Compton Mackenzie with a pastiche of Wells thrown in at the end," he wrote several months before the book was published. "I wish you had not chosen such bad masters. . . . Your hero is an intellectual fake of the first water and I read his views on art, politics, religion and society with more riotous mirth than I should care to have you know."[27]

In lesser measure, *This Side of Paradise* was also indebted to several other writers. Not only was Fitzgerald an admirer of Owen Johnson's popular *Stover at Yale,* but the scenes in *Paradise* devoted to undergraduate bull sessions in the dormitory and to the behavior of Princeton students at the movies, as well as the device of listing periodically all the books Amory has been reading, had their source in Johnson's novel. Fitzgerald also profited from his study of the plays of Bernard Shaw. He later said that the "sub-titles" he introduced to head the various episodes in his chapters came from Shaw's "prefaces." And Anne Whitefield, the emancipated heroine of *Man and Superman*, one of Fitzgerald's favorite plays, is an unmistakable forerunner of his own flappers.

The improvement in *This Side of Paradise* over Fitzgerald's earlier versions cannot, however, be explained merely in terms of literary influences. One invaluable aid was the critical advice Fitzgerald received from his classmates, John Peale Bishop and "Sap" Donahoe. Unlike Father Fay and Shane Leslie, they were not allowed to see the manuscript of "The Romantic Egotist" until it was completed. But when they did read it, they were much more outspoken about its faults than either Fay or Leslie had been. They were also much less impressed by the author's efforts to imitate Compton Mackenzie's aureate prose. After reading the five chapters Fitzgerald sent him of the second version of his novel, Donahoe candidly wrote that he had been bored stiff by much of it, notably Stephen Palm's long-winded account of all the little girls he had ever known. This part, especially, he said, reminded him of gushy popular novels with titles like *Men Who Have Made Love to Me*. John Bishop went even further in offering practical technical advice. He thought Fitzgerald should prune out a great deal of his soggy exposition and turn the rest into sharply focused scenes. "I have a theory novels should be written in scenes," he said, adding that Fitzgerald would profit from study of the techniques of Dostoevski and Anatole France. It was all good advice, and if Fitzgerald failed to study France and Dostoevski, he at least turned back in his subsequent revision to that dramatic rendering which was his natural style.[28]

Thanks to the survival of some of the chapter from the second version of "The Romantic Egotist," we are able to see how Fitzgerald went about revising this material for *This Side of Paradise*. Take, for example, the first big scene in Chapter I, "A Kiss for Amory." So far as emotional content is concerned, this encounter between Amory Blaine and thirteen-year-old Myra St. Claire is admittedly banal. But from a functional standpoint, it is one of the most important episodes in the book. It is Amory's first big dramatic scene (so far his history has been straightforward narrative) and, therefore, the first in which the reader has an opportunity to identify with Amory's emotions. It is also the first of those romantic encounters that form the narrative backbone of the story. Here, too, Fitzgerald introduces us to one of the central ideas of *This Side of Paradise*—that Amory, for all his sophistication, is unable to cope with the feminine mind, and never more so than when he is involved in a sexual relationship.

The manuscript of Chapter I that has survived from "The Romantic Egotist" shows that "A Kiss for Amory" was skillfully constructed from two quite independent incidents, neither of which has the emotional impact of the final version. The first was a literal rendering of a conversation that might have come right out of the autobiographical Thought-book which Fitzgerald had kept when he was thirteen:[29]

> I thought I'd found the answer to most things one night in a dark haired girl who had come to Minneapolis from Canada. Her name was Ruth Dodge and she was athletic and graceful and had a laugh that rang far over the snowy fields. I sat beside her on the sleigh and was sentimental about the moon.
>
> "Pale moons like that one" (gesture).
>
> "What?"
>
> "Pale moons like that make some people pretty—and, and not others."
>
> "Why?"
>
> "You look good in that pale moon. You look like a witch."
>
> "Why you horrid boy," cried Ruth; "I look like a witch?"
>
> "Not an old witch," I hastened to say: "a young witch with her hair flying over her eyes—" (Hurried fixing of hair to my great discouragement)
>
> "Ruth."
>
> "What?"
>
> "Don't you like boys at all?"
>
> "No," she said considering. "I'd like to be one, but I don't like them."
>
> "They're not as entertaining as girls," I said, thinking Ruth hopelessly unsentimental. . . .

Three pages further along in the same manuscript of "The Romantic Egotist," Fitzgerald describes an encounter with another girl.

> I met a girl named Bessie Gordon from Portland, who was staying at the club; kissed her under a grape arbor one night and the disillusion of this made me a temporary misogynist. . . . I borrowed her ring one night, and made a dash away with it; she caught me by the grape arbor and, as she bent to snatch it, I kissed her on the cheek.
>
> "Why," she said[,] startled, "Why did you do that?"

"I don't know" I answered frankly.

She sat down on a bench.

"I like you too," she said as if in agreement with something that I'd offered.

"Do you?" I responded nervously; my sentiment had vanished with the kiss.

"Why don't you sit down here beside me and we'll talk?"

"I've gotta go back to the club."

"No you don't."

"Yes I do." I was desperately afraid that she had fallen in love with me. "I got to—really."

She rose slowly and walked toward the club house. I followed unhappily, and we strolled in silence. At the door of the club she turned around and faced me.

"I hate you," she said slowly; "and I'm going to tell my mother you kissed me."

"What?" I gasped, and stood there in stupefaction as the screen door banged in my face. But the next night I danced the Boston with her frantically at the weekly hop and she seemed to have forgotten that she had ever liked me or hated me. This aroused a faint interest but I decided to let well-enough alone.

From these two passages and his imagination, Fitzgerald shaped the much more amusing and appealing episode, "A Kiss for Amory." Colorless Ruth Dodge and Bessie Gordon have now been transformed into glamorous Myra St. Claire, one of the richest and prettiest thirteen-year-old girls in town. In this episode, Amory receives an invitation from Myra to her sleighing party, which is to wind up with a dance at the local country club. Arriving at what he assumes is a fashionably late hour, Amory finds that the sleighing party has already started off for the club, leaving an exasperated Myra and the family chauffeur to bring Amory with them in the St. Claire limousine. After Amory and Myra are comfortably settled in the back seat of her car, the following conversation ensues:[30]

"Myra," he said, lowering his voice and choosing his words carefully, "I beg a thousand pardons. Can you ever forgive me?"

She regarded him gravely, his intent green eyes, his mouth, that to her thirteen-year-old, arrow-collar taste was the quintessence of romance. Yes, Myra could forgive him very easily.

"Why—yes—sure."

He looked at her again, and then dropped his eyes. He had lashes.

"I'm awful," he said sadly. "I'm diff'runt. I don't know why I make faux pas. 'Cause I don't care, I s'pose." Then, recklessly: "I been smoking too much. I've got t'bacca heart."

Myra pictured an all-night tobacco debauch, with Amory pale and reeling from the effect of nicotined lungs. She gave a little gasp. "Oh, *Amory*, don't smoke. You'll stunt your *growth!*"

"I don't care," he persisted gloomily. "I gotta. I got the habit. I've done a lot of things that if my fambly knew"—he hesitated, giving her imagination time to picture dark horrors—"I went to the burlesque show last week."

Myra was quite overcome. He turned his green eyes on her again.

"You're the only girl in town I like much," he exclaimed in a rush of sentiment. "You're simpatico."

Myra was not sure that she was, but it sounded stylish though vaguely improper. . . .

"You shouldn't smoke, Amory," she whispered. "Don't you know that?"

He shook his head.

"Nobody cares."

Myra hesitated.

"*I* care."

Something stirred within Amory.

"Oh, yes, you do! You've got a crush on Froggy Parker. I guess everybody knows that."

"No, I haven't," very slowly.

A silence, while Amory thrilled. . . . He reached over with a violent, jerky effort, and clutched Myra's hand—her thumb, to be exact.

"Tell him to go to the Minnehaha straight," he whispered. "I wanta talk to you—I *got* to talk to you."

Myra made out the party ahead, had an instant vision of her mother, and then—alas for convention—glanced into the eyes beside. . . .

"I can kiss her," he thought. "I'll bet I can. I'll *bet* I can!"

Overhead the sky was half crystalline, half misty, and the night around was chill and vibrant with rich tension. From the Country Club steps the roads stretched away, dark creases on the white blanket; huge heaps of snow lining the sides like the tracks of giant moles. They lingered for a moment on the steps, and watched the white holiday moon. . . .

They drifted up the stairs and Myra led the way into the little den of his dreams, where a cosy fire was burning before a big sink-down couch...

"You're such a funny boy," puzzled Myra.

"How d'ya mean?" Amory gave immediate attention, on his own ground at last.

"Oh—always talking about crazy things. Why don't you come ski-ing with Marylyn and I tomorrow?"

"I don't like girls in the day time," he said shortly, and then, thinking this a bit abrupt, he added: "But I like you." He cleared his throat. "I like you first and second and third. . . ."

"I like you the first twenty-five," she confessed, her voice trembling, "and Froggy Parker twenty-sixth."

Froggy had fallen twenty-five places in one hour. As yet he had not even noticed it.

But Amory, being on the spot, leaned over quickly and kissed Myra's cheek. He had never kissed a girl before, and he tasted his lips curiously, as if he had munched some new fruit. Then their lips brushed like wild young flowers in the wind.

"We're awful," rejoiced Myra gently. She slipped her hand into his, her head drooped against his shoulder. Sudden revulsion seized Amory, disgust, loathing for the whole incident. He desired frantically to be away, never to see Myra again, never to kiss any one; he became conscious of his face and hers, of their clinging hands, and he wanted to creep out of his body and hide somewhere safe out of sight, up in the corner of his mind.

"Kiss me again." Her voice came out of a great void.

"I don't want to," he heard himself saying. There was another pause.

"I don't want to!" he repeated passionately.

Myra sprang up, her cheeks pink with bruised vanity, the great bow on the back of her head trembling sympathetically.

"I hate you!" she cried. "Don't you ever dare speak to me again!"

"What?" stammered Amory.

"I'll tell mama you kissed me. I will too! I will too! I'll tell mama, and she won't let me play with you!"

Amory rose and stared at her helplessly, as though she were a new animal of whose presence on earth he had not heretofore been aware.

The door opened suddenly, and Myra's mother appeared on the threshold, fumbling with her lorgnette.

"Well," she began, adjusting it benignantly, "the man at the desk told me you children were up here—How do you do, Amory."

Amory watched Myra and waited for the crash—but none came. The pout faded, the high pink subsided, and Myra's voice was placid as a summer lake when she answered her mother.

"Oh, we started so late, mama, that I thought we might as well—"

He heard from below the shrieks of laughter, and smelled the vapid odor of hot chocolate and tea-cakes as he silently followed mother and daughter down-stairs. . . .

Though there may be more memorable passages in *This Side of Paradise*, none is stamped more sharply with the imprint of Fitzgerald's personal style. Here is prose free of the borrowed finery of *Youth's Encounter* as well as of the fuzzy intellectualism of *The New Machiavelli* and *The Research Magnificent*. Fitzgerald has returned to the dramatic narrative.

Artistically, "A Kiss for Amory" is composed of two literary elements: realistic dialogue and sensuous imagery. In this respect, it is like "Babes in the Woods," the Princeton story he had written two years earlier. But by comparing the two (and this can easily be done since the latter was also included in *This Side of Paradise*), we can see that Fitzgerald has become much more adept in "A Kiss for Amory" in combining these two elements so that they release a greater amount of emotion. Although, in revising "The Romantic Egotist," he has abandoned the first-person narration, the scene is skillfully presented from Amory's point of view. And as Myra's physical presence gradually rouses vague sexual longings in Amory, each of his five senses becomes awakened: taste, touch, and smell, as well as sight and hearing. Fitzgerald has inserted all kinds of timely sensory images in order to evoke in the susceptible reader something of Amory's own changing state of mind.

Five years later—that is, by the time he was at work on *The Great Gatsby*—Fitzgerald had begun to realize that it was in scenes like "A Kiss for Amory" that his unique gifts as a writer of fiction emerged, and that his task was to develop and mature this highly personal literary technique. But, while writing *This Side of Paradise*, he was still discovering what his potential resources were, and he was also only incidentally aware of how much a scene like "A Kiss for Amory" revealed about his own deepest feelings and of how much he could learn about himself from the study of his own fiction. In this first novel, his conscious purpose had been only to set down as honestly and as accurately as he could the record of an adolescence and youth that he believed was typical of his generation. Because of this honesty, the writing in this scene is as valid today as it was when it was first published, though it no longer exercises the impact that it did in 1920. Most authors of popular novels, in their treatment of incipient teen-age sexual relations, either hastily glossed over them or larded them with romantic sentiment. Owen Johnson's *Stover at Yale,* for example, was one of the best-known American novels about adolescence to appear during the World War I decade. Yet, although Johnson treated the masculine side of college life realistically enough, when Dink Stover (a rugged fullback on the Yale football team) finally mustered up enough courage to hold the hand of his roommate's beautiful sister, convention demanded that Dink kneel and propose to her immediately. Whereupon the young lady jerked back her hand and said, in shocked tones, "Mr. Stover, you have done a very wrong thing . . . If what you said were true [even in a crisis like this a "nice" girl always remembered to use the subjunctive case!], and you are too young to have said such solemn words, may I ask what right you had to say them to me? You are a boy and I am not yet a woman . . . I want always to keep the respect I had for you."[31]

At another extreme there was the example of H.G. Wells. For all his eager desire to discuss sex in the abstract in his novels, Wells suffered from the traditional middle-class English dislike of any public discussion of feelings. The emancipated narrator-hero of *The New Machiavelli* analyzes his sexual problems with fashionable candor. But when it comes to describing exactly how he behaved during courtship he can only say: "I find it not a little difficult to state what kept me back from proposing marriage that summer, and what urged me forward at last to marry her. It is so much easier to remember one's resolutions than to remember the moods and suggestions that produced them."

Readers of *The New Machiavelli* will remember that Wells' hero was suffering from the same ambiguous combination of attraction and disgust as Amory. But Wells was more interested in describing his hero's thoughts and "resolutions" about sex, whereas Fitzgerald, from the beginning of his writing career, was more interested in conveying the "moods and suggestions" that produced them.[32]

Fitzgerald knew from personal observation that the romantic behavior of the boys and girls with whom he had grown up from 1910 to 1920 was quite different from the accounts to be found in the works of such widely read authors as Wells, Mackenzie, Owen Johnson, or their rivals. From childhood he had been in the habit of recording his experiences with girls in his diaries and Thoughtbook. By the time he entered Princeton he was carrying on an extensive correspondence with Midwestern girls who were still back in St. Paul, or who had come East to boarding school or college. A number of their letters to him have been preserved, and from them we can see that the heroines of *This Side of Paradise* and of his *Nassau Lit* short stories were faithful and accurate descriptions of the behavior of the wealthy, privileged, middle-class girls from the Midwest with whom he had grown up during these years.

"You haven't changed a bit," we find one of them writing Fitzgerald in 1916. "I was interested in your last [letter], in the things you've learned from different girls." In exchange for his confidences they offered their own. For example, during an Eastern vacation with her family at a resort hotel, one girl writes that she has let herself be kissed by a strange boy, and now the boy she really loves has found out about it. "Of course my darling with the ideals wouldn't understand," she tells Fitzgerald. "He thinks I'm the kind of a girl who'll stand for anything." In another letter she reports that her father has promised to buy her a new Jeffries sports runabout when she goes back home for the summer. "Think of the romances that are made possible by a car! I've planned a hundred. (1) To run over every good looking boy I see, bring him home to recuperate then—(2) To have punctures whenever adventure seems available."[33]

Fitzgerald, in short, did not have to exaggerate the behavior of his heroes or heroines in order to create a brand-new popular American literary convention. The older generation, lulled into false complacency by a Puritan glossing over of sex, was shocked and then angered by Fitzgerald's realism, and accused him of being immoral. But Fitzgerald's contemporaries knew, or at least suspected, that he was merely telling the truth.

We are all familiar with the history of that revolution in the manners and morals of American young people that occurred so dramatically during the World War I decade. Its roots went back far into the national past. During most of the country's history, the problem of securing a living had obliged American boys and girls to pass quickly from childhood into the adult responsibilities of pursuing a calling and raising a family. Besides, the prevailing Puritan philosophy hardly favored the leisurely enjoyment of a carefree youth. Youth was regarded as merely an awkward stage in the difficult process of growing up—"the sooner over the better." Count Alexis de Tocqueville, the French traveler who had observed the American scene in the 1830's, was struck by the number of young people who yielded up the pleasures of youth almost before their youth had begun. Most Americans, he noted, "enter upon their calling at fifteen, and so their education ends where ours begins." As late as 1909, the young literary critic Van Wyck Brooks (himself only a year or so out of college) could not see that conditions had improved much since de Tocqueville's day. "We are all grown up in America," he asserted in his *The Wine of the Puritans.* "We are the most grown-up race in the world. America has never had a childhood. . . . For most of us, living means getting a living."[34]

But the fact was that, as the benefits of the Industrial Revolution were diffused more widely through the social fabric, more and more American boys and girls postponed marriage and a job in order to attend college. A higher standard of living, increased educational opportunities, and the impulse of European nineteenth-century romanticism (with its emphasis on the validity of youthful feeling and experience), all conspired to emancipate and glorify the idea of "youth." Youth, increasingly, began to be valued as possessing qualities distinctively different from either childhood or adulthood—qualities to be savored and enjoyed as long as possible. By 1919, the young critic Randolph Bourne was proclaiming that only "youth has all the really valuable experience." Within a few years these words would become a universal cry.[35]

But though the "New Freedom" (in Woodrow Wilson's words) was winning many battles on the political and social fronts, it had not yet emerged as a theme in popular American fiction. This explains in large measure the tremendous impact of *This Side of Paradise* when it appeared in 1920—an impact far out of proportion to the book's literary merits. It was the first popular American novel to illustrate the implications of this new freedom as it was expressed in adolescent behavior. It was easy for the more knowing critics to point out the novel's intellectual and literary shortcomings. But who listened? Certainly the average American parent was poorly prepared to defend his tottering position. Amory and his Isabelles and Rosalinds were better-read, more sophisticated, and considerably more sure of themselves than their parents. After all, how many fathers had gone to college and read Tolstoy and Dostoevski and Marx and Freud, as Amory claimed he had? How many mothers could quote Verlaine's poetry in the original French, or defend themselves on the back seat of a car as gracefully as Fitzgerald's heroines? Until more attractive and appealing heroes and heroines emerged, these would symbolize the dreams and aspirations of a young and increasingly assertive segment of American society.

Another quite different reason for the notoriety of *This Side of Paradise* was that it introduced to many of its more youthful feminine readers, especially in the East, a brand-new kind of heroine—an emancipated American girl whose behavior was quite different from the code of manners to which they were expected to conform. Unlike her Western counterpart, who was a product of the more free-and-easy frontier, the Eastern girl was still subject to such old-fashioned European customs as the chaperon, an elaborately formal system of etiquette, and an educational philosophy which advocated the separation of the sexes and the incarceration of the girls into prisonlike boarding schools.

It is not surprising, therefore, that the largest sales of *Paradise* were concentrated in the Eastern States. Arbiters of Eastern etiquette, like Mrs. Frank Learned, the author of a popular handbook entitled *The Etiquette of New York Today*, had long maintained that the Western regions were inhabited by barbarians who permitted their daughters greater license. *This Side of Paradise*, on the other hand, demonstrated that for all their independence and lack of inhibitions, these Midwestern girls were no less attractive or desirable than those of the more strait-laced East. Fitzgerald had naïvely assumed that, in describing the girls with whom he had grown up in St. Paul, he was describing the behavior of most wealthy American girls. No wonder he was so puzzled by the Boston and Philadelphia ministers and editors who accused him of trying to corrupt their daughters, and puzzled by the daughters themselves who saw his novel as a clarion call to revolt.[36]

This Side of Paradise also represented the frontier point of view in its glamorization of the image of New York City—an image that in 1920 had only just begun to emerge as the symbol of the most sophisticated and cosmopolitan aspects of the national culture. Here again, as in the case of his description of his heroines, Fitzgerald was innocent of any revolutionary motive. He merely thought that he was describing New York City realistically. And so he was. But it was a Western tourist's New York that he described; and it was this new image that was destined to emerge as the popular one in the years that followed the appearance of *This Side of Paradise*. Hitherto, the few writers who had written imaginatively about New York had seen little or nothing to glamorize. "The New York streets are fatal to the imagination," according to Henry James, who had moved permanently to Europe and Edith Wharton, an even more authentic New Yorker, had been primarily concerned in her fiction with showing the destruction of the "Old New York" she loved by that bustling, commercial, and hotel civilization which was the very thing Fitzgerald would later glamorize. For writers like James and Wharton and even Sinclair Lewis (an outlander like Fitzgerald), the European capitals, especially Paris, symbolized metropolitan glamour and mystery. Other American writers like Stephen

Crane, O. Henry, and Fannie Hurst, who knew New York intimately, wrote only about its seamier, uglier aspects.

But Fitzgerald, in his first novel as well as his early stories, limited himself exclusively to that tiny segment of the city bordered by Times Square, Central Park, and the fashionable hotel and shopping districts. By concentrating on this "white sparkling city," most of which had sprung up during the World War I decade, he created a brand-new image of New York in the popular consciousness. Indeed, to his amazement, he found himself hailed overnight as the city's laureate. "I, who knew less of New York than any reporter of six months standing and less of its society than any hall-room boy in the Ritz stag line, was pushed into the position not only of spokesman for the time but of the typical product of that same moment. . . . To my bewilderment I was adopted, not as a Middle Westerner, not even as a detached observer, but as the arch type of what New York wanted."[37]

The new uptown New York north of Forty-second Street was essentially a Western city. It shared more with such burgeoning metropolises as Detroit, Houston, and Chicago than it did with such older neighbors as Boston, Baltimore, and Philadelphia. And it was this circumscribed but Western image of New York—shimmering with the romance of un-fulfilled possibilities—that Fitzgerald celebrated for the first time in our fiction.

His friend Edmund Wilson was one of the first to point out Fitzgerald's limitations as an observer of the New York scene. "It seems to me a great pity," Wilson wrote, "that he has not written more of the West; it is perhaps the only milieu that he understands. When he approaches the East he brings to it the standards of the wealthy West—the preoccupation with display, the love of magnificence and jazz, the vigorous social atmosphere of amiable flappers and youths, comparatively unpoisoned as yet by the snobbery of the East." But, ironically, it was Wilson's image of New York, a New York sharing so much with the older East Coast cities, that was already fading. For what is New York today, to the average American, but an extension of Western America, largely inhabited by transplanted Midwesterners? It was this image of New York City—the unreal metropolis of skyscrapers, luxurious shops, and hotels—that was first glamorized by Fitzgerald and that has since become the setting for more than half of all our motion pictures, the setting for most of our expensive advertising illustrations, and one of the dominant factors in our national culture.[38]

But subject matter alone, no matter how fresh and timely, was not the main reason for the popularity of *This Side of Paradise*. If it were, then Stephen Vincent Benét's first novel, *The Beginning of Wisdom,* which was published within the year, should have enjoyed a comparable success. Instead, it dropped stillborn from the press. Superficially, the two books were much alike. Both authors were the same age and had undergone very similar experiences. Benét was a member of the class of 1919 at Yale. Both extravagantly admired and owed a debt to Compton Mackenzie's *Youth's Encounter.* In form, both novels were loose collections of anecdotes, letters, poems, long-winded monologues, held together by the personality of a hero who resembled his creator. Both carried their heroes from childhood and boarding school, through college and into war-time military service. Like Stephen Palms, Benét's hero was born in San Francisco. Both heroes struggled with the perennial problems of growing up—teachers, girls, college success, the choice of a career, the problem of reconciling their newly awakened love of beauty with the ugliness and sordidness of everyday life.

Artistically, Benét was not only a better poet but a more skillful literary craftsman than Fitzgerald. Still, *This Side of Paradise* is a more compelling piece of writing than is *The Beginning of Wisdom.* The reason is simply that Fitzgerald surpassed Benét in that instinctive concern for the dramatic aspects of life that marks the genuine novelist. In the best pages of *This Side of Paradise,* life is a drama; everything else is subordinated to this end. Thin as his characters are, their behavior dominates Fitzgerald's material, whereas Benét's heroes and heroines are continually getting lost in fancy writing and philosophical disquisitions. Benét possessed little dramatic sense at this stage in his career; when he did attempt a dramatic scene the dialogue was too literary and derivative to be convincing. Instead, as in his later work, his gifts found their greatest fulfillment in verse. Fitzgerald may well have had the authors of first novels like *The Beginning of Wisdom* in mind when he said at the end of his own career: "The men of promise who fade out in a year have never been able to subordinate all thinking and feeling to the business of thinking and feeling dramatically."[39]

IV
The
Short
Stories:
1919-1925

On September 18, 1919, as soon as he had word from Maxwell Perkins that Scribner's had accepted *This Side of Paradise*, Fitzgerald wrote his editor a long letter outlining his plans for the future. He wanted to get married as soon as Zelda would have him, and he wanted to start work on a second novel. Since both projects required money, he hoped that *Paradise* would be brought out immediately. He already had a title ("The Demon Lover") in mind for this next novel which he estimated would take him about a year to write. In his reply, Perkins was obliged to explain that Scribner's winter book list had been made up weeks before and that *This Side of Paradise* could not possibly be published until spring. Besides, he warned, Fitzgerald should not count too heavily on his royalties. First novels rarely sold more than a few thousand copies.[1]

Under these circumstances, Fitzgerald decided to put the new novel aside and take another look at the magazine fiction market. So far, his only customers had been H.L. Mencken and George Jean Nathan at *Smart Set*. While they were interested in seeing more of his work, they were unwilling to pay him more than forty dollars a story. During the next several months he sold them eight additional stories and sketches —but only after he was convinced that no other editor would pay more.

A more likely market was *Scribner's Magazine*. Robert Bridges, the editor, was a loyal Princetonian who welcomed the opportunity to publish the work of fellow alumni. But his tastes, like his audience, were conservative, and so far he had returned every story or poem that Fitzgerald had sent him. Now that *This Side of Paradise* was to be published under the Scribner imprint, however, Bridges expressed a fresh interest in the young author's work. Of the six short stories that Fitzgerald subsequently sent him, most of them leftovers from the previous spring, Bridges took two and paid $150 apiece. One of them, to Fitzgerald's amusement, was a story Bridges had turned down several months earlier, apparently unread. Neither was typical of Fitzgerald's best work; both lacked the vitality and humor of the pieces he was currently selling to *Smart Set*. They were wooden, uninspired but conscientious copies of the more conventional stories of the day—highly moral and heavily plotted, but with no roots in Fitzgerald's own experience. "The Four Fists" was a thinly contrived allegory about a spoiled rich boy who gets some sense knocked into him. Possibly the design, as well as the title, had been inspired by Henry James's similar early short story, "The Four Meetings." "The Cut-Glass Bowl" was an unconvincing domestic tragedy in which the glass bowl of the title had an obscure symbolic function.[2]

With the $300 that he received from Bridges, Fitzgerald could afford a train ticket from St. Paul to Montgomery and New York. Neglecting, as usual, to tell his parents his plans or his destination, he set off early in November hoping that Zelda would finally capitulate now that he was an author. "I may be a wreck by the time I see you," he wrote a classmate in New York just before he left. "I'm going to try to settle it definately one way or the other." But in Montgomery he found Zelda still adamant. After all, so far he had only a few hundred dollars to show for his summer's work, most of which had gone into his trip East. After a disheartening weekend of arguments and tearful but inconclusive reconciliations, he boarded a train for New York, convinced that the cold he had contracted in Alabama was now turning into tuberculosis.[3]

One of his reasons for going to New York was to discuss with a literary agent the possibility of selling stories to the bigger magazines. The agent was Paul Revere Reynolds, who was recommended to him by a St. Paul friend, Grace Flandrau. Before going East, Fitzgerald had sent Reynolds several stories he had been unable to sell on his own. To his great delight, on visiting Reynolds' office, he learned that one of them, "Variety," had been sold to George Horace Lorimer, the editor of *The Saturday Evening Post*, for $400. Lorimer, who retitled the story "Head and Shoulders," was interested in seeing more of Fitzgerald's work. During this New York visit, Fitzgerald also made the acquaintance of Harold Ober, a young man on Reynolds' staff who had been assigned to handle Fitzgerald's fiction. Ober was to become one of

Fitzgerald's closest friends and advisers, continuing to handle Fitzgerald's business affairs after he set up his own office ten years later.[4]

"Head and Shoulders" was the first in a long line of light, tongue-in-cheek stories that Fitzgerald would write for *The Saturday Evening Post*. For all its triviality, it was a more original and a better-written piece than either of the two stories he had sold to *Scribner's*. The college setting, the unexpected twist in the plot at the end, and the characters —a shy young hero and an attractive, aggressive working-girl heroine (from a vaudeville show)—were to become familiar staples in his subsequent commercial fiction.

Reynolds' news had a marked restorative effect on his health, and Fitzgerald returned much encouraged to St. Paul. Here he wrote "The Ice Palace." It was inspired by his recent trip to Montgomery, and it reflected his mixed feelings not only about Zelda and himself but also about the South and Minnesota. The heroine, Sally Carrol Happer, is bored by her life in a small Southern town and longs for romance and adventure. So, instead of marrying a local boy and settling down like most of her friends, she becomes engaged to an outlander, the aggressive son of a wealthy businessman from the North. The rest of the story takes place during Sally Carrol's first visit to her fiancé's home in Minnesota; and although St. Paul is not specifically named, it obviously provided the setting. Each year Fitzgerald's native city held a colorful winter carnival which figures prominently in the story.[5]

During her visit, Sally Carrol is extensively entertained by her young man's wealthy family. But the more she sees of Minnesota and his friends, the more alien she feels. She dislikes their cold-blooded bustle and efficiency, so different from the relaxed tempo of the South. One afternoon she goes with a crowd of young people to explore the ice palace, one of the carnival's star attractions. While they are investigating it Sally Carrol wanders off, becomes lost, and roams in terror through its ghostly corridors until she is finally rescued. This disturbing adventure brings to the surface the deep-seated misgivings that have been troubling her ever since her arrival. For all its frozen beauty, the glittering ice palace reminds her too much of her fiancé and his world. Breaking off her engagement, she happily goes back home, ready at last to accept her own heritage.

Lorimer promptly bought "The Ice Palace" in December, and, encouraged by this, Fitzgerald rummaged through his backlog of rejected stories to see what else he might have for the *Post*. Lorimer evidently liked stories written in a light, comic vein with attractive, strong-willed young women as heroines. With this in mind, Fitzgerald rewrote two earlier pieces, "Lilah Meets His Family" and "Barbara Bobs Her Hair," that had recently been sent back by *Scribner's*. In his revisions he exaggerated the humorous elements and the heroines' unconventional behavior. Both were artificially contrived and plotted, and neither had the freshness nor the depth of "The Ice Palace." But Lorimer was delighted and took them both. The first, retitled "Myra Meets His Family," told how a poor but honest chorus girl took revenge on her lover's rich, snobbish family—only to find out at the end that their snobbery had just been a way of testing her. Fitzgerald was so ashamed of this story that later he refused to have it included with his collected stories. The second, retitled "Bernice Bobs Her Hair," was more original, and described how a wallflower transformed herself into a belle by daring to cut her hair like a boy's. The basis for it was a list of instructions telling how a girl could make herself popular, which Fitzgerald had prepared for the edification of his younger sister.[6]

With the money from these stories, he now felt that he could afford to go off somewhere alone and work on his second novel. Early in January, he left St. Paul and headed for New Orleans, where he holed up in a room at 2900 Prytania Street. But for several reasons, all somehow connected with Zelda, he was unable to make headway with the book. By now, far more than his passions were involved with the girl. She had become the symbol of the success he had pursued for so long. She would be satisfied by nothing less than fame and fortune; winning her would mean that he had finally reached his goal. And the quickest way to win her, obviously, was to sell more stories to *The Saturday Evening Post*. In this divided state of mind, he found himself unable to write his novel; one corner of his mind kept thinking up clever ideas for magazine stories. "I want to start it," he wrote Perkins from New Orleans, "but I don't want to get broke in the middle and start in and have to write short stories again—because I don't enjoy it and just do it for money. . . . I have two stories for Mr. Bridges both stuck in the middle and two *Post* stories cut off in their first paragraph."[7]

But clever magazine stories, even on the most trivial subjects, required skill and effort. He was forced to discard many beginnings before he hit on a promising idea, and then he had to keep working furiously before he forgot what he had set out to say. He started writing one story at eight o'clock one morning and had it in the mail twenty-one hours later, but it left him exhausted and discouraged. This particular tale, "The Camel's Back," was a smooth little comedy inspired by a fancy-dress party in St. Paul, and Harold Ober had no trouble placing it with the *Post*. But Fitzgerald's failure to make progress with his novel, combined with such frantic writing sprees, had their unfortunate effects. During most of his stay in New Orleans, as he ruefully admitted to Maxwell Perkins, he had been in a "nervous alcoholic state."[8]

His next *Saturday Evening Post* contribution was an even more artificial story called "The Offshore Pirate," which Lorimer accepted even though Ober had now raised Fitzgerald's price. Here the heroine, a beautiful spoiled rich girl, disdainfully rejects one suitor after another. Finally she is kidnapped from her luxurious yacht by a dashing river pirate who forcefully reduces her to abjection. Then it turns out that her kidnapper is really a wealthy young man of impeccable background who has taken this unconventional way of wooing her. The two are obviously made for each other, and their implausible romance ends in a hackneyed but colorful motion-picture embrace.

Gradually, in such stories as these, Fitzgerald was evolving the formula for that frothy, humorous romance featuring an unconventional young American girl as heroine, that would be popularly associated with his name for the rest of his life. But as long as he kept writing this kind of fiction, it was difficult to settle down to sustained work on a serious novel. Less than a month after he arrived in New Orleans, he realized that the project had been a failure. If he were going to spend his time writing nothing but magazine stories, he might as well be in New York; indeed, he was eager to be there, for *This Side of Paradise* was scheduled for publication toward the end of March and he wanted to be on hand when it appeared. By February eleventh, he was living in a room in New York at the Hotel Allerton on East Thirty-ninth Street.

During the next six weeks, while he waited for his novel to appear, he worked on two new stories, both more ambitious than anything he had written so far. The first was "The Jelly-Bean," planned as a vague sequel to "The Ice Palace"; the setting was the same sleepy Southern town. The heroine is a friend of Sally Carrol's named Nancy Lamar. Nancy is not only a more striking and original character than Sally Carrol, but she is much more appealing. Like Zelda Sayre, Nancy Lamar combined the charm and social instincts of a well-nurtured Southern belle with the rebelliousness and daring of the newly emancipated post-World War I American girl.[9]

Nancy's story is presented through the eyes of Jim Powell, who represents the best and worst qualities of the Old South. Good-looking, proud but penniless, Jim is adrift in the new commercialized society whose money-making philosophy he refuses to accept. His own family has lost its property, but instead of learning a trade or skill and making his own way, Jim turns his back on the twentieth century and becomes an unambitious onlooker—a "jelly-bean."

Nancy, another unreconstructed rebel, shares Jim's aristocratic disdain of money grubbing. But whereas Jim is slowly sinking, Nancy is determined to surmount and dominate the post-World War I world. Like Sally Carrol in "The Ice Palace," she gets herself engaged to the son of a rich out-of-state tycoon. But during an epic crapshooting spree at the country club, Nancy and Jim become allies and, falling desperately in love with her, Jim finds a reason for trying to make something of himself. For several hours he is a new man, but the change has come too late to do any good. Nancy is a reckless drinker. Like Jim's loafing, her drinking is a way of protesting against conditions she is unwilling to accept. But in the end it betrays her. While drunk, she elopes with her wealthy outlander and wakes up unhappily to find herself married. Hearing of her plight, Jim bitterly slumps back into his old "jelly-bean" role.

Nancy Lamar was Fitzgerald's first fully drawn portrait of the post-World War I "flapper." "The Jelly-Bean" is also one of the more perceptive stories about the recent South to have been written by a Northerner. Much as Fitzgerald sympathized with Nancy and Jim, he carefully avoided glamorizing them. Even so, Nancy emerges as a vital and attractive person. Like so many pretty Southern girls of her generation, her loyalties were divided between the older, traditional way of life and the new freedom. Where Southern writers like Faulkner and Robert Penn Warren, in such novels as *Sanctuary* and *At Heaven's Gate*, depicted the emancipated flapper as a traitor to the established code, emphasizing her tawdriness and hard-boiled manner, Fitzgerald saw her more sympathetically as one of the South's more poignant heroines.

The Saturday Evening Post, however, turned down "The Jelly-Bean" because of the "unhappy ending," and several other magazine editors also rejected it for this reason. It was only some months later, after the publication of *This Side of Paradise* had made Fitzgerald famous, that Harold Ober was finally able to place this excellent story—and then only in Bernarr Macfadden's almost bankrupt *Metropolitan*, "the fiction-lover's magazine."[10]

In March—still at the Allerton—Fitzgerald wrote another notable short story, "May Day." There is good reason to believe that it was originally the opening part of the novel on which he had been working in New Orleans. Soon after his arrival in New York, he told Max Perkins that he had decided "to break up the start of my novel and sell it as three little character stories to *Smart Set*." Nothing else he wrote that spring, or that *Smart Set* published, seems to fit this description except "May Day," which is really three independent episodes tied together by an unconvincing plot—probably imposed at the last minute. If this is the case, it would help explain "May Day's" prose texture, which had been polished to a much higher luster than was usual in Fitzgerald's commercial fiction. It would also account for the melodramatic ending, which, in all likelihood, was a last-minute addition. For all its structural faults, however, "May Day" surpassed Fitzgerald's earlier fiction in general excellence, and it remained his finest work until *The Great Gatsby* appeared four years later. The editors of *Smart Set* were so pleased with it that, instead of their usual $40 fee, they paid $200.[11]

This impressionistic story is one of the best accounts of what it was like to be young in New York immediately after the war. Many of "May Day's" dramatic incidents—the parade of ex-doughboys up Fifth Avenue, and their looting of the offices of a left-wing newspaper—were based on fact. The mood is especially striking, reflecting not only Fitzgerald's personal disillusion, but the more generalized disenchantment of many of his contemporaries. For them, the feverish idealism of the war years was now being supplanted by disillusion and a sense of betrayal. In May, 1919, Fitzgerald himself had been working at his New York advertising job, despairing of ever becoming a successful author. In his story this personal unhappiness is fused with the public mood. Ever afterwards he would think of that particular May Day as having marked the end of American innocence and the beginning of a new epoch—the Jazz Age—just as the end of that epoch would be marked a decade later by the October, 1929, stock-market crash.[12]

The best parts are the kaleidoscopic scenes in which Fitzgerald expresses the confusions and uncertainties—and the resultant irresponsibility—that characterized a cross section of young people from widely differing backgrounds. The story's weakest features are its melodramatic ending and its unconvincing hero. In fact, Gordon Sterrett is so much like Anthony Patch, the hero of *The Beautiful and Damned*—which Fitzgerald began several months later—that it seems likely that the original novel from which "May Day" was presumably salvaged resembled *The Beautiful and Damned* in its general outlines. If this was the case, it is too bad that Fitzgerald did not save his "May Day" material for *The Beautiful and Damned*, instead of piecing it together in this hasty fashion. The chronicle of Gordon Sterrett's decline and fall needed the more ample space of a novel to do it justice. Indeed, the only convincing thing about Gordon is the intensity of his passion for luxury—a lust with which Fitzgerald himself sympathized but which, nonetheless, he believed to be evil. Gordon's trouble is his inability to distinguish between money and morality. When an old friend accuses him of having gone "bankrupt—morally as well as financially," he answers characteristically, "Don't they usually go together?" Too weak to suppress his lust for self-indulgence or to assert the will to gratify it, Gordon makes a mess of his life and finally puts a bullet through his head.[13]

Gordon's moral confusion and despair undoubtedly reflect Fitzgerald's during those winter months of 1920, while he was struggling to establish himself as both a serious and a successful magazine writer. He was discovering that the magazine audience was much more interested in skillfully written light entertainment than it was in careful craft. *The Saturday Evening Post* wanted bold farce like "The Offshore Pirate," while the more genteel readers of *Scribner's* preferred safe moral tales like his "The Four Fists." The literary taste of one distinguished *Scribner's* subscriber, President John Grier Hibben of Princeton, finds expression in a letter Hibben wrote Fitzgerald soon after *This Side of Paradise* appeared. Hibben was shocked, he said, by Fitzgerald's portrayal of his alma mater in *Paradise* as a country club. Nonetheless, he confessed he had read and enjoyed "The Four Fists." Fitzgerald's response to this letter was an exasperated snort. He had written his heart out in his novel, while "The Four Fists" was nothing but a contrived fake, from its implausible hero to its cheap moral ending. "I wrote it in desperation one evening because I had a three-inch pile of rejection slips and it was financially necessary for me to give the magazines what they wanted," he wrote Hibben in reply. To Max Perkins he said more bluntly: "I've always hated and been ashamed of that damned story, 'The Four Fists.' Not that it is any cheaper than 'The Offshore Pirate' because it isn't but simply because it's a mere plant, a moral tale and utterly lacks vitality."[14]

Just as Fitzgerald was wondering what to do next, his world turned topsy-turvy, leaving him with a new set of problems. In March, 1920, Harold Ober sold the movie rights of "Head and Shoulders" to Metro for $2,500, and subsequently persuaded three other film studios to pay a total of $4,500 for the film rights to three other *Post* stories. Whereupon Zelda capitulated. Their engagement was announced in the Montgomery newspapers on March 20, and *This Side of Paradise*, published six days later, was a splendid success. They were married on April third in the rectory of St. Patrick's Cathedral in New York.[15]

Now Fitzgerald hoped that he could give up writing for the magazines, and that he could support himself on best-selling novels like *Paradise*, varied with an occasional Broadway play. To this end he dedicated himself—unsuccessfully, as things turned out.

For the next half-dozen years he was occasionally obliged to grind out a magazine potboiler to pay his bills. Over the next several years the temptation became harder to resist as Ober pushed his price up to $2,500 a story and as he saw lesser writers earning this much merely by copying his formula. Even so, in contrast to the sixteen magazine stories that he had written during the winter of 1919–1920, he was to write only ten more during the next three years. Of these, only four were truly commercials. The other six were unconventional pieces he had written just for the fun of it; and, characteristically, Ober had difficulty getting them placed.[16]

Trivial, hastily contrived pieces like "Hot and Cold Blood" and "Dice, Brass Knuckles, and Guitar," which he would later be ashamed to republish, brought increasingly higher prices, while serious stories like "The Diamond as Big as the Ritz" or "Absolution" were returned by all the popular magazines and finally went to Mencken's *Smart Set*, or its successor, *The American Mercury*, for as little as $300 and $118, respectively. "I find that what I enjoy writing is always my best," Fitzgerald had written Max Perkins back in the fall of 1919. But the stories that earned the most were usually those that left him most dissatisfied. "I am rather discouraged that a cheap story like *The Popular Girl* written in one week while the baby was being born brings $1,500," he wrote Ober in 1921, "and a genuinely imaginative thing . . . like *The Diamond in the Sky* [as he had originally called "The Diamond as Big as the Ritz"] brings not a thing. But, by God and Lorimer, I'm going to make a fortune yet."[17]

Looking back from the perspective of forty years, we can see more readily than Fitzgerald's contemporaries could why his commercial stories were so admired by George Horace Lorimer, the shrewd editor of *The Saturday Evening Post*. At the start they were useful ammunition for Lorimer in the struggle that was then being politely waged for circulation between Lorimer's *Post* and the *Ladies Home Journal*—which enjoyed the biggest circulation of any magazine in the world. Both publications were the property of the Curtis Publishing Company of Philadelphia. As editor of the *Post* for the past twenty years, Lorimer had been obliged to bask in the shadow of his more famous colleague, Edward Bok, the great editor of the *Journal*. Much of the *Journal's* success had been due to Bok's policy of making it a magazine for the entire family. Meanwhile, the *Saturday Evening Post* had been aimed at a smaller, primarily male audience—"the magazine for the tired businessman," as some of its rivals claimed.[18]

When Bok retired from the editorship in November, 1919, the *Journal* was selling over two million copies and enjoyed a monthly advertising revenue of over a million dollars. One secret of Bok's success had been his invention of the policy of publishing stories and articles which aroused in his readers the desire for the gadgets and other material comforts that were also featured in the *Journal's* advertisements. By 1919, the *Journal's* vulnerability lay in its old-fashioned, Victorian image of the American family. The wives in its stories were invariably demure and uncomplaining, the husbands aggressive and virile, and the children obedient and well-mannered. In spite of its advertising revenue, the record-breaking November, 1919, issue of the *Ladies Home Journal,* which signaled Bok's retirement, carried only four inconspicuous advertisements selling cosmetics. Of these, only one was bold enough to suggest that ladies would benefit from the use of "lip-rouge" —and even this one quickly explained that its effects would be "imperceptible if properly applied."[19]

The *Journal's* conservative tastes in fiction merely reflected those of the other successful magazines of the era. If there was any American author who had reason to complain against the vapid idealism of popular taste, it was Theodore Dreiser, whose novel, *Sister Carrie,* had been issued in the smallest possible edition by a conscience-stricken publisher on the grounds that it was an immoral book. Yet when Dreiser himself assumed the editorship of the *Delineator* magazine shortly before World War I, he cheerfully insisted on an insipid editorial policy that automatically excluded his own serious work. "We like sentiment, we like humor, we like realism," he instructed his staff, "but it must be tinged with sufficient idealism to make it of truly uplifting character. . . . We cannot admit stories which deal with false or immoral relations, or which deal with things degrading, such as drunkenness. . . . The finer things of life—the idealistic is [sic] the answer for us, and we find really splendid material within these limitations." Under no circumstances, Dreiser insisted, should the *Delineator's* illustrations depict people with glasses of wine or cigarettes in their hands.[20]

By 1919, two important new developments had taken place in American life, both greatly accelerated by the recent war. The behavior of teen-agers was no longer that described in popular magazine fiction. Moreover, American youth was asserting itself as a new economic market with tastes and expectations quite different from those of its parents, and with increasingly more money at its disposal to gratify these desires. If a magazine like *The Saturday Evening Post* could somehow identify itself with these new values and attitudes, it could supplant the *Ladies Home Journal* as the world's biggest magazine. In November, 1919 (the month Bok resigned), when Lorimer read the manuscript of his first Fitzgerald story, "Head and Shoulders," he promptly bought it and asked to see more of this author's work.

Publishing stories like "Head and Shoulders" or "Myra Meets His Family" undoubtedly involved a certain amount of risk. After all, what would Lorimer's tired businessmen think of young girls who swore, smoked, drank, wore tight one-piece bathing suits, and talked back impudently to their parents? After the heroine of his story, "Bernice Bobs Her Hair," walked into a men's barber shop and asked for a short haircut, Fitzgerald and Lorimer both were swamped with letters from angry parents accusing them of corrupting their daughters' morals.[21]

Lorimer's courage paid off, however. Advertisements illustrating how other girls could be similarly popular on a moderate budget promptly blossomed in the columns adjoining these *Saturday Evening Post* stories. Fitzgerald, of course, cannot be credited with having engineered this revolution in manners single-handedly, but he led the way. The skeptic has only to examine back-files of the *Post*, and other popular magazines, to see how quickly the unconventional attitudes and values described in Fitzgerald's early stories were reflected in the magazine advertisements as well as in the pictures illustrating his fiction. Parents might protest angrily against heroines like Bernice, but their daughters promptly imitated her. Before long the *Post*'s cover-girls were wearing bobbed hair too.[22]

No wonder Lorimer preferred a light, hastily written story like "Myra Meets His Family" to a better but more pathetic tale like "The Jelly-Bean." Fitzgerald experienced considerable difficulty adjusting himself to this hard reality. But once he grasped the situation he temporarily put his tongue in his cheek and, in "The Offshore Pirate," produced for Lorimer's edification an extravaganza of pure advertising-copy prose. Actually, this was the last story Fitzgerald was to write for the *Post* for several years. But for many readers it represented the kind of fiction they would continue to associate with him for the rest of his life. "The Offshore Pirate" began as follows:[23]

This unlikely story opens on a sea that was a blue dream, as colorful as blue-silk stockings, and beneath a sky as blue as the irises of children's eyes. From the western half of the sky the sun was shying little golden disks at the sea—if you gazed intently enough you could see them skip from wave-tip to wave-tip until they joined a broad collar of golden coin that was collecting half a mile out and would eventually be a dazzling sunset. About half-way between the Florida shore and the golden collar a white steam-yacht, very young and graceful, was riding at anchor and under a blue-and-white awning aft a yellow-haired girl reclined in a wicker settee reading The Revolt of the Angels, by Anatole France.

She was about nineteen, slender and supple, with a spoiled alluring mouth and quick gray eyes full of a radiant curiosity. Her feet, stockingless, and adorned rather than clad in blue-satin slippers which swung nonchalantly from her toes, were perched on the arm of a settee adjoining the one she occupied. And as she read she intermittently regaled herself by a faint application to her tongue of a half-lemon that she held in her hand. The other half, sucked dry, lay on the deck at her feet and rocked very gently to and fro at the almost imperceptible motion of the tide.

The second half-lemon was well-nigh pulpless and the golden collar had grown astonishing in width, when suddenly the drowsy silence which enveloped the yacht was broken by the sound of heavy footsteps and an elderly man topped with orderly gray hair and clad in a white-flannel suit appeared at the head of the companionway. There he paused for a moment until his eyes became accustomed to the sun, and then seeing the girl under the awning he uttered a long even grunt of disapproval.

"Ardita!" said the gray-haired man sternly.

Ardita uttered a small sound indicating nothing.

"Ardita!" he repeated. "Ardita!"

Ardita raised the lemon languidly, allowing three words to slip out before it reached her tongue.

"Oh, shut up."

Once this new kind of story had caught on, it made little difference to Lorimer or other rival editors *who* wrote the stories, so long as they read like Fitzgerald's. If Fitzgerald preferred to write stories with unhappy endings for editors like Mencken, there were others who were not too proud to exploit the vein of gold he had unearthed. By August, 1920, stories by other writers bearing title such as "Maroon Colored, with Wire Wheels," were regularly appearing in the *Post*. And when

College Humor, that spectacularly successful and most representative magazine of the Jazz Age, appeared on the scene in 1922, Fitzgerald's influence could be recognized everywhere in its glittering prose. Describing the kind of serial novel he was looking for, *College Humor's* editor told Katharine Brush: "What I want is a novel like *This Side of Paradise.* Give me glamor and plenty of it. Give me the cry of horns and the whisper of dancing feet."[24]

> And I did [said Miss Brush]. There was practically a prom on every page. And a prom girl, naturally. A gilded babe. . . . They all had tiny feet in snub-nosed slippers, with tall heels. They were ultra-modern. They had incredible eyelashes and most of them were brown-eyed blondes. . . . Their names were usually Jean Amidon or Charmian Phillips, or something; they were in love with jaunty gentlemen called Perry Leonard or "Snake" Otterbridge, who played the banjo, stroked the crew, captained the football team, flunked all their studies—understandably enough—and went about in coonskin coats, with their hair parted in the middle.

Thus Fitzgerald continued to be popularly associated with material of this kind, even though the greater part of his writing from 1921 to 1926 was in a different vein. His next two novels, *The Beautiful and Damned* and *The Great Gatsby,* as well as his play, *The Vegetable,* attempted to explore and expose the values that he had so naïvely glamorized in his early *Saturday Evening Post* stories and *This Side of Paradise.*

The failure of his play, *The Vegetable,* during its Atlantic City opening in the autumn of 1923, however, left Fitzgerald $5,000 in debt. And again he turned back to commercial magazine fiction as he had during the winter of 1919–1920. Between November, 1923, and April, 1924, he ground out the amazing total of eleven stories and seven essays and articles, which Harold Ober easily sold for a total of some $22,000. But now it was all the most obvious kind of hack work. Fitzgerald knew what the editors expected of him and gave it to them. In three stories, "The Baby Party," "Gretchen's Forty Winks," and "The Sensible Thing," he tried to make use of personal experience, notably his feelings about Zelda. But even the best of this group, "The Sensible Thing," failed because of the compromises he made in order to sell it. "On re-reading this story it doesn't seem good," he wrote Ober, apologetically. "I started with one mood and plot and finished it with another and somewhere between there is a joint that shows." Ober, however, had no difficulty in selling the story to Liberty for $1,750.[25]

The best of the magazine stories that Fitzgerald wrote from 1919 to 1925, that is between *This Side of Paradise* and *The Great Gatsby*, were collected and published in three volumes: *Flappers and Philosophers* (1920), *Tales of the Jazz Age* (1922), and *All the Sad Young Men* (1926). Since there has never been a very large market in this country for books of short stories, it was Scribner's practice to schedule the publication date of each volume so that it coincided as nearly as possible with the appearance of one of Fitzgerald's novels. In this way, the stories benefited from the fanfare accompanying the novels. The first collection, *Flappers and Philosophers*, representing the best stories he had written for *Smart Set* and the *Post* during the winter of 1919–1920, contained eight pieces of fairly uniform quality. Even "The Offshore Pirate," for all its tongue-in-cheek manner, still makes amusing reading.

The second, *Tales of the Jazz Age*, illustrated the deterioration that had set in, now that he understood how little interest the magazines took in his more serious writing. The two best pieces in the book, "May Day" and "The Jelly-Bean," dated back to the winter of 1919–1920 and would have been included in *Flappers and Philosophers* except for the fact that they were still waiting for publication in a magazine. The only other notable stories in this second volume were two that Fitzgerald had written primarily for his own entertainment, "The Diamond as Big as the Ritz" and "The Curious Case of Benjamin Button." Of these "The Diamond" was not only the better one, but for that very reason had been rejected by more magazine editors than any other story in the volume.

"The Diamond as Big as the Ritz" is an example of a literary genre that Fitzgerald extravagantly admired at the time but rarely brought off successfully—whimsical fantasy. Like the rest of his generation, he had grown up admiring such Victorian classics as *Alice in Wonderland*, the Savoy operas, and *Peter Pan*. But fantasy as a literary form demanded certain qualities of wit and taste that he did not possess. When he tried to write clever whimsy, he usually succeeded only in being cute or coy. Edmund Wilson, who shared Fitzgerald's predilection, encouraged him in this direction. *Tales of the Jazz Age* includes a number of Fitzgerald's feebler ventures; his play, *The Vegetable*, would be his most catastrophic experiment with the form.

What saved "The Diamond as Big as the Ritz" from a similar fate was the fact that Fitzgerald was able to make use of the exaggerations and other comic devices of fantasy to express his convictions about the fantastic power of money in our society. Here, as nowhere else in his fantasies, form and content were perfectly fused. The result was an authentic American fairy tale, a Jazz-Age variant of the story of Jack the Giant-Killer. Jack, in this instance, is a sixteen-year-old boy from the Midwest named John T. Unger, whose money-worshiping parents have sent him East to St. Midas' School, "the most expensive and the most exclusive boys' preparatory school in the world." Here John becomes acquainted with a classmate from Montana, Percy Washington, who invites him home for the holidays. On the trip west, John learns that Percy's father is "the richest man in the world."

The Washingtons live in isolated splendor in a secret valley hidden deep in the Rocky Mountains, where they own a diamond "bigger than the Ritz-Carlton Hotel." They have preserved their passion for anonymity for three generations by corrupting government officials and incarcerating unsuspecting intruders. Soon after John's arrival, he learns that at the end of his visit he is destined to be imprisoned for life or destroyed. Percy's father, Braddock Washington, a direct descendant of George Washington and Lord Baltimore, combines the worst traits of a Southern plantation owner (he is waited on by an army of two hundred and fifty enslaved Negroes) and a Gilded Age tycoon. The Washingtons eat from diamond plates and their gold-and-platinum palace is defended by a battery of the most up-to-date anti-aircraft guns. Their existence is a blend of Arabian Nights extravaganza and ingenious American gadgetry. John Unger has only to press a button to be propelled gently from his bed into the adjoining perfumed bath.

Also, with the press of a button Mr. Washington is able to blow up and destroy his secluded fortress. This he does when Army bombers discover him and render his defenses useless. Luckily, John is saved by Percy's beautiful sixteen-year-old sister, Kismine, who helps him escape before the palace goes up in smoke and flames. Fitzgerald later said that he had written this story to satisfy his craving for luxury. Of all his fantasies, this one best conveys his envy of—his almost sensual lust for— the power and possessions of the very rich.

Aside from "The Diamond," "May Day," and "The Jelly-Bean," however, *Tales of the Jazz Age* consisted only of hack work. During the two years that had elapsed since the appearance of *Flappers and Philosophers,* Fitzgerald had not written enough good pieces to warrant the publication of a second collection. He himself hinted as much in the apologetic prefaces he wrote for each story in the table of contents. But, in spite of its padding, *Tales of the Jazz Age* sold thirteen thousand copies, a thousand more than its much better predecessor, *Flappers and Philosophers*.

All the Sad Young Men, Fitzgerald's third volume of short stories, was also heavily padded with second-rate material. Although it was published in 1926, a year after *The Great Gatsby,* all but one of the stories dated back to the period between 1922 and 1924. Therefore, the contents deserve to be included in any consideration of Fitzgerald's early or "pre-*Gatsby*" fiction. Only three stories in the volume were really outstanding: "Winter Dreams," "Absolution," and "The Rich Boy" (which Fitzgerald wrote immediately after finishing his proof-corrections for *Gatsby*). All three were connected in some way with the impulse that inspired *The Great Gatsby,* and so discussion of them will be postponed until they can be treated in their relation to that book.

The rest of the stories in *All the Sad Young Men* were written during the hectic winter of 1923–1924 to get Fitzgerald out of debt. What he wrote in a letter to Harold Ober about a typical *Post* story of the period, "The Popular Girl," holds for these other hasty commercial pieces too.[26]

> You notice that The Popular Girl hasn't the vitality of my earlier, popular stories, even though I've learned my tricks better and am technically more proficient. I don't believe it's possible to stand still —you've either got to go ahead or slide back and in The Popular Girl I was merely repeating the matter of my earlier period without being able to capture the exuberant manner.

Thus, the quality of Fitzgerald's magazine fiction generally declined between 1920 and 1925, while the price he received for his stories steadily climbed. And *The Saturday Evening Post,* his old stand-by, forged ahead, in circulation as well as in advertising revenue. By 1925 it had a circulation of over three million, and a typical two-hundred-page issue carried five million dollars' worth of advertising. More than any other magazine of the era, the *Post* served as the spokesman for the typical American middle-class mind.[27]

Because of Fitzgerald's early popular fame and pervasive influence, one can understand why the public that admired *This Side of Paradise* and his early magazine stories showed little interest in a serious novel like *The Great Gatsby.* Even as late as 1940, many readers learning of his death still associated him with a kind of fiction that he had not been writing for many years. Somewhat more astonishing is the fact that so many literary pundits made the same error. Take such self-appointed custodians of the short story as Blanche Colton Williams and Edward J. O'Brien, whose annual volumes of the "best" or "prize" stories from the magazines were familiar landmarks of the era. They too were so dazzled by Fitzgerald's commercial success that they generally overlooked his really good work. Thus, Miss Williams passed over such excellent stories as "May Day" and "The Jelly-Bean," and included the more trivial "The Camel's Back" in her *O. Henry Memorial Prize Award Stories for 1920*. And her rival, that grand panjandrum of the short-story anthology, Edward O'Brien, skipped over all these stories and cited "The Four Fists" and "The Cut-Glass Bowl" as among *The Best Short Stories of 1920*. Two years later he ignored first-rate stories like "Winter Dreams" and "The Diamond as Big as the Ritz," and selected instead the mediocre "Two for a Cent" for inclusion in his *The Best Short Stories of 1922*. O'Brien, who remained an enthusiastic if undiscriminating reader of Fitzgerald's magazine stories over the years and continued to reprint them in his collections, was, in Fitzgerald's opinion, "the world's greatest admirer of mediocre short stories."[28]

In general, the leading literary critics—with the exception of his friend, Edmund Wilson—ignored Fitzgerald's work prior to the publication of *The Great Gatsby* in 1925. The only really perceptive essay that appeared was written by Paul Rosenfeld, better known for his sensitive essays on music and painting than as a literary scholar. Rosenfeld pointed out that Fitzgerald was not the skilled professional magazine author many people took him to be. He lacked the rational habits of mind, the sense of structure, and the knack for plots that mark the true expert in this narrow but rigorous discipline. Fitzgerald was at his best when he explored dramatically conflicting human emotions. "May Day" —hardly a proper short story at all—was, in Rosenfeld's opinion, "perhaps the most mature of all his tales." In a passage that shrewdly gauged the distance Fitzgerald must travel before he would reach the higher ground of *The Great Gatsby*, Rosenfeld went on to say:[29]

. . . And yet, in spite of "May Day," Fitzgerald has not yet crossed the line that bounds the field of art. He has seen his material from its own point of view, and he has seen it completely from without. But he has not done what the artist does: seen it simultaneously from within and without; and loved it and judged it, too. For "May Day" lacks a focal point and merely juxtaposes a small number of pieces. Should Fitzgerald finally break his mould, and free himself of the compulsions of the civilization in which he grew, it might go badly with his popularity. It will be a pathetic story he will have to tell, the legend of a moon that never rose; and that is precisely the story a certain America does not wish to hear. Nevertheless, we would like hugely to hear him tell it. And Fitzgerald might scarcely miss his following.

V

*The Beautiful
and Damned* and
The Vegetable

Fitzgerald had unsuccessfully pursued a number of ideas for a second novel before finally settling on the unhappy history of Anthony Patch, the hero of *The Beautiful and Damned*. His first plan was to write something called "The Demon Lover"; it is mentioned briefly in his letter of September 18, 1919, to Maxwell Perkins. But what this was about remains a mystery. He apparently abandoned the idea after a few weeks and there is no further mention of it. By mid-October he was busily planning a new novel of about twenty thousand words to be called "The Diary of a Literary Failure." He now hoped to persuade *Scribner's Magazine* to publish this in several parts. It would consist, he wrote Robert Bridges, of:[1]

> . . . selections from the note-books of a man who is a complete literary radical from the time he's in college thru two years in New York. . . .
>
> It will be in turns cynical, ingenuous, life-saturated, critical and bitter. It will be racy and startling with opinions and personalities. I have a journal I have kept for 3½ years which my book didn't begin to exhaust, which I don't seem to be able to draw on for stories. . . . This thoroughly edited and revised plus some imagination and ½ doz ingredients I have in mind will be the bulk of it. . . . The tremendous success of Butler's notebooks and of Barbellion's (Wells) Dissapointed Man makes me think that the public loves to find out the workings of active minds in their personal problems. It will be

bound to have that streak of coarseness that both Wells and Butler have but there won't be any James Joyce flavor to it.

But no "journal" like the one which he described in this letter has ever come to light. Neither his childhood Thoughtbook nor the auto-biographical Ledger in which he set down the month-by-month account of his life seems to fit this description. Instead, what he seems to have had in mind was some leftover autobiographical material from "The Romantic Egotist" that he had been unable to incorporate into *This Side of Paradise*. Whatever it was, Robert Bridges showed no interest in buying it for *Scribner's*.

Nonetheless, Fitzgerald did not give up the project. Several weeks later, in a letter to Harold Ober, we find him writing about it in greater detail. It was to be a collection of episodes strung together loosely in the manner of *This Side of Paradise* and would include "one long thing which might make a novelette for the *Post* called *The Diary of a Popular Girl*, half a dozen cynical incidents that might do for *Smart Set*, and perhaps a story or two for *Scribner's* or *Harper's*." He hoped that Ober might be able to sell some of this material to the magazines before it appeared in book form, just as he himself had recently disposed of two episodes from *This Side of Paradise* to *Smart Set*.[2]

But before long "The Diary of a Literary Failure" was also put aside; further references to it cease, and by December Fitzgerald was writing Max Perkins about a new novel to be called "The Drunkard's Holiday." Either this project was also discarded or it was given a new title, for when Fitzgerald went off to New Orleans soon afterwards in January, 1920, to work on a novel, it was now referred to in his letters to Perkins as "Darling Heart." As we have already seen, he made little progress with this project in New Orleans, and, when he returned to New York in February, it was presumably the fragments of "Darling Heart" that he used for the story, "May Day." Except for that story, nothing else remains of these abortive attempts to get started on a second novel.[3]

Fitzgerald intended this next novel to be professional in every sense of the word—entertaining enough to make a lot of money, and well-written enough to satisfy readers like Edmund Wilson and John Peale Bishop, both of whom were writing criticism for New York magazines. But as long as he needed to prove himself to Zelda by writing magazine stories, he found it hard to get really started on a serious piece of work. And yet whenever he succeeded with magazine stories, his literary conscience bothered him. As soon as he sold "The Offshore Pirate" to the

Post, he wrote Max Perkins a conscience-stricken letter in which he promised, "I'm going to obey my own mandate and write every book as if it were the last work I'd have on earth."[4]

Another development that kept him from getting on with the novel was his discovery of the new school of American realists—among them Frank Norris and his brother Charles Norris, Theodore Dreiser and Harold Frederic. They were of more somber temperament than Wells and Mackenzie, and Fitzgerald worried about whether the popular magazines would buy fiction in this style. "How about it," he inquired of Harold Ober. ". . . Do you think a story like C.G. Norris' *Salt* or Cabell's *Jurgen* or Dreiser's *Jennie Gerhardt* would have one chance in a million to be sold serially—it will have an influence on my future plans."[5]

Fitzgerald's indecision was due in large part to his inability to find a subject that suited both his literary ambitions and his financial needs. But his difficulty in getting started ceased once *Paradise* had established him professionally and he was married. In June, 1920, Ober sold the serial rights for this still-unwritten second novel to the *Metropolitan* for $7,000 and six weeks later Fitzgerald was making such good progress that he promised Ober the first draft would be finished by October first.[6]

His tentative title, he wrote Charles Scribner several weeks later, was "The Flight of the Rocket." His hero was to be "one of those many with the tastes and weaknesses of an artist but with no actual creative inspiration. How he and his beautiful young wife are wrecked on the shoals of dissipation is told in the story. This sounds sordid but its really a most sensational book and I hope won't disappoint the critics who liked my first one. I hope it'll be in your hands by November 1st." There were continual interruptions, however, and the delivery date was repeatedly postponed. In August, the Fitzgeralds drove south to visit the Sayre family in Montgomery. When they returned, in September, they gave up their Westport house and took an apartment in New York at 38 West 59th Street. In November, they moved again to 381 East 59th Street. But by now, the Manhattan season was in full swing, and the famous author of *This Side of Paradise* and his attractive young wife were quickly swept up in a whirl of parties and other distractions.[7]

Further progress on *The Beautiful and Damned* (as it had now been retitled) was also delayed by the author's chronic financial worries. It is easy to laugh at these, especially since *This Side of Paradise* was selling well and his price for a magazine story had climbed to $1,000. Nonetheless, Fitzgerald had very real fears. Not only were Zelda and he both spending money like water but he had no sense at all about business matters. The mathematics of money bored when it did not exasperate him. To the intricacies of everyday economics he brought only a few simple childhood principles: borrowing was a sin, and the only way to overcome it was to work hard enough to pay off one's debts. But principles like these were awkward for the would-be free-lance writer, who must often get by on publisher's advances against work still to be done.

When the seven thousand dollars from the *Metropolitan* evaporated, Fitzgerald found it hard to resist Reynolds' offer to make advances against unwritten magazine stories—stories that he was sure he could dash off in his spare time. But the stories did not come that easily. The manuscript of *The Beautiful and Damned* was put aside while he struggled with a story that would not take shape and fretted nervously over the novel that was gathering dust on the shelf. Before long he would blow up, and Max Perkins would receive a desperate appeal. "Here with the novel within two weeks of completion," one typical letter goes, "am I with six hundred dollars worth of bills and owing Reynolds $650.00 for an advance on a story that I'm utterly unable to write. I've made half a dozen starts yesterday and today and I'll go mad if I have to do another debutante [story,] which is what they want. . . . I need *$1600.00*."[8]

Usually Perkins would have the necessary amount promptly deposited to Fitzgerald's account. But one afternoon Fitzgerald thoughtlessly cashed a check for a bigger sum than he had in his bank; then he discovered that, because the next day was a holiday, Scribner's would not be able to cover his overdraft in time. The result was that he spent the interim in a cold sweat, momentarily expecting the police to arrive and carry him off to jail. This was one lesson in economics that he would never forget. Several years later he put his anguish and humiliation into a short story, "The Rubber Check."

Zelda was not a great deal of help on these occasions. Her solution to the problem of how to keep from spending too much money was to hide it. One morning Fitzgerald awoke to discover that she had concealed $500 so ingeniously that neither of them was ever able to find it.[9]

Occasionally there were periods when work on the novel progressed rapidly—even too rapidly. "Done 15,000 words in last three days," one note to Perkins reports. After many interruptions, the first draft of *The Beautiful and Damned* was finished in January, 1921, and, after further revision, the manuscript was delivered to the *Metropolitan* on April twenty-seventh. On May third the Fitzgeralds sailed for Europe. It was their first trip, and they had been looking forward to it eagerly. But Zelda was pregnant and, as the weeks passed, traveling about became increasingly uncomfortable for her. They cut their trip short and by midsummer were back with her family in Alabama. In late August they moved from Montgomery to St. Paul where they remained for the next fourteen months. Here in October their only child, Frances Scott Key Fitzgerald, was born.[10]

By now the magazine serial version of *The Beautiful and Damned* had begun to appear, and Fitzgerald learned to his dismay that the *Metropolitan* editor had cut his original 130,000-word story to less than 90,000 words. The rule adopted for cutting seemed to be to take out everything that did not advance the plot. And since plot had always been Fitzgerald's nemesis, the result of this butchery was to emphasize the book's weakest points. We can see this by comparing the chopped-up magazine version of *The Beautiful and Damned* with the full-length text that Scribner's subsequently published in book form. In his eagerness to emphasize the story-line the *Metropolitan's* editor had cut out most of the dramatic episodes and the passages of evocative prose which created and sustained that atmosphere of dissipation and irresponsibility that was the book's most distinguishing feature.[11]

Rereading his novel after his European holiday, Fitzgerald realized that it had been written much too hastily and in the midst of too many distractions. The whole manuscript needed a thorough revision before it appeared in book form. It was twice as long as *This Side of Paradise* and much more intricate and ambitious in structure and theme. But where that first novel had taken shape over a period of three years, and most of it had been revised at least three different times, *The Beautiful and Damned* had been written in six months and revised in less than three. His plan now was to spend the autumn of 1921 in St. Paul carefully revising his manuscript before Scribner's published it in book form. His mood at the time was one of discouragement. ". . . I've loafed for 5 months and I want to get to work," he had written Perkins in August. "Loafing puts me in this particularly obnoxious and abominable gloom. My third novel, if I ever write another, will I am sure be as black as death with gloom. . . . If it wasn't for Zelda I think I'd disappear out of sight for three years. Ship as a sailor or something & get hard—I'm sick of the flabby semi-intellectual softness in which I flounder with my generation."[12]

Friends like Harold Ober and Edmund Wilson, whose critical judgments he valued, were admonished to disregard the emasculated version of *The Beautiful and Damned* currently running in the *Metropolitan*. When the book version appeared, he promised, it would be "almost entirely rewritten." It was a brave resolution, but one that he was unable to carry out. A comparison of the magazine and book versions shows that he actually did very little revising for the Scribner text. He began by smoothing up a number of clumsy sentences at the beginning, but he undertook no major structural changes of any kind. After a few chapters he stopped polishing altogether. He probably realized that to do justice to his material he would have to start over from scratch.[13]

There were also several other reasons for this decision. Perkins wanted to get the book version into print as soon as possible, to take advantage of the advertising that accompanied the serialization in the *Metropolitan*. Besides, Fitzgerald was now so popular that the book would probably have a respectable sale despite its literary flaws. (And this proved to be the case, for it sold more copies during its first year than *This Side of Paradise*.) In his usual nervous funk over money, he postponed work on his novel while he wrote another story for *The Saturday Evening Post*. Then, in November, he was suddenly inspired with the idea of writing a satirical play about Washington politics, *The Vegetable*, which he decided was bound to make his fortune on Broadway.

The trouble with *The Beautiful and Damned* was that Fitzgerald was really trying to write two stories. One was a tragedy of modern married life inspired by the new Dreiser-Norris kind of realism. The second was a brittle comedy of ideas in the manner of Shaw or Wilde. Of the two, the second was the more difficult. Too much of the humor of *The Beautiful and Damned* consisted of private jokes. To appreciate them, the reader needed to know the extent to which Gloria and Anthony and their companions were exaggerated portraits of the Fitzgeralds themselves and their friends, notably Edmund Wilson, George Jean Nathan, H.L. Mencken and Fitzgerald's Princeton classmate, Ludlow Fowler. The episodes involving the Japanese house servant named Tana, for instance, are more amusing if the reader has been told that the Fitzgeralds had an oriental servant of this name whom Mencken and Nathan pretended was an enemy agent in disguise. Fitzgerald had talked so much about immortalizing his friends in his next book that new he felt obligated to do so at any price.[14]

The long-winded conversations in which Anthony, Richard, and Maury discuss sex, marriage, love, education, and the meaning of life, were based on similar discussions the Fitzgeralds had enjoyed with their friends over glasses of bootleg gin during that first summer of their marriage in Westport. To enliven the quality of the repartee, Fitzgerald drew heavily on his memories of Shaw's *Prefaces* and Wilde's *Picture of Dorian Gray*. Another recent discovery was the *Notebooks* of Samuel Butler. ("The most interesting book ever written," he had noted enthusiastically on the fly-leaf of his well-thumbed, heavily underlined copy.) Occasionally (i.e., "Life is one long process of getting tired"), he even quoted Butler's pithy aphorisms as if they were his own.[15]

On a somewhat different level, *The Beautiful and Damned* was intended to be a sort of latter-day *Vanity Fair*, a moral commentary on certain aspects of postwar American society. During the four years that had elapsed since he started writing *This Side of Paradise*, Fitzgerald's point of view toward the contemporary scene had radically changed. Many of the values he had so innocently glamorized in this first novel and his early short stories were now losing their luster. "While I took a little time off," Fitzgerald said of the period that elapsed between the writing of these two novels, "a fresh picture of life in America began to form before my eyes. The uncertainties of 1919 were over—there seemed little doubt about what was going to happen—America was going on the greatest, gaudiest spree in history and there was going to be plenty to tell about it. The whole golden boom was in the air. . . . All the stories that came into my head had a touch of disaster in them—the lovely young creatures in my novels went to ruin, the diamond mountains of my short stories blew up, my millionaires were as beautiful and damned as Thomas Hardy's peasants. In life these things hadn't happened yet, but I was pretty sure living wasn't the reckless, careless business these people thought—this younger generation just younger than me."[16]

For this new point of view Fitzgerald was indebted especially to Dreiser, Norris, and the other realists whose work he had discovered during the summer of 1919, just as he was finishing *This Side of Paradise*. By then it was too late for them to have had much influence on the writing of his first novel. But toward the end of the book he had recorded how Amory Blaine had been "rather surprised by his discovery through a critic named Mencken of several excellent novels: 'Vandover and the Brute,' 'The Damnation of Theron Ware' and 'Jennie Gerhardt.' "[17]

It is easy to understand how Fitzgerald was attracted to *The Damnation of Theron Ware*, not only because it was an outstanding novel but one that had dealt sympathetically with the American conflict between Catholic and Protestant that he himself had experienced. Despite certain differences in background and viewpoint, he also admired Theodore Dreiser, another renegade Catholic. Several years later, Fitzgerald was to tell Maxwell Perkins that he considered Dreiser's portrait of Hurstwood in *Sister Carrie* to be one of the few really great achievements in American fiction.[18]

But of these three—Harold Frederic, Theodore Dreiser, Frank Norris—it was Norris whose influence is most conspicuous in *The Beautiful and Damned*. It was Norris with whom Fitzgerald most easily identified himself as a fellow American author. The parallels between their two careers are striking. Both had been dedicated writers from childhood. Norris' first ambitious boyhood work was a long medieval poem, "Yvernelle," reminiscent of Fitzgerald's childhood narrative, "Elavoe." Westerners in upbringing, both had gone East to college—Norris to Harvard —where they began writing their first novels. Both had burst spectacularly on the American literary scene in their early twenties. Perhaps there was a certain significance too for Fitzgerald (who disliked the idea of growing old) in the fact that Norris had died tragically at the height of his fame when he was only thirty-one years old.

Norris served Fitzgerald in *The Beautiful and Damned* as the kind of literary model that Compton Mackenzie had been for *This Side of Paradise*. "There are things in *Paradise* that might have been written by Norris—those drunken scenes for instance—in fact, all the realism," he wrote Max Perkins during the spring of 1920. "I wish I'd stuck to it throughout!" Later, in 1921, reviewing a new novel entitled *Brass* by Norris' brother, Charles G. Norris, Fitzgerald described his original excitement in discovering the school of naturalistic fiction: "To me it was utterly new. I had never read Zola or Frank Norris or Dreiser. . . . No one of my English professors in college had ever suggested to his class that books were being written in America. Poor souls, they were as ignorant as I." With characteristic enthusiasm Fitzgerald wrote Charles Norris and H.L. Mencken in 1920 suggesting that Norris' fiction be republished in a uniform collected edition—a project that materialized several years later under Mencken's supervision. Fitzgerald's admiration for Norris is also evident in one of the deleted passages of *The Beautiful and Damned*, in which Richard Caramel, the successful novelist whose career is based on Fitzgerald's own recent history, describes himself proudly as "the only authentic American realist since Frank Norris."[19]

Of Norris' novels and stories, *Vandover and the Brute* was by far the most influential. Unlike Norris' other stories, it was about a wealthy upper-middle-class young American—indeed, it is the most autobiographical of all his work. He had written it in the early 1890's while he was a Harvard undergraduate. In its forthright treatment of love and sex it was much closer to the spirit of 1920—so much so that Norris' publishers had withheld publication until 1912, twelve years after his death. Even then it was ahead of its time and was treated gingerly by most of the critics. Today, however, *Vandover* is among the most admired of Norris' works.[20]

There are a number of parallels between it and *The Beautiful and*

Damned. Perhaps the most obvious is the atmosphere of moral decay that pervades both stories. There are also striking similarities between the two heroes. Frank Vandover and Anthony Patch both come from wealthy families; both go to Harvard; later, both pursue dissipated, aimless careers as dilettantes and men about town. Both drift into casual affairs with innocent girls from a poorer background, treat them shabbily, are later found out, and as a result forfeit the affection and respect of the girl they really love. Whereupon, both heroes go into a moral tail spin. Vandover loses his reason and sinks into bestiality. According to Edmund Wilson, Fitzgerald planned at one stage to have *The Beautiful and Damned* end similarly "in a carnival of disaster for which the reader was imperfectly prepared; . . . [he] removed his characters wholesale with a set of catastrophes so arbitrary that, beside them, the worst perversities of Hardy were like the working of natural law." Eventually, however, Fitzgerald settled on an ending that merely reduced Anthony to a state of childish imbecility.[21]

Yet in spite of its debts to *Vandover and the Brute* and to the fiction of Dreiser and Harold Frederic, *The Beautiful and Damned* cannot be regarded as an authentic example of American naturalistic fiction. Fitzgerald's point of view toward his material, especially toward his hero and heroine, Gloria and Anthony Patch, was too wavering and inconsistent. Most of the time Anthony is nothing more than a weak, spoiled rich boy. But Fitzgerald is continually struggling to give his history tragic dimensions. On page 144, for example, we are told that Anthony is the victim of an implacable fate "more profound, more powerful than the God made in the image of man, and before which that God, did he exist, would be equally impotent." Yet two pages later Anthony is described as a kind of Jazz Age Hamlet reduced to impotence by his own powers of mind and heart, by "that quality of understanding too well to blame—that quality which was the best of him and had worked swiftly and ceaselessly toward his ruin." Is Anthony supposed to be a naturalistic hero victimized by a world he never made, or a Shakespearean protagonist of Hamlet-like stature?

In the *Metropolitan* serial version of *The Beautiful and Damned*, Fitzgerald went so far as to end his novel with the following paragraph (subsequently deleted from the book text), which was clearly intended to elevate poor Anthony and Gloria to the stature of tragic characters:[22]

Beneath the sordid dress and near the bruised heart of this transaction there was a motive which was not weak but only futile and sad. In the search for happiness, which search is the greatest and possibly the only crime of which we in our petty misery are capable, these two people were marked as guilty chiefly by the freshness and fullness of their desire. Their disillusion was always a comparative thing—they sought glamour and color through their respective worlds with a steadfast loyalty—sought it and it alone in kisses and in wine, sought it with the same ingenuousness in the wanton moonlight as under the bold sun of inviolate chastity. Their fault was not that they doubted but that they believed.

The sympathetic ending in the *Metropolitan* version contrasted sharply with the ironic view of Anthony and Gloria that predominated in the first half of the novel. Fitzgerald had begun with the idea that Anthony was to be the victim of an implacable fate, with Gloria the providential instrument of his destruction—a *dea ex machina*. In the course of telling their story, he became absorbed in their relationship to each other. He had come to see their incompatibility, their unhappy marriage, their need for each other, and their struggle to hold their marriage together, as a doomed and tragic theme.

Even so, the *Metropolitan* ending was out of line with the ironic comedy of manners he had intended to write, and that his readers expected from him. So in the book version, he replaced it with a final scene in which, Anthony, now a hopeless wreck, is awarded a windfall inheritance of thirty million dollars. This absurd conclusion is in keeping with the opening chapters. But it weakens the impact of the novel as a whole. For the best part is not the clever side shows, the private jokes, smart wise-cracks, and passages of flashy prose, but rather the relationship that develops between Anthony and Gloria. In this respect *The Beautiful and Damned* was a major artistic advance over *This Side of Paradise*. Anthony and Gloria are more solid and more completely imagined characters than Amory Blaine and his debutantes.

Besides the problem of maintaining a consistent point of view toward his characters, a second difficulty that Fitzgerald faced was that of giving his material adequate form. *This Side of Paradise* had been little more than a series of episodes held together by the force of Amory Blaine's personality. Now Fitzgerald had to cope with a much longer and more complex plot as well as a larger cast of characters. He was consciously aware of the problem from the beginning. "I am now working on my second novel—much more *objective* this time and hence harder sledding," he wrote Shane Leslie in September, 1920. ". . . I'm taking your advice and writing very slowly and paying much attention to form. Sometimes I think this new novel has nothing much else but form." But as the writing progressed he became so absorbed in his story that he forgot to heed his own advice. The novel's chief fault, he told John Peale Bishop after *The Beautiful and Damned* had appeared, was that "I devoted so much more care myself to the *detail* of the book than I did to thinking out the general scheme."[23]

All the evidence—Fitzgerald's comments in his correspondence as well as the original manuscript of *The Beautiful and Damned* now at Princeton—indicates that Fitzgerald intended Anthony Patch to be the novel's main center of interest. Gloria was to take a back seat; she was originally intended to be a more humorous character—the most complete portrait Fitzgerald had yet drawn of the Jazz Age flapper. Yet as the novel took shape she gradually emerged as the most vital and consistently interesting person in the story. Like Rosalind, her paler counterpart in *This Side of Paradise,* she derived from Zelda. Fifteen years later Fitzgerald would protest to his daughter that she "was a much more trivial and vulgar person than your mother." The truth is that he probably did not realize how much of his feelings about Zelda and their marriage had unconsciously crept into his novel. He tried to maintain a detached, ironic attitude toward both Gloria and Anthony, but he was writing much too close to actual experience. Take, for example, a passage like the following in which Gloria teases Anthony about his erratic writing habits:[24]

> "Work . . . Oh, you sad bird! You bluffer! Work—that means a great arranging of the desk and the lights, a great sharpening of pencils, and 'Gloria, don't sing!' and 'Please keep that damn Tana away from me,' and 'Let me read you my opening sentence,' and 'I won't be through for a long time, Gloria, so don't stay up for me,' and a tremendous consumption of tea or coffee. And that's all. In just about an hour I hear the old pencil stop scratching and look over. You've got out a book and you're 'looking up' something. Then you're reading. Then yawns—then bed and a great tossing about because you're all full of caffeine and can't sleep. Two weeks later the whole performance over again."

Up until this passage, Fitzgerald has never taken Anthony's literary ambitions seriously. Earlier, he had stated quite emphatically that Anthony had no talent whatsoever, and that he would never finish writing the long history of the Popes at which he has been working for years. Yet in this scene, Fitzgerald's guard drops and we find ourselves sympathizing with Anthony and blaming Gloria, rather than his own shortcomings, for his failure to finish his book. Instead of writing a novel, Fitzgerald is suddenly writing about himself. And Zelda is close beside him, taunting him and jealously begrudging the time he devotes to his writing instead of to her. Before long, her envy of his disciplined habits of work, as well as of his success, will become an insane compulsion.

Unlike Anthony's, Fitzgerald's work habits consisted of more than fiddling with the objects on his desk and sharpening his pencils. The heavily revised manuscript of *The Beautiful and Damned* shows how much judicious pruning and painstaking rewriting went into shaping his story. Yet for all the rewriting, it never received the final polishing it should have had. For example, at one point Gloria tells Anthony that she is pregnant—but we never hear anything more about this interesting development. Whatever happened to her baby? Only from a deleted passage in the manuscript do we learn that Anthony wanted a son very much but that Gloria insisted that he find her an abortionist. According to his Ledger, Fitzgerald had recently performed the same service for Zelda. In his haste to delete such personal allusions, Fitzgerald often failed to cover his tracks.

What power the novel has—and many have testified to this power—does not come from its overall structure but rather from the accumulative effect of many excellent separate episodes. As William Troy has written in an especially perceptive essay, *The Beautiful and Damned* "is not so much a study in failure as in the atmosphere of failure." The reasons for Anthony's fall from grace may not be clear, but there is no denying the force with which the emotions of horror and pity are conveyed in Fitzgerald's chronicle of that fall.[25]

By now, even more than in *This Side of Paradise*, Fitzgerald had become a master of the expanded image, which he used effectively to express complex feelings. For example, in the following passage, Gloria's feelings of loneliness and futility are conveyed by a series of images that foreshadow the surrealistic imagery of *The Great Gatsby*:[26]

[She] came back into the room, turned out the lamp, and leaning her elbows on the window-sill looked out at the Palisades Park, where the brilliant revolving circle of the ferris wheel was like a trembling mirror catching the yellow reflection of the moon. The street was quiet now; the children had gone in—over the way she could see a family at dinner. Pointlessly, ridiculously, they rose and walked about the table; seen thus, all that they did appeared incongruous—

it was as though they were being juggled carelessly and to no purpose by invisible overhead wires.

The last third of the book is not only the most dramatic but contains the best writing. The atmosphere of doom and retribution that echoes through the closing chapters is relieved and at the same time intensified by several excellent comic scenes. One of the funniest occurs when Anthony, in a desperate attempt to be a successful businessman, drunkenly tries to sell a briefcase full of securities to a line of women in a grocery store. Then there is Anthony's thirsty and bewildered safari up the dusty pavement of Sixth Avenue, from pawnshop to pawnshop, in a futile attempt to raise money for another bottle of liquor. This brief but haunting episode was later to become an important source for one of the best chapters in Charles Jackson's well-known novel, *The Lost Weekend*. This fact alone is impressive evidence of the power of *The Beautiful and Damned*. Indeed, no author has been more generous or more outspoken than Jackson in his admiration of Fitzgerald's work. "Don't be fooled by what the Sunday reviewers say of his jazz-age *Saturday Evening Post* popularity, et cetera," Jackson wrote in *The Lost Weekend* back in 1944 when Fitzgerald's reputation was at lowest ebb. "People will be going back to Fitzgerald one day as they now go back to Henry James. . . . His writing is the finest, purest, the most entertaining and most readable that we have in America today."[27]

Fitzgerald began writing *The Vegetable*, his only full-length published play, as we have already noted, in November, 1921, immediately after sending back his half-hearted corrections of the proofs of *The Beautiful and Damned*. As soon as it was finished the following March he took it to New York to have it read by George Jean Nathan, then one of the country's most influential drama critics, and Edmund Wilson. Considering its limitations as drama as well as its subsequent unhappy stage history, one wonders why these friends didn't advise him to put it aside and go back to writing novels. But both admired the frothy vaudeville skits he had published in *Smart Set* several years earlier and encouraged his ambitions to become a successful Broadway playwright. Discussing his friend in a recent book, Nathan wrote:[28]

I hope that young F. Scott Fitzgerald will turn from the one-act form to the three-act form one of these days: I feel that he will confect a genuinely diverting comedy. He has a good sense of character, a sharp eye, a gracious humor, and an aptitude for setting down adolescent dialogue that Tarkington has rarely matched.

Nathan was eager to do all that he could to help get the script produced. And Wilson wrote its author: "So far as I am concerned, I think it is one of the best things you ever wrote . . . marvelous—no doubt the best American comedy ever written. . . . I think you have a gift for comic dialogue even though you can never resist a stupid gag—and should go on writing plays." *The best American comedy ever written!* This was heady praise indeed. Whether Wilson meant it seriously or not, Fitzgerald assumed that he did, and quoted Wilson's opinion proudly in a letter to Max Perkins. But unfortunately Nathan's and Wilson's opinions regarding Fitzgerald's dramatic talent were not universally shared. One producer after another—Gilbert Miller, Arthur Hopkins, George Selwyn, Jed Harris—turned down the script as did Frank Craven the actor, whom Fitzgerald had hoped would take the leading role. Everyone had ideas for improving it, and, after spending almost a year tinkering with it, Fitzgerald's efforts were rewarded when Sam Harris agreed to put it on with Ernest Truex as the star. An Atlantic City tryout was scheduled for early November, 1923, to be followed by a premiere on Broadway.[29]

Fitzgerald devoted the summer and fall of 1923 to revising the script for Harris and Truex, and he persuaded himself that he had a great success on his hands. "Harris wants the play because he thinks it will be *the* flapper play," he wrote Ober not long before it opened. ". . . I feel that Acts I and III are probably the best pieces of dramatic comedy in English in the last five years." But the first night audience in Atlantic City thought otherwise, and the production folded a few performances later.[30]

The idea of *The Vegetable*, a spoof on Washington politics, was an excellent one. The story centers on a henpecked little man, Jerry Frost, who is married to a shrew named Charlotte. Most of the time Charlotte sits around the house eating chocolates and reading popular magazines, notably *The Saturday Evening Post*. She is unhappy because Jerry hasn't risen in the world and become rich and successful like the heroes in her favorite magazine stories. Recently, Jerry has taken a genteel white-collar job as a clerk in a railroad office because Charlotte wants him in a respectable position. But he is bored by the tedious routine and dislikes being cooped up inside all day. What Jerry would like to be more than anything else is a postman. He wants to work outside and likes the idea of bringing people good news. If Charlotte would let him take a postman's job, he would try to be "the best postman in the world."

But to Charlotte Frost, her husband is a hopeless failure, a vegetable. The play's title comes from a passage which Fitzgerald, on his title page, credited as having come "From a Current Magazine."

> Any man who doesn't want to get on in the world, to make a million dollars, and maybe even park his toothbrush in the White House, hasn't got as much to him as a good dog has—he's nothing more or less than a vegetable.

The first act of the play takes place on that fateful night in 1920 when Senator Warren G. Harding of Ohio was selected by the Republican Party as its candidate for President of the United States. While Jerry is sitting at home drinking bootleg gin and waiting for news of the convention's choice, he falls asleep and dreams that he himself has been elected President. The second act is a comic nightmare purporting to show what happens when a well-intentioned incompetent like Jerry is put in the White House. Everyone takes advantage of him—not least, his closest friends and relatives. Washington is honeycombed with corruption, and Jerry is finally impeached and convicted. On waking, he is so upset by this dream that he quits the railway clerk's job he has always disliked and runs away. Before long, we get news that he has become a postman and is happy doing the job that he likes best. The third act ends happily with a tearful, lonely Charlotte ready at last to take Jerry back on his own terms.

Perhaps if *The Vegetable* had appeared on the scene a year or so later, it might have found a more responsive audience. When it opened in the autumn of 1923 President Harding had been dead only a few months. Teapot Dome had not yet assumed the proportions of a national scandal, and the average theater-goer was not ready to ridicule the White House. John Farrar expressed the Babbitt-like complacency of the era when, reviewing *The Vegetable* in the influential *Bookman* magazine, he called it "impudent" and "more of a commentary on Fitzgerald's generation than upon American life."[31]

The remarkable thing was that Fitzgerald, with his chronic lack of interest in political matters, had guessed so well what was really going on in Washington. If impudence and a lack of respect for the tribal gods were the play's only faults, then it would be ripe for revival today. But it had other shortcomings. A decade later Kaufman and Ryskind's *Of Thee I Sing* showed what could be done with first-rate political satire. Fitzgerald once claimed that *Of Thee I Sing* had been plagiarized from *The Vegetable* and thought seriously of bringing suit. Luckily, he did not.

Comparison of the two shows that the musical owed little if anything to *The Vegetable*.

In spite of his teen-age triumphs as an impresario, and his later Triangle successes, Fitzgerald did not know enough about the professional stage to write successful full-length plays. For all the cleverness of its theme and dialogue, *The Vegetable* lacked the one thing that is essential—unified progression toward a climax. A lot is said, but nothing ever happens. This sense of the theater was the one important talent that George Jean Nathan had omitted from his list of Fitzgerald's qualifications as a dramatist. But not to possess it was fatal; without it Fitzgerald's comic sense and his ear for dialogue counted for very little.

Indeed, Fitzgerald is an excellent example of the novelist whose sense of drama can be conveyed only by means of the written page. *The Vegetable* was dramatic only in a literary sense. It relied entirely on words and failed to exploit those non-verbal elements which are as important to a play as language. The result was something that read much better than it acted. One wonders if Edmund Wilson's and George Jean Nathan's failure to take account of this shortcoming was the result of their thinking of the play in literary rather than theatrical terms.

Another fault of the play was its half-baked fantasy. The dream sequence in the second act was intended to contrast with the comic realism of the first and third acts. It should have been the most striking and original feature of the play. To do justice to the stupidity and corruption of Washington at that time, Fitzgerald needed the merciless satire of a Swift or the absurd surrealism of a Bosch or a Kafka. Instead, in his second act nightmare, he fell back on the gentle whimsy and spoofing of *Trial by Jury* and *Alice in Wonderland*. The result was the arch nonsense and coy fantasy that shows up in some of his poorer magazine stories.

Here again the advice of Nathan and Wilson was not especially helpful. Nathan, as co-editor of *Smart Set*, had not only encouraged Fitzgerald to write such trivial dramatic skits as "Mr. Icky" and "Porcelain and Pink," but he had gone out of his way to praise them in his essays. Wilson in his occasional essays and reviews seems to have regarded Fitzgerald more as an accomplished author of librettos and vaudeville skits than as a serious moralist—a kind of Noel Coward or Cole Porter. In his 1922 *Bookman* review of *Tales of the Jazz Age*, Wilson ignored the only two first-rate stories in the collection and gave his attention to such smart-aleck nonsense as "Mr. Icky" and "Jemina." Overlooking the larger human problems raised by such excellent pieces as "May Day" and "The Jelly-Bean," Wilson said that the stories in *Tales of the Jazz Age* were "the most charming of ballets—something like the Greenwich Village Follies with overtones of unearthly music." When he reached out for other authors with whom to compare Fitzgerald, those who came to mind were Lewis Carroll, W.S. Gilbert, and Edward Lear.[32]

Like *The Beautiful and Damned*, *The Vegetable* also suffered from the effort to make it serve too many different purposes. Fitzgerald began by wanting to make his play a protest against the contemporary dream of success from which he himself had only recently awakened. Jerry Frost wants only to do the job for which he is best qualified. But in order to satisfy his producer, Fitzgerald was obliged to reshape his play to amuse the same audiences that read his magazine stories. Among Fitzgerald's papers are a number of scenes that he wrote for the stage version that opened in Atlantic City. In his attempt to obtain all the laughs that he could for Sam Harris, he had drifted away from his original idea, cluttering his script with jokes about everything of topical interest he could think of—flappers, bootleggers, politicians, Washington, morticians, marriage.

Max Perkins, with his usual insight, had been particularly disturbed about what had happened to Fitzgerald's original idea. The shrewd analysis Perkins wrote in pencil on the back of one of Fitzgerald's letters to him (a comment Fitzgerald may never have seen) is the best account that has been written about what Fitzgerald had initially intended to say:[33]

The underlying idea [is that] . . . God meant Jerry to be a good egg and a postman; but having been created, in a democratic age, Free and Equal, he was persuaded that he ought to want to rise in the world. . . . He is therefore very unhappy, and so is his wife, who holds the same democratic doctrine.

Your story shows, or should, that this doctrine is sentimental bunk; and to do this is worthwhile because the doctrine is almost universal: Jerry and his wife are products of a theory of democracy which you reduce to the absurd. . . .

But when you come to the second act, which is the critical point of the play, and so in the expression of your idea, you seem to lose sense of your true motive. Partly, this is because you have three motives here, the main motive of Jerry's story and its meaning, and two subordinate motives—(1) of conveying through the fantastic visions and incidents which are the stuff of a dream caused by a 1923 prohibition brew *the sense of a comic nightmare,* and (2) of satirizing the general phenomena of our national scene. You have, I think, simply got more or less lost in the maze of these three motives by a failure to follow the green line of the chief one—Jerry's actual story, or that stage of it which shows him that he doesn't want to be President. Satirize as much as you can, the government, the army, and everything else, and be as fantastic as you please, but keep one eye always on your chief motive. Throughout the entire wild second act there should still be a kind of *wild logic*.

In spite of its limitations as a stage play, *The Vegetable* is an authentic document of the Jazz Age. A year before the lid blew off Teapot Dome and exposed the corruption of the Harding administration, Fitzgerald had already sensed the absurdity of electing someone like Harding to the Presidency. He had seen, too, the connection between such a phenomenon and the American dream of success that he himself had once accepted so unquestioningly. Yet, not only did his contemporaries miss the drift of *The Vegetable*, but readers since then have continued to do so. In a recent essay, Maxwell Geismar, a critic who is usually at his best in dealing with the social implications of literature, dismisses Fitzgerald's play as a trivial satire "of the moneyed elite [written] for the bourgeois makers of money." "Fitzgerald," Geismar continues, "is not at all concerned, as Dos Passos, with the human implications of our cultural patterns." But frail as it is as a play, *The Vegetable* is more than a "trivial satire." It fails because of its dramatic ineptitudes, not because it deals trivially with a trivial problem.[34]

VI
The Great Gatsby:
Finding a Theme

It is not clear exactly when Fitzgerald began to plan his third novel, *The Great Gatsby*. In May, 1921, after finishing *The Beautiful and Damned*, he wrote Max Perkins from Europe that he "hoped" to start work on a new novel later that summer. But instead he and Zelda came home, and there had been the problem of revising *The Beautiful*, followed by his work on *The Vegetable*. Meanwhile, the harsh treatment *The Beautiful and Damned* received from the reviewers persuaded him that he had been writing much too fast. He was wondering also if he had not been mistaken in trying to imitate the new school of realists. "I shall not right [sic] another novel for a year," he wrote Perkins from St. Paul that spring of 1922, "but when I do it will not be a realistic one."[1]

The decision to make St. Paul their permanent home, he soon realized, had also not been a happy one. Everything he had predicted back in 1919 in his story, "The Ice Palace," about Zelda's fundamental incompatibility with St. Paul and the Midwest turned out to be true. The city's staid respectability irritated her and she was soon restless for New York. Fitzgerald's own feelings about his native city were considerably more complicated. Although he had lived there very little since he was fourteen, his emotions were still deeply involved with St. Paul. When he became a celebrity, he felt a compulsion to return and make his peace with Summit Avenue. It seemed fitting that his first child should be born there. He even hoped to settle down there permanently. But a year was enough. By the end of September, 1922, the Fitzgeralds were back in their beloved Hotel Plaza, searching for a suitable suburban house not too distant from the bustle of Times Square.

The St. Paul episode had one important consequence, however. It gave Fitzgerald the idea for a third novel. "I have been lazy this month, trying to outline a new novel," he wrote Perkins around the end of May. And in another letter that summer: "Its locale will be the middle west and New York of 1885 I think. It will concern less superlative beauties than I run to usually and will be centered on a smaller period of time. It will have a catholic element."[2]

Exactly what this "catholic" novel was to have been about we can only guess. A few weeks before the Fitzgeralds moved from St. Paul to New York, however, Fitzgerald sat down and wrote a better-than-average magazine story, "Winter Dreams," that dramatized many of the mixed feelings about the Midwest and his own youth that he would later incorporate into *The Great Gatsby*. This story describes the fruitless love of a successful young Minnesota business man named Dexter Green for a beautiful rich girl named Judy Jones. Judy is the daughter of one of the city's most prominent families, and Dexter has admired her from afar ever since, as a poor boy, he caddied for her at the country club. Now that he has built up a prosperous business he is able to meet her on her own grounds. At first she is attracted by his success and his romantic devotion. But she finally decides that she cannot overlook his origins, turns him down, and marries a man from her own set. Some years later, when Dexter hears that she is being treated badly by her husband, he is "possessed with a wild notion of rushing out into the streets" to save her. But soon common sense asserts itself, and he reconciles himself to the fact that he cannot repeat the past. "The dream was gone. . . . He wanted to care, and he could not care. For he had gone away and he could never go back any more. . . . Even the grief he could have borne was left behind in the country of illusion, of youth, of the richness of life, where his winter dreams had flourished."[3]

Closely associated with "Winter Dreams" in theme is another story, "The Sensible Thing," that Fitzgerald wrote the next year. Based on his own hectic courtship of Zelda, it tells how a young civil engineer just starting his career is turned down by an attractive Southern girl who loves him but refuses to marry him because he has no money. Embittered, George O'Kelly goes off to South America where he strikes it rich and makes his fortune. On his return he is surprised to find that his girl is not only ready now to marry him but sees nothing odd about her previous behavior. George still loves her, but something important to him has disappeared from their relationship. "For an instant as he kissed her," Fitzgerald says, "he knew that though he searched through eternity he could never recapture those lost April hours." But in spite of his disappointment George O'Kelly, like Dexter Green in "Winter Dreams," is "at bottom hard-headed." So he does "the sensible thing," accepts the situation, and marries his girl. "Well, let it pass, he thought; April is over, April is over."[4]

The Great Gatsby, which was slowly taking shape in Fitzgerald's imagination during this time, bears a certain family resemblance to both these short stories. Gatsby is the foolhardy idealist who cannot take the common-sense view, who refuses to accept an equivocal love. It is almost as though Fitzgerald first had to explore the limits of the common-sense view in these two stories before he could celebrate the romantic view he himself shared with Jay Gatsby.

Despite the stories' literary shortcomings, Harold Ober had no difficulty selling them to the magazines—"Winter Dreams" for $900 to the *Metropolitan* and "The Sensible Thing" to *Liberty* for $1,750. Fitzgerald had no illusions about their quality, however. The first, he wrote Ober, was "pretty bad stuff" while the second, he wrote both Ober and Perkins, "didn't seem good" to him because it had been "done under pressure" for ready cash. His next novel—*The Great Gatsby*—would be something quite different in every way.[5]

But New York, as things turned out, did not offer any more opportunity for leisurely writing than St. Paul. After several weeks of house-hunting, the Fitzgeralds leased a spacious, comfortable new house on Gateway Drive in Great Neck, where they lived for the next eighteen months. The Great Neck section had attracted them because of its convenient commuting distance to the city; also, it had recently become popular with a great many actors, directors, editors, and other people connected with the New York entertainment and publishing worlds. Nearby, overlooking Long Island Sound, were the magnificent estates of wealthy business tycoons. The Fitzgeralds, with characteristic enthusiasm, plunged headlong into the community's extravagant social life. "Great Neck is a great place for celebrities—" he wrote his cousin "Ceci" Taylor soon after their arrival, "it being the habitat of Frank Craven, Herbert Swope, Arthur Hopkins, Jane Cowl, . . . Samuel Goldwyn, Ring Lardner, Fontayne Fox, . . . Gene Buck, Donald Bryan, Tom Wise, Jack Hazard, General Pershing. It is most amusing after the dull healthy Middle West. For instance at a party last night where we went were John McCormack, Hugh Walpole, FPA, Neysa McMien, Arthur William Brown, Rudolph Friml and Deems Taylor. They have no mock-modesty and all perform their various stunts upon the faintest request so it's like a sustained concert."[6]

Thus, with one thing and another, Fitzgerald made little progress with *The Great Gatsby* during the eighteen months in Great Neck. Most of 1922 and 1923 were taken up with *The Vegetable.* When it failed he spent the winter of 1923–1924 writing magazine stories and articles to clear his debts, and to earn enough extra so that he could go somewhere else and work on his novel. So many New York friends had gotten into the habit of treating the Fitzgerald residence as if it were a roadhouse that serious, sustained writing had become impossible. "Weekend parties" there had a way of stretching from one weekend to the next. Ring Lardner, who lived nearby on East Shore Drive, became incensed at the way people imposed on the Fitzgeralds. The only alternative for them was to make a clean break. Concealing their plans from everyone except the Lardners and the Maxwell Perkinses, they slipped away May 3, 1924, on the S.S. *Minnewaska* bound for France.[7]

The idea was to live inexpensively on the French Riviera until *The Great Gatsby* was finished. After several weeks' holiday in Paris they headed south, stopping at Grimm's Hotel at Hyères until they found an attractive villa overlooking the Mediterranean at nearby St. Raphaël. Here Fitzgerald worked quietly and without serious interruption for the next five months, mailing his completed manuscript to Perkins on October 27, 1924.[8]

During the eighteen months he lived in Great Neck he had only been able to complete a fraction of his novel—about three chapters—almost all written during the summer of 1923. When he had an opportunity to get back to work on it in the spring of 1924, he discovered that his conception of the story had changed so radically that he felt obliged to begin it all over again.[9]

Much of what I wrote last summer was good, [he wrote Perkins from Great Neck in late April, 1924, just before sailing for France] but it was so interrupted that it was ragged and in approaching it from a new angle I've had to discard a lot of it—in one case 18,000 [words] (part of which will appear in the *Mercury* as a short story). It is only in the last four months that I've realized how much I've— well, almost *deteriorated* in the three years since I finished the Beautiful and Damned.

The story referred to in this letter was "Absolution," which H.L. Mencken published in the June, 1924, issue of *The American Mercury.* According to Fitzgerald's records it was written in June, 1923. At this time, he apparently was still planning a novel with a "Catholic element" and a Middle Western setting, and "Absolution" seems to have been part of the opening chapter.

"I'm glad you liked it," Fitzgerald wrote Perkins after "Absolution" had appeared in the *Mercury*. "As you know it was to have been the prologue of the novel but it interfered with the neatness of the plan." Ten years later, in a letter to an admirer, he again mentioned the connection between *The Great Gatsby* and "Absolution," saying that the latter had been "intended to be a picture of his [Gatsby's] early life, but . . . I cut it because I preferred to preserve the sense of mystery."[10]

In April, 1924, when Fitzgerald returned to his novel after a nine-month interruption, he not only changed the setting from the Midwest of the Gilded Age to Jazz Age Long Island, but he also abandoned the conventional third-person narrative he had used in his previous novels, adopting instead the device of a first-person narrator. He also de-emphasized the Roman Catholic element. Any attempt to come to terms with *The Great Gatsby*, therefore, cannot afford to overlook its relationship with "Absolution." The story is important because it makes explicit the religious considerations which underlie the longer work.

"Absolution" is the story of an eleven-year-old boy's first encounter with evil. It begins one Saturday afternoon when Rudolph Miller impulsively tells a lie while he is attending confession. Rudolph is bored with the monotonous catalogue of trivial sins that he recites week after week. So, when the priest unexpectedly asks him if he doesn't sometimes tell lies, Rudolph seizes the opportunity to make a dramatic gesture. No, he proudly tells Father Schwartz, he never lies. Afterwards, walking home, he momentarily savors the aesthetic delight of a dramatic performance skillfully executed. Then, before long, his overdeveloped conscience reasserts itself. It was bad enough to deceive the priest, for of course Rudolph sometimes tells lies. But he has made matters worse by lying during confession. Later he further compounds his sin by accepting Holy Communion in this unshriven state.

His first impulse, once he has realized the magnitude of his error, is to pretend that it wasn't really he himself who told the lie. It was Blatchford Sarnemington—an imaginary playmate who is the lonely boy's closest friend. Blatchford, Rudolph's alter ego, represents everything Rudolph is not and longs to be. Where Rudolph must mind his parents, his teachers, and Father Schwartz, Blatchford soars above such mundane obligations. He is beyond good and evil, responsible only to his imagination. Rudolph's persuasive performance in the confessional booth is just the kind of thing that Blatchford would have admired.

But Rudolph's severe religious training will not allow him to shift the blame to Blatchford for very long. After an unhappy weekend during which he expects momentarily to be stricken down by the hand of an angry God, Rudolph finally seeks out Father Schwartz and blurts out the whole story. Now, however, it is the priest who fails to do his duty. For Father Schwartz is also an incurable romantic. In Rudolph's action he sees mirrored his own frustrated longing for a fuller, more aesthetically satisfying and adventurous life. Instead of disciplining the child, exacting the penance he has been taught to expect as his due, and then absolving him, Father Schwartz merely excuses Rudolph's conduct with a formula of words whose meaning the child does not comprehend. "Apostasy implies absolute damnation only on the supposition of a previously perfect faith," he tells the conscience-stricken child. "Does that fix it?" Then he increases Rudolph's consternation by launching out into a crazy speech that the boy interprets as a justification of his sin.[11]

Frightened by this turn of events, Rudolph rushes away home. Instead of absolving the boy's sin, the priest has actually fertilized the seeds of religious doubt latent in Rudolph's mind. Rudolph now believes that his old suspicions about God and the church have been confirmed. Somewhere, as Father Schwartz has said, there is a glittering world where Rudolph can exist apart from God, responsible only to his own imagination.[12]

. . . [U]nderneath his terror he felt his own inner convictions were confirmed. There was something ineffably gorgeous somewhere that had nothing to do with God. He no longer thought that God was angry with him about the original lie, because He must have understood that Rudolph had done it to make things finer in the confessional, brightening up the dinginess of his own admissions by saying a thing radiant and proud. At the moment when he had affirmed immaculate honor a silver pennon had flapped out in the breeze somewhere and there had been the crunch of leather and the shine of silver spurs and a troop of horsemen waiting for the dawn on a low green hill.

In short, Rudolph is free at last to become Blatchford Sarnemington.[13]

In *The Great Gatsby* Rudolph reappears as Jimmie Gatz, while Blatchford Sarnemington has been renamed Jay Gatsby. Jimmie's decision to change his name, Fitzgerald tells us, was "the specific moment that witnessed the beginning of his career." And that career began, as we know from "Absolution," when eleven-year-old Jimmie Gatz decided to commit himself to the moral world of his own imagination—a world where he could be "safe from God." "The truth was that Jay Gatsby of West Egg, Long Island, sprang from his Platonic conception of himself. He was a Son of God—a phrase which, if it means anything, means just that—and he must be about his Father's business, the service of a vast, vulgar, meretricious beauty."[14]

The source of "Absolution" was the similar incident in Fitzgerald's childhood when he too had inadvertently told a lie in confession. Many years later he still shivered at the recollection of that "very chilling experience." (While he had not gone so far as to change his name as the result, still he had pretended that he was no longer a Fitzgerald, but the scion instead of the House of Stuart.) Like Rudolph Miller and Jimmie Gatz, he had persuaded himself that the world of his imagination was a better world—both aesthetically and morally—than the ordinary one governed by his parents and their faith. It was precisely because of the intensity of his belief in the world of his imagination that he succeeded through his early writing in realizing so many of these childhood dreams.[15]

But by 1922, when he began the discarded novel represented by "Absolution," most of the fruits of this success were beginning to turn to ashes in his mouth. Here we see him first undertaking that sober scrutiny of his past in the light of this new hard-won wisdom that was to be the subject of all his later serious fiction. He was not yet ready to disown completely the romantic idealism that had served him so well in his youth. But it was no longer the moral guide that it had once been. "That's the whole burden of this novel," he would write Ludlow Fowler two years later, in the summer of 1924, when he was finishing the final draft of *The Great Gatsby*, "the loss of those illusions that give such color to the world that you don't care whether things are true or false so long as they partake of the magical glory."[16]

The trouble with "Absolution" is that Fitzgerald had not yet worked out clearly what the system was that he was using as the basis for moral judgment in this story. A careful reading of it in the light of *The Great Gatsby* discloses that the source in both works was that of the faith in which he had been reared. Both Rudolph and his successor, Jimmie Gatz, are irretrievably damned. Yet when "Absolution" first appeared in *The American Mercury* Fitzgerald's Catholic friends accused him of having written a sacrilegious story. The difficulty was that Rudolph is so much more attractive a character than Father Schwartz that it is hard to accept the foolish priest as an appropriate symbol of the faith he so unworthily serves. Fitzgerald's personal dislike obscures the priest's aesthetic function in the story. He was undoubtedly a portrait of some-one Fitzgerald had known, and it is pretty clear that Schwartz's treatment of Rudolph is connected in some way with Schwartz's latent homosexuality.

What saves *The Great Gatsby* from the pitfalls of "Absolution" was Fitzgerald's decision to start all over again and approach his novel "from a new angle." One important innovation was his introduction of the device of a unifying first-person narrator, Nick Carraway. Nick performs the function of Father Schwartz and makes the necessary final moral judgments. But, unlike the priest, Nick enjoys a more clearly defined and more sympathetic relationship with the story's hero. Indeed, in the earliest draft that survives of this new version, Nick and Gatsby are so alike in temperament that it was only after extensive revision that Fitzgerald succeeded in endowing them with separate personalities.

In this new version Fitzgerald also eliminated most of the Catholicism that had earlier provided "Absolution's" moral scaffolding. Nick, in spite of his many resemblances to Gatsby, is saved from his neighbor's fate by two new and somewhat different sources of moral knowledge.

The first is that heritage of traditional values that he has learned from his father. He is indebted to Mr. Carraway, he says at the beginning, both for that "habit of reserving all judgments" which allows him, alone of all of Gatsby's acquaintances, to value his neighbor's romantic idealism, and for that "sense of the fundamental decencies of life" which makes it possible for him to see the shabby limitations of Gatsby's dreams. At the start of the story Nick was ready to reject this moral heritage, along with the Carraway name. That is, Nick refused to take the job awaiting him in the Middle Western wholesale hardware business that had been in his family for three generations. Instead he left the "bored, sprawling, swollen towns beyond the Ohio" and came East to take a job in a Wall Street brokerage firm. But by the end of the novel it is the values represented for Nick by the image of his father that have saved him from Gatsby's terrible mistake. Realizing this, Nick is ready at last to return home.

The second kind of knowledge that Nick possesses, in contrast to his neighbor, is his ever-present awareness of man's mortality. For Nick the fact of death stands inexorably between man's dreams and the chances of realizing them during his brief lifetime. Not only is Nick continually aware of death, and his narrative strewn with death images, but the entire novel seems to have been conceived by Fitzgerald as the expression of a death wish—a wish that, in the earliest surviving draft of *The*

Great Gatsby, Nick actually voices at the conclusion of Chapter I. At this initial stage of his conception of *The Great Gatsby,* Nick resembled Gatsby not only in his Midwestern origins and his romantic setting off for the East, but by the fact that Nick had also been in love with Daisy Buchanan before her marriage to Tom. In this draft Nick, it turns out, has not seen Daisy since her marriage. So, when he learns the unhappy facts about the Buchanan menage he is profoundly disturbed. It is bad enough to discover that Tom is having an affair with another woman. What disturbs Nick even more is Daisy's puzzling attitude toward the situation, her "basic insincerity," as he calls it. It is as though the virginal Daisy of Nick's dreams has been contaminated by an evil so pervasive that everything else has also been corrupted by it—not only his Long Island surroundings, but the whole American continent stretching out to the Western sea. Indeed so intense is Nick's mood of disillusion at this point in Chapter I that it inspired Fitzgerald to write that long threnody to the memory of the continent's lost innocence that he eventually moved to the end of chapter nine, where it provides a fitting coda to the entire story.[17]

> The sense of being in an unfamiliar place deepened on me, and as the moon rose higher the inessential houses began to melt away until I was aware of the old island here that flowered once for Dutch sailors' eyes—a fresh, green breast of the new world. Its vanished trees, the trees that had made way for Gatsby's house, had once pandered in whispers to the last and greatest of all human dreams; for a transitory enchanted moment man must have held his breath in the presence of this continent, compelled into an aesthetic contemplation he neither understood nor desired, face to face for the last time in history with something commensurate to his capacity for wonder.
>
> And as I sat there brooding on the old, unknown world, I too held my breath and waited until I could feel the motion of America as it turned through the hours—my own blue lawn and the tall incandescent city on the water and beyond that the dark fields of the republic rolling under the night.

At this point in this first draft of Chapter I, Nick also says (in a passage later altered):[18]

> It was already deep summer on roadhouse roofs and on the dark murmurous little porches and around the garages where new red gas-pumps sat out in pools of light—and summer always promised

fulfillment of my old childish dreams. I wanted something definite to happen to *me*, something that would wear me out a little—for I suppose the urge to adventure is one and the same with the obscure craving of our bodies for a certain death.

Then, looking out across the bay, Nick notices for the first time the shadowy silhouette of his mysterious neighbor, Gatsby, standing on the beach nearby. Thus, everything that is still to happen—all of Gatsby's subsequent history—is to serve Nick as a kind of moral exemplum, a cautionary tale illustrating the kind of fate Nick himself might have suffered if his love for Daisy had blinded him, as it did Gatsby, to the evil that is as much a part of her nature as it is of any other mortal being.

But Nick, unlike Gatsby, is continually aware of the fact that man must die. Indeed the odor of mortality is everywhere in the novel, even more in the early drafts than in the published version of the text. In one draft, when Gatsby proudly shows Nick his oversized yellow sports car ("the death car," as the New York newspapers will later call it after Myrtle's death), Nick is automatically reminded of a hearse. A few paragraphs further on, when Nick is riding in Gatsby's car to New York, he passes a funeral and is confronted with the image of "a dead man . . . in a hearse heaped full of flowers." The most persistent death image in the novel is that of the waste land of dust and ashes over which Gatsby and his neighbors must pass every time they go to New York. From this limbo blows that "foul dust" that "floated in the wake of Gatsby's dreams." Tom Buchanan, after having helped to contrive Gatsby's murder, arrogantly tells Nick, "He [Gatsby] threw dust in your eyes just like he did Daisy's." At one time Fitzgerald even planned to call his novel, "Among the Ash-Heaps and Millionaires."[19]

Over this portentous waste land brood the sightless eyes of Dr. T.J. Eckleburg—rooted (as Fitzgerald says in another deleted passage) "in a spot that reeks of death." Nearby stands the squalid, ash-covered garage of George Wilson, the insane agent of Gatsby's doom. In his manuscript Fitzgerald carefully changed the color of Wilson's hair from "yellow" to the more deathly hue of "pale."[20]

At the end, the simple fact of Gatsby's death is quickly stated in a sentence. But the implications of that death necessitate a long concluding chapter. No one besides Nick is willing to confront those implications. Gatsby's fatuous father, an obvious contrast to Nick's father, consoles himself with the sordid lie of his dead son's "success." Gatsby's other friends all stay away, presumably following the corrupt Wolfshiem's maxim that in matters connected with death "it is better to leave

everything alone." Only Nick is incapable of letting things alone. His
neighbor's death rouses Nick—the hitherto passive onlooker—to one of
the few positive actions of his career.

> As he lay in his house and didn't move or breathe or speak, hour
> upon hour, it grew upon me that I was responsible because no one
> else was interested—interested, I mean, with that intense personal
> interest to which every one has some vague right at the end.

Whereupon Nick sees that his dead friend has a decent funeral and
then, taking up one more responsibility, goes back home.[21]

Nick's vicarious involvement in Gatsby's destiny, in other words,
permitted him to see the world for a brief space through the glasses of
Dr. T.J. Eckleburg. What he sees is a world without moral sanctions of
any kind, an anarchy in which romantic idealists like Gatsby are the
most vulnerable of all. "After Gatsby's death," Nick says, "the East was
haunted for me . . . distorted beyond my eyes' power of correction. So
. . . I decided to come back home." Dr. Eckleburg is the symbol of a
world without the idea of God, a kind of anti-God. When George Wilson
discovers that his wife has been unfaithful he drags her to the window
of his garage and there, in front of the eyes of Dr. Eckleburg, tells her:
"God knows what you've been doing. You may fool me but you can't
fool God." "God sees everything," Wilson tells Michaelis after Myrtle's
death, just before setting off on his crazy quest for vengeance. He only
succeeds in killing the wrong man.[22]

Thus, "Absolution" provides a gloss for the religious background of
The Great Gatsby. Nick in one important sense is an aspect of Fitzgerald
judging another aspect of himself. In seeking the basis for this judgment,
Fitzgerald initially attempted to fall back on his childhood religious
training. But his feelings about the Church of Rome by now were so
chaotic that he could not use them objectively. Indeed his views of the
Church as an institution were probably not much different from those
expressed by Amory Blaine at the end of *This Side of Paradise*.[23]

> The idea was strong in him that there was an intrinsic lack in
> those to whom religion was necessary, and religion to Amory meant
> the Church of Rome. Quite conceivably it was an empty ritual, but
> it was seemingly the only assimilitative traditionary bulwark against
> the decay of morals. . . . Yet acceptance was, for the present, impos-
> sible. He wanted time and the absence of ulterior pressure. He
> wanted to keep the tree without the ornaments.

Fitzgerald's solution, in *The Great Gatsby*, was to retain the tree—the residual tradition of moral values represented by the advice given Nick by his father—without the sectarian dogma. Underlying this was his profound, perhaps unconscious, awareness of death.

The result was a moral position that permitted Fitzgerald to value the romantic impulse he shared in common with Nick and Gatsby (a "heightened sensitivity to the promises of life"), as well as to see its limitations. Thus, *The Great Gatsby* became a criticism of the romantic egotism Fitzgerald had celebrated in *This Side of Paradise*. It was a retreat toward, though by no means into, the bosom of Mother Church. That Nick longs for such a moral absolute at the end of *Gatsby* is suggested by his remark, "When I came back from the East last summer I wanted the world to be in uniform and at a sort of moral attention forever." The closest Nick can come to such an absolute, however, is to go back home and take up his responsibilities as a member of the Carraway clan.[24]

Several months after *Gatsby* was published, Fitzgerald complained to Edmund Wilson that "of all the reviews, even the most enthusiastic, no one has the slightest idea what the book is about." What it was about, he told John Peale Bishop, was himself. To this Bishop objected strenuously. "I can't understand your resentment of the critics' failure to perceive your countenance behind Gatsby's mask. . . . It seems to me to be interesting, if at all, privately only." What Fitzgerald meant, however, was not his literal, but rather his moral countenance. Like T.S. Eliot's *The Waste Land*, *The Great Gatsby* is a religious work because it has as its source a deeply felt religious emotion. This, perhaps, was what Mr. Eliot had in mind when, soon after it was published, he called it "the first step the American novel has taken since Henry James."[25]

VII
The
Great Gatsby:
Finding a
Hero

Max Perkins was tremendously impressed by the manuscript of *The Great Gatsby* which Fitzgerald sent him from St. Raphaël on October 27, 1924. "Extraordinary . . . magnificent . . . ," he wrote Fitzgerald on November twentieth; it was a novel that suggested "all sorts of thoughts and moods." "It's got his old vitality," Perkins wrote Ring Lardner enthusiastically a few days later, "—vitality enough to sweep away the faults you could, critically, find with it,—which relate, in my view, chiefly to Gatsby himself."[1]

It was to Gatsby's shortcomings as a character that Perkins devoted the greater part of his long letter of November twentieth, in which he summarized for Fitzgerald his reactions to the manuscript. He had two major criticisms of the hero:

> One is that among a set of characters marvelously palpable and vital—I would know Tom Buchanan if I met him on the street and would avoid him—Gatsby is somewhat vague. The reader's eyes can never quite focus upon him, his outlines are dim. Now everything about Gatsby is more or less a mystery, i.e. more or less vague, and this may be somewhat of an artistic intention, but I think it is mistaken. Couldn't *he* be physically described as distinctly as the others, and couldn't you add one or two characteristics like the use of that phrase "old sport"—not verbal, but physical ones, perhaps. . . . I do not think your scheme would be impaired if you made him so.
>
> The other point is also about Gatsby: his career must remain

mysterious, of course. But in the end you make it pretty clear that his wealth came through his connection with Wolfsheim. You also suggest this much earlier. Now almost all readers numerically are going to be puzzled by his having all this wealth and are going to feel entitled to an explanation. To give a distinct and definite one would be, of course, utterly absurd. It did occur to me, though, that you might here and there interpolate some phrases, and possibly incidents, little touches of various kinds, that might suggest that he was in some active way mysteriously engaged. . . . Whether he was an innocent tool in the hands of somebody else, or to what degree he was this, ought not to be explained. But if some sort of business activity of his were simply adumbrated, it would lend further probability to that part of the story.

In December, Fitzgerald wrote Perkins from Italy, where he and Zelda had gone for the winter, that he was confident he could remedy these defects during his revision of the galley proofs.[2]

Strange to say my notion of Gatsby's vagueness was O.K. What you and Louise [Mrs. Perkins] and Mr. Charles Scribner found wanting was that:

I myself didn't know what Gatsby looked like or was engaged in and you felt it. If I'd known it and kept it from you you'd have been *too impressed with my knowledge to protest.* This is a complicated idea but I'm sure you'll understand. But I know now—and as a penalty for not having known first, in other words to make sure, I'm going to tell more. . . .

Anyhow after careful searching of the files (of a man's mind here) for the Fuller McGee [sic] case . . . I know Gatsby better than I know my own child. My first instinct after your letter was to let him go and have Tom Buchanan dominate the book (I suppose he's the best character I've ever done—I think he and the brother in "Salt" and Hurstwood in "Sister Carrie" are the three best characters in American fiction in the last twenty years, perhaps and perhaps not) but Gatsby sticks in my heart. I had him for a while, then lost him and now I know I have him again.

The trouble, as we know from "Absolution," was that Gatsby was nothing more than the figment of a small boy's imagination. How was Fitzgerald to make something as vague as "Blatchford Sarnemington" the hero of his novel? Quite likely, when Fitzgerald began to plan the

F. Scott Fitzgerald

book, he expected to model the mature Gatsby after some typical Midwestern tycoon—perhaps his own grandfather, or Grandfather Mc-
Quillan's friend, James J. Hill. "If he'd of lived he'd of been a great man,"
Mr. Gatz proudly tells Nick. "A man like James J. Hill. He'd of helped
build up the country."[3]

If this was the case, then Fitzgerald, after coming to Great Neck, no
longer continued to think of his novel as a Midwestern story of the
Gilded Age. By 1923, it was evident that the Twenties would surpass
even that earlier era in glitter and irresponsibility. Moving his setting
to New York did not, however, materially alter the story's meaning. For
what was New York but an extension of Fitzgerald's Midwest, with all
its bustle and excitement and easy money? "I see now that this has been
a story of the West, after all," Nick says at the end of the novel. "Tom
and Gatsby, Daisy and Jordan and I, were all Westerners and perhaps
we possessed some deficiency in common which made us subtly un-
adaptable to Eastern life."[4]

Almost every Sunday the society columns and rotogravure sections
of the New York newspapers carried accounts of wealthy young Midwesterners like the Buchanans who had moved to Long Island to enjoy
the yachting, polo, and other expensive pastimes of the very rich. The
financial sections of the same papers almost as regularly reported the
mysterious appearance of Gatsby-like figures who had suddenly
emerged from the West with millions of dollars at their command. A
typical example was Charles Victor Bob, who turned up in Wall Street
from Colorado, claiming to be the owner of tin mines in South America
and copper mines in Canada. He spent money like water, throwing lav-
ish parties for Broadway celebrities who had never heard of him before,
and selling gilt-edged mining securities. He was finally indicted on a
six-million-dollar mail fraud charge, but, in spite of the evidence, three
successive juries refused to convict him. So far as the Twenties were
concerned, anyone as rich, colorful, and successful as Charles Victor
Bob deserved a better fate than jail.[5]

Knowing of Fitzgerald's interest in "success" stories like this, his
friends collected them for him. The outskirts of Great Neck, where
palatial estates fronted on Long Island Sound, made an especially good
hunting ground. "He [Ring Lardner] told me of a newcomer who'd
made money in the drug business—not dope but the regular line," Max
Perkins wrote the Fitzgeralds shortly after they went to France:[6]

This gentleman had evidently taken to Ring. One morning he
called early with another man and a girl and Ring was not dressed.

But he hurried down, unshaven. He [Ring] was introduced to the *girl only,* and said he was sorry to appear that way but didn't want to keep them waiting while he shaved.

At this point the drug man signals to the other, who goes to the car for a black bag and from it produces razors, strops, etc., etc., and publicly shaves Ring. *This* was the drug man's private barber; the girl was his private manicurist. But as he was lonely he had made them also his companions. Ring declares this is true!

Lardner himself sent the Fitzgeralds an account of a Fourth of July celebration that might have come from the pages of *The Great Gatsby:*[7]

On the Fourth of July, Ed Wynn gave a fireworks display at his new estate in the Grenwolde division. After the children had been sent home, everybody got pie-eyed and I never enjoyed a night so much. All the Great Neck professionals did their stuff, the former chorus girls danced, Blanche Ring kissed me and sang, etc. The party lasted through the next day and wound up next evening at Tom Meighan's where the principal entertainment was provided by Lila Lee and another dame, who did some very funny imitations (really funny) in the moonlight on the tennis court. We would ask them to imitate Houdini, or Leon Errol, or Will Rogers or Elsie Janis; the imitations were all the same, consisting of an aesthetic dance which ended with an unaesthetic fall onto the tennis court.

Of all Fitzgerald's Long Island neighbors, the one whose outlines are most clearly discernible in *The Great Gatsby* was a certain Great Neck resident by the name of Edward M. Fuller. This was the Fuller of the "Fuller-McGee" case which Fitzgerald told Perkins he had studied until he felt he knew Gatsby better than he knew his own child. A thirty-nine-year-old bachelor and man about town, Fuller was president of the New York brokerage firm of E.M. Fuller and Co., with offices at 50 Broad Street. Of obscure origins, he had emerged suddenly on Wall Street in 1916 as a member of the Consolidated Stock Exchange and the head of his own company. Before long, he was being mentioned in the newspapers as one of a fashionable set that included Gertrude Vanderbilt, Charles A. Stoneham, the owner of the New York Giants baseball team, and Walter B. Silkworth, prominent clubman and president of the Consolidated Exchange. Fuller, an aviation enthusiast, was one of the first Long Island residents to commute weekly by airplane from his Great Neck estate to Atlantic City while the horse-racing season was on.[8]

On June 22, 1922, however, E.M. Fuller and Co. declared itself bankrupt, with some six million dollars in debts and assets of less than seventy thousand dollars. Fuller and his vice-president, William F. McGee, were promptly indicted on a twelve-count charge that included operating a "bucket shop"—i.e., illegally gambling with their customers' funds. It took four trials to put them behind prison bars, and it is significant that the first opened two months after the Fitzgeralds moved to Great Neck, and ended several days later with a hung jury. The second trial, in December, ended in a mistrial after the state admitted its inability to produce a key witness, who had unaccountably disappeared. The third, which began the following April, 1923, also resulted in a hung jury. During this trial it was revealed that Fuller's lawyer, a prominent New York attorney named William J. Fallon, had tried to bribe one of the jurors. For this Fallon was subsequently convicted and imprisoned, disgraced for life.

During this third trial, a leading state's witness was temporarily kidnapped by another of Fuller's attorneys, and vital records and other evidence also disappeared. By now the "Fuller-McGee" case was being featured on the front pages of the New York newspapers, and the fourth trial opened on June 11, 1923, amid a rash of rumors that Fuller and McGee were going to throw themselves on the mercy of the court and make a full confession. A deal had been arranged, it was reported, whereby they were to receive light sentences in exchange for confessions implicating a number of prominent New York officials, politicians, and businessmen with whom they had been associated in their financial ventures. Instead, however, both Fuller and McGee merely pleaded guilty to the more innocuous charges and were promptly sentenced to five years in Sing Sing—a sentence that was subsequently reduced to twelve months for "good behavior."

By coincidence, McGee's wife, a former New York showgirl named Louise Groody, arrived in Paris the same day that Fuller and her husband confessed their guilt. According to the Paris newspapers, Mrs. McGee disembarked from the liner at Cherbourg covered with diamonds and other jewels valued at several hundred thousand dollars. It was subsequently revealed that she had cashed a check of her husband's for $300,000 just a few hours before E.M. Fuller and Company went bankrupt.

Actually, the state of New York had difficulty establishing conclusive proof for most of the charges brought against Fuller and McGee. Nonetheless, it was obvious that they were part of a tangled web of corruption that included some of New York's wealthiest and most powerful business and political leaders. Fuller, according to his testimony, owed his business success mainly to his friendship with Charles A. Stoneham, another mysterious Gatsby-like figure who began life as a board boy in a broker's office and rose swiftly in the Wall Street financial hierarchy, emerging eventually as president of the brokerage house of C.A. Stoneham and Company. In 1921, he had sold out his firm's interest to E.M. Fuller and Co. and three other investment houses (E.D. Dier and Co., E.H. Clarke and Co., and Dillon and Co.) and plunged heavily into big-time gambling and sporting enterprises. Besides his controlling interest in the New York Giants baseball club, Stoneham owned a race track, a gambling casino, a newspaper, and other associated interests in Havana. By 1923, all four of the firms which had bought the assets of Stoneham and Co. had gone bankrupt, with debts totaling more than twenty million dollars.[9]

Fuller testified under oath that, after the dissolution of Stoneham and Co., Charles Stoneham had become a silent partner in the Fuller firm; he further claimed that his friend had advanced some two hundred thousand dollars in checks drawn against the Giants club, in a fruitless attempt to stave off Fuller and Co.'s impending bankruptcy. Stoneham insisted, however, that the money had merely been a private loan to Fuller, which he had advanced at the request of his friend Thomas F. Foley, former New York sheriff and Tammany Hall official. Foley, who had himself loaned Fuller $15,000, explained that he had come to Fuller's assistance purely out of friendship for one of McGee's former wives, a certain Nellie Sheean, who had remarried and was now living in Paris (the residence, also, of the current Mrs. McGee).

Fuller and Company, it turned out, had a rather dubious financial history. In 1920, the firm was indicted for having systematically defrauded its customers over the past three years by sale of worthless oil securities, but the case was thrown out of court on the grounds of insufficient evidence. On February 24, 1923, while awaiting his third bankruptcy trial, Fuller was arrested on another charge along with seven other men and women, most of whom had criminal records. They were seized in a suite of the Hotel Embassy, where they were accused of having attempted to sell fraudulent securities over the telephone. It was further claimed by the police that Fuller and his friends were planning to organize a new securities firm for the purpose of selling worthless stocks. This case, however, was also dismissed by the court because of lack of evidence.

On June 13, 1922, Fuller had again been involved with the police, but under more romantic circumstances. On this occasion, his Broad Street offices had been invaded by "a fashionably dressed young lady" who, according to the New York *Times,* had threatened Fuller with severe bodily harm. Later, in the police court, the woman identified herself as Nellie Burke, twenty-seven, of 245 West Seventy-fifth Street. Miss Burke, who at the time of her arrest was wearing $20,000 worth of what she told newspaper reporters was "borrowed" jewelry, testified that she had become acquainted with Fuller in 1915, in the bar of the Hotel Knickerbocker. Their subsequent friendship had terminated in a breach-of-promise suit which she had brought against him in 1921. On June sixth of that year, she said, she had been visited by Fuller's friend and business associate, the notorious Arnold Rothstein, who had promised her $10,000 if she would sign a paper dropping the suit and agreeing not to pester Fuller any more. She had signed the paper and received $5,000 from Rothstein, but the rest of the money had been withheld. Her visit to Fuller's office the following June had, she claimed, been merely to collect the $5,000 in cash still due her. The magistrate found her guilty of assault but agreed to suspend sentence if she would promise not to give Fuller any more trouble. (Fuller's failure to pay her the additional $5,000 was explained several days later, on June twenty-second, when his firm went into bankruptcy!)

Many intimations of a mysterious tie between Fuller and the gambler, Arnold Rothstein, appeared during the Fuller trials, but the precise nature of this relationship was never fully clarified. Rothstein— "the walking bank, the pawnbroker of the underworld, the fugitive, unhealthy man who sidled along doorways," as Stanley Walker has described him in *The Night Club Era*—testified that Fuller owed him $336,768, most of which consisted of unpaid gambling debts. Fuller countered this statement with the charge that Rothstein personally owed him some $385,000. In subsequent testimony, Rothstein admitted having borrowed $187,000 at one time from Fuller and Co., for which he had put up $25,000 worth of collateral. But Fuller and Co.'s financial records (those that could be located) were so confused that this testimony was of little significance. More informative was Rothstein's statement that Fuller was a shrewd gambler who usually won his bets. Beyond this, Rothstein refused to testify. It was generally suspected that the firm's assets had been squandered by Fuller, McGee, Rothstein, and their friends on racing, baseball, boxing, and other sporting interests. Rothstein was believed to have "fixed" the World Series in 1919, although, again, nothing conclusive was ever proved against him. He was also reputed to be engaged in numerous other criminal activities, including the operation of gambling houses, shops selling stolen gems, brothels, and a lucrative bootlegging business—enterprises which did not affect his social standing. Like Fuller, he was frequently seen in the company of respected New York business and society figures, whom he entertained lavishly in his expensive Park Avenue apartment.[10]

Another interesting friendship disclosed during the trials was that between Edward Fuller and Walter S. Silkworth, the president of the Consolidated Stock Exchange. For months prior to the collapse of Fuller and Company, Silkworth had repeatedly ignored requests from Fuller's customers that Fuller and Co. be suspended from the exchange for fraudulent practices. Silkworth's brother was one of Fuller's employees, and during the trial Silkworth himself was unable to account for $133,000 in his private banking account—$55,175 of which had been deposited in cash. After Fuller's and McGee's convictions, Silkworth was obliged to resign from his presidency of the Consolidated Exchange.

Fitzgerald borrowed heavily from the newspaper accounts of Fuller's business affairs in creating Gatsby than he had from the details of Fuller's personality. For example, it seems unlikely that Fuller's friendship with Nellie Burke inspired Gatsby's idealistic attachment to Daisy Buchanan. However, Charles Stoneham's paternal interest in young Fuller, as it came out during the trial, is paralleled in the novel by Dan Cody's friendship for Gatsby, and Meyer Wolfshiem obviously was suggested by Fuller's friend, Arnold Rothstein. From the newspaper accounts of Fuller's career Fitzgerald also borrowed such details as Gatsby's airplane, the young stock-and-bond salesmen who haunted his parties, his mysterious connections with "the oil business" as well as his efforts to find a "small town" in which to start up some new and unmistakably shady enterprise, and his connections with New York society people like Tom Buchanan's friend Walter Chase. "That drug store business was just small change," Tom says after he has investigated Gatsby's business connections with Chase, "but you've got something on now that Walter's afraid to tell me about." What that "something" was Fitzgerald had spelled out in more detail in one of the earlier drafts of *The Great Gatsby.* "Until last summer when Wolfshiem was tried (but not convicted) on charges of grand larceny, forgery, bribery, and dealing in stolen bonds," Nick Carraway says, "I wasn't sure what it all included." Later, however, Fitzgerald omitted this passage, preferring to leave most of the facts about his hero's business affairs to the reader's imagination.[11]

For after all, in a world where people like Tom and Daisy and Jordan

Baker survived and continued to be admired, what difference did it make what crimes Gatsby had committed? Besides, who in the real world of the Twenties, or in the novel that mirrored it, was free of the universal stain? The files of the Fuller-McGee case prove concretely what *The Great Gatsby* implies indirectly: that society leaders, financial tycoons, politicians, magistrates, pimps, jurors, lawyers, baseball players, sheriffs, bond salesmen, debutantes, and prostitutes—all shared in some degree the responsibility for Gatsby's fate.

Gatsby's murder was a grimmer fate than that meted out to Edward Fuller, who successfully delayed going to Sing Sing for several years and who was then paroled at the end of a year. Even so, Fitzgerald's premonition that careers like Fuller's and Rothstein's were destined to end violently was borne out by later history. Rothstein was fated to die in almost exactly the same manner as Meyer Wolfshiem's friend Rosy Rosenthal, who was shot "three times in his full belly" at four A.M. in the morning outside the old Metropole, where he had spent the night plotting with five of his mobsters. Rothstein was finally killed by an anonymous gunman in 1928 just as he was leaving a conference of big-time bootleggers and gangsters in the Park Central Hotel. In Rothstein's case, however, there were no witnesses to eulogize the manner of his passing, as Wolfshiem did so lyrically for Rosy Rosenthal. Afterwards, the New York police were not only reluctant to investigate Rothstein's murder, but devoted their efforts instead to seizing and suppressing his papers, lest his connections with other prominent New Yorkers be brought to light. Ultimately it was the public hue and cry over the police's inability to solve the mystery of the Rothstein slaying that triggered the historic Seabury investigation into New York City politics a year later, in 1929. As Judge Seabury gradually compiled enough evidence to force the resignation of Mayor Jimmy Walker and his top officials, intimate ties were disclosed between money, politics, sports, crime, and business—ties which Fitzgerald had already described in *Gatsby* some years earlier. The further the 1920's recede, the more that novel emerges as one of the most penetrating criticisms of that incredible decade.

The newspaper clippings of Edward Fuller's career, however, by no means account for Gatsby himself or for the novel's vitality as a literary work. Few heroes of fiction have spent so much time off stage and yet dominated the action as he does. He does not speak his first line until the story is one-fourth of the way along, and he is dead by the time it is three-quarters finished. So far as the narrative is concerned, we are much better acquainted with Nick Carraway than we ever are with his mysterious neighbor. Yet *The Great Gatsby* for many of its admirers remains exclusively Gatsby's story. To the suggestion that Nick Carraway is the real hero of the novel and Gatsby only a figment of Nick's imagination, John O'Hara, for example, objects strenuously. "Gatsby not real. Why he's as real as you are sitting there in that chair!"[12]

Fitzgerald himself was not, however, so confident of his success in establishing the credibility of his hero. ". . . [Y]ou are right about Gatsby being blurred and patchy," he wrote John Peale Bishop several months after his novel was published. "I never at any one time saw him clear myself—for he started as one man I knew and then changed into myself—the amalgam was never complete in my mind." When Fitzgerald wrote this in the summer of 1925, *The Great Gatsby* was selling badly and he was groping for reasons to explain its disappointing reception. But now that his novel has become an established classic, it is not so apparent that Gatsby's vagueness is the flaw Fitzgerald thought it was. The puppet-carver, for example, knows that it is a mistake to carve his puppet's features too meticulously. At the distance from which the audience views his figures, reality is as much a factor of the on-looker's imagination as the carver's faithfulness to literal detail.[13]

Gatsby, too, is a puppet figure. It is useless to demand that he approximate the reality of the other characters in the novel, since the question of his reality is itself the subject matter of the story. He is an ideal figure, and the focal distance that separates him from the reader is greater than that of any of the other characters. What credibility he finally attains in the reader's imagination is not due to any specific action that he performs as much as to what he represents. Essentially, Gatsby is a mythic character, and the reality he achieves is that of the myth that creates and sustains him.

Lord Raglan, in his classic study of *The Hero,* points out that the career of the typical hero of Western folk literature generally follows a familiar pattern. Nothing illustrates Gatsby's mythopoeic nature better than his many resemblances to this archetype. According to Lord Raglan, the traditional hero of legend is the son of royal parents who has been wrongfully deprived of his birthright and sent away to the hinterland to be reared by humble foster parents. He is ignorant of his origins, yet his natural grace and talents soon mark him as a superior being. Suspecting that he is different from his companions, he leaves home and sets off for the king's court to seek his fortune. There he proves himself by some onerous test and eventually regains his rightful heritage.[14]

Most striking of all is Gatsby's resemblance to one particularly well-known variation of this pattern—the so-called Great or Noble Fool. This story was especially popular with Celtic bards, and served as the source for the histories of two famous Arthurian heroes, Sir Galahad and Sir Perceval. Here the rude country lad on his way to court meets a beautiful lady of high degree, wins her favor and spends a memorable night with her. Proceeding to court, he is mocked by the king's followers because of his rude ways and given a menial position, usually in the castle kitchen. There he is ridiculed by the evil cook (or steward) until an opportunity arrives for him to prove himself. The lovely lady whom he met earlier appears on the scene, begging the king for a champion to defend her against some evil being who has her in thrall—an enchanter or cruel dragon or, in some versions, a cruel husband. Since everyone else is too frightened to volunteer, our hero steps forth, follows her to battle, destroys the wrong-doer, and wins her hand in marriage.[15]

The resemblances between this ancient pattern and *The Great Gatsby* are self-evident. That Fitzgerald had them consciously in mind when he was writing his novel is unlikely. But there is no doubt at all about his familiarity with the great fool motif. As a boy he had not only read Sir Walter Scott's famous version, *Ivanhoe,* but had written an imitation in verse, "Elavoe." During the years that he was growing up, a number of popular sentimental treatments of the great fool theme appeared in fiction—notably Sir James Barrie's *Sentimental Tommy* and *The Little Minister,* and John William Locke's *The Beloved Vagabond.* In *This Side of Paradise* Amory listed all three among the favorite books of his childhood. Also, in a 1923 review of Sherwood Anderson's *Many Marriages,* written while Fitzgerald was planning *The Great Gatsby,* he refers to the theme of "the noble fool which has dominated tragedy from *Don Quixote* to *Lord Jim.*"[16]

In one of the best-known renditions of this myth, the legend of Sir Parzival, the hero ultimately renounces the various worldly trophies that he has won by his prowess, including sexual love, and dedicates himself to the quest for the Holy Grail, the symbol of the perfect life. It was an unattainable goal in this world, but, purified by long years of self-denial and a simple life, Parzival is finally rewarded with a vision of the Grail as he dies and ascends to Heaven.

Gatsby too, as Fitzgerald says, had "committed himself to a following of the Grail." But the Grail he pursues is the modern one of worldly success. Much of the force of his story lies in the fact that it combines two of the most pervasive myths in modern Western culture, with each serving as a critique of the other. One is the medieval and fundamentally Christian myth of the grail knight, and his lifelong pursuit of the good, the beautiful, and the true. The other is the modern secular myth of the self-made man—based on the belief that anyone, no matter how lowly his origins, could rise and become a success, provided he worked hard and made the most of his talents. The symbols of success were those that Fitzgerald himself had pursued with such diligence—wealth, prestige, and the possession of a beautiful, popular girl.[17]

Somewhere between the closing of the Middle Ages and the beginning of the modern era, the Parzival myth was supplanted by the present-day myth of the poor boy who makes good. The most convincing evidence for this is the dramatic emergence of a popular culture hero embodying the values of the new industrial society—Dick Whittington, best-known and best-loved of modern business tycoons.

Within the space of a few years, from 1600 to 1610 or so, Renaissance London experienced a sudden outpouring of broadsides, ballads, plays, and stories in prose and verse, all glorifying this hitherto unknown hero of the new rising middle class. The real Sir Richard Whittington had been dead and forgotten for almost two hundred years. The facts of his life, except that he owned a cat and had been Lord Mayor of London, bore little relation to the new Elizabethan legend. What was needed was a popular folk hero whose history would inculcate the virtues of the new philosophy of hard work and the opportunity to rise in the world. So sudden and so dramatic was Dick Whittington's appearance on the scene, full-blown, that one suspects the machinations of an Elizabethan public relations expert—just as the American "Paul Bunyan" would later spring in full panoply from the brain of a smart lumber industry advertising executive.[18]

Thus was the tale of the great fool changed to suit the needs of the new dispensation. During the years that followed Dick became the established ideal middle-class hero. Nowhere was he better-known or more admired than in the U.S.A., where his history went through edition after edition. Among some of his more famous offspring were Benjamin Franklin's "Poor Richard" and Horatio Alger's poor-boy heroes—Ragged Dick, Frank Fearless, and the sturdy lads of *Making His Way, Strive and Succeed,* and *From Canal Boy to President.*

It was hardly necessary for Fitzgerald to know the writings of Alger or Franklin to have been familiar with their philosophy of business success. Their maxims were promulgated weekly in the pages of popular magazines like *The Saturday Evening Post* (which claimed to have been founded by Franklin). In fact, one scholar has recently shown that Fitzgerald actually based Gatsby's pathetic list of rules for self-improvement on "Poor Richard's" popular precepts for getting ahead in the world.

And in a deleted passage of an early draft of *The Great Gatsby*, Fitzgerald actually called one of Gatsby's sinister business acquaintances "Mr. Franklin Dick." Such was his ironic tribute to the Dick Whittingtons, Ragged Dicks, Poor Richards, and their forerunners to whom Gatsby owed his shabby glamorous dreams.[19]

Like the rest of his generation, Fitzgerald also knew his Horatio Alger. In "Absolution," Rudolph Miller's tiny library consists exclusively of that author's works. In "Forging Ahead," another autobiographical story written several years later for the *Post*, celebrating the virtues of hard work and determination, Fitzgerald said that after his hero decided to become a business success he "took down half a dozen dusty volumes of Horatio Alger . . . then much as a postwar young man might consult The George Washington Condensed Business Course, he sat at his desk and slowly began to turn the pages of 'Bound to Rise.' "[20]

Thus like Fitzgerald's earlier play, *The Vegetable*, *The Great Gatsby* was a conscious indictment of the American dream of success. Like *The Vegetable*, it was another attempt to atone for stories like "The Popular Girl," "The Off-shore Pirate," and "Forging Ahead," which accepted this precept, and which he would continue to write (as long as his conscience would let him) whenever he needed money. But unlike *The Vegetable*, *The Great Gatsby* succeeded because, by turning to his own past, Fitzgerald was able to make use of the wealth of mythology that had shaped his own experience.

Gatsby, like Fitzgerald, wants it both ways. He must be a Grail Knight as well as a Wall Street tycoon. He expects Daisy to be the innocent maiden in distress waiting stoically for her knight-errant. At the same time he insists that she be a typical "popular" girl—rich, pretty, and consequently self-centered and unadventurous. Confused by these conflicting aims and goals, the vulnerable Gatsby is easily betrayed and destroyed. But his story affirms the unique value as well as the limitations of the philosophy of romantic individualism. More than any other American novel, *The Great Gatsby* demonstrates the tragic quality of this faith—still one of the most pervasive and vigorous beliefs of Western man.

VIII
The Great Gatsby:
Finding a Form

Technically, *The Great Gatsby* was the most carefully planned and most flawlessly executed of all Fitzgerald's novels—although, had he lived to finish it, *The Last Tycoon* might have surpassed it on both counts. Unlike its immediate predecessor, *The Beautiful and Damned*, *Gatsby* took shape in his imagination gradually over a period of at least three years. "I want to write something *new*—something extraordinary and beautiful and simple and intricately patterned," he had written Max Perkins when he first began to think of it in the spring of 1922. Two more years would elapse, however, before he finally decided on its form. After that he spent ten uninterrupted months in the south of France and in Italy writing and revising it. "Never before," he later said of those months in his Modern Library introduction to *Gatsby*, "did one try to keep his artistic conscience as pure. . . ."[1]

Several years afterwards, in a 1927 newspaper interview, Fitzgerald spoke of "that inspired hush that people make for themselves in which they want to be or do on the scale . . . with which great races make their dreams." Altogether, there were only three such hushed moments in Fitzgerald's creative life. The first was that hot summer of 1919 when, despairing of ever becoming a business success, he had thrown up his advertising copywriter's job in New York and gone home to rewrite *This Side of Paradise*. Later, he would look back on it as one of the most heroic moments of his life. The second was the ten months from April, 1924, to February, 1925, that he spent in Europe writing and polishing

The Great Gatsby. The third would be the lonely autumn of 1940 in Hollywood, when, tired and ill, he wrote most of *The Last Tycoon.*[2]

That summer of 1924 was not entirely free from distractions. While he worked alone at his desk in the Villa Marie day after day on *Gatsby,* Zelda and two-year-old Scottie were left to amuse themselves as best they could on the nearby St. Raphaël beach. It was here, in July, that Zelda encountered "René Silvé" ("Edouard Josanne"), the gallant and handsome young French aviation officer who devoted himself to keeping the lonely young *américaine* from becoming bored.

How far Zelda let this affair with René go, and how much it disturbed her husband's writing, is obscure. Arthur Mizener is convinced that it marked the turning point in the Fitzgeralds' marriage and that the emotional effect on Fitzgerald himself was enormous. This is certainly the impression Zelda gave when she wrote a thinly disguised account of that summer eight years later in her autobiographical novel, *Save Me the Waltz.* But her version must be partially discounted. It was written in a mental clinic where she was being treated for schizophrenia, and one of the symptoms of her illness was a frantic jealousy of her husband's literary success. Her novel was an expression of this envy and a bitter attack on Fitzgerald. Thus she had a motive, both at this time and back in 1924 when she first met René Silvé, for exaggerating her account of their friendship in the hopes of arousing Fitzgerald. A Southern belle accustomed to a great deal of masculine attention, Zelda increasingly resented the time Fitzgerald had begun to spend on the slow, careful writing and extensive revision that were necessary for his best work. A novel as ambitious as *The Great Gatsby* was just the thing to antagonize her, especially when he could easily make all the money they needed from his magazine stories. (I can still remember the irritated note in her voice when she told me, not long before her death in 1948, "I don't see why Scott objected so to those *Post* stories when he got such wonderful prices for them.")[3]

If Fitzgerald was seriously disturbed by Zelda's behavior that summer, the laconic entries in his Ledger do not indicate it.[4]

> July: "The big crisis. Zelda swimming every day."
> August: "Good work on the novel. Zelda and I close together."
> September: "The novel finished. Trouble clearing away."

"Zelda and I are contemplating a careful revision after a week's complete rest," he wrote Max Perkins at the end of August. ". . . It's been a fair summer. I've been unhappy but my work hasn't suffered from it. I am grown at last."[5]

Whatever his feelings were about the René Silvé episode, they did not dampen his satisfaction with *Gatsby.* "Artistically," he wrote Harold Ober that autumn, "it's head and shoulders over everything I've done." And to Edmund Wilson: "My book is wonderful. . . . I have got my health back—I no longer cough and itch and roll from one side of the bed to the other all night and have a hollow ache in my stomach after two cups of black coffee." "The cheerfulest things in my life are first Zelda," he wrote John Peale Bishop several weeks later, "and second the hope that my book has something extraordinary about it. I want to be extravagantly admired again. Zelda and I sometimes indulge in terrible four day rows that always start with a drinking party but we're still in love and about the only truly happily married people I know." As for the novel: "I'm tired of being the author of *This Side of Paradise* and I want to start over," he wrote Perkins in his October 27, 1924 letter accompanying the manuscript of *Gatsby.* ". . . I think that at last I've done something really my own."[6]

Gilbert Seldes, who visited the Fitzgeralds in France while *Gatsby* was being written, said in a *Dial* review that it owed its structure to the fiction of Edith Wharton, and through her to Henry James. Fitzgerald had great personal admiration for Mrs. Wharton, who was a good friend of Father Fay, and of his other friends, Mrs. Winthrop Chanler and "Peevie" Parrott, although he never mentioned her work in his letters. When *The Great Gatsby* was published in the spring of 1925 the Fitzgeralds were in Paris, and Mrs. Wharton was in residence in her handsome villa, the Pavillon Colombe, nearby. Fitzgerald sent her an inscribed copy of *Gatsby* and was rewarded with an appreciative letter as well as a note inviting him and Zelda to tea with Parrott and Mrs. Chanler's son, Theodore Chanler the composer.[7]

So far as Edith Wharton's novels are concerned, the only one that resembles *Gatsby* particularly is *Ethan Frome* (a copy of which Fitzgerald owned). Like *Ethan Frome, Gatsby* is short and dramatically structured and has a similar violent ending, but it lacks the stark inevitability of Mrs. Wharton's New England tragedy. Fitzgerald may also have been impressed by the device of the first-person narrator, although the anonymous young engineer who tells the story of Ethan Frome plays a much less important role in the action than does Nick Carraway.

At this stage in his career Fitzgerald seems to have been even less familiar with the fiction of Henry James than he was with that of Mrs. Wharton. Edmund Wilson, who was certainly in a position to know, published an amusing, fictitious interview in 1924 between his friend and Van Wyck Brooks (who had just written a biography of Henry James) in which Fitzgerald says, "I don't know anything about James, myself. I've never read a word of him." Of James's novels, *Daisy Miller* most resembled *Gatsby* in form. Both describe the attempt of a sensitive young man to understand the ambiguous social behavior of a less sophisticated compatriot. Both are set in an unfamiliar setting—*Gatsby* in the alien East, *Daisy Miller* in Europe. But although the latter novel is presented from the point of view of a young man, Frederick Winterbourne, he does not tell the story himself as does Nick Carraway. Consequently, Winterbourne's sensibility is much less of a controlling artistic factor. What Fitzgerald sees as a romantic drama fraught with tragic overtones James presents as an ironic comedy of manners.[8]

There is no evidence that Fitzgerald knew *Daisy Miller* when he wrote *The Great Gatsby*. But it eventually became one of his favorite novels, the only novel of James that he seems to have admired. It invariably shows up on the lists of the favorite books that he prepared during the last few years of his life for the edification of friends or the instruction of his college-age daughter. Was it because he had been struck by the many parallels between *Daisy Miller* and *Gatsby*? Despite their differences in temperament, both James and Fitzgerald shared an obsessive concern for the moral life of upper-middle-class American society. On his return to the United States in 1904, after an absence of twenty-five years, James had noted the emerging themes and symbols which, he prophesied, would preoccupy the American novelist of the next generation: the new hotel life of New York, the suburban country club, and above all, the recently emancipated American girl. It was these that Fitzgerald would shortly make the subject matter of his fiction.[9]

Although *The Great Gatsby* is closer to *Daisy Miller* in form than to James's other novels, philosophically its theme is more reminiscent of James's *The American*. The problem Nick confronts at the end of *Gatsby* is remarkably like that which confronted James's hero, Christopher Newman, as James described it in the Preface he wrote for the "New York" edition of *The American*. It was, James said,[10]

the situation, in another country and an aristocratic society, of some robust but insidiously beguiled and betrayed, some cruelly wronged, compatriot: the point being in especial that he should suffer at the hands of persons pretending to represent the highest civilization and to be of an order in every way superior to his own. What would he

'do' in that predicament, how would he right himself, or how, fail-
ing a remedy, would he conduct himself under his wrong?

For James the answer was a forthright one:

> . . . he would simply turn, at the supreme moment, away, the bitter-
> ness of his personal loss yielding to the very force of his aversion.
> All that he would have at the end would be therefore just the moral
> convenience, indeed the moral necessity, of his practical but quite
> unappreciated magnanimity.

Nick Carraway, at the end of *The Great Gatsby,* confronts the same
situation that James had raised in *The American* fifty years earlier. But
Nick's response is different from that of Christopher Newman. Henry
James's essentially Victorian cast of mind is revealed in his confident
assertion that his hero's bitter disillusion will be counteracted by his
intrinsic "magnanimity." Fitzgerald, on the other hand, shared the Jazz
Age's distrust of all such moral abstractions. Nick's response at the end
of the story is expressed in more concrete terms by his altered attitude
toward the symbols of home and family.

Although James himself was fascinated by the artistic possibilities
of the "point of view," and experimented with it widely, he actually made
very little use in his own fiction of a first-person observer-narrator like
Nick Carraway. Parallels to Nick appear only in James's obscure novel,
The Sacred Fount, and a few shorter stories. The most probable source
for the idea of Nick was neither Henry James nor Edith Wharton, but
rather Joseph Conrad in those works in which the story is narrated by
Marlow: *Lord Jim, Youth, Chance, Victory,* and *Heart of Darkness.* (But
this does not mean that James was not an influence on Fitzgerald, if
only indirectly. For Conrad, like Edith Wharton, owed an appreciable
debt to "The Master." In fact, Conrad was, according to F.W. Dupee,
James's "greatest disciple.")[11]

Fitzgerald owed much more to Conrad than the device of the first-
person narrator. Just as Fitzgerald's discovery of Keats at Princeton had
been responsible for his awareness of the resources of language and
imagery, so his subsequent study of Conrad taught him most of what he
learned from others about form and structure. His earlier models—
Mackenzie, Norris, *et al*—served him briefly and then were discarded.
But Keats and Conrad were to be Fitzgerald's indispensible literary
touchstones for the rest of his life.

He came upon Conrad's work for the first time during the winter of

1919–1920, probably having heard about it from H.L. Mencken, who at the moment was waging a one-man campaign for both Conrad and Theodore Dreiser. At first it had been Conrad's pessimism rather than his art that impressed Fitzgerald—a pessimism which he (like Mencken) believed to be similar to Dreiser's. Like Mencken, too, he welcomed it as an antidote to the saccharine optimism expressed by so much contemporary writing. "My view of life," Fitzgerald wrote grandiloquently at this time to President Hibben of Princeton, ". . . is the view of the Theodore Dreisers and Joseph Conrads—that life is too strong and remorseless for the sons of men."[12]

Even after Fitzgerald had cut adrift from the naturalists he continued to admire Conrad—but now more for his art than for his philosophy. The extent of this admiration can be seen in the eleven book reviews that he wrote between 1922 and 1925. For example, in one review he calls *Nostromo* "the greatest novel since 'Vanity Fair' (possibly excluding 'Madame Bovary')." In another, he cites the first sentence of Conrad's *Youth* as "one of the most remarkable passages of English prose written these thirty years."[13]

When, in his 1934 introduction to the Modern Library edition of *The Great Gatsby,* Fitzgerald tried to explain how he had written that novel ten years before, he said simply: "I had just re-read Joseph Conrad's Preface to *The Nigger* [*of the 'Narcissus'*]," as though that fact alone accounted for the tremendous advance *Gatsby* represented over his previous work. And when H.L. Mencken, in an unperceptive review of *Gatsby,* dismissed it as "in form no more than a glorified anecdote," Fitzgerald objected strenuously to Edmund Wilson, "That is because he [Mencken] has forgotten his admiration for Conrad and adjusted himself to the sprawling novel." Several years later, he would tell Max Perkins flatly: "Conrad has been, after all, the healthy influence on the technique of the novel."[14]

The Preface to *The Nigger of the "Narcissus"* offered Fitzgerald a credo especially well suited for his talent and temperament. "My task, which I am trying to achieve," Conrad wrote, "is, by the power of the written word to make you hear, to make you feel—it is before all, to make you see." Distinguishing the artist from the thinker (who is concerned with ideas) and the scientist (concerned with facts), Conrad defined the artist's task as that of descending within himself and discovering there the source of truth. "He speaks to our capacity for delight and wonder, to the sense of mystery surrounding our lives; to our sense of pity, and beauty and pain."

Then there was Conrad's ubiquitous Marlow. At the time he was writing *The Great Gatsby*, Fitzgerald not only had read *Lord Jim* and *Youth*, but was probably familiar with the other tales in which Marlow officiates. *Gatsby* is especially reminiscent of *Lord Jim*; and Nick Carraway resembles Marlow in his effort to probe beneath the crust of legend surrounding Gatsby to the reality beneath. In their attempts to attain moral insight into the respective heroes of these two stories, both Nick and Marlow advance haltingly, alternately attracted to and repelled by the object of their scrutiny. Marlow's apology for the vagueness of his portrait of "Lord Jim" might have been voiced by Nick. "I don't pretend to understand him. The views he let me have of himself were like those gleams through the shifting rents in a thick fog—bits of vivid and vanishing detail."[15]

Robert Stallman has ingeniously ferreted out just about every intimation to be found in *Gatsby* of Conrad's influence. We do not have to accept every scrap of his evidence in order to agree with his conclusion that the novel owes Conrad a profound debt. It seems unlikely, however, that Fitzgerald realized how varied and extensive these borrowings were. He never troubled to conceal his *conscious* debts to other writers. Indeed, he took great pleasure in admitting the intentional echoes in *The Great Gatsby* of lines from Keat's *Eve of St. Agnes* and *An Ode to a Nightingale*. But although he often expresses his great admiration for Conrad, nowhere in his letters does he mention having been specifically indebted to him.[16]

Temperamentally Fitzgerald and Conrad were somewhat alike. Both were essentially poets rather than prose writers in the sense that both were more concerned in their fiction with rendering states of feeling than with ideas or facts. Both were moralists. But neither was at home in the popular third-person expository tradition of the nineteenth-century British novel which treated moral questions confidently and abstractly. In his first novels, *An Outcast of the Islands* and *Almayer's Folly*, Conrad had struggled to use this method of narration, but without much success. In his attempts to indicate the complex ramifications of moral issues, he indulged in long-winded philosophical reflections that slowed up the story, or he piled image upon purple image in order to evoke moods and feelings he could not convey by direct statement. Similarly, in *This Side of Paradise* and *The Beautiful and Damned*, Fitzgerald had been unable to cope with the moral issues raised by his subject matter, and had indulged in long subjective speculations, or had brushed them off with an inconclusive irony.[17]

In Conrad's case, his discovery of Marlow as a device provided him with an artistic solution to his problem. Marlow is free to raise moral questions about the events he observes—even to suggest tentative answers. But Conrad's philosophical proclivities are disciplined by the necessity of having to filter them through Marlow's sensibility. In Marlow, Conrad found a method of dramatizing and objectifying his compulsion to moralize. Marlow's conversations with other people, his tentative questionings, musings, moral reflections, take the place of the heavy-footed expository statements that Conrad had used so unskillfully in his earlier fiction. Indeed, so delighted was Conrad by his discovery of the device of Marlow that he refused to lay aside the "short story" in which Marlow first appeared, and kept on writing until it had turned into one of his finest novels, *Lord Jim*!

This device was especially well-suited for the twentieth century novelist interested in moral ideas but unable to treat them with the detached third-person assurance of such Victorian moralists as Dickens, Thackeray, or George Eliot. In this country, not only Fitzgerald, but Willa Cather, Hemingway (in *A Farewell to Arms*), Faulkner (in *Absalom! Absalom!*), and Robert Penn Warren (in *All the King's Men*) were to make brilliant use of the intellectually detached but emotionally and morally involved first-person narrator.

Finally, *The Great Gatsby* owes a debt—not always beneficial—to Conrad's mellifluous, image-encrusted prose style. A typical image from *Lord Jim*—

> The thin gold shaving of the moon floating slowly downwards had lost itself on the darkened surface of the waters . . .

finds a corresponding, if somewhat more syncopated echo in *Gatsby*:[18]

> The moon had risen higher, and floating in the Sound was a triangle of silver scales, trembling a little to the stiff, tinny drip of the banjoes on the lawn.

Fitzgerald's attempts to copy Conrad's habit of piling image upon image were occasionally less successful. In the following passage from *Lord Jim*, for instance, Conrad succeeds brilliantly in his use of poetic imagery to suggest the ineffable:

> The ship moved so smoothly that her onward motion was imperceptible to the senses of men, as though she had been a crowded planet speeding through the dark spaces of ether behind the swarm

of senses in the appalling and calm solitudes awaiting the breath of future creations.

Here image, rhythm, rhyme, all combine to evoke a concrete impression which resists literal translation. Fitzgerald's attempts to express Gatsby's cosmic longings in this manner, however, often landed him in a quagmire.[19]

> Out of the corner of his eye Gatsby saw that the blocks of the sidewalks really formed a ladder and mounted to a secret place above the trees—he could climb out of it, if he climbed alone, and once there he could suck on the pap of life, gulp down the incomparable milk of wonder.

The earlier drafts of *Gatsby* are full of such over-written prose.

Another novelist whose influence in *The Great Gatsby* was almost as important as that of Conrad was Willa Cather. She, too, had started out by writing long, expository novels told from the viewpoint of a third-person historian. *The Song of the Lark* (1915) was her most ambitious early venture of this kind. But in two later novels which Fitzgerald admired, *My Ántonia* (1918) and *A Lost Lady* (1923), she had adopted the Conradian device of presenting her material from the point of view of only one of her characters, with the same liberating consequences.

My Ántonia is the story of Ántonia Shimerda, a Bohemian immigrant girl from a small town in the Midwest. It is narrated by a successful, middle-aged railroad lawyer named Jim Burden. Jim and Ántonia grew up in the same primitive prairie community. But Jim escaped—going East, marrying into a prominent New York family, and becoming a respected man of affairs. Ántonia remained behind, slaving away as a servant and finally making a marriage of convenience with a man twice her age. On the surface Ántonia's life of hardship and poverty appears to have been much less satisfying than Jim Burden's. But as Jim investigates the past they shared together, the reader realizes that it is really Jim who has failed. Bitter, disillusioned, married to a woman with whom he has less in common than he has with Ántonia, Jim discovers that his memory of the heroic, misunderstood Ántonia—"my Ántonia"—is the most precious thing he possesses.

Fitzgerald not only echoed the rhythmic final sentence of *My Ántonia* —"We proved together the precious, the incommunicable past."—in the closing sentence of *The Great Gatsby*, but in an essay that he wrote sixteen years later, during the last year of his life, he says:[20] "And this tragic year, so like another year, I keep thinking of Willa Cather's, 'We possess [sic] together the precious, the incommunicable past.' "

Like Conrad, whom she greatly admired, Miss Cather conveyed mood and atmosphere primarily by means of images. *My Antonia* contains a number of passages like that given below, which find echoes in *Gatsby*:[21]

> As we walked home across the fields, the sun dropped and lay like a great golden globe in the low west. While it hung there the moon rose in the east, as big as a cartwheel, pale silver and streaked with rose color, thin as a bubble or a ghost moon. . . . I felt the old pull of the earth, the solemn magic that came out of those fields at nightfall. I wished that I could be a little boy again and that my way could end there.

A Lost Lady is another investigation of the difference between appearance and reality. Here the story is presented through the eyes of a young man named Niel Herbert, who is trying to get at the truth about Marian Forrester, an older woman who fascinates him by her perplexing blend of charm and decadence. Niel does not narrate the story, but everything is focused through his sensibility. As a result *A Lost Lady*, like *My Antonia*, has a dramatic intensity missing from Miss Cather's more sprawling, expository narratives. This point was brought out by Edmund Wilson in a review of *A Lost Lady* in the January, 1924, *Dial*, that Fitzgerald undoubtedly read. Wilson's enthusiasm for the point-of-view method in both *A Lost Lady* and *My Antonia* may even have had something to do with Fitzgerald's decision three months later to abandon the third-person approach to his story, and to tell it by means of Nick Carraway. Nick resembles Willa Cather's ineffectual young men even more than he does Conrad's Marlow.

When *The Great Gatsby* was published the following April, 1925, Fitzgerald sent Miss Cather a copy with an inscribed note mentioning a passage in his novel that he had borrowed from *A Lost Lady*. Like that novel, *Gatsby* was a pastoral tragedy in which the less pleasant features of urban life were contrasted unfavorably with the more innocent frontier West of the author's youth. Miss Cather's conviction that "the Old West had been settled by dreamers, great-hearted adventurers who were impractical to the point of magnificence; a courteous brotherhood, strong in attack but weak in defence," found an echo in the moral geography of *The Great Gatsby*. Her description of one of her novel's less attractive personages—

His whole figure seemed very much alive under his clothes with a restless muscular energy that had something of the cruelty of wild animals in it—

could have applied equally to Tom Buchanan, whose powerful frame, Fitzgerald said, bulged out his riding habit and boots—

until he strained the top lacing, and you could see a great pack of muscle shifting when his shoulder moved under his thin coat. It was a body capable of enormous leverage—a cruel body.[22]

Henry James, Edith Wharton—more important, Joseph Conrad and Willa Cather—what different models from the ones Fitzgerald had chosen for his first two novels! Apart from the debts he owed them in style and themes, there was also the example they set for him in craftsmanship. Fitzgerald's new preoccupation with craft at this time can be seen in the heavily revised pages of his manuscript for *The Great Gatsby* and also in the eleven book reviews that he wrote during the three years, 1921–1924. Like the earlier reviews he had written at Princeton for the *Nassau Literary Magazine*, these were not especially distinguished literary criticism since they revealed more about Fitzgerald's own concern with literary problems than they did about the books he was reviewing. But in them we find him giving greater attention than ever to the technical aspects of craft, especially to the subject of literary form.

For example, his deprecating criticisms of Sherwood Anderson's *Many Marriages* and Woodward Boyd's *The Love Legend* are due primarily to these novels' formlessness. Such lack of form might be excused in a "first novel," he admitted (probably thinking of his own), on the grounds that "this lack of pattern gives the young novelist more of a chance to assert his or her individuality, which is the principal thing." Indeed, when formless first novels really were successful, he continued, they could be "amazing documents . . . utterly national and of today. And when our Conrad or Joyce or Anatole France comes, such books as they will have cleared the way. Out of these enormous and often muddy lakes will flow the clear stream—if there is to be a clear stream at all."[23]

It is evident from these reviews that Fitzgerald was more interested in the clear stream of literature represented by Conrad, Joyce, and France, than in the muddy lakes represented by his own previous novels. Everything that he finds praiseworthy in these eleven reviews relates in some way to problems of craft. "This is all very careful work," he says of John Dos Passos' *Three Soldiers*. "There is none of that uncorrelated

detail, which shows in all but one or two pieces of American realism."
Of his friend Tom Boyd's World War I novel, *Through the Wheat,* he
wrote:[24]

> . . . without one single recourse to sentiment, to hysteria, or to
> trickery, the author strikes one clear and unmistakable note of hero-
> ism, . . . and with this note vibrating sharply in the reader's con-
> sciousness the books ends.
>
> There is a fine unity about it all which only becomes fully ap-
> parent when this note is struck. The effect is cumulative in the sheer-
> est sense. . . . The whole book is written in the light of one sharp
> emotion and hence it is as a work of art rather than as a textbook
> for patrioteer or pacifist that the book is interesting.

Through the Wheat hardly deserved this praise; Fitzgerald was describing instead the kind of novel he himself hoped to write. Elsewhere
in his reviews, he discussed subtle technical details about which he had
troubled very little in the past, but which would preoccupy him during
the composition of *The Great Gatsby.* Thus, in his review of his friend
Grace Flandrau's novel, *Being Respectable,* he called attention to her
method of introducing one of her minor characters in such a way that
"the entire charm and personality of the woman is conveyed at second-
hand. We have scarcely a glimpse of her and she says only one line
throughout. Yet the portrait is vivid and complete." This detail was
hardly worthy of attention in a short newspaper review. But it was the
method Fitzgerald would use in introducing his readers to Jay Gatsby.[25]

Ironically, at the moment that Fitzgerald himself was abandoning
the baggy shapelessness of his first two novels, other authors were adopting them as models. Thus, when the editor of *College Humor* commissioned Katherine Brush in 1924 to write a new novel for him, his instructions to her amounted to little more than an order to imitate *This
Side of Paradise:*[26]

> Don't think of it as a novel and then you'll be all right. Think of
> it as a lot of little plots strung together; episodes and incidents and
> some really fine character studies. If you've got ideas in mind right
> now that you were going to use for short college stories, put them
> together, hitch them up, give them one main character to which all
> these different things happen—and there you are, you'll have it.
> First thing you know, it'll be a novel. It might even be a good one
> if the characters are real enough. . . . I want a novel like Fitzgerald's

This Side of Paradise. . . . I cabled Fitzgerald to see if I could get him to do it for me but I can't afford his price.

But the identification of sources and influences, although a fascinating pastime, cannot account adequately for *The Great Gatsby* as a work of art. For this we must turn to the text itself. And here the evidence of Fitzgerald's manuscript is illuminating. Unfortunately, as we noted earlier, nothing except "Absolution" survives from the version of *Gatsby* which Fitzgerald discarded in April, 1924. But of the final version, with Nick Carraway as narrator, we have the following material:

(1) A complete draft, mostly in pencil, that was probably the first completed draft of *Gatsby.* Many pages have been heavily revised, while others appear to be smooth copies of earlier drafts no longer extant. The erratic pagination of certain episodes, and the crude prose in other sections, suggest that this was pieced together, chapter by chapter, from earlier drafts during the summer of 1924. The detailed revisions give us some idea of how Fitzgerald went about revising his material.

(2) A set of uncorrected galley proofs. The discrepancies between these proofs and the pencil manuscript described above indicate that Fitzgerald probably made a smooth typescript (no longer extant) of the above manuscript, which he further revised slightly and sent Max Perkins on October 27, 1924.

(3) A second set of the same proofs, corrected and extensively revised by Fitzgerald. There are a few unimportant discrepancies between the text of this set and that of the published text of *Gatsby.* Either these were duplicates on which Fitzgerald failed to note all the revisions, or further changes were made by him (or Perkins) in page proofs no longer extant.[27]

The most striking thing about the earliest extant manuscript version of *Gatsby* is that so much of it is badly written. The apparent spontaneity and effortlessness of the published version was attained only by the most painstaking revision.

The next point to be noted is that Fitzgerald began writing with a surprisingly vague idea of what Daisy and Nick and Gatsby were really like as people. Nick, for example, was much more crudely defined in Chapters I and III (II was an afterthought) than he would be in the later versions. At one moment he is a rather unpleasant smart-aleck, full of cynical wise-cracks. A few paragraphs later, he is fretting about his lack of money, sure that the chauffeurs of his rich Long Island neighbors are snubbing him because he drives a battered old car.

Jordan Baker and Daisy Buchanan are also less clearly defined, especially in the opening chapters. And Daisy is less appealing. In Chapter I, after telling Nick about the birth of her daughter, she says coarsely: "I woke up feeling as if I'd just been raped by a company of soldiers and left out on a field to die." It is a good line, but out of keeping with Daisy's personality, and was later deleted. At this stage Tom Buchanan was the most fully developed of all the characters, probably because a profound dislike of Tom was the only emotion Fitzgerald had been thus far able to feel about his cast.[28]

Someday we will have a variorum edition of *The Great Gatsby* based on the extant manuscripts and revised galley proofs. Until that is available, the best way of showing how the novel took form is to describe the textual evolution of each of its nine chapters. Chapter I, in which Nick Carraway introduces himself to the reader, has already been discussed in considerable detail in Chapter VI of this book. We have seen how this opening chapter had its origin in a single flooding emotion— an emotion that eventually was to unify the entire work. "Whether it's something that happened twenty years ago or only yesterday," Fitzgerald would later say, "I must start out with an emotion—one that's close to me and that I can understand."[29]

Nick's sense of disenchantment comes from his discovery that the Buchanan marriage is a farce, and that Tom is having an affair which Daisy knows about and cynically accepts. But why does this knowledge have such a shattering effect on Nick? Why is he seized with foreboding merely upon entering the Buchanans' residence, before he has even learned what is going on? Nick says in a deleted passage:[30]

> A curious mood took possession of me as we went in that door, a sensation I had experienced before when as a little boy I went from a dark open street into a bright little shop on the corner. It was an absurd sensation, of the futility of things being one way rather than another. I felt as though I should have come in on all fours or standing on my hands.

This emotional reaction was a private one which Fitzgerald at this stage has imposed on Nick without providing enough justification. Apparently Fitzgerald intended to imply that Nick's discovery of the truth about Daisy's marriage would serve as his initiation into the knowledge of evil. From the very beginning, Fitzgerald had conceived of Tom as the embodiment of evil; thus, through her marriage Daisy has become contaminated. Both Daisy's contamination and Nick's betrayal, in the first version of this chapter, were symbolized by the defilement of the green American continent by the first Dutch sailors and European colonizers and settlers. There is a strong hint that the evil Daisy has experienced, and that Nick senses in the atmosphere of the Buchanan household, is involved with sex, with Daisy's physical relationship to Tom. Here we are reminded of the intimations in "Absolution," expressed through imagery, that Father Schwartz's treatment of little Rudolph Miller was due to repressed homosexual desires. Was Gatsby's idealized love of Daisy only a kind of sexual impotence?

Be that as it may, at this point in the pencil manuscript, Nick's visit to Tom and Daisy results in his being overtaken by a profound melancholy. His thoughts turn to death, and he longs for some violent experience that will jar him out of this state of mind. Both Nick's initial infatuation with Daisy, and the disillusion and death wish that followed, were later deleted from Chapter I. But they are evidence of the powerful emotion that gripped Fitzgerald at the time. Gatsby's love affair with Daisy, ending in his death, served Fitzgerald as an "objective correlative" for that emotion of romantic disillusion that had possessed Nick with such force at the end of this first draft of Chapter I. By shifting the emphasis away from Nick's static emotional state to the more dynamic relationship existing between Gatsby and Daisy, Fitzgerald was able to make more objective use of Nick as the detached observer and moralist. The story of Gatsby's betrayal and his violent death and of Daisy's collusion, was a more appropriate vehicle for the emotion that had initially inspired Fitzgerald.

As the writing of that first draft progressed and Fitzgerald plunged deeper into his story, he got to know his characters better. Nick threw off the narcissistic self-pity of the first chapter and developed a more mature understanding of the romantic impulse that had led him (and Gatsby) to idealize and thus overvalue Daisy. By the end of Fitzgerald's first draft of the novel, Nick had progressed to the point where he could not only sympathize with this alter ego, but could also see the more ridiculous aspects of Gatsby's behavior.

Chapter II, the highly comic chapter in which Nick accompanies Tom and Myrtle to their West Side New York love nest, was a splendid afterthought. Apparently Fitzgerald did not write it until the rest of his first draft, or most of it, had been completed. As far as plot is concerned, Chapter II is an unnecessary digression. But this merely underlines once again the minor role that the element of plot played in Fitzgerald's art. Artistically, this second chapter is one of the most inspired things in the book. In contrast to the cool, orderly elegance of Tom's and Daisy's spacious Georgian mansion in Chapter I, we now move through the ash-strewn valley of death to the blurred disorder of Tom's and Myrtle's drunken party. Nick bears little resemblance either to the wisecracking young cynic we met at the opening of the preceding chapter, or to the victim of dissillusioned self-pity we left at the end. This supports the other evidence indicating that Chapter II was a late addition. Throughout this second chapter Nick actually says very little. He has been transformed into an alert, thoughtful observer, although, as he gets drunker, he finds this role difficult to sustain. Eventually his vision becomes so cloudy that everything he sees has a blurred look about it, from Catherine's "blurred eyebrows," and Mr. McKee's ridiculous photograph of "a hen sitting on a blurred rock," to Nick's last hazy view of the lower level of Penn Station at four o'clock in the morning.

It would require the corrective lenses of Dr. T.J. Eckleburg to give focus and clarity to the disorder of Tom Buchanan's sex life, as we see it demonstrated in this chapter. Nick Carraway's lone moment of insight comes midway in the party when, in spite of his alienation from Tom and Myrtle and their raucous friends, he discovers that he is too deeply involved with them to be able to escape.[31]

> I wanted to get out and walk eastward toward the Park through the soft twilight [he says as he looks out of the apartment window], but each time I tried to go I became entangled in some wild, strident argument which pulled me back, as if with ropes, into my chair. Yet high over the city our line of yellow windows must have contributed their share of human secrecy to the casual watcher in the darkening streets, and I saw him, too, looking up and wondering. I was within and without, simultaneously enchanted and repelled by the inexhaustible variety of life.

Here, for the moment, Nick and Fitzgerald are one. Here, too, is the first intimation that we have had of Nick's tragic sense, of that capacity for compassion coupled with moral judgment that is the hallmark of his humanity. In a way *The Great Gatsby* is the story of how Nick developed a genuinely tragic sense of life—"that ability to hold two opposed ideas in the mind at the same time and still retain the ability to function," that Fitzgerald in one of his later *Crack-up* essays would describe as "the mark of a first-rate intelligence." It is because of Nick's artistic existence as a controlling point of view that Fitzgerald was able to treat his own personal history with a detachment missing from his previous novels; consequently, *Gatsby* succeeds as a work of art where the other two failed. Here, finally, Fitzgerald has done "what the artist does"—as Paul

Rosenfeld, in his 1922 essay, had hoped he someday might: He has "seen [his material] simultaneously from within and without; and loved it and judged it, too."[32]

The insertion of Chapter II between the first and third chapters further retarded the already belated entrance of the novel's hero, Jay Gatsby. But this was all to the good. It was essential to the novel's success that Gatsby at first should be accepted by the audience on his own idealized terms. And one of the best ways of persuading the skeptical modern reader to accept a heroic figure—as Homer long ago proved in the *Odyssey*—was to keep him off stage long enough for the other characters to build up an ideal impression of him. Chapters I and II, and the first part of Chapter III, were therefore, carefully sprinkled with a number of casual allusions to Gatsby in order to create a plausible suspense regarding his origins and business affairs.

Physically, Gatsby is in evidence only a short time during Chapter III, but we are continually aware of his presence. This is *his* chapter, as Chapter I belonged to Nick, and Chapter II to Tom and Myrtle. When we finally meet Gatsby unexpectedly, like Nick, we are easily taken in by his public mask—the elegant "mine host," suave, urbane, debonair. Gatsby is at the zenith of his social career, and for the moment we are willing to accept him and his glittering party on his own terms. By contrast with the seedy goings-on we have just witnessed in Tom's and Myrtle's apartment, Gatsby's party fairly shimmers with color and beauty. So impressed are we by all this glamour that we overlook the fact that most of his "interesting" guests are not much different from the drunken crew we just left at the end of Chapter II.

To obtain this effect was not easy. Fitzgerald spent many hours over Chapter III, revising and polishing. At first, he was still as unsure about Nick and Gatsby as he had been at the end of Chapter I. Nick was still the wisecracking exhibitionist, and Nick's initial impression of his host in this first draft was originally blurred and overwritten:[33]

> He was undoubtedly one of the handsomest men I had ever seen [Nick says]—the dark blue eyes opening out into lashes of shiny jet were arresting and unforgettable. A sort of hesitant candor opened them wide when he listened but when he spoke the hesitancy was transferred to his voice and I got a distinct impression that he was picking his words with care.
>
> He was older than me—somehow I had expected a florid and corpulent person in his middle years—yet he was somehow not like a young man at all. There was a tremendous dignity about him, a reti-

cence which you could fear or respect according to your temperament but on the other hand a formality that just barely missed being absurd, that always trembled on the verge of absurdity until you found yourself wondering why you didn't laugh.

In the final version of *Gatsby*, this passage has been sharpened and improved:[34]

> He smiled understandingly—much more than understandingly. It was one of those rare smiles with a quality of eternal reassurance in it, that you may come across four or five times in life. It faced—or seemed to face—the whole external world for an instant, and then concentrated on *you* with an irresistible prejudice in your favor. It understood you just as far as you wanted to be understood, believed in you as you would like to believe in yourself, and assured you that it had precisely the impression of you that, at your best, you hoped to convey. Precisely at that point it vanished—and I was looking at an elegant roughneck, a year or two over thirty, whose elaborate formality of speech just missed being absurd. Some time before he introduced himself I'd got a strong impression that he was picking his words with care.

Besides introducing us to Gatsby, Chapter III also has the function of developing Nick's friendship with Jordan Baker, whom he had met briefly in Chapter I. Jordan plays an essential role in the plot, since it is through her that Nick learns about Gatsby's earlier friendship with Daisy Buchanan. In what was apparently his first plan for this chapter, Fitzgerald intended to have Nick fall in love with Jordan. She was to have thrown him over at the end of the novel as a kind of parallel to Daisy's treatment of Gatsby. But later Fitzgerald changed his mind, probably because a romance between Nick and Jordan would have detracted from the much more important relationship between Nick and Gatsby. Consequently, in his subsequent revisions of Chapter III and of the chapters that followed, Fitzgerald cut out several episodes in which Nick and Jordan became increasingly involved with each other. He also deleted several passages in which Nick excused to himself Jordan's dishonesty and her recklessness. The result of all of this was to reinforce Nick's feelings of skepticism toward Jordan—feelings which were in contrast to Gatsby's feelings toward Daisy, rather than paralleling them. At the end of the story, Daisy betrays Gatsby, but Nick has the vicarious satisfaction of snubbing Jordan. Here, Fitzgerald seems to imply, is the kind of girl Nick could have loved if she had not been corrupted by so much money and by irresponsible friends.

Where Chapter III introduced us to the public Gatsby, Chapter IV shows us the private one—a puzzling mixture of romantic idealism, vulgarity, and ruthlessness. Most of Fitzgerald's revisions here were minor, their object being to sharpen and clarify Nick's feelings about his mysterious neighbor. In the course of these revisions, Gatsby gradually emerged as a more innocent and sympathetic character than Fitzgerald had first conceived. Nick is less eager to write him off as merely "a fatuous idealist," as he impatiently calls him in one deleted passage.

Chapter V, the tea party in the rain that finally brings Gatsby and Daisy together, is the emotional as well as the structural center of the novel. It was the shortest and most dramatic of the nine chapters, and it was also Fitzgerald's favorite. The earliest version we have differs very little from the published text, suggesting that it was easy to write. Most of his revisions were subtle improvements in the rhythm and melody of his prose. At the last minute, he added three new passages to his galley proofs. All of them provided additional information about Gatsby's business affairs, and all were lifted from newspaper reports of the career of Edward M. Fuller: the account of Gatsby's friendship with Dan Cody, Gatsby's offer to set Nick up in a job selling fraudulent securities, and the mysterious telephone call from Detroit that hints Gatsby is mixed up in some shady enterprise.[35]

Chapters VI and VII gave Fitzgerald more trouble than any of the others. The former centers around Gatsby's second and last party; the latter takes Nick, Gatsby, Tom, Daisy, and Jordan on their ill-fated expedition to New York. Originally, both chapters formed one long, rambling chapter. Fitzgerald had been making excellent headway with his writing until he became dissatisfied with this section. In August, 1924, he had written Perkins that he had finished his manuscript; then, reading it over, he decided this chapter was much too long and involved and that he would have to break it up into two parts. In doing so, he wrote what were essentially two new chapters. "I've had to rewrite practically half of it," he write Perkins in September, "—at present it's stored away for a week so I can take a last look at it and see what I've left out. There's some intangible sequence lacking somewhere in the middle and a break in interest there invariably means the failure of the book." This "last look" involved at least several more weeks of revising, for, although Fitzgerald had promised to have the manuscript in the mail by the first of October, it did not go off until the end of the month. Even then, Fitzgerald was still dissatisfied with Chapter VII, and, in his subsequent proof revisions, he gave more attention to this chapter than to any other.[36]

His trouble was the old one of having to come to terms with a plot. The preceding five chapters of *The Great Gatsby* had been practically plotless. Each was an independent unit built around a single dramatic incident: Nick's visit to the Buchanans, his visit to Tom's and Myrtle's apartment, his visit to Gatsby's party, his trip to New York with Gatsby, and his tea party for Daisy and Gatsby. What linked them together was Nick's growing intimacy with Gatsby, and the drama of Gatsby's rediscovery of Daisy. But so far as the plot was concerned, these five chapters were merely the overture. Now that Daisy and Gatsby had been reunited in Chapter V, the consequences of their reunion had still to be developed. Fitzgerald had to awaken Tom's jealousy, to motivate Daisy's growing coolness to Gatsby, to provide the opportunity for her to throw him over, to contrive the automobile accident in which Daisy kills Myrtle, and thus to establish the circumstances leading to Gatsby's death.

Gatsby's second party at the beginning of Chapter VI, therefore, was intended from its original conception to serve two different functions. It not only parallels the earlier party in Chapter III but also subtly contrasts with it. The first party was presented entirely from Nick's point of view. Now Tom and Daisy are present, and things are different. Where Fitzgerald emphasized the gaiety and glamor of the first occasion, he now wanted to underscore the more corrupt and sinister aspects. This was not easily accomplished. He started out by turning the second party into a fancy-dress ball, where the vulgar tastes of the guests were reflected in the absurdity of their extravagant costumes. The whimsical comedy of the first party is replaced by a mood of reckless dissipation. In this first version, Tom, who has been drinking too much, slyly sneaks off into the bushes every few minutes with a different girl. Meanwhile Daisy tells Nick loudly that she has decided to run away with Gatsby and Tom, overhearing, gets into a noisy quarrel with his host.

All this violence, combined with the trip to New York that followed, made a long, confusing chapter. In reworking it, Fitzgerald made Chapter VI more compact, centering around the party. Now, instead of trying to contrast the second party with the first by exaggerating the former's absurdities, he made his point more subtly and effectively merely by showing us the identical party we attended in Chapter III, only from a different angle—Daisy's. Where the first affair was presented exclusively from the impressionable Nick's point of view, at this second party Nick hovers constantly around his cousin and is more interested in observing *her* reaction. What will she think of Gatsby's "interesting" friends and his awful taste? Will her love survive them? Daisy, after all, knows a good party when she sees one. Though she tries to have a good time, she is not amused. At the end of Chapter VI Nick senses that some kind of qualitative change in her attitude toward Gatsby has already occurred.

Thus, during his revision, the costume-ball material was deleted and such distracting incidents as Daisy's plan to run off with Gatsby, Tom's goatish behavior, and his quarrel with Gatsby, were either deleted or postponed to a later chapter. Then, since this new version was not long enough to make a chapter of respectable size, Fitzgerald added several new incidents that improved the story in various ways.

The first of these was the episode at the start of Chapter VI where a newspaper reporter knocks at Gatsby's front door. Initially, this incident came after the party where VII now begins. But Fitzgerald moved it up to the beginning of VI so that it could add further luster to Gatsby's still glamorous and mysterious reputation. To parallel this incident, he subsequently planted another at the beginning of Chapter VII. This time, however, it is Nick who knocks on Gatsby's door, to be greeted not by the butler, as before, but by a sinister-looking gangster—presumably one of Gatsby's henchmen. By framing Chapter VI with these two slightly different episodes, Fitzgerald intimated the qualitative change that was overtaking Gatsby's fortunes—not only in his relations with Daisy but in his business affairs as well.

The other major incident in Chapter VI is the scene in which Tom Buchanan and some of his horsy friends call on Gatsby and snub him. One of the guests invites Gatsby to go riding with them, but, while Gatsby is changing his clothes, Tom persuades the others to sneak away without waiting. Fitzgerald's first plan was to end this episode with a long speech in which Gatsby tells Nick how rude Tom and his friends have been. Eventually, however, he improved the scene merely by deleting Gatsby's speech. Instead, the passage ends with the poignant image of Gatsby standing in his doorway, unaware of what has been done to him, politely waiting for the guests who have already ridden away.

All these revisions emphasized the major role that rhythm, pattern, and repetition played in the composition of *Gatsby:* the parallel parties in Chapters III and VI, the parallel openings of Chapters VI and VII, and especially the portrait of Gatsby the gracious host standing expectantly by his great front door. This image of Gatsby waving a silent farewell—to his drunken guests, to the neighbors who have deceived him, and finally to Nick as they part for the last time—is among the most powerful in the book.

Chapter VII, which culminates in the memorable scene in the Hotel Plaza, is the climax of the novel. Just as Gatsby's meeting with Daisy in the rain in Chapter V was the crisis which set the plot in motion, here, in the hotel suite, the story reaches its highest peak of emotional intensity. Once Fitzgerald had decided to separate this episode from Gatsby's party, he was able to construct Chapter VII around the quarrel between Gatsby and Tom that ends with Daisy's return to Tom and the collapse of Gatsby's dream. His greatest problem in this chapter was finding an effective setting for the quarrel. First, he took his party of five to the Polo Grounds to watch a baseball game between the New York Giants and Chicago Cubs (inspired, no doubt, by Edward Fuller's friendship with the Giants' owner, Charles Stoneham). After the game they moved on to a tavern in Central Park, where Tom and Daisy and Gatsby argued back and forth interminably.

Once he had hit on the idea of a suite at the Hotel Plaza, however, he was able to give this chapter the necessary unity and tension. The Plaza had always represented Fitzgerald's idea of sophisticated elegance. The wedding reception that takes place downstairs was a stroke of genius; the sounds of merrymaking drifting up from the ballroom comment ironically on the fashionable Buchanan marriage that is breaking up before our eyes. With superb art, Fitzgerald condensed and pruned the tedious bickering between Tom and Daisy in his earlier draft, counterpointing it against both the clamor of the wedding party below and Nick's and Jordan's desultory small talk.

Then, just as the tension between Tom and Daisy reaches its peak, Tom Buchanan cleverly shifts the ground of his attack; turning from Daisy to Gatsby, he calmly proceeds to strip away the latter's mask of contrived gentility. Here, for a few moments, Fitzgerald's conception of his hero seems to have faltered and blurred, as Gatsby is abruptly transformed from a naïve idealist into Edward Fuller, the hard-eyed crook and intimate associate of Arnold Rothstein. Then, before we have had time enough to adjust to this more realistic version of Gatsby, he changes back again into his old, pathetic self. Tom's appeal to Daisy to come back to him is based as much on his physical virility as it is on his charges against Gatsby. Before the power of this entreaty, the Platonic Gatsby is defenseless; at this point he begins to evaporate before our eyes.

Once Fitzgerald had the Hotel Plaza scene firmly in mind, he was able to go back and smooth up the other incidents that lead up to it. One point bothering him was the appropriate moment at which Daisy should announce her intention of running off with Gatsby. He originally had her do this at Gatsby's party in Chapter VI, but this introduced a complication he was not yet ready to develop. Next he moved the incident to her luncheon at the beginning of Chapter VII, but here again he was unable to follow it up satisfactorily, and it weakened the rest of that scene. So, finally, he delayed the announcement until they were all comfortably settled at the Plaza. Here it naturally triggers the argument that is to be the main incident of this episode. Much of Fitzgerald's structural revision of *The Great Gatsby* involved this kind of rearrangement of essential incidents in the plot, moving them from isolated positions and grouping them with others with which they had more dramatic relationship.

In a similar manner, Fitzgerald revised the passage in which Tom and Nick stop at Wilson's garage for gas on the way to New York. It is important for the plot that Wilson should see Tom driving Gatsby's yellow car, and also that he should begin to suspect his wife's infidelity. In the earliest version of this scene Wilson expostulated with Tom about these suspicions at great length. But the final version, in which Wilson's doubts are merely implied, is much more effective. Throughout this chapter, everything that preceded the hotel scene was soft-pedaled so that it would not detract from this climactic episode.

Thus Daisy's luncheon party, as Fitzgerald rewrote it, became a kind of lull before the storm. Originally, it was keyed with passion and jealousy. Gatsby nervously talked too much and behaved erratically, but all this was deleted. During the luncheon the only thing that prepares us for the coming tension is the atmosphere of oppressive heat; and this contrasts with the cool rain of Chapter V and the crisp autumn weather that will prevail next day—the day of Gatsby's murder.

There are many other fine touches that show the thought and care Fitzgerald put into his repeated revisions of Chapter VII. In the earlier draft, it was Tom Buchanan who invited Nick to Daisy's luncheon party. But, by having Gatsby relay Daisy's invitation to Nick, Fitzgerald delicately implies the growing intimacy that has developed between them. Another wonderful moment occurs in the hotel scene when Nick suddenly realizes that it is his thirtieth birthday. At first, this thought came to him in the middle of Daisy's quarrel with Tom, where it was obscured by the general confusion. Later, Fitzgerald moved it to its present position, where it falls with a deafening crash into the silence that follows the quarrel, and so ends that episode. The moment deserves the emphasis he has given it. Nick is saved from Gatsby's fate—in the very nick of time, as it were—by his own sense of time. Because Nick lives in the temporal as well as the ideal world, and knows how old he is, he is able to grow up. But Gatsby lives outside time, in that dream world where past, present, and future are all one. He has no sense of the past and so is never able to come to terms with it.

In spite of all the attention he had given to it, Fitzgerald was never completely satisfied with this part of the book. "The Chapter VII (the hotel scene) will never be quite up to the mark," he wrote Perkins in December, 1924, just before he began correcting and revising his galley proofs. "—I've worried about it too long and I can't quite place Daisy's reaction. But I can improve it a lot. It isn't imaginative energy that's lacking—it's because I'm automatically prevented from thinking it out over again *because I must get all these characters to New York* in order to have the catastrophe on the road going back and I must have it pretty much that way. So there's no chance of bringing the freshness to it that a new free conception sometimes gives." When the proofs arrived, he spent three weeks reworking the hotel scene until he felt that it was "really almost perfect of its kind." But as soon as his final revisions were in the mail he began to fret about the mistakes he had failed to correct. "I wrote it over at least five times," he said in the letter he sent Perkins on April 10, 1925, the day *The Great Gatsby* was published, "and I still feel that what should be the strong scene (in the hotel) is hurried and ineffective."[37]

The main problem that he faced in Chapter VIII was that of disclosing the details of Gatsby's past to the reader. His first plan was to have Gatsby tell Nick about his boyhood and youth in a long monologue at the beginning of the chapter. But at this point in his first draft Fitzgerald so identified himself with his hero that he had difficulty controlling his prose; the result was a long, soggy autobiographical confession as bad as the poorer parts of "The Romantic Egotist." Next he adopted the more objective approach of having Nick summarize the information. But even then Fitzgerald could not avoid long stretches of inflated writing.

When Max Perkins suggested that he break up this material and distribute it throughout the text, Fitzgerald at first resisted the idea. "Zelda also thought it was a little out of key," he admitted, "but it is good writing and I don't think I could bear to sacrifice any of it." Eventually, however, he changed his mind, moving a great deal of Gatsby's history to Chapters IV and VI, where Jordan Baker and Nick, respectively, disclose it.[38]

The extent to which Fitzgerald had identified himself with Gatsby in the earliest version of Chapter VIII can be seen in the following pas-

sage taken from Gatsby's original long monologue. After telling Nick
how he used to compose song lyrics when he was fourteen years old,
Gatsby jumps up and sings seven lines from a sentimental ballad that
Fitzgerald had probably written himself at that age. Then he says:[39]

> "That's what I've got to do—live the past all over again. And I
> don't want to start by running away. Why, I could be a great man if
> I could just forget that once I lost out on something I wanted . . . I
> want to turn the whole world upside down and give people some-
> thing to think about. I don't care how much people talk about me,
> hate me. Just so I could make them admire me, make everybody
> admire me—like my company did in the war. They knew I was a
> good man. They gave me a watch! . . . Jay Gatsby! . . . There goes
> Jay Gatsby. That's what people are going to say—wait and see."

Eventually, the scene in which this passage occurs was transformed
into the much less sentimental conversation between Nick and Gatsby at
the end of Chapter VI.

In the process of redistributing Gatsby's monologue Fitzgerald did
not succeed in getting all the threads tied back together again. Thus, in
a passage immediately following the one just quoted, he originally
wrote:

> [Gatsby] jumped up and began walking back and forth franti-
> cally, as if the past that he had wanted to repeat were lurking here
> under the very shadow of his house, just out of reach of his hand. His
> impassioned sentimentality possessed him so thoroughly that he
> seemed in some fantastic consummation with space and time—and
> they must have given him an answer then and there in the moonlight,
> for he sat down suddenly and put his face in his hands and began
> to sob.
>   "Why I'm only thirty two. I might be a great man if I could forget
> that once I lost Daisy. But my career has got to be like this—." He
> drew a slanting line from the lawn to the stars. "It's got to keep going
> up. I used to think wonderful things were going to happen to me, be-
> fore I met her. And I know it was a great mistake for a man like me
> to fall in love—and then one night I let myself go, and it was too
> late— . . .
>   "I felt as if there'd been a trick played on me. I went and told her
> part of the truth, sort of hoping that she'd throw me over—but it
> didn't make any difference because she was in love with me, too. She

150   F. Scott Fitzgerald

seemed to think I knew a lot about life, and it was just because I knew different things from her. Then we took that walk together one night and suddenly I decided that she was what my dreams had been about all along. That made it all right. I thought out my life over again with Daisy in it, trying to figure how we could marry and struggle along on so many dollars a month. I didn't want to be great any more because I wouldn't admit to myself that there could be anything better than having her."

In the final version of the novel this passage was taken away from Gatsby and given to Nick. In the process it was condensed and sharpened, part was moved to the beginning of Chapter VI and part to the end of Chapter VII. But even then Fitzgerald was unable to remove entirely the autobiographical details. For, in rewriting it, he inserted the following passage:[40]

Out of the corner of his eye Gatsby saw that the blocks of the sidewalk really formed a ladder and mounted to a secret place above the trees—he could climb to it, if he climbed alone, and once there he could suck on the pap of life, gulp down the incomparable wonder.

Here the words "if he climbed alone" make sense only if they are put back into the context of the original passage. There is nothing explicit in the final version of the novel to indicate that Gatsby felt shackled by his first affair with Daisy or that he wanted to escape from her. Fitzgerald momentarily confused Gatsby's feeling toward Daisy with his own growing concern over Zelda—specifically her increasingly irrational resentment of the amount of time he was spending on his writing.[41]

Once these problems of handling Gatsby's previous history had been worked out, Fitzgerald had only to add the series of incidents leading up to Gatsby's murder, in order to complete Chapter VIII. In sharp contrast with the violence generated in the Hotel Plaza scene at the end of the preceding chapter, Gatsby's even more violent death is treated with masterly understatement. This is because Gatsby has already become for us a disembodied ghost. He has been gradually fading away ever since we began to question the permanence of his dream. One of Fitzgerald's most inspired last-minute additions to this chapter is the passage in which Gatsby tells Nick that Daisy never really loved Tom—or, if she did, "in any case it was just personal." In the long process of making himself into a public figure, a man of distinction, Gatsby has lost contact with flesh-and-blood reality and is no longer capable of experiencing a personal relationship.[42]

Here perhaps is the reason why Fitzgerald did not allow Gatsby that final moment of self-knowledge vouchsafed all heroes of genuinely tragic stature. Gatsby's sensibility is not sufficiently developed for him to realize the full implications of his situation. Instead, as Nick leaves him hopefully and hopelessly waiting for the phone call from Daisy that will never come, it is Nick who senses the terror and the grandeur implicit in what would otherwise have been only a pathetic anecdote about a bootlegger.[43]

> I have an idea that Gatsby himself didn't believe it would come, and perhaps he no longer cared. If that was true he must have felt that he had lost the old warm world, paid a high price for living too long with a single dream. He must have looked up at an unfamiliar sky through frightening leaves and shivered. . . . A new world, material without being real, where poor ghosts, breathing dreams like air, drifted fortuitously about . . . like that ashen, fantastic figure gliding toward him through the amorphous trees.

Chapter IX, the long last chapter, like Chapter I, is entirely Nick Carraway's. Its function is to disclose to Nick the full meaning of his neighbor's career. At first, it was not easy for Fitzgerald to adopt the right tone in making his final judgment. In stressing the moral of his story, he made Nick sound rather like a Sunday-school prig. "I don't like casualness," Nick observes righteously in one later-deleted passage. "I don't like waters that close over your head without a bubble or a ripple when you go. The feeling that they shouldn't became a sort of obsession —then finally a horror to me." In the end, Fitzgerald crossed out most of Nick's gratuitous comments about the other characters. Instead of lecturing Jordan, as he did at first, Nick merely reminds her, just before he hangs up the phone, that, after all, he is thirty years old now. Instead of snubbing Tom, as he did in one early draft, Nick shakes his hand, feeling "as though I were talking to a child."[44]

This last chapter ends with a burst of images that conveys Nick's feelings far better than any rational statement. The story's conclusion, as we have seen, had originally been anticipated at the end of Chapter I by Nick's death wish. In Chapter IX, his desire for physical annihilation is expressed by the nightmare image of "a night scene by El Greco" in which four men in evening clothes carry the glittering body of a drunken woman into a house "—the wrong house. But no one knows the woman's name and no one cares." Sharply contrasted with this is the image of Nick's homecoming from school as a boy.[45]

> One of my most vivid memories is of coming back West from prep school and later from college at Christmas time. Those who went farther than Chicago would gather at the dim old Union Station at six o'clock of a December evening, with a few Chicago friends, already caught up in their own holiday gaieties, to bid them a hasty good-by. I remember the fur coats of the girls returning from Miss This-or-That's and the chatter of frozen breath and the hands waving overhead as we caught sight of old acquaintances, and the matchings of invitations . . . and the long green tickets clasped tight in our gloved hands. And last the murky yellow cars of the Chicago, Milwaukee & St. Paul railroad looking cheerful as Christmas itself on the tracks beside the gate.
>
> When we pulled out into the winter night and the real snow, our snow, began to stretch out beside us and twinkle against the windows, and the dim lights of small Wisconsin stations moved by, a sharp wild brace came suddenly into the air. We drew in deep breaths of it as we walked back from dinner through the cold vestibules, unutterably aware of our identity with this country for one strange hour, before we melted indistinguishably into it again.
>
> That's my Middle West—not the wheat or the prairies or the lost Swede towns, but the thrilling returning trains of my youth, and the street lamps and sleigh bells in the frosty dark and the shadows of holly wreaths thrown by lighted windows on the snow. I am part of that, a little solemn with the feel of those long winters, a little complacent from growing up in the Carraway house in a city where dwellings are still called through decades by a family's name.

Although this passage was woven out of the memory of many homeward trips from school and college, the chief source was one particular trip: the first Christmas vacation that Fitzgerald had come home from Newman School in 1911, when he was fifteen. It had been an especially unhappy trip, contrasting as it did the high hopes of the previous September when he had eagerly set forth, with his present status as one of the most unpopular boys in the school. When he had first described that homecoming some years earlier in "The Romantic Egotist," his memory of it was still mixed with feelings of guilt and shame:[46]

Christmas came at last and as the train drew out of Chicago and struck the cool, crisp air of Wisconsin, my heart rose in the joy of homecoming. Three weeks of comfort and friendliness and even sentiment were before me, I thought. No one at home knew about my life at Markle. I had written nothing of the state of things to the family, it would have horrified me that they should know. My vanity would not have allowed it. When next morning the familiar buildings and the exhilarating cold of Minneapolis flooded into my consciousness from the chilly observation platform of the train where I lingered hungrily, I felt Markle drop its cloudy weight from my mind like a bad dream.

These two passages measure the distance Fitzgerald had traveled as a craftsman during the seven years from 1917 to 1924. They also emphasize the extent to which his art was nourished by his feelings. The sparkling imagery in the memorable *Gatsby* passage was possible because it mirrored an emotion over which Fitzgerald had brooded for thirteen years.

Many other striking images also had their source in Fitzgerald's remorse over wasted opportunities. For several years now his sleep had been troubled by nightmares that woke him in the small hours of the morning. Some years later he would describe these dreams in an essay, "Sleeping and Waking." The mood of depression they generated, as he described it in the following passage from that essay, resembled so closely Nick Carraway's feelings both at the end of Chapter I (in the first draft) as well as at the end of the novel, that they surely had their origin in a common source:[47]

I see the real horror develop over the roof-tops and in the strident horns of the night-owl taxis and the shrill monody of reveler's arrival over the way. Horror and waste—

—Waste and horror. . . .

The horror has come now like a storm—what if this prefigured the night after death—what if all thereafter was an eternal quivering on the edge of an abyss, with everything base and vicious in oneself urging one forward and the baseness and viciousness of the world just ahead. No choice, no road, no hope—only the endless repetition of the sordid and the semi-tragic. Or to stand forever, perhaps, on the threshold of life unable to pass it and return to it. I am a ghost now as the clock strikes four.

Out of a welter of moods, memories, doubts, questionings, regrets, reveries—about himself, God, good and evil, man's nature and his destiny—Fitzgerald wove the texture of the most ambitious novel he had so far attempted. Writing it was an act of self-discovery, but attained only by the most arduous revision. His language, especially, required extensive refurbishing. Chunky Latinate words were replaced by the more colloquial Anglo-Saxon forms: "recognized" became "knew," "emerged" became "moved out," "altercations" became "fights." No subtleties of rhythm or tone were too insignificant to be overlooked. If George Wilson's hair was more appropriately described by the adjective "pale" than by its former "yellow," for similar reasons of harmony and congruence it was necessary to change the "gray" dress of a chorus girl at Gatsby's party in Chapter III to the gayer hue of "gas blue."

The final proof corrections, he had already warned Max Perkins, were to be "one of the most expensive affairs since 'Madame Bovary.'" On the whole, he wrote after he had finished, he felt the six weeks he had devoted to them had been "very successful labor."

(1) I've brought Gatsby to life.
(2) I've accounted for his money.
(3) I've fixed up the two weak chapters (VI and VII)
(4) I've improved his first party.
(5) I've broken up his long narrative in Chapter VIII.

Yet, as the April 10, 1925 publication date approached, he continued to wonder uneasily if perhaps it hadn't been written too hastily, after all. If he had just been able to take more time. Not only was the Hotel Plaza scene still "hurried and ineffective," he wrote Perkins the day the book appeared, but "also the last chapter, the burial, Gatsby's father, etc., is faulty. It's too bad because the first five chapters and parts of the 7th and 8th are the best things I've ever done."[48]

IX
The
Short Stories:
1925-1934

The seven thousand dollars in savings that the Fitzgeralds brought with them to France in the spring of 1924 evaporated sooner than they had expected. "I'm about broke and as soon as the novel gets off I will write a story immediately either for the *Post* or for Wheeler [of *Hearst's International*]," Fitzgerald wrote Harold Ober in September, when he was putting the finishing touches to his manuscript of *The Great Gatsby*. ". . . . That story will be followed within a month by two more. I think I've had hard luck with the movies. I must try some love stories with more action this time. I'm going to write three that'll do for Famous-Players as well as for the *Post*."[1]

It is disconcerting—"heartbreaking" was Fitzgerald's word—to turn from the careful prose of *Gatsby* to the crude banalities of the three stories that he ground out while he was waiting for the galley proofs of his novel. "Love stories with more action" describes them perfectly. None of them—"Love in the Night," "The Adjuster," "Not in the Guidebook"—was bought by the movie industry as their author had hoped. But Ober had no difficulty disposing of them to the magazines. By now Fitzgerald's price had gone up from $1,750 to $2,000. All three, however, were contrived and labored. "Good stories write themselves; bad ones have to be written so this took up about three weeks, and look at it," Fitzgerald said in the apologetic note to Ober that accompanied "Not in the Guidebook." "I'd rather not offer it to the *Post* because everybody sees the *Post* but I know it's saleable and I need the money. I leave it to you."[2]

For some reason the manuscript of "Not in the Guidebook" did not get to Ober, but was returned to the hotel in Rome where the Fitzgeralds were staying. Instead of readdressing it, Fitzgerald made the mistake of rereading his story and was so embarrassed that he took precious time away from correcting the proofs of *The Great Gatsby* to rewrite it one more time.

Once the revised proofs of his novel were on their way back to Max Perkins, however, Fitzgerald devoted the spring and summer of 1925 to writing a different kind of short story from his three previous pot-boilers. This was "The Rich Boy"—one of the best-known of all his shorter pieces. He began it at Capri (where they had gone from Rome in February) and worked at it on and off for the next six months. It was written while he was still exhilarated by a sense of having accomplished something really first-rate in *Gatsby,* and before he had yet realized that his novel was destined to be a popular and financial failure. "The Rich Boy" was the best story he had written since "May Day," and the best he would write until "Babylon Revisited" in 1930, five years later.

Anson Hunter, the hero, was based on Ludlow Fowler, Fitzgerald's Princeton classmate who had already provided certain details for the portrait of Maury Noble in *The Beautiful and Damned.* "I have written a fifteen thousand word story about you called *The Rich Boy,*" Fitzgerald wrote him after it was finished, "—it is so disguised that no one except you and maybe two of the girls concerned would recognize [it], unless you give it away, but it is in a large measure the story of your life, toned down here and there and symplified. Also many gaps had to come out of my imagination. It is frank, unsparing but sympathetic and I think you will like it—it is one of the best things I have ever done."[3]

Here, as in *The Great Gatsby,* Fitzgerald was again writing about the relation of money to American society. But whereas his novel was primarily about wealthy Westerners, in "The Rich Boy" he was attempting to come to terms with the somewhat different nature of Eastern moneyed society. Anson Hunter's family was probably not as rich as Tom Buchanan's, but the Hunters had been used to money for several generations; the Buchanans were of the new plutocracy. Fitzgerald's aim in "The Rich Boy" was to analyze Anson and his circle with the same "unsparing but sympathetic" objectivity that he had brought to bear on the *nouveaux riches* of Great Neck in *The Great Gatsby.* The tone of his inquiry was established at the beginning of the story:[4]

Let me tell you about the very rich. They are different from you and me. They possess and enjoy early, and it does something to them, makes them soft where we are hard, and cynical where we are trust-ful, in a way that, unless you were born rich, it is very difficult to un-derstand. They think, deep in their hearts, that they are better than we are because we had to discover the compensations and refuges of life for ourselves.

But the mask of cool objectivity that Fitzgerald assumed here was one he was unable to hold in place for very long. He had difficulty sym-pathizing imaginatively with someone as different from himself as Anson Hunter; he could not temper his judgment of Anson with the compas-sion he had felt for Gatsby. In *The Great Gatsby*, Fitzgerald had per-sonal affinities with Nick Carraway and Gatsby. Because of this Nick also shared with Gatsby a secret bond. But no such tie exists between Fitzgerald and Anson Hunter, nor between Anson and the anonymous narrator of his story. The latter of course is Fitzgerald. His childhood also has been spent "in a series of small and medium-sized houses" where he "was never far out of the reach of [his] mother's voice, of the sense of her presence, her approval or disapproval." But envious as he was of the Hunter wealth and social background, Fitzgerald could not bring to Anson's story the double vision he brought to *The Great Gatsby*.[5]

Thus, in spite of the tone of clinical detachment with which "The Rich Boy" begins, Fitzgerald gives the whole show away on the second page when he says of Anson that, although he had the ordinary human aspirations, "there was no mist over them, none of that quality which is variously known as 'idealism' or 'illusion.'" So, where "most of our lives end as a compromise—it was as a compromise that his life began." The dice are loaded against Anson from the start. Indeed, the only really attractive character in "The Rich Boy" is Paula Legendre, the girl Anson could have married if his stuffy sense of superiority had not gotten in the way. Paula, as we might expect, comes from the West—from "somewhere in California." Unlike Anson Hunter, she has the Gatsby-like attributes of "sincerity" and "emotional simplicity"; and Anson loves her because "he felt that if he could enter into Paula's warm safe life he would be happy." But because he is unable to commit himself wholly to another human being, Paula finally marries someone else. Afterwards, as Anson's life grows more sterile, he characteristically refuses to put the blame where it belongs, on himself. "I could settle down if women were differ-ent," he tells Paula, "if I didn't understand so much about them, if women didn't spoil you for other women, if they had only a little pride."[6]

The implication of "The Rich Boy" is that Anson's failure as a human being is due to his having been brought up with too much money. But Anson's trouble is really a lack of imagination—a quality that Fitzgerald, with his faith in the virtue of hard work, begrudged the rich and privileged. He wrote about them with an authority and a veracity of detail based on intimate knowledge and observation. But, despite his lifelong association with the rich, Fitzgerald never succeeded in portraying them sympathetically. None of his wealthy characters, from his early debutantes through Tom and Daisy Buchanan, Jordan Baker, and Anson Hunter, to the fabulous Warren family in *Tender Is the Night,* is presented with the understanding he reserves for such heroes as Jay Gatsby, Dick Diver, Monroe Stahr—all poor boys struggling to make good. When Fitzgerald writes about the rich, it is always as an outsider. He either endows them from a distance with a romantic glamor or, moving closer, judges them by the standards of a disillusioned member of the middle class.

In 1922, when Maxwell Perkins learned from John Biggs (Fitzgerald's Princeton roommate) that Biggs's talented friend, John P. Marquand, was going to marry into one of Boston's most exclusive Brahmin families, he wrote to Fitzgerald:[7]

> What an environment for a novelist! I said I thought it would be a fine experience for you to have to do it for a time, because there is in your books, so far, no recognition of the existence of the 'highly respectables,'—and yet, however uninteresting they may be, they are an essential element in society, both upper and lower case.

But Fitzgerald was too much of a frontier idealist to view the respectable members of upper-crust American society with the understanding he instinctively felt for the aspiring bourgeoisie. People with money, he believed, had a moral obligation to behave better than those without it. In his copy of H.L. Mencken's *Prejudices: Second Series,* he marked approvingly such passages as:[8]

> I need not set out at any length, I hope, the intellectual deficiencies of the plutocracy—its utter failure to show anything even remotely resembling the makings of an aristocracy. It is badly educated, it is stupid. . . . Out of this class comes *the grotesque, fashionable society of our big towns.* . . . It shows all the stigmata of inferiority—*moral certainty, cruelty, suspicion of ideas, fear* [here in the margin Fitzgerald had written in the names of several wealthy St. Paul families].

If Fitzgerald failed to come to terms with the American rich, he at least saw the more typical middle-class American as a complex and tragic human being; and this, in the long run, may turn out to have been his most lasting literary achievement.

As the year 1925 advanced, it became increasingly clear that *The Great Gatsby* was not destined to enjoy the popular success of Fitzgerald's two previous novels. In January, Fitzgerald had optimistically predicted to Perkins that the book would sell at least eighty thousand copies—almost twice that of his other books. He had even volunteered to cut his regular twenty percent royalty back to fifteen as a reward to Scribner's for its continued faith in him! When *College Humor* offered $10,000 for the pre-publication serial rights to *Gatsby*, he turned it down in the hope that they would bring at least $35,000. But both *Cosmopolitan* and *Liberty*, to his surprise, rejected the chance to serialize it. "Too ripe for us," the fiction editor of *Liberty* explained after reading the manuscript. ". . . We could not publish this story with as many mistresses and as much adultery as there is in it."[9]

On the heels of this disappointment came word that a number of booksellers had canceled their advance orders for the novel after discovering that it was to be only 218 pages long. The American reading public, one of them explained to Perkins, expected a great deal more reading matter than that in a two-dollar novel. After all, *The Saturday Evening Post* contained two hundred pages every week, and only cost a nickel! Next, William Collins Sons, the London publishing house that had brought out overseas editions of both of Fitzgerald's previous novels, announced after reading the manuscript that it did not want to publish a British edition of *Gatsby*. "The British public would not make head or tail of it, and . . . it would not sell . . . ," Collin's representative explained to Scribner's London agent. "The point is that the atmosphere of the book is extraordinarily foreign to the English reader, and he simply would not believe in it." More than a year elapsed before Chatto and Windus finally undertook an English edition.[10]

Altogether, the first year's sale of *The Great Gatsby* amounted to around 20,000 copies, barely enough to repay Scribner's for its advances to the author. The obvious conclusion was that Fitzgerald could no longer count on his novels to pay the greater part of his expenses, as he had for the past five years. He was still reluctant to accept the full implications of this fact, however. During the spring of 1925, he had begun to plan a fourth novel—a story about American expatriates in Europe to be called "The World's Fair"—which he hoped would not only be as good artistically as *Gatsby* but more of a commercial success. For the time being, he planned to continue as in the past, turning out just enough trashy magazine stories to finance the completion of this project.[11]

> Now I shall write some cheap ones until I've accumulated enough [money] for my next novel [he had written Perkins from Paris that spring]. When that is finished and published I'll wait and see. If it will support me with no more intervals of trash I'll go on as a novelist. If not I'm going to quit, come home, go to Hollywood and learn the movie business. I can't reduce our scale of living and I can't stand this financial insecurity. Anyhow there's no point in trying to be an artist if you can't do your best. I had my chance back in 1920 to start my life on a sensible scale and I lost it and so I'll have to pay the penalty. Then perhaps at 40 I can start writing again without this constant worry and interruption.

The novel, however, was not to be finished for nine more years. Instead of writing it, he loafed and traveled about France and then devoted the winter of 1925–1926 to writing five undistinguished magazine stories. As usual, he was embarrassed by their quality. "This is one of the lousiest stories I've ever written," he wrote Ober in the letter enclosing "Your Way and Mine." "Just *terrible!*" And to Max Perkins of his stories in general: "Trash doesn't come as easily as it used to and I've grown to hate the poor old debauched form itself."[12]

Then fate stepped in, abruptly, as it so often did in his life, and reversed his fortune, relieving him for the next several years of further financial worries. In February, 1926, William Brady's production of *The Great Gatsby,* dramatized by Owen Davis, opened successfully on Broadway and settled down to a comfortable run. From the sale of the dramatic rights, Fitzgerald received $6,000, as well as an additional $16,000 from the sale of the motion picture rights of the play to Warner Brothers. In February, also, Scribner's brought out his third volume of collected short stories, *All the Sad Young Men,* which brought in some $2,000 in royalties during 1926. And in June, Ober arranged a contract with *Liberty* whereby that magazine agreed to pay $35,000 for the prepublication serial rights to Fitzgerald's next novel, providing it met with *Liberty's* approval and the manuscript was delivered before January 1, 1927. The contract also gave *Liberty* first refusal on the next ten magazine stories that Fitzgerald might write during 1927, for which it agreed to pay not less than $3,500 apiece—almost twice Ftizgerald's current *Saturday Evening Post* price.[13]

For the rest of 1926, Fitzgerald had no obligations except to finish his novel. His letters from the south of France, where he and Zelda had gone for the summer, were most encouraging. "With the play going well & my new novel growing absorbing & with our being back in a nice villa on my beloved Rivierra," he wrote Perkins from Juan-les-Pins, "I'm happier than I've ever been for years. It is one of those strange, precious, and all too transitory moments when everything in one's life seems to be going well." They booked passage on a ship to New York leaving Genoa December tenth. It had been an unforgettable two years, but they were glad to be going home. "We have had a fine summer—and now all the gay decorative people have left taking with them the sense of carnival and impending disaster," Zelda wrote Perkins later that autumn. ". . . I think being here has been good for us in some obscure way I can't define—Anyway, it's helped our manners."[14]

"God, how much I've learned in these two and a half years in Europe," Fitzgerald wrote Perkins shortly before they sailed for home. "It seems like a decade & I feel pretty old but I wouldn't have missed it, even in its most unpleasant and painful aspects." But, in spite of his optimistic letters, Fitzgerald was still far from the end of his novel. Avoiding Perkins and Ober when they landed in New York, they hurried on to Montgomery for Christmas. There was no likelihood of his being able to fulfill his contract with *Liberty*, and, since their funds were running out, it looked as though he would have to go back once more to the magazines. Then, on December thirtieth, he received a wire from John Considine, Jr., of United Artists offering him $12,000 to come to Hollywood for ten weeks to write a script about college life for a silent motion picture starring Constance Talmadge.[15]

Without consulting Ober, Fitzgerald promptly accepted, and a few days later he and Zelda were en route by train for California. Actually, it was not an especially advantageous contract. United Artists was to pay him $3,500 in advance, but the remaining $8,500 would be forthcoming only if the studio decided to film his script. In Hollywood, everyone lionized the new arrivals, and in the midst of the parties and excursions, it was hard to settle down to serious work. The "fine modern college story," entitled "Lipstick," that Fitzgerald turned out for Considine was extremely bad—about on a par with his poorest magazine fiction. The plot featured a beautiful heiress who had been unjustly imprisoned in the New Jersey State Penitentiary. There she met a troupe of Princeton students on a sociology field trip and fell in love with the handsomest,

who was also the university's star varsity football player. After sur-
mounting many obstacles, the two lovers were finally reunited during
Princeton's Houseparties Weekend. Comic relief for this cliché-ridden
script was supplied by several shopworn characters—a fat boy, a
spinsterish college professor, and the latter's domineering mother. The
title, "Lipstick," derived from an enchanted lipstick whose magical
properties helped in the unraveling of the plot. After submitting this
script to Considine, Fitzgerald made things worse by quarreling with
Miss Talmadge. The upshot was that Considine shelved the whole project, and Fitzgerald ended up with less money for his ten weeks' work
than he would have received for a magazine story.[16]

However, he learned one thing. Writing for the movies was not the
easy work he had thought it to be. For two years he had been loafing
on the assumption that, if worst came to worst, he could always go out
to Hollywood and make money writing film scripts. Now he was obliged
to face up to the fact that, with his novel far from finished, the sole
source of steady income he could count on was the magazines. Providing,
that is, that he took his stories seriously and did not antagonize any more
magazine editors as he had done in the case of *Liberty*.

So, in the spring of 1927, on his return from California, Fitzgerald
settled down to a career as practically full-time writer of magazine
stories. Instead of scattering them around as he had in the past, he decided to aim them primarily at George Horace Lorimer and *The Saturday Evening Post*. Lorimer still admired his work, and Ober had been
able to talk Lorimer into meeting *Liberty's* price of $3,500 per story.
Since most of the *Post's* writers and illustrators lived within easy commuting distance of Lorimer's office in Philadelphia, Fitzgerald decided
to do likewise. John Biggs, his college roommate, was a prominent young
attorney in Wilmington, Delaware, and also a talented writer of fiction.
With Biggs's help, Fitzgerald rented a fine old estate, "Ellerslie," on the
west shore of the Delaware several miles up the river road from Wilmington.[17]

Beginning in June, 1927, Fitzgerald produced a *Post* story regularly
every six or seven weeks for the next six years—a grand total of 55 short
stories. By 1929, his price had climbed to $4,000, and during these years
his income from his magazine fiction averaged around $30,000 annually.
But it was not the best of times. Fresh ideas came more slowly now, and,
when they did, it was increasingly hard to convert them into smooth,
swift-moving magazine stories. Meanwhile, the novel lay neglected while
he fretted over his failure to find time for uninterrupted work.

"Ellerslie," with its handsome, high-ceilinged rooms and its shaded lawns sloping down to the river, made an ideal setting for parties. At first, various Princeton friends and *Post* authors like Joseph Herge-sheimer motored over. The Biggses introduced the Fitzgeralds to Wil-mington society. And Max Perkins, Dorothy Parker, Carl Van Vechten, Ludlow Fowler, Thornton Wilder (who was then a young English in-structor at the Lawrenceville School), and other friends came down on the Friday afternoon train from New York for lively weekends. But the parties had a way of ending up in quarrels, with the host angry at every-one. And Biggs soon got tired of having to bail Fitzgerald out of jail for foolish escapades. Eventually, his friends began to wonder if Fitzgerald would kill himself by his drinking. When Perkins visited "Ellerslie" in the fall of 1927, he was so shocked by Fitzgerald's state of health that he tried, unsuccessfully, to get him to take the cure for alcoholism at Mul-doon's, a well-known sanatorium. Several weeks later, after a visit to his Manhattan physician, Fitzgerald turned up at Scribner's and asked for a desk in a quiet corner where he might write. "He worked here for an hour," Perkins reported to Ring Lardner, "and then got one of his ner-vous fits, and could not work any more and wanted to go out and have a drink.—So we did it on condition that it would be one drink only, and that is all we had."[18]

Stopping after one drink was not always that easy. Moreover, Zelda's new obsession with the ballet did not help matters. There was little hope of her ever becoming a prima ballerina, but, soon after they moved to "Ellerslie," at the advanced age of twenty-seven, she started taking ballet lessons with Catharine Littlefield, the Philadelphia dancer and impresario. Before long her dancing became a fixation, a means by which she might rival her husband's fame as a successful writer. While Zelda sweated and pirouetted relentlessly before the huge mirror in the parlor of "Ellerslie," Fitzgerald wrote in the library, where he also kept his supply of gin slyly concealed behind the books lining the walls. Often when he could not write, he would take to the nearby dirt roads for long solitary walks. It was an isolated corner of the world; their only close neighbors were a few fishing families who knew little about the Fitz-geralds except the servants' gossip about the pretty young wife who danced madly for hours alone in the big house, and the liquor bottles hid-den in the library. Occasionally a fisherman would encounter Fitzgerald, white-faced and haggard, strolling alone in an empty lane, and feel sorry for him.[19]

For some months Zelda had been eager to return to France. She felt her dancing had progressed to the point where she was ready to take more advanced training in one of several Paris studios where exiled

Russian ballerinas trained replacements for Diaghilev's ballet corps. So, in the late spring of 1928, after Fitzgerald had recovered from a serious attack of the flu, they went abroad for the summer. They planned to rent an apartment in Paris, where Fitzgerald would work uninterruptedly on the novel while Zelda kept busy with her lessons. But when they returned the following autumn, all Fitzgerald had to show for his summer's work was six *Saturday Evening Post* stories.

By now he was so depressed by his inability to get on with his novel that he did not want to talk about it any more to Perkins. Indeed, Perkins heard little more from him until the following March, 1929, when he received an apologetic note announcing that the Fitzgeralds were aboard a transatlantic liner en route to Europe. The lease had expired on "Ellerslie," and it seemed a good time to make a break with the past. Fitzgerald was ashamed to be "sneaking away like a thief," without seeing Ober or Perkins, but this time, he promised, he would remain abroad until he had finished the novel.[20]

In spite of these promises, the manuscript of the novel gathered dust while Fitzgerald continued to turn out his regular supply of stories for Lorimer. His production rate slowed up only temporarily when Zelda collapsed in Paris the following April, 1930, and had to be placed in a mental institution. Afterwards, her prolonged convalescence only increased Fitzgerald's expenses, and he was obliged to make up for the interruptions of 1930 by writing even more *Post* stories than usual during 1931.

Actually, Zelda's behavior for the preceding several years had been so erratic that it seems odd that Fitzgerald should have been so shocked when she broke completely. He had made their precarious marriage the basis for several recent stories, and had only to scrutinize the portraits of Zelda he had drawn there to see that she had been in need of mental therapy for some time. The truth, however, is that it was difficult for him to examine his marriage with much objectivity, except as material for his fiction. That, as a matter of fact, was one of the reasons why Zelda was so unhappy and disturbed. For example, back in 1928, a few days after they had landed in France from a trans-Atlantic crossing, Fitzgerald was able to sit down and write a brilliant and moving story about some of the more hectic aspects of their trip, entitled "The Rough Crossing." It concerns the insane jealousy of an attractive young American woman for her famous and talented husband. His irresponsible but innocent shipboard flirtations drive her at one point almost to suicide. Her fits of hysteria are touching and convincing, but her husband's unwillingness to face up to the gravity of her illness is disturbing. At the

end of the story Fitzgerald, without realizing how implausible his conclusion is, has the husband fatuously tell his wife that "the real truth
is that none of it happened. . . . It was a nightmare—an incredibly awful
nightmare." Did he really think Zelda's fits were bad dreams that she
would outgrow if they refused to take them seriously?[21]

In August, 1930, four months after her collapse, he tried for the first
time to come to terms in his fiction with their marriage in the light of
this devastating development. "One Trip Abroad" is the story of Nicole
and Nelson Kelly, a carefree young American couple who have decided
to live in Europe in the belief they will find there a measure of self-
fulfillment impossible at home. They pursue their dream for five irresponsible years, until finally they realize the futility of their lives. The
moment of insight comes as their trail crosses that of another expatriate
American couple whom they have casually encountered on previous
occasions. This time, however, the Kellys realize that this jaded, dissipated pair are really their own doubles—ghostly premonitions of the
rootless kind of people they are destined to become if they do not change
their ways. "It's just that we don't understand what's the matter," poor
Nicole cries pathetically to Nelson at the end of this haunting tale.
"Why did we lose peace and love and health, one after the other? If we
knew, if there was anybody to tell us, I believe I could try. I'd try so
hard."[22]

A few months later, in December, 1930, Fitzgerald again returned to
the subject of himself and Zelda in what is probably the finest of all his
short stories, "Babylon Revisited." One reason it is so much better than
"The Rough Crossing" and "One Trip Abroad" is that this time he consciously avoided the problem of the wife's point of view. When the story
begins she is dead, and everything is shown from the husband's viewpoint. Also, instead of trying to narrate the entire history of their marriage, he built up his story dramatically around a single central incident
—the husband s effort to expiate his sense of guilt for his wife's death
by asserting his responsibility for their small daughter.

During the four months that intervened between the writing of "One
Trip Abroad" and "Babylon Revisited," Fitzgerald had himself spent
several weeks in a Swiss sanatorium in the hope of restoring his frayed
nerves. Meanwhile, certain members of the Sayre family had accused
him of having been the cause of Zelda's collapse, and had even raised
the question of his fitness to care for nine-year-old Scottie during her
mother's illness. Fitzgerald's remorse, and his resentment of these im-
putations, played a significant part in the shaping of "Babylon Re-

visited." The hero of the story is an American expatriate named Charles Wales who hopes to regain custody of his daughter, Honoria, by rehabilitating himself to the satisfaction of his dead wife's neurotic sister. Prior to his wife's death, the Wales had traveled with a rich, dissolute crowd of Americans living in Paris; afterwards the sister-in-law has insisted on keeping Honoria because she dislikes Charles and blames him for her sister's death.[23]

The story begins with Charles's return to Paris in the hope of retrieving his daughter. He has stopped drinking and has settled down in another part of Europe and established himself in a successful business career. Convinced that he has mended his ways, the sister-in-law reluctantly consents to Honoria's joining him. Then, at the most inopportune moment, two of Charles's disreputable former friends turn up and make a scene. Whereupon the sister-in-law hysterically refuses to let Honoria go back to him, and he faces a further period of penance, his guilty past still not fully absolved.

These events of 1930, beginning with Zelda's breakdown and ending with the writing of "Babylon Revisited," left Fitzgerald in a state of exhaustion, physical as well as emotional. The nine magazine stories that he ground out in 1931 to meet his exorbitant hospital and medical expenses were to be among the poorest he had yet written.

Back in Montgomery, Judge Sayre was suffering what was ultimately to prove a fatal illness. By September, 1931, Zelda was well enough to leave the Swiss sanatorium where she had been undergoing psychiatric treatment and return home. From the pier in New York the Fitzgeralds hurried directly to Alabama. Several weeks later, Harold Ober arranged a lucrative Hollywood contract for Fitzgerald, this time to work on the movie version of Katherine Brush's recent best-selling novel, *Red-Headed Woman*, for Metro-Goldwyn-Mayer. Leaving Zelda and Scottie in Montgomery with the stricken judge, he went to California at the beginning of November.[24]

During his four-year absence from the film colony, the advent of talking pictures had revolutionized the industry. Popular novelists, especially those reputed to be skillful writers of dialogue, were in great demand. But scriptwriting for the talkies was technically quite different from what it had been in the old silent-film days. Fitzgerald was teamed up with a studio hack who ruthlessly cut out what Fitzgerald thought were the best parts of his script. After six weeks of this kind of collaboration, he blew up and flew back to Alabama. He would later write his daughter about this episode:[25]

... [W]hile all was serene on top, with your mother apparently recovered in Montgomery, I was jittery underneath and beginning to drink more than I ought to. Far from approaching it too confidently I was far too humble. I ran afoul of a bastard named de Sano, since a suicide, and let myself be gypped out of command. I wrote the picture & he changed as I wrote. I tried to get at Thalberg [i.e., Irving Thalberg, head of M-G-M production] but was erroneously warned against it as "bad taste." Result—a bad script. I left with the money—for this was a contract for weekly payments[—]but disillusioned and disgusted, vowing never to go back, tho they said it wasn't my fault & asked me to stay. I wanted to get East when the contract expired to see how your mother was. This was later interpreted as "running out on them" & held against me.

When he came East in December he tried unsuccessfully to sell several magazine editors the idea of an article to be called "Hollywood Revisited," in which he would contrast the new Hollywood of the talkies with the old silent-film community he had visited four years earlier. When no one indicated interest in the proposal he wove his impressions of his recent visit into a short story, "Crazy Sunday," that revolved about his mixed feelings of admiration and dislike for Irving Thalberg, the young production genius in charge of the Metro-Goldwyn-Mayer studio. Thalberg symbolized for Fitzgerald all that was good and bad about the remarkable men and women—actors, directors, producers —who had transformed the screen from a cheap form of entertainment into what was, in Fitzgerald's opinion, the most powerful medium that had ever existed for the expression of dramatic art. Dedicated, neurotic, sensitive, hard-working, egotistical, these leaders of the industry drove themselves and everyone else at such a pace that when the weekend rolled around they did not know how to relax, and wasted their "crazy Sundays" quarreling and making love with the same intensity they put into their work the rest of the week.[26]

Since "Crazy Sunday" has a special relevance to *The Last Tycoon,* further discussion has been postponed to Chapter XV. The point to be made here is that this story was in every way the best short story Fitzgerald had written since "Babylon Revisited." But it was turned down by *The Saturday Evening Post, Cosmopolitan,* and *Redbook* on the grounds that its publication might anger the movie studios and jeopardize these magazines' lucrative movie-advertising accounts. Fitzgerald finally gave it to H.L. Mencken for *The American Mercury,* for a price of two hundred dollars.[27]

Meanwhile, during Fitzgerald's absence in California, Judge Sayre had died in Montgomery on November seventeenth, and in January Zelda, unnerved by this event, underwent a second breakdown and was taken to the mental clinic at Johns Hopkins hospital. By April, 1932, it was evident that her recovery, if she recovered at all, would be slow, and Fitzgerald and Scottie, who had remained behind in Montgomery, made plans to move to Baltimore. In May they rented a rambling old Victorian house, "La Paix," on the Bayard Turnbull estate in suburban Towson. Here Zelda was able to visit them, and eventually to make her home with them, until a third breakdown in 1935 necessitated her confinement for many years in a private mental institution.

One of Fitzgerald's last acts before leaving Montgomery in April had been the writing of a short story, "Family in the Wind," which, while it does not equal his finest stories, stands out sharply from the usual potboilers of this period. Into it he put his affection for Scottie and for the countryside around Montgomery, which he sensed that he was quitting for the last time. There, back in 1918, he had known some of the happiest moments of his life, but without Zelda it could never be the same.

"Family in the Wind" is the story of Dr. Forrest Janney, a skillful surgeon who has wrecked his career because of his heavy drinking, and who has come back to live in the Alabama farm community where he was raised. But his brother's family, who have remained dirt-farmers, resent his education and his having thrown away his advantages. Like Fitzgerald, Dr. Janney has learned that domestic fractures are beyond the cure of the cleverest physician. "He knew that the present family quarrel would never heal, nothing would ever be the same, it would all be bitter forever. . . . There was no peace here. Move on!" The story is spoiled by two rather melodramatic hurricanes and certain sentimentalities. But at the end Dr. Janney decides to adopt a small orphaned girl, and make himself into a responsible person once more. It is Fitzgerald's farewell to the South, as well as the expression of his determination to turn over a new leaf. It was also the last noteworthy story he would write for *The Saturday Evening Post*.[28]

He was to keep writing stories for several more years, however—as long as editors were willing to buy them. By now he realized that the quality of his magazine fiction had dropped badly ever since Zelda's breakdown two years before. But so far no one but Fitzgerald appeared to be troubled by this; certainly not the editors of the big magazines. At the beginning of 1932 *The Saturday Evening Post's* rival, *Cosmopolitan*, tried to lure him into an exclusive contract under which it agreed to pay him $5,000 a story—$1,000 more than his current *Post* price. But, worried about the decline in the quality of his commercial work, Fitzgerald decided it was safer to stick to his old standby, the *Post*. A year earlier, when Ober had tried to persuade Fitzgerald into letting him pressure Lorimer into raising his price, Fitzgerald had nervously refused. "Please don't try to push the Post up any more," he had written from Switzerland even though he had heavy expenses to meet. "I've gotten self-conscious and don't think my stuff is worth half what I get now."[29]

The truth was that most of his stories now had little intrinsic value at all, and were worth only what the market would bring. As things turned out, Fitzgerald would probably have been better off to have taken the *Cosmopolitan's* offer. When Lorimer relinquished the editorship of the *Post* several months later, in 1932, and was made head of all the Curtis Company's publishing ventures, his successor promptly began sending Fitzgerald's stories back with the advice that they either be scrapped or improved. Lorimer still liked them—after all, he had practically invented them himself! But for most of mid-Depression America, Fitzgerald's 1920 formula love stories were as old-fashioned as Lorimer's political opinions—one of the reasons why Lorimer had been kicked upstairs.

The Saturday Evening Post's criticism of his stories, however, merely increased Fitzgerald's already growing uncertainty about his ability to write good commercial fiction of any kind. When Ober relayed to him one editor's unfavorable comments, Fitzgerald replied angrily, "The only way I can write a decent story is to imagine no one's going to accept it and who cares. Self-consciousness about stories is *ruinous* to me." But he was only deluding himself. If he wasn't writing these potboilers solely for the magazine editors, who was he writing them for?[30]

By the summer of 1933, so many of his stories were being rejected by the *Post*, and he was so irritated by Harold Ober's well-meaning attempts to tell him how to go about making them more saleable, that he began to ignore Ober altogether in his dealings with the magazines. Instead of working through Ober, he would mail his revisions to the *Post's* fiction department, and then get on the phone and call every day, insisting on an immediate acceptance. Until he knew the fate of the story under consideration, he could not settle down to work on a new one. His concern is understandable, but his behavior merely angered the editors and embarrassed Ober. Ever since Lorimer's departure, Fitzgerald's reputation with the *Post* had been slipping. Where it had regularly published eight or nine of his stories each year from 1927 through 1931, it bought only five during 1932, three in 1933, three more in 1934, and one —the last—in 1935.

The difficulty was that, as a storyteller dependent on personal experience for his subject matter, Fitzgerald had temporarily run out of material. After five years of writing nothing but magazine stories, his past was depleted; and, ever since Zelda's breakdown, the present had been too confused and too unpleasant to serve for breezy popular entertainment. Although he was unable to do much about the situation in which he found himself, he could still analyze his strength and limitations with remarkable detachment. "I am thirty-six years old. For eighteen years, save for a short space during the war, writing has been my chief interest in life, and I am in every sense a professional," he said in a revealing essay, "One Hundred False Starts," which the *Post* published in 1931.[31]

Yet even now when, at the recurrent cry of "Baby needs shoes," I sit down facing my sharpened pencils and block of legal-sized paper, I have a feeling of utter helplessness. I may write my story in three days or, as is more frequently the case, it may be six weeks before I have assembled anything worthy to be sent out. I can open a volume from a criminal-law library and find a thousand plots. I can go into highway and byway, parlor and kitchen, and listen to personal revelations that, at the hands of other writers, might endure forever. But all that is nothing—not even enough for a false start. . . .

Mostly, we authors must repeat ourselves—that's the truth. We have two or three great and moving experiences in our lives—experiences so great and moving that it doesn't seem at the time that anyone else has ever been so caught up and pounded and dazzled and astonished and beaten and broken and rescued and illuminated and rewarded and humbled in just that way ever before.

Then we learn our trade, well or less well, and we tell our two or three stories—each time in a new disguise—maybe ten times, maybe a hundred, as long as people will listen. . . .

When I face the fact that all my stories are going to have a certain family resemblance, I am taking a step toward avoiding false starts. . . . Whether it's something that happened twenty years ago or only yesterday, I must start out with an emotion—one that's close to me and that I can understand.

Lacking the inspiration of such personal emotions, he turned more and more after 1930 to elaborately constructed plots as the way out of his dilemma. But in the presence of a contrived plot his imagination lost its power and magic. Practically all of his poorer stories suffer from the burden of too much plot. Among his papers he left the outline of an unfinished story, "I Take Hard Cases," that shows where his trouble lay. In its finished state it was to have run to some six thousand words and to have consisted of "three or four brisk parts" arranged as follows:

I	up to Marriage	1 big scene
II	up to 2nd Marriage	2 big scenes
III	up to Despair	3 big scenes
IV	Partial Recovery	3 big scenes

For a writer who depended so much for his effects on the creation of mood and atmosphere, and on the slow building up of dramatic climaxes, nine scenes of approximately 700 words each simply did not offer enough scope. He should have cut the structure back to one or two big scenes at the most. *The Great Gatsby* was built around only nine major scenes, and to tell that story had taken him sixty thousand words![32]

During the nine years between *The Great Gatsby* and *Tender Is the Night*, Fitzgerald published fifty-five magazine stories, more or less—depending on the classification of several semi-autobiographical sketches. The quality of these stories reached its highest peak in 1928 and 1929, when practically every one was a deft, smoothly executed, and interesting piece of work. During these years, he wrote "The Last of the Belles," "Outside the Cabinet Maker's," "The Rough Crossing," and two series of stories grouped respectively around fourteen-year-old Basil Duke Lee and eighteen-year-old Josephine Perry. Following Zelda's collapse in 1930, the quality of his stories fell off sharply, though this decline was occasionally interrupted by a piece like "Babylon Revisited" or "Crazy Sunday." The latter were hardly classifiable as magazine fiction, however. As we have seen, "Crazy Sunday" was rejected by the better-known magazines. And although *The Saturday Evening Post* bought "Babylon Revisited," it promptly complained to Harold Ober that Fitzgerald was writing too much about Europe and that it wanted more good one-hundred-per-cent American backgrounds in his stories! After Zelda's breakdown, Fitzgerald never really recovered his old knack for turning out slick, light, commercial fiction.[33]

Unfortunately, he did not save the manuscripts or work sheets of his published stories, so that we cannot watch them take shape as we could *The Great Gatsby*. Instead, he kept tearsheets from the magazines in which they appeared. Sometime during the early 1930's he began dividing them into two categories: those stories that he considered worthy of republication, and those that he preferred to leave interred in the magazines. It was his habit to go over the tearsheets of the latter stories carefully with a red pencil before filing them away, underlining any passages that he thought worth preserving for future use. These passages were then typed up and filed away under an appropriate heading in his scrapbook: "Descriptions of Things and Atmosphere," "Descriptions of Girls," etc. The stort stories that had been stripped in this manner were then marked "Scrapped and to be Permanently Buried." In a note to his literary executor dated March 26, 1935, he explained that the reason none of these stories were to be reprinted was that:[34]

> The best . . . have been stripped of their high spots which were woven into novels . . . also because each story contains some special fault—sentimentality, faulty construction, confusing change of pace —or else was too obviously made for the trade.

In a similar manner he made it a practice to strip and file away under the appropriate scrapbook heading the best passages from the discarded drafts of unfinished or completed stories that he had discarded because they would not sell. He also salvaged similar material from discarded drafts of the novel on which he was then working, "The Boy Who Killed His Mother." Much of this material, including many passages from his scrapped magazine stories, was later incorporated into *Tender Is the Night.*

After Fitzgerald's death Edmund Wilson came across these files and published the greater part of their contents in 1945 in his *Crack-up* volume. At that time Mr. Wilson mistakenly assumed that the material consisted primarily of hitherto unpublished passages that Fitzgerald had written down in inspired moments and saved for future use. On the contrary, the largest proportion consisted of passages salvaged from his published, and in a few cases, unpublished, stories. Hence, "The Scrapbooks" is probably a better title for this collection than "The Notebooks."

Altogether, during his lifetime, Fitzgerald published around one hundred and fifty magazine stories (excluding the amateur pieces he wrote before 1920). The twenty-eight stories that Malcolm Crowley collected in *The Stories of F. Scott Fitzgerald* include all of Fitzgerald's better stories (except for the "Jelly-Bean") as well as a generous sampling from the others. Arthur Mizener included several more in his volume of hitherto uncollected stories and sketches by Fitzgerald, *Afternoon of an Author*. As a result, among the uncollected material very few stories remain whose republication will add any luster to their author's reputation. Yet even Fitzgerald's poorest work contains many passages of good writing. Two stories that were published in the Cowley volume ("Magnetism" and "The Bridal Party") and four in *Afternoon of an Author* ("A Night at the Fair," "Forging Ahead," "Basil and Cleopatra," and " 'I Didn't Get Over' ") were among the ones Fitzgerald specifically said he did not want republished. Although opinions differ, strong evidence can be found to support the argument that he was a severe and conscientious critic of his work.[35]

The popular magazine story, conventional in form and content, was never a medium well-suited to Fitzgerald's talent. He found greater freedom in the novel, the casual autobiographical essay, and those occasional unorthodox stories that were rarely bought by the bigger magazines. One of his most perfect stories was the short piece, "Outside the Cabinet Maker's," written in 1928. It describes an afternoon he spent alone with seven-year-old Scottie, while they were waiting for Zelda to return from some shopping. In its charm, its precision of language and image, its cool detached humor and affection, it foreshadowed such notable essays as his "Crack-up" pieces, "The Lost Decade," "Author's House," and "Afternoon of an Author." But as so often happened with Fitzgerald's better work, "Outside the Cabinet Maker's" was turned down by seven different magazines before Fitzgerald finally gave it to the old *Century* for one hundred and fifty dollars.[36]

In spite of their triviality, Fitzgerald's magazine stories are interesting because of what they reveal about him personally, as well as for the light they throw on his career as a professional magazinist. One practice that he followed several times in his magazine work was that of creating a hero attractive enough to his readers to be used as the subject for a series of stories. This was the practice of a number of other successful *Saturday Evening Post* authors at the time, notably Arthur Train, Booth Tarkington, and Mary Roberts Rinehart. One advantage was that the series could later be collected and sold in book form. The first such series that Fitzgerald wrote centered around the adventures of Basil Duke Lee, a fourteen-year-old boy based on Tarkington's Penrod and Fitzgerald's own schoolboy memories. Many of Basil's adventures had already been described by Fitzgerald in "The Romantic Egotist." But there they were colored by the bitterness and resentment of their twenty-one-year-old author. Now, ten years afterwards, he was able to look back on that unhappy adolescence with a comic detachment. The Basil series got off to a fine start in 1928 with "The Scandal Detectives," "The Captured Shadow," and "The Perfect Life." Then Fitzgerald ran out of ideas and began writing off the top of his mind. "Forging Ahead" and "Basil and Cleopatra" were strained and unconvincing; the last, "That Kind of Party," was so bad no one would buy it. Altogether there were nine in the series, but there were not enough good ones to make an independent volume, as he had hoped.[37]

The following year he started a new series, this time centered around the adventures of an eighteen-year-old debutante from the Chicago suburbs, named Josephine Perry, who was created from his memories of Ginevra King. Like the heroines of *This Side of Paradise*, Josephine embodied certain values and aspirations which, while they dated back much earlier, were to find wide literary expression only after World War I. In these stories Fitzgerald dissected his heroine with a humor and insight that had been missing when he had known her original some ten years before. Today, however, the series has a distinctly dated air. Pretty, pampered, self-centered, badly read, Josephine Perry is an amusing example of that "finishing school" type that was to be one of the lesser casualties of the Depression and World War II. During the Thirties Fitzgerald replaced her, in his more serious fiction, with a more capable and more responsible kind of heroine—notably eighteen-year-old Rosemary Hoyt in *Tender Is the Night* and Cecilia Brady, the Bennington College girl in *The Last Tycoon*.[38]

The magazine stories Fitzgerald wrote between *The Great Gatsby* and *Tender Is the Night*, i.e., between 1925 and 1934, are also of interest because we see him encountering themes and situations that he was to explore more fully in the second of these novels. One recurring situation is that of a middle-aged man in love with a young girl of eighteen. Sometimes the hero is a bachelor, sometimes he is married—usually to a violently jealous wife. In both "The Love Boat" (1927) and "The Rough Crossing" (1929) he is led to believe, erroneously, that his philandering has driven his wife to suicide. The circumstances are changed in "A New Leaf" (1931), which was written after Zelda's breakdown. Here it is the older man, a hopeless alcoholic, who commits suicide, leaving the girl to marry a man nearer her own age.

No matter how Fitzgerald treated this theme in his stories, the man's love for the younger girl was usually frustrated in some way, and he suffered for his foolish infatuation, just as Dick Diver suffers in *Tender Is the Night*. In "Two Wrongs" (1930), the straying husband is "punished" by contracting tuberculosis. His career as a theatrical producer ends and his wife leaves him to become a successful ballerina. "He realized perfectly that he had brought all this on himself, and that there was some law of compensation involved," Fitzgerald comments at the end of this involved story. ". . . He felt beyond everything, even beyond his grief, an almost comfortable sensation of being in the hands of something bigger than himself. . . ."[39]

In the stories of this period, most of them from *The Saturday Evening Post*, we find Fitzgerald applying the middle-class values of hard work and individual enterprise to the exploits of his heroines as well as of his youthful heroes. "The Bowl" (1928), for example, describes the rivalry of two girls for the affections of a handsome football player. One of them is the well-groomed, beautiful but spoiled daughter of a wealthy family who foreshadows Nicole Warren in *Tender Is the Night*. The other is a talented, hard-working young movie starlet like Rosemary Hoyt in that novel. Indeed, like Rosemary, she even jumps into a swimming pool with a high fever, because it is part of her job as an actress and the show must go on. Here, as in *Tender*, Fitzgerald makes no bones about his prejudice in favor of the poor girl who makes her own way. "She was eighteen," he says, "and . . . [as] I compared her background of courage, independence, and achievement based on co-operation, with most girls I had known, there was no way in which she was not immeasurably superior."[40]

Closely associated with this dislike of the children of the rich was a strong prejudice against the wealthy as a class—a prejudice that becomes especially pronounced in the magazine stories Fitzgerald wrote after 1930. Earlier pieces like "The Diamond as Big as the Ritz," "May Day," and *The Great Gatsby* had softened this antipathy toward great wealth by feelings of awe and envy, and an ironic humor. There the very rich possessed a color and glamor that made up in some degree for their egotism and irresponsibility. But after 1930 they are rarely portrayed as attractive. One reason for this undoubtedly was the October, 1929, stock market crash and the ensuing Depression. The miseries of the Thirties fulfilled all the prophecies about the dangers of reckless, uncontrolled wealth that Fitzgerald had voiced so often in his stories during the previous years.

Like many of his friends, Fitzgerald was attracted to Marxism after 1929 because he shared with it a skepticism concerning the popular philosophy of laissez-faire capitalism. While he was living outside Baltimore from 1932 until 1934, he even let "La Paix" be used for meetings organized by local Communists. But it was not classical capitalism that Fitzgerald resented so much as the unbridled license of moneyed people—especially the arrogant behavior of their children. No one believed more whole-heartedly in the virtues of individual initiative and free enterprise. His 1932 short story, "The Rubber Check," is a vigorous defense of a poor but capable young man who has been cruelly humiliated by some rich boys because he inadvertently cashed a bad check— as Fitzgerald himself had once done. "Six of One," another *Saturday Evening Post* story of that year, tells how a certain Mr. Barnes, a self-made Minnesota millionaire, has his faith restored in the American system of free enterprise as the result of an ingenious experiment. He had begun to question the American dream because the children of his rich friends were so weak and pampered. So he gave an equal sum of money to twelve young men, six rich boys and six poor boys. Naturally, his wealthy friends assured him their sons would make best use of it. Instead the rich boys frittered it away, while the poor boys put it to work and were soon collecting dividends and clipping coupons.[41]

Careful reading of these stories also reveals the fact that Fitzgerald, in spite of his great affection for Gertrude Stein, refused to accept that label of "a lost generation" that she had applied to himself and Hemingway and their post-War I contemporaries. If any generation deserved to be called "lost," in Fitzgerald's opinion, it was the pre-War I generation of his parents—and of Miss Stein, herself. It was they who deserved the blame for the stupid war, as well as the Boom and Bust that followed. If Fitzgerald and his friends behaved badly, it was because of the poor training and education provided for them by their parents. "No generation in the history of America has ever been so dull, so worthless, so devoid of ideas, as that generation which is now between forty and sixty years old—the men who were young in the nineties," he had written in a magazine article in 1924.

The attack continued in his subsequent magazine stories, stimulated especially by the catastrophe of the depression. Of one typical parent he said in "A Freeze Out" (1931):

> She and her husband and all their friends had no principles. They were good or bad according to their natures; often they struck attitudes remembered from the past, but they were never sure as her father and grandfather had been sure. Confusedly she thought it was something about religion. But how could you get principles just by wishing for them?

In contrast to the kind of parents described here, Fitzgerald offered the hard-working young men portrayed in "Six of One," who had restored Mr. Barnes's faith in the future of America. "He was glad," Fitzgerald said of Mr. Barnes, "that he was able to feel that the republic could survive the mistakes of a whole generation, pushing the waste aside, sending ahead the vital and strong. Only it was too bad and very American that there should be all that waste at the top."[42]

Fitzgerald, by accepting the positive aspects of the American dream, still exercised his right to criticize or condemn its excesses. The expatriate American who stands at the rail of a transatlantic liner watching the fading shoreline of his native land in his 1929 short story, "The Swimmers," was Fitzgerald himself:[43]

> Watching the fading city, the fading shore . . . , he had a sense of overwhelming gratitude and gladness that America was still there, that under the ugly debris of industry the rich land still pushed up, incorrigibly lavish and fertile and that in the heart of the people the old generosities and devotions fought on, breaking out sometimes in fanaticism and excess but indomitable and undefeated. There was a lost generation in the saddle at the moment, but it seemed to him that the men coming on, the men of the war, were better, and all his old feeling that America was a bizarre accident, a sort of historical sport, was gone forever. The best of America was the best of the world. . . .
>
> France was a land, England was a people, but America, having about it still that quality of an idea, was harder to utter—it was the graves at Shiloh, and the tired, drawn, nervous faces of its great men, and the country boys dying in the Argonne for a phrase that was empty before their hearts withered. It was a willingness of the heart.

X
"The Boy Who Killed His Mother":
1924-1932

The idea of a novel about Americans living in Europe—the germ of *Tender Is the Night*—seems to have first occurred to Fitzgerald sometime during the autumn of 1924, just as he was finishing *The Great Gatsby*. The manuscript of *Gatsby* had gone off to Maxwell Perkins from St. Raphaël on October twenty-seventh, and several days later the Fitzgeralds themselves departed for Italy. By mid-November we find Zelda writing Perkins from Rome: "Scott thinks he would like to begin a new novel right away. He says he's full of stuff he doesn't want to waste on short stories." And in December Fitzgerald himself wrote Perkins: "I've got a new novel to write—title and all, that'll take about a year."[1]

But first the necessity of having to write some stories to pay their bills, and then the extensive proof revisions of Gatsby, kept him otherwise occupied for the rest of the winter. During the spring, while the waited in Paris for *Gatsby* to appear, he loafed and worked at a leisurely pace on "The Rich Boy." Meanwhile, the idea for his next book was gradually taking shape in his mind. "The happiest thought I have is of my new novel," he wrote Perkins in May, 1925, "—it is something really NEW in form, idea, structure, the model for the age that Joyce and Stien [sic] are searching for, that Conrad didn't find." And to John Peale Bishop in early August: "I'm beginning a new novel next month on the Riviera."[2]

Several days later the Fitzgeralds left Paris to spend a month at Antibes, the Riviera resort midway between Cannes and Nice. Europeans who wintered in the south of France traditionally went north in hot weather to the cooler beaches along the Atlantic coast. But during the past several years the hitherto empty summer Riviera had become increasingly popular with Americans, who were accustomed to the hotter beaches at home. Besides, prices were cheaper there than at the more fashionable Biarritz and Deauville. Among the other expatriate Americans at Antibes that summer were the Archibald MacLeishes, the John Dos Passoses, the Ernest Hemingways, the Rex Ingrams, the Max Eastmans, and the Gerald Murphys. It was in the garden of Gerald and Sara Murphy's lovely home, the Villa Americana, that Fitzgerald's novel was formally "conceived." By the end of August he had progressed to the point where he was at last ready to announce his plans. It would be called "Our Type," he wrote Max Perkins, and was to be "about several things, one of which is an intellectual murder on the Leopold-Loeb idea. Incidently it is about Zelda & me & the hysteria of last May and June in Paris (Confidential)."[3]

In September the Fitzgeralds joined the Murphys in Paris, where the annual social season was just getting under way. The Murphys knew everyone, and a gala international exposition was in full swing on the banks of the Seine. All the parties and the Paris color and excitement furnished fresh background material for the new novel, and during the rest of the year Fitzgerald sent enthusiastic reports of his progress to Perkins, Ober, Paul Reynolds, Ring Lardner, John Peale Bishop, and other literary friends. The manuscript, he wrote Reynolds, would be finished in about a year. His failure to serialize *The Great Gatsby* he now believed had been a mistake. The resulting magazine publicity would have helped rather than harmed its sale; therefore, he asked Reynolds to see what could be done about the serialization of "Our Type." "The novel progresses slowly & carefully with much destroying & revision," he wrote Perkins in October. However, when Harold Ober (at Reynolds' request) wrote asking for more specific details so that he could arrange for the sale of the serial rights, Fitzgerald grew suspiciously vague. "I'd rather not tell about the new novel yet," he replied,"—as part of it isn't clear in my mind and I don't want it to chrystalize [sic] too soon."[4]

"The book is wonderful," he wrote Perkins at Christmas. "I honestly think that when it's published I shall be the best American novelist (which isn't saying a lot) but the end seems far away." The following May, 1926, he was at last ready to give Ober a few more details. "The novel is about one-fourth done and will be delivered for possible serialization about January 1," he wrote from Juan-les-Pins. "It will be about

75,000 words long, divided into twelve chapters concerning (and this is absolutely confidential) such a case as that girl who shot her mother on the Pacific Coast last year. In other words like *Gatsby* it is highly sensational. Not only would this bar it from the *Post* but they are also hostile, as you know, to the general cast of thought that permeates my serious work." Ober then arranged the $35,000 agreement with *Liberty*, providing that Fitzgerald met the January 1927 deadline.[5]

He did not meet *Liberty's* January deadline and by the following June there was still no manuscript. In fact, Fitzgerald, now at "Ellerslie," had embarked on that regular schedule of *Saturday Evening Post* stories that was to consume most of his creative energy for the next half-dozen years. Yet he continued to hold out all kinds of promises. Max Perkins, who had so far not seen a word of it, had the impression that it was practically done. "I am sure anyhow, that if he will finish up his novel, which is about five thousand words from completion, and will then take a real rest and regular exercise, he will be in good shape again," Perkins wrote Ring Lardner in October, 1927. But both autumn and winter passed without further progress except a vague "hope I'm nearly done" in a note to Perkins in February, 1928.[6]

When Fitzgerald decided to spend the summer of 1928 abroad, Perkins encouraged the plan in the hope that he would be able to rest and finish the novel. "We are settled and not a soul in the world knows where we are, on the absolute wagon & working on the novel, the whole novel, and nothing but the novel. I'm coming back in August with it or on it," Fitzgerald wrote him from Paris in July. "The novel goes fine," he reported several weeks later. "I think it's quite wonderful & I think those who've seen it (for I've read it around a little) have been quite excited. I was encouraged the other day, when James Joyce came to dinner, when he said, 'yes, I expect to finish my novel in three or four years more at the *latest*' and he works 11 hrs a day to my intermittent 8. Mine will be done *sure* in September."[7]

But this was bluff, or wishful thinking, or (more likely) a mixture of both. The true history of that summer of 1928 is chronicled in his Ledger: "Drinking and general unpleasantness. First trip jail. C—R— and dive in Lido, second trip jail. General carelessness and boredom. . . . No real progress in anything and wrecked myself with dozens of people."[8]

When they returned to "Ellerslie" in the autumn, Fitzgerald decided to set himself an elaborate, Gatsby-like work schedule. "Am going to send you two chapters a month of the final version of book beginning next week and ending in February," he wrote Perkins. "I think this will help me get it straight in my own mind—I've been alone with it too long." Several days later, he mailed Perkins "the first fourth of the book (2 chapters, 18,000 words). Now comes another short story, then I'll patch up Chaps. 3 and 4 the same way, and send them, I hope, about the 1st of December."[9]

> Chapter 1 here is good.
> Chapter 2 has caused me more trouble than anything in the book. You'll realize this when I tell you it was once 27,000 words long! It started its career as Chapter 1. I am far from satisfied with it even now. . . .

Perkins was impressed by what he read and replied enthusiastically that both chapters; especially the second, contained "some of the best writing you've ever done." But at this point Fitzgerald's plan to follow a schedule petered out. Despite Perkins' repeated inquiries, no more installments arrived at Scribner's. Again, the explanation can be found in Fitzgerald's autobiographical month-by-month record of that winter of 1928–1929. "More parties. Accidents . . . Cornelius Vanderbilt and various rows." The next word Perkins received was a note written from a transatlantic liner in March in which Fitzgerald confessed he was "sneaking away like a thief without leaving the chapters." He still had lots of work to do "straighten[ing] them out." Nevertheless, the finished manuscript, he promised, would be in Perkins' hands in "a few months."[10]

Three months passed before Perkins had another letter. Indeed, Perkins was reduced to having to write to Lardner asking for news of Fitzgerald, but Lardner was just as much in the dark. Finally, in June, a note arrived for Perkins explaining that Fitzgerald had been having trouble with certain technical problems but was now "working day & night on novel from new angle that I think will solve previous difficulties." In September, he assured Perkins again that he was "working hard on the novel and have sworn not to come back this fall without completing it. Prospects bright." But as things turned out they were not to come back for two more years—and even then with the novel still unfinished. The reports of "hard work" that summer are pathetically contradicted by the evidence of his Ledger: "Being drunk and snubbed. . . . Fairies, breakdown . . . Zelda dancing and sweating. . . . Rows and indifference. . . . The Murphy yatch [yacht] and a last row."[11]

After two years of nothing but magazine stories, Fitzgerald was no further ahead financially than before, and Perkins began to wonder if under the present circumstances the novel would ever materialize. "You know, Scott, that if you want money ever you've just to ask for it," he wrote in November. "And I know that while there is a balance here against you, our debt to you is really much greater than that balance. I'm a Yankee, and at talk, not so good, but this I know and so do 'we.' "[12]

Earlier that month Fitzgerald had written him from Paris that "For the first time since August I see my way clear to a long stretch on the novel." But, instead, Zelda and he became involved in the usual round of expatriate parties. The following March, 1930, Fitzgerald promised Harold Ober to have half the novel ready for a reading by April first, if any magazine editor still wanted to serialize it. But this promise, too, failed to materialize. Instead, March and April swept by in a festive blaze, ending abruptly on April twenty-third with Zelda's collapse. For several weeks thereafter, no further word of any kind was forthcoming from Fitzgerald. His worried mother had to write to Perkins, asking for news of her son, but Perkins had heard nothing from him either. Fitzgerald's explanation of his silence, when it finally arrived, was neither enlightening nor reassuring. "Powell Fowler & his wedding party arrived & I got unfortunately involved in dinners & nightclubs & drinking; then Zelda got a sort of nervous breakdown from overwork & consequently I haven't done a line of work or written a letter for twenty-one days."[13]

Between Zelda's illness and his *Saturday Evening Post* stories, he was able to give the novel no time at all during the next eighteen months. Inquiries about it only made him angry. "I wrote young & I wrote a lot & the pot takes longer to fill up now," he replied irritably to one such letter from Perkins, "but the novel, my novel, is a different matter than if I'd hurriedly finished it up a year and a half ago. . . . *I know what I'm doing* —honestly, Max. . . . I think it [i.e., time] seems to go by quicker there in America but time put in is time eventually taken out—and whatever this thing of mine is it's certainly not a mediocrity like *The Woman of Andros* and *The Forty-Second Parallel*." And to Ober, still waiting for the manuscript he had promised to *Liberty* four years ago: "The other night I read one great hunk of it to John Peale Bishop and we both agreed that it would be ruinous to let *Liberty* start it uncompleted. . . . Suppose *Liberty* didn't like even the first part and went around saying it was rotten before it was even finished. . . . At one time I was about to send 4 chapters out of eight done, to you. Then I cut one of those chapters absolutely to pieces. I know you're losing faith in me and Max too, but God knows one has to rely in the end on one's own judgment. I could have published four lousy halfbaked books in the last 5 years and people would have thought I was at least a worthy young man not drinking myself to pieces in the south seas—but I'd be dead as Michael Arlen, Bromfield, Tom Boyd, Callaghan and the others who think they can trick the world with the hurried and second-rate."[14]

When younger American writers encountered him in Paris or on the Riviera—Robert Penn Warren, Thornton Wilder, Allen Tate—and asked him about his work, he became angry, or changed the subject and said that now that Hemingway was writing, he no longer had anything to say. "Haven't touched novel for four months, save for one week," he wrote Ober from Switzerland in November, 1930, after a summer's silence. "In mid-summer from the combination of worry and work my lungs sprang a leak. That's all right now, thank heaven. I went up to Caux and rested for a month. All this is between you and me—even Max doesn't know. Then Scotty fell ill. I figure I've written about 40,000 words to Forel (the psychiatrist) on the subject of Zelda, trying to get at the root of things."[15]

"Hope to Christ I'll have the novel for you this year," he wrote Perkins at the beginning of 1931. But in February his father died and he made a hurried trip to Maryland for the funeral. Then to Montgomery to report on Zelda's illness to her family—and back to Switzerland, tired and discouraged. "The trip South was not so fortunate as it might have been," he wrote his cousin "Ceci" from the *Olympic* en route to France. "Life got very crowded after I left you, and I am damned glad to be going back to Europe where I am away from most of the people I care about and can *think* instead of feeling."[16]

By the following September Zelda was well enough to travel and they hurried back to Montgomery so that she could be with her dying father. Judge Sayre's death in November, while Fitzgerald was working in Hollywood, left her badly shaken. So at Christmas he took her to Florida for a holiday. There, while she sunned herself on the beach at St. Petersburg, he turned once more to "The Boy Who Killed His Mother"—the title on which Perkins and he had now mutually agreed. "At last for the first time in two years and ½ I am going to spend five consecutive months on my novel," he wrote Perkins happily. "I am actually six thousand dollars ahead. Am replanning it to include what's good in what I have, adding 41,000 new words and publishing. Don't tell Ernest [Hemingway] or anyone—let them think what they want— you're the only one whose [sic] ever consistently felt faith in me any-how."[17]

But again his plans went awry. Zelda, as we know, collapsed again and it was the summer of 1932 before Fitzgerald and Scottie were settled at "La Paix" near her hospital in Baltimore. In July, Ober and

Perkins worked out an arrangement whereby he would receive a monthly allowance from Scribner's, so that he could stop writing stories and devote his time exclusively to the book. By mid-August *Tender Is the Night* had been "plotted and planned," as he noted in his Ledger, "nevermore to be interrupted." The first draft was finished the following September, 1933, and the first installment of the four-part serialization appeared in the January, 1934, *Scribner's Monthly*. The book version was published the following April.

Tender Is the Night was, however, an altogether different book from the novel on which Fitzgerald had been working ever since the summer of 1925, and that he had successively entitled "Our Type," "The World's Fair," and "The Boy Who Killed His Mother." Occasionally, in his correspondence, he had also called it "The Melarky Case." But had there ever really been such a novel? And if there were, had it ever been only 5,000 words from completion, as Max Perkins had been led to believe as early as 1927? Had Fitzgerald spent the years from 1925 to 1932 nursing a dream—or a lie?[18]

The manuscript evidence for this discarded novel is certainly voluminous enough: hundreds of pages of material in all stages of revision. Fitzgerald may have destroyed a certain amount of reworked material, but inspection of the mass he did preserve does not indicate that any significant portions are missing. On the contrary, he seems to have taken pains to save as much as he could. And what he did save presumably represents those "three hundred thousand words" which, he told Malcolm Cowley in 1933, he had discarded before he began *Tender Is the Night*. If this is so, then we are obliged to conclude from this evidence that he really never progressed very far with "The Boy Who Killed His Mother," despite his statements to the contrary. In 1926 he had told Harold Ober that it would run to twelve chapters, yet we have nothing in his manuscript beyond the first four. Instead of writing out a crude first draft and then going back and revising what he had written, as he had done for *The Great Gatsby*, Fitzgerald seems to have devoted seven years, off and on, to polishing and repolishing these first four chapters! Not only did he neglect to make a preliminary written outline for the story, but he never seems to have had such an outline firmly in mind. Indeed the impression one reluctantly carries away from a careful reading of this mass of material is that Fitzgerald finally abandoned the novel on which he had been at work so long, simply because he no longer knew precisely what it was he wanted to say.[19]

The nature of that original intention can be reconstructed fairly well from the chapters we have. In the earliest surviving version of Chapter I we are introduced to two Americans, a young man named Francis Melarky and his mother, Charlotte, who are staying at a hotel in Rome. Francis, we learn, was born in Tennessee and attended West Point, from which he was expelled for some unspecified infraction of the regulations. Later he worked as a film-cutter in Hollywood until some other misdemeanor (also unspecified) made it necessary for him to leave the country to avoid imprisonment—hence his presence in Europe. His father is at the moment in jail somewhere in the United States for a crime vaguely described as a "government fraud." Mrs. Melarky (or "Megary," as it is occasionally spelled) is a red-faced, loud-mouthed, unattractive woman. She tells Francis that by bringing him away to Italy she has saved him from his father's fate. Now that he is safe, she is determined to do all she can to keep him from "making a fool of himself."

Francis resents his mother, however, and spends a great deal of time quarreling with her. She, on the other hand, insists that he is "going to pieces" and needs her care. They are not an especially prepossessing couple, although Francis is good-looking in a dark, romantic way:

> At first glance [Fitzgerald says in a passage that also illustrates the overblown prose of this early draft] he was conventionally handsome, the "ideal" of a young girl—only after this impression was minimized by the faint disgust nearly always present in his face, did those who continued to look at him react to the full lustre of his wet, brilliant brown eyes. Wide open, they were a glittering world, spinning on the axis of a bright soul you guessed at. For a moment you lived in them so eagerly, so confidently, that if they closed up you vanished. They were mature eyes, vivid as a child's—but rich in urgency rather than in promise, in arrival rather than in aspiration. You found them, you who had forgotten the dull inability of the mouth to endure boredom and the nervous young forehead, already lined with fretful and unprofitable pain.

Leaving his mother at the hotel, Francis goes out alone for a night on the town. But when his attempt to pick up a girl in an expensive nightclub is rebuffed, he gets drunk, attacks a policeman, and is badly roughed up and thrown into jail. Later his release is obtained through the joint efforts of Mrs. Melarky and an American vice-consul whose reluctant services she has commandeered.

Fitzgerald himself had been involved in a similar scrape in Rome in the autumn of 1924, not long after Zelda and he arrived there from France to spend the winter. Afterwards he would describe it as "the most humiliating experience that ever happened to me." The first evidence we have that he was planning to write a new novel, it will be recalled, occurs in a letter he wrote Max Perkins from Rome about the time this fracas took place. Quite likely, then, it was his humiliation and remorse over this affair—emotions that he effectively conveys in this first chapter—that provided the initial inspiration for this new novel. If this was the case, then the inspiration for "The Boy Who Killed His Mother" closely resembled the emotions of despair and humiliation which had inspired the first draft of the first chapter of *The Great Gatsby*. By the time Fitzgerald decided to discard the story of Francis Melarky, this opening chapter had been revised and polished to such a high luster that he was able to incorporate it practically verbatim into *Tender Is the Night*, where it comprises Chapters XXII and XXIII of Book II.[20]

After this humiliating interlude, the Melarkys decide to continue on their travels. At the beginning of Chapter II we find them staying at a beachfront hotel on the French Riviera midway between Nice and Cannes. Here they become acquainted with two Americans named Abe and Mary Grant (who in other versions are also referred to as Abe and Mary Graw, Abe and Mary Herkimer, Walter and Mary Caswell, and Walter and Mary Naaman). Abe is connected in some obscure way with the U.S. State Department. He is also an amateur violinist, though not an especially good one. In the earlier versions of this chapter Francis is kept busy trying to seduce Mary, whose marriage is going on the rocks. Although the Grants spend much of their time drinking and gambling at the hotel and adjoining casino, they live in a handsome villa overlooking the ocean. Among their neighbors is another rich, expatriate American couple, Seth and Dinah Piper ("Rorebacher" in some drafts). Gradually, as Fitzgerald rewrote, the Grants receded into the background, and the Pipers—who superficially resembled the Gerald Murphys—advanced to the center of the stage. Eventually, the Pipers were moved into the attractive hillside villa, and the Grants ended up living in Francis' hotel.

Chapter III, which does not appear to have been written until most of Chapter II had been thought out, is mainly concerned with a big dinner party at the Piper villa, and the absurd duel that followed. In the earliest version Francis and his mother are merely taken up to the Pipers by the Grants for an afternoon social call. Once Fitzgerald has got the Pipers and Francis together, however, he began to envision all sorts of consequences developing from this friendship. Seth's afternoon tea party becomes a gala dinner not only for Francis and his mother but for all the other Americans at the hotel: the Grants, an American novelist named McKisco and his wife, a Mrs. Abrams and a French soldier of fortune named Brugerol. During the evening Brugerol insults Mrs. McKisco, and her husband drunkenly challenges him to a duel. The amusing encounter that follows is practically identical with the duel at the beginning of *Tender Is the Night*.

Meanwhile, Mrs. Melarky has gone back to the hotel; and when Francis returns after witnessing the duel he learns from her that he has had a visit from an American producer named Earl Brady, who is making a movie in the vicinity and wants his services. Francis, who is looking for something interesting to do, is delighted. But Mrs. Melarky adds that she has sent Brady packing because she thinks he is a dope addict and a bad influence. At this point their quarrel is interrupted by the Pipers, who have come by to invite Francis to go to Paris with them to celebrate the Grants' departure for the States. Flattered by this attention, Francis eagerly accepts.

Chapter IV exists in numerous drafts, the last of which Fitzgerald never completed. The setting is Paris, where the Pipers and Grants and Francis (and his ubiquitous mother) are staying at the same hotel. By now we can see the outlines of a plot beginning to emerge. Seth and Dinah Piper, both of whom have been attracted by Francis' sultry good looks, are ready to introduce him to the glittering world of Paris society. But Charlotte is determined to prevent her son from being debauched by these libertines who, in her view, are not much better than a dope addict like Earl Brady. If Francis is to enjoy the entrée offered him by the Pipers, he must first cut his silver cord. As her naggings and warnings become more frequent, Francis' resentment builds up until the atmosphere between them crackles with emotion.

At this point the manuscript of "The Boy Who Killed His Mother" stops. But even without the title, we can guess the rest of the plot from Fitzgerald's letters. His novel, he had told Max Perkins even before he began the actual writing, was to be about "an intellectual murder on the Leopold-Loeb idea." The cold-blooded killing of little Bobby Franks by two wealthy Chicago youths, Leopold and Loeb, had reached the front pages of the newspapers in May, 1924, just as the Fitzgeralds were leaving Great Neck for France. The June 28, 1924 issue of *Liberty* Magazine, which carried one of Fitzgerald's short stories, featured an especially lurid article about the affair, which Fitzgerald carefully filed among his papers. Fitzgerald thought of it as "an intellectual murder" in the sense that it so perfectly exemplified his theory about the moral irresponsibility of the pampered rich. Leopold and Loeb were two spoiled rich boys who had killed an innocent child for no other motive than to demonstrate their superiority to a society whose values they refused to accept. In "The Boy Who Killed His Mother," Francis Melarky's murder of his mother was to express a similar idea. Only by freeing himself from his mother's domination, Francis thinks, can he gratify his aesthetic lust for the kind of life represented by the glamorous, charming Seth and Dinah Piper. "In regard to my novel," Fitzgerald wrote Perkins several months later, "will you ask somebody what is done if one American murders another in France? Would an American marshall come over for him? From his state of residence? Who would hold him meanwhile—the consul or the French police? . . . It's important that I find this out and I can't seem to."[21]

When he heard that Theodore Dreiser had a new novel coming out in January, 1926, with the title *An American Tragedy*, he wondered at first if Dreiser had appropriated his story. But a reading of the novel soon set his mind at rest. "In a certain sense my plot is not unlike Dreiser's . . . ," he wrote Perkins in February. "At first this worried me but now it doesn't for our minds are so different." In both novels, willful murder is the price that the two young heroes must be willing to pay if they are to enter the "best" society. From what we know of Fitzgerald's other work, however, it seems likely that he planned to dwell more on the moral dilemma confronting Francis than on the consequences— whereas it was the ironic consequences which so fascinated Dreiser in his *American Tragedy*. Morally the inhabitants of Fitzgerald's glamorous expatriate world were no better than the dull, middle-class businessmen and their families whom Clyde Griffiths admired. But Fitzgerald was more interested than Dreiser in the problem of evoking in the reader a sense of the tangible color and beauty of that world. For there lay the only possible moral excuse for Francis' conduct. Could Fitzgerald have succeeded in conveying the effect of the Pipers' way of life on the impressionable Francis so that his subsequent actions would appear to be justified? In spite of his crudeness and brutality, Francis was to be at least partially redeemed (as Jay Gatsby had been) by the purity of his aesthetic passion. Who, after all, is really to blame for the murder—Francis, or the ugly civilization that had spawned him and then starved his imagination for so long?[22]

It was a theme worthy of the talent of a Hawthorne or a Henry James. But once Fitzgerald had introduced his main characters and es-

tablished the nature of Francis' moral conflict, he seemed unable to continue with his story. We know that he let Max Perkins see the first two
chapters in 1928, and promised to send two more when they were
ready, but never did. One trouble was that, according to his original
plan, when he reached the end of the fourth chapter he should have
been one-third of the way through the plot; actually he had hardly
begun! And so far, not one appealing character had emerged. The more
he reworked his material, the staler his inspiration became. By the time
he began to write the last version of Chapter IV, his cast of characters
had become so tiresome that he finally quit the whole story in mid-
sentence—apparently too bored to keep on! At this stage Abe Grant has
turned into a prig who preaches to his old friends, Seth and Dinah
Piper. The Pipers reciprocate by gossiping unpleasantly about Abe and
Mary to Francis. Francis, when we take our final leave of him, is busy
trying to find some way to seduce his benefactor's wife Dinah without
Seth's knowledge.

At some point during his revision of this material, Fitzgerald decided
to move the chapter with the Roman setting, and to have the book begin
instead with the Riviera hotel setting. He also became dissatisfied with
the third-person method of narration that he had adopted, and started
over with a first-person narrator: an anonymous young American who
says he once knew Francis Melarky back in the United States. But he
soon abandoned this device, probably because he was unable to develop
any kind of fruitful relationship between the narrator and the hero, as
he had in *The Great Gatsby*. Instead he returned to a third-person
method of narration that limited itself primarily to Francis' point of
view.

Then, in June, 1929, Fitzgerald wrote Max Perkins that he had been
"working night and day on the novel from new angle." Whether he
actually decided to discard Francis Melarky and begin a new story, as
Arthur Mizener believes, or merely to write a fresh opening, we do not
know. But it was at this time that he wrote the eleven-thousand-word
fragment that represented a new beginning. The setting is a transatlantic
liner en route to Europe. Instead of Francis and his friends, we are introduced to a group of first-class passengers consisting of a young
American couple, Lew and Nicole Kelly, a young Hollywood actress
named Rosemary who is traveling with her mother, and a Yale ex-under-
graduate named Curly. Lew Kelly, we are informed, is a famous movie
director only twenty-seven years old—"save for Griffith, the most successful motion-picture director in the United States." Tired out from
overwork and "the eternal triangle of money, assertiveness and stupidity

[that] made him want to drink and be as rude as possible," Lew has decided to throw up his lucrative Hollywood job and go to Europe to live. He has never been abroad and his impulsive decision to spend the rest of his life on the French Riviera is due to a romantic novel he has recently read. His wife Nicole drinks more than she should and is irrationally jealous of Lew.[23]

Once these characters have been introduced, not much else happens except when Curly inexplicably jumps overboard. This incident disturbs Lew, and after the boy is rescued he goes up and introduces himself. But at this point Fitzgerald once again lost control of his material, which trails off in a long, maudlin monologue of Lew's. Among other things, Lew admits to himself that he dislikes Curly because the boy reminds him so much of the other rich boys at Yale who stole away his girl, Marva.

In certain respects Lew bears a striking resemblance to Rex Ingram, the young American movie director whom Fitzgerald met at Antibes during the summer of 1925. Like Lew, Ingram attended Yale and then became a celebrity while he was still in his twenties, through his direction of such spectacular silent films as *The Four Horsemen of the Apocalypse, The Prisoner of Zenda,* and *Scaramouche.* Then tiring of Hollywood, he went abroad to live.[24]

According to Arthur Mizener, it was about the time that this new opening was written, in the summer of 1929, that Fitzgerald decided to abandon the idea of Francis Melarky altogether and began the novel about Dick Diver that was eventually to become *Tender Is the Night.* But this seems unlikely for several reasons. Nowhere in his correspondence did Fitzgerald indicate that he had decided to scratch the Melarky story and start over again. On the contrary, his letters suggest that he is making even better progress than usual with the old plan. In one letter of September, 1929, for example, he refers quite specifically to his plans for the novel on which he has been working now "for about five years." Furthermore, so much of the subject matter of *Tender Is the Night* (except what he salvaged from "The Boy Who Killed His Mother") was based on the events that followed Zelda's breakdown in 1930, that it is difficult to see what portion of that book could have been written in 1929. While we do not know what Fitzgerald planned to do with the material about Lew Kelly, it is quite possible that this was merely a new start for "The Boy Who Killed His Mother." At the time the episode was written, those who envied Rex Ingram his success were saying that he owed it chiefly to the talents of a young film cutter, and that without this man's help he would be unable to make a first-rate film.

Francis Melarky had been a Hollywood film cutter. Perhaps Lew Kelly is on his way to Europe in search of the young man who is so necessary to his professional success?[25]

Whatever his original intention may have been, Fitzgerald afterwards made very little use of this "shipboard" material in *Tender Is the Night*. Both the figures of Rosemary and her mother, and of the husband and jealous wife en route to Europe, had already been much more fully developed in his magazines stories. Indeed the only incident he incorporated into *Tender* was the episode of Curly's jumping into the Atlantic. It later turns up in Chapter XIX, Book II (of the magazine serial version) where Dick Diver's boat trip back to France after his father's funeral is described. Actually it makes no more sense at this point in *Tender Is the Night* than it did in the fragment, but Fitzgerald clung to it through the many revisions of Chapter XIX, and retained it in the *Scribner's* magazine version, though he finally deleted it at the last minute from the book version. Chapter XIX was confused enough without this additional episode.

What Fitzgerald's plans were in June, 1929, when he wrote his new opening for "The Boy Who Killed His Mother," is an academic question. He was to have little opportunity of any kind to work on a novel for the next several years. He was already busy meeting his schedule of a new *Saturday Evening Post* story every six weeks, and after Zelda's collapse the following spring there was even less time to devote to the novel. Thus it was not until the beginning of 1932, after he had returned from his second Hollywood visit, that he was financially secure enough to settle down to a period of sustained writing. By now, so much had happened to his marriage and to his feelings about Zelda and Europe, that he viewed his material somewhat differently. Rather than starting afresh, he decided instead to narrow his scope, and to write a shorter novel of around 70,000 words. That, at any rate, had been his intention in December, 1931. But Zelda's second breakdown several weeks later and the necessity of taking her to Johns Hopkins had forced him to delay this plan. It was mid-summer before he was settled at "La Paix" and ready to begin work again. By this time his plan was once more radically changed.[26]

The reason for this was *Save Me the Waltz*, the autobiographical novel that Zelda had written during a furious six weeks in January and February, 1932, soon after she entered Johns Hopkins Hospital. It was a desperate and moving attempt to give order to her confused memories. It was also a bitter attack on Fitzgerald, who was thinly disguised in her manuscript as "Amory Blaine." She had sent it to Max Perkins in

March without Fitzgerald's knowledge, and Perkins was enough impressed to be willing to publish it. Besides its obvious merits, both he and Fitzgerald agreed with Zelda's physicians that bringing it out would be good for her shattered ego. It would help to resolve the jealousy of her husband's success that was one of her most serious obsessions. Fitzgerald insisted on going over her manuscript, however, changing or deleting considerable revealing material about their marriage. At first, Zelda refused to undertake the necessary revision, but—with Fitzgerald's encouragement—finally reworked it. She also corrected the galley proofs; but Fitzgerald's handwriting on them shows that he took time out during July and August to rework them too.[27]

When he finally returned to his own novel in July, 1932, he viewed it from a new vantage point. Now it would include a defense of his marriage against the attacks of neglect and irresponsibility that had been leveled at him in *Save Me the Waltz*. He had been greatly affected by his reading of Zelda's novel, and the portrait she had painted of their marriage, and this is evident in the intensity with which he attacked his work. He now drew up a work schedule according to which his first draft would not be finished for at least twelve more months. Instead of the short novel of some 70,000 words that he planned in January, he now outlined a new one that would run to some 130,000 words. *Tender Is the Night* was to be both a reply to *Save Me the Waltz* and a defense: a defense not so much of himself as of a point of view quite different from the one presented in Zelda's story.

Thus, *Tender Is the Night*, upon which Fitzgerald worked for the next year and a half, evolved into a much more complex and ambitious piece of work than "The Boy Who Killed His Mother." Any attempt to come to terms with it must take account of *Save Me the Waltz*. Together, these two chronicles of the same marriage seen from the wife's and the husband's points of view, form one of the most unusual pairs of novels in recent literary history.

XI
Save Me the Waltz:
1932

Quite apart from its connection with *Tender Is the Night,* Zelda Fitz-gerald's novel, *Save Me the Waltz,* deserves attention for several other reasons. It was one of the first and still is one of the best stories that has been written by an American about the career of a ballerina. It is also one of the authentic literary documents of the post-World War I decade. Who, after all, was better qualified to write the history of the American girl during that era than Zelda? A child of the century, born in 1900, she had sat for her portrait as Rosalind, first of the flappers, in *This Side of Paradise* and had married its author before she was twenty years old.

During the decade that followed, no one accepted the new phi-losophy of the flapper more completely nor defended it more outspokenly than did Zelda. "All neurotic women of thirty and all divorce cases, according to the papers, . . . [can] be traced to the flapper," she had written in 1922 in a popular magazine article vindicating her way of life. "As a matter of fact she hasn't yet been given a chance. I know of no divorcées and no neurotic women of thirty who were flappers." But be-fore she herself was thirty, her own marriage had fallen apart and she was confined to a mental institution. Exactly a decade elapsed between her marriage in April, 1920, and her collapse into schizophrenia in Paris in April, 1930.[1]

During the decade preceding World War I, the American girl had won her freedom, so to speak, at the barricades—striking for better working conditions, going to jail for the right to vote, and otherwise assuming the traditional male prerogatives. As a result, her younger sister, the post-war flapper, was given her freedom before she had actually earned it. For the girl whose twentieth birthday fell during the year 1920, as Zelda's did, it seemed for one historic moment as though there were nothing she could not do or be, if she tried hard enough. But only at a price. Few documents surviving from the 1920's record more movingly than Zelda's novel the price the women of her generation paid for their boundless sense of freedom. *Save Me the Waltz* deserves to be read by everyone who ever shared Zelda's belief that happiness consists in doing just what one wants, or who ever envied her because she had the opportunity to live by that principle.

But a word of caution. The reader who opens *Save Me the Waltz* for the first time without advance warning is bound to be puzzled and exasperated by Zelda's baffling literary style. What, for example, is he to make of a passage such as this, right at the beginning of the story?[2]

> Incubated in the mystic pungence of Negro mammies, the family hatched into girls. From the personification of an extra penny, a street-car ride to whitewashed picnic grounds, a pocketful of peppermints, the Judge became, with their matured perceptions, a retributory organ, an inexorable fate, the force of law, order, and established discipline. Youth and age: a hydraulic funicular, and age, having less of the waters of conviction in its carriage, insistent on equalizing the ballast of youth. The girls, then, grew into the attributes of femininity, seeking respite in their mother from the exposition of their young-lady years as they would have haunted a shady grove to escape a blinding glare.

Fortunately this turgid prose clears up about a third of the way through *Save Me the Waltz*, and Zelda's writing begins to take on professional luster and sparkle. By then, the reader has discovered that he is participating in a remarkable experience. Before the reader's eyes, as it were, Zelda has succeeded in imposing imaginative order on the raw material of her shattered past, and in giving it objective structure and meaning. What began as a haunted nightmare has been transformed into a lucid and moving story. Understandably, the reader accustomed to a Faulkner's or a Dostoevski's more artful rendering of a diseased state of mind flinches at first before Zelda's much cruder transcriptions of reality. But, before long, he is watching fascinated as her imagination detaches itself from the crazy burden of personal history and creates a story capable of commanding his attention and sympathy. The result is a novel of cumulative power that continues to reverberate in the memory long after it has been laid aside.

The facts of Zelda Fitzgerald's life differed little from those of her heroine, "Alabama Beggs." Like Alabama, she was born in 1900, the youngest of a family of four girls. Zelda's own father, Anthony Dickinson Sayre, was a typical Southern gentleman of the old school—poor, genteel, proud. His father, Daniel Sayre, had been a well-known Alabama newspaper publisher. His mother, the former Musidora Morgan, was the sister of John Tyler Morgan, a brigadier general in the Confederate army who later served for over thirty years as United States Senator from Alabama. Anthony Dickinson Sayre, born in 1858, attended Roanoke College in Virginia and then returned to Montgomery, the state capital of Alabama, where he read for the law, practiced as an attorney, and served successively as clerk of the city court, state representative, state senator, and president of the senate. In 1909, he was named a justice of the state supreme court and adorned that bench until his death in 1931 at the age of seventy-four.

In 1884 he married Minnie Buchner Machen, the daughter of Senator Willis B. Machen of Kentucky. Like his good friend Senator Morgan from Alabama, Machen was an unreconstructed rebel. During the Civil War, while Kentucky had been ruled for a time by two rival governments, Machen served as president of the Confederate Council, until he was forced to flee with a price on his head. After his flight his wife and children were incarcerated in a Federal prison where, it was said, their hardships and suffering brought about one daughter's death and temporarily deranged his wife's mind. Their second daughter, Minnie, had both dramatic and literary talents, and dreamed for a time of a professional career in the legitimate theater. But her hope of going to Philadelphia to study dramatics was cut short when, in 1884, there was serious talk by many Southern Democrats of nominating her father for the Presidency. No aspirant for that high office could risk having a daughter connected with the stage![3]

Instead she went to Montgomery to visit the family of Senator Morgan, and there at a New Year's Eve ball she met and was courted by the Senator's nephew, Anthony Dickinson Sayre. In time she bore him six children: two sons who did not survive their early youth, and four daughters, Marjorie, Rosalind, Clothilde, and Zelda. They were high-strung, strong-willed children, and it was said they inherited the Machen taint of melancholia. Zelda, the youngest and prettiest, was also the most spoiled. Judge Sayre was forty-two when she was born. And to Zelda, growing up during the restless World War I years, her father's

courtly manners and pompous dignity made him seem a monument to a
fading way of life. Though she believed that his moral scruples were as
out-of-date as his manners, she depended on him far more than she realized. Adopting his self-assurance as well as his ramrod posture, she always behaved as though her conduct, too, were above reproach. It was
not, however. When she graduated from high school in June, 1918, she
had the reputation of being not only one of the prettiest and most
popular, but one of the fastest girls in the class.

Quite likely many of the stories about her drinking and petting and
swimming in the nude were exaggerated. If they were, no one cared
less than Zelda. Certainly, they did nothing to diminish her popularity
with the college boys at Alabama State and Georgia Tech, where she was
in constant demand for dances and house parties, or with the young
officers stationed at nearby Camp Sheridan. Like her heroine, Alabama
Beggs, she was eager to marry and escape "from the sense of suffocation
that seemed to her to be eclipsing her family, her sisters and mother."
But as she frankly admitted to Fitzgerald, she did not intend to do so
until she had found someone with enough money to gratify her desire
for expensive adventures.[4]

> She, she told herself, would move brightly along high places and
> stop to trespass and admire, and if the fine was a heavy one—well,
> there was no good in saving up beforehand to pay it. Full of these
> presumptuous resolves, she promised herself that if, in the future,
> her soul should come starving and crying for bread it should eat
> the stone she might have to offer without complaint or remorse. Re-
> lentlessly she convinced herself that the only thing of significance was
> to take what she wanted when she could.

Like Alabama, too, Zelda "want[ed] life to be easy and full of
pleasant reminiscences. . . . Obligations were to Alabama a plan and a
trap laid by civilization to ensnare and cripple her happiness and hobble
the feet of time." Marriage, instead of an assumption of new responsibilities, was an escape from old ones. "I believe it has always been
understood between us," Alabama reminds David Knight, her artist
husband, after their marriage, "that we would not interfere with each
other." To this principle Zelda herself clung determinedly during the
next ten years. When, successively, New York, St. Paul, Long Island, and
Wilmington bored her, there was always her beloved Paris, where the
parties never ceased. "Nobody knew whose party it was," she wrote in
Save Me the Waltz. "It had been going on for weeks. When you felt

you couldn't survive another night you went home and slept, and when you got back a new set of people had consecrated themselves to keeping it alive." Later, in a Paris night club, when the waiter brings the check, Alabama insists on paying for everything herself. "This is my party," she tipsily insists, ". . . I've been giving it for years."[5]

But finally even the Paris parties lose their savor. "I can't stand this any longer," she cries pathetically to her husband after one especially hectic evening. "I don't want to sleep with the men or imitate the women, and I can't stand it! . . . Oh, David . . . I'm much too proud to care—pride keeps me from feeling half the things I ought to feel." But David, who by now is tired of her drinking and carousing, and who has his own career as a successful painter to occupy him, can only answer impatiently, "Care about what? Haven't you had a good time?"[6]

Then one evening Alabama's life suddenly assumes fresh purpose and meaning. Like all the other evenings, this particular one has begun in the usual way with a crowd of drunken expatriates in the American bar of a fashionable Paris hotel. Besides Alabama and David, there are Dickie Axton ("She shot her husband in the Gare de l'Est"), Dickie's friend, a certain Miss Douglas ("She was English. You couldn't tell whom she had slept with"), and Miss Douglas' companion, an American musician named Hastings ("an intangible reprobate, discouraging people and living like a moral pirate"). From the American bar, these charming people move on restlessly to one entertainment after another, including a program of Russian ballet at the Théâtre du Châtelet. Here, watching the dancing, Alabama is struck by the contrast between its disciplined grace and beauty and the ugly confusion of her own existence. Afterwards, in a crowded, smoke-filled night club, she is introduced to a Russian princess who has once been a star with the Imperial ballet corps, and who now trains dancers in her own studio for Diaghilev. Impressed once more by the contrast between the noisy disorder of their surroundings and this woman's poised serenity, Alabama impetuously persuades the princess to let her attend one of her ballet classes.[7]

Once Alabama's dance lessons begin, the muddy language of *Save Me the Waltz* immediately starts to clear up. Instead of image-encrusted expository prose, we get dramatic scenes of great power. Leaving the chaos of her youth behind, Zelda has now reached the most satisfying period of her life: those afternoons in 1928 and 1929 that she spent dancing in the Paris studio of Lubov Egorova, the Princess Troubetsky. Following her retirement from the Russian Imperial ballet, where she had been a famous prima ballerina, Egorova had opened a school in

Paris in 1923 at the instigation of Diaghilev. Zelda met her two years later through the Gerald Murphys, whose small daughter attended one of her ballet classes.[8]

Alabama's husband, the successful David Knight, has nothing but scorn for his wife's dream of becoming a professional dancer. She is much too old to begin; and her grueling afternoons, sweating in front of a mirror at the ballet bar, exasperate him. "Are you under the illusion that you'll ever be any good at that stuff?" he inquires patronizingly. "There's no use killing yourself. I hope that you realize that the biggest difference in the world is that between the amateur and the professional in the arts." When she tries to tell him about the pleasure she finds in her lessons, he laughs and calls her a mystic. "You're not the first person who's ever tried to dance. . . . You don't need to be so sanctimonious about it."[9]

Finally, after long weeks of practice, Alabama is given the chance to make her professional debut in a theater in Naples. On Madame's recommendation, she has been invited to dance with the ballet corps of an Italian opera company. The scenes describing her adventures living in a seedy boardinghouse, and performing with a broken-down troupe of Neapolitan singers and dancers, are among the funniest in the novel. Equally comic, but more poignant, are Zelda's descriptions of Alabama's husband and their small daughter impatiently waiting in a dull Swiss summer hotel for news of her opening night triumph. It is hard to believe that the dazed mind which began this story has been able to attain such mastery over her material. But now Zelda is completely detached from her past, and can shape it with cool, controlled prose.

She has finally left her personal tragedy behind and soared off on the wings of her imagination. Actually, the invitation to dance professionally that Zelda had longed for with such impatience never came. Nor was she ever able to convince Fitzgerald that she too had creative talent. Instead she wore herself out in Egorova's studio until she broke down and was forced to give up her dreams of becoming a professional *danseuse.*

Once Alabama has achieved her triumphant debut as a ballerina, *Save Me the Waltz* plunges back again into nightmarish fantasy. Alabama's foot becomes infected, and she eventually collapses into raving delirium. When she awakens in a hospital, she learns that, in order to save her foot, the surgeon has had to cut the tendons; she will never be able to dance again. Her husband, who has hurried from Switzerland, does his best to comfort her. But because he has never realized what her dancing meant to her, his words are of little help. "We have each other," he says. "Yes—what's left," is her bitter reply. "She had always meant to take what she wanted from life. Well—she hadn't wanted this."[10]

Soon afterward she gets word that her father is seriously ill, and with David and their daughter, Bonnie, she hastens home. Faced for the first time with the realization that her father is going to die, Alabama wonders how she will survive her loss.

> She thought of the time when she was little and had been near her father—by his aloof distance he had presented himself as an infallible source of wisdom, a bed of sureness. She could trust her father. She half-hated the unrest of David, hating that of herself that she found in him. Their mutual experiences had formed them mutually into an unhappy compromise. That was the trouble; they hadn't thought that they would have to make any adjustments as their comprehensions broadened their horizons, so they accepted those necessary reluctantly, as compromise instead of change. They had thought they were perfect. . . .

Without her father, Alabama thinks, she will have lost her last resource. Or will she? "It will be me who is the last resource," she tells herself, "when my father is dead."[11]

After his funeral Alabama withdraws more and more into her own secret world. At the end of the novel, when David finds her brooding alone in a dark corner and asks what she is thinking about, she can only tell him, "Forms, shapes of things." These words remind us of the incident several chapters earlier in which Alabama had come into Madame's studio one day and discovered the old princess serenely sitting all alone studying the vacant distance. "What do you find in the air that way?" Alabama had inquired. "Forms, child, shapes of things." "Is it beautiful?" she asked. "Yes." "I will dance it," Alabama had promised. Now she can only weave and reweave the shattered fragments of her dreams into a private ballet of her own.[12]

"Why have we practically wasted the best years of our lives?" David asks impatiently in the novel's concluding pages. "So that there will be no time left on our hands at the end," is Alabama's answer. ". . . [T]he object of the game is to fit things together so that when Bonnie [their small daughter] is as old as we and investigates our lives, she will find a beautiful harmonious mosaic." To the making of this secret mosaic Zelda was to devote the rest of her life, until she died in a disastrous fire (along with eight other women patients) at Highland Hospital for Nervous Diseases near Asheville, North Carolina, on March 11, 1948.[13]

Thus, *Save Me the Waltz* is a great deal more than a clinical document of schizophrenia. "It's very difficult to be two simple people at once—one who wants to have a law to itself and the other who wants to keep all the nice old things and be loved and safe and protected," she says of her heroine in a passage that combines Zelda's own lawless grammar with her pathetic need for order and security. With one side of her nature she continued to cling to the moral certainties represented by her father, while at the same time she let herself be swept up in the hectic quest for new experiences. "We grew up founding our dreams on the infinite promises of American advertising," Alabama admits ruefully at one point toward the end of the novel. "I *still* believe that one can learn to play the piano by mail and that mud will give you a perfect complexion."[14]

What makes Zelda's novel such a remarkable experience is that we are able to participate to such a degree in her effort to impose imaginative unity on her divided and shattered past. She begins by trying to write conventional, straightforward narrative history. But because she has no stable point of view from which to judge her experience, the result is chaos. She cannot reduce her past to an orderly chronological arrangement of facts, nor can she establish fruitful cause-and-effect relationships, nor make meaningful generalizations. Take, for example, the passage quoted at the beginning of this chapter, in which she confronts for the first time the problem of writing about her father. Unable to sort out or to control her feelings about Judge Sayre, she can only pile on top of one another the welter of images that are associated in her memory with him.

However, once Zelda reaches the point where her life takes on purpose and meaning—in the dancing studio of Egorova—the chaos in her writing (and her mind) disappears. No wonder she clung to those dancing lessons as persistently as she did, despite Fitzgerald's objections and lack of sympathy. They gave her the first security she had known since leaving Montgomery. Her dancing became for her a total—a religious—commitment. When, in *Save Me the Waltz*, she later tried to express what dancing meant to her, she inevitably fell back on religious metaphor and imagery. "My friend tells me you want to dance. Why?" Madame asks Alabama curiously at the first lesson. "You have friends and money already." "[Because] . . . it seemed to me—Oh, I don't know.

As if it held all the things I've always tried to find in everything else,"
Alabama replies intensely.[15]

> This first glimpse of the dance as an art opened up a world. "Sacri-
> lege," she felt like crying out to the posturing abandon of the past.
> . . . It seemed to Alabama that, reaching her goal, she would drive
> the devils that had driven her—that, in proving herself, she would
> achieve that peace which she imagined went only in surety of one's
> self—that she would be able, through the medium of the dance, to
> command her emotions, to summon love or pity or happiness at will,
> having provided a channel through which they might flow. . . .
> David's success was his own—he had earned his right to be critical
> —Alabama felt that she had nothing to give the world and no way to
> dispose of what she took away.
>   The hope of entering Diaghilev's ballet loomed before her like a
> protecting cathedral.

Afterwards, when a friend asks Alabama why she insists on wearing
herself out at her lessons day after day, Zelda says in her defense:[16]

> [She] had never felt so close to a purpose as she did at that moment.
> . . . She felt that she would know [the answer] when she could listen
> with her arms and see with her feet. It was incomprehensible that
> her friends should feel only the necessity to hear with their ears. That
> was "Why."

This longing for total communication—to speak, as it were, with
the voice of God—was for Zelda a passionate compulsion. In her writing,
as in her dancing and her painting, she was continually trying to transcend the limits of physical reality, to "listen with her arms and see with
her feet." It was mad, of course, but it was the madness of the artist.[17]
It shows up also in the painting to which she turned with considerable
success after she was no longer able to dance. In 1934, a showing of her
work was held in a Manhattan gallery. One painting of which she was
especially fond, now in the municipal art gallery in Montgomery, represented two dancers in motion, their legs and arms oddly distorted. "I
painted them that way to express the pure quality of what it was they
were dancing," she told me when she showed it to me in 1947. "It wasn't
the dancers but the step itself that I wanted to paint."[17]

The need to go beyond the borders of the senses, to express the in-
expressible, was also responsible for her weird, synesthetic prose. In

writing of this type, the senses become confused. Trumpets blare scarlet colors, the blue sky feels cool, the deserts burn with a yellow intensity, and smells, odors, tastes, visual images, and tactile sensations pile up on another. It is a kind of writing frequently exhibited by schizoid personalities, often with fresh and striking results. Although it is disturbing when first encountered at the beginning of *Save Me the Waltz*, where it often rages uncontrolled, it sometimes endows Zelda's prose with an elegant intensity.

High parabolas of Schumann fell through the narrow brick court and splashed against the red walls in jangling crescendo . . . Asthmatic Christmas bells tolled over Naples: flat metallic sheets of sound like rustled sheafs of roofing. . . . The afternoon . . . scratched itself on the yellow flowers. . . .

Yellow roses she bought with her money like Empire satin brocade, and white lilacs and pink tulips like moulded confectioner's frosting, and deep-red roses like a Villon poem, black and velvety as as insect wing, cold blue hydrangeas clean as a newly calcimined wall, the crystalline drops of lily-of-the-valley, a bowl of nasturtiums like beaten brass, anemones pieced out of wash material, and malignant parrot tulips scratching the air with their jagged barbs, and the voluptuous scrambled convolutions of Parma violets. She bought lemon-yellow carnations perfumed with the taste of hard candy, and garden roses purple as raspberry puddings, and every kind of white flower the florist knew how to grow. She gave Madame gardenias like white kid gloves, and forget-me-nots from the Madeleine stalls, threatening sprays of gladioli and the soft, even purr of black tulips. She bought flowers like salads and flowers like fruits, jonquils and narcissus, poppies and ragged robins, and flowers with the brilliant carnivorous qualities of Van Gogh. She chose from windows filled with metal balls and cactus gardens of the florists near the rue de la Paix, and from the florists uptown who sold mostly plants and purple iris, and from florists on the left bank whose shops were lumbered up with wire frames of designs, and from outdoor markets where the peasants dyed their roses to a bright apricot, and stuck wires through the heads of the dyed peonies.[18]

Such jagged imagery is especially suited to the nightmare agonies that Alabama undergoes while she is in the hospital in Naples. Here Zelda was remembering her own delirium in the Swiss mental sanatorium in 1930:[19]

The walls of the room slid quietly past, dropping one over the other like the leaves of a heavy album. They were all shades of grey and rose and mauve. There was no sound when they fell.

Two doctors came and talked together. What did Salonika have to do with her back?

"I've got to have a pillow," she said feebly. "Something broke my neck!"

The doctors stood impersonally at the end of the bed. . . . "This afternoon, then, at three," said one of the men, and left. The other went on talking to himself.

"I can't operate," she thought he said, "because I've got to stand here and count the white butterflies today."

"And so the girl was raped by a calla-lilly," he said, "—or, no, I believe it was the spray of a shower bath that did the trick!" he said triumphantly.

He laughed fiendishly. How could he laugh so much of "Pucinello." And he as thin as a matchstick and tall as the Eiffel Tower! . . .

. . . The walls began again. She decided to lie there and frustrate the walls if they thought they could press her between their pages like a bud from a wedding bouquet. For weeks Alabama lay there. The smell of the stuff in the bowl took the skin off her throat and she spat red mucous. . . .

. . . Sometimes her foot hurt her so terribly that she closed her eyes and floated off on the waves of the afternoon. Invariably she went to the same delirious place. There was a lake there so clear that she could not tell the bottom from the top; a pointed island lay heavy on the waters like an abandoned thunderbolt. Phallic poplars and bursts of pink geranium and a forest of white-trunked trees whose foliage flowed out of the sky covered the land. Nebulous weeds swung on the current: purple stems with fat animal leaves, long tentacular stems with no leaves at all, swishing balls of iodine and curious chemical growths of stagnant waters. Crows cawed from one deep mist to another.

Save Me the Waltz ultimately fails as a novel. Except for a few comic scenes in the second half, it rarely arouses any emotion except pity. Its humanity lies less in its art than in its documentary proof of the remarkable survival powers of the imagination. Although Zelda, when she wrote it, was unable to cope rationally with either her literal past or the immediate everyday world, she was still capable of inventing an imaginary world of striking beauty and order. The world in which Alabama dances and fulfills herself is a true one—a finer and more convincing one than the ruins from which it had been created by Zelda's imagination. It is a world that she was able to view with humor and detachment, and she succeeded in conveying her feelings about it with insight and passion.

Certainly, *Save Me the Waltz* offers a more sensitive account of the deranged wife's view of her marriage than we find in her husband's version, *Tender Is the Night*. The disturbing thing about both novels is their authors' mutual failure to comprehend the other's point of view. Dick Diver and Alabama Beggs, the two centers of interest, are proof that the more unsympathetic portraits of their respective spouses, Nicole Diver and David Knight, must be heavily discounted. No wonder the Fitzgerald marriage failed. Nor is it surprising that, after spending the spring and summer of 1932 correcting both the manuscript and the galley proofs of *Save Me the Waltz*, Fitzgerald, on returning to his novel, should have extensively overhauled and expanded his plans. How elaborate that overhauling was we do not know precisely. But in the process, *Tender Is the Night* clearly became a defense of his role in their marriage. This new purpose had the advantage of involving Fitzgerald more deeply in his subject matter than he had ever been in "The Boy Who Killed His Mother." But it meant that he would have to discover a form and structure that would allow him to make use of his experience, and yet keep him from getting lost in self-pity and remorse.

XII
Tender
Is the Night:
1932-1934

Unlike *The Great Gatsby, Tender Is the Night*[*] was written under the most difficult circumstances. Rarely during the twenty months that Fitzgerald was occupied with it (from July, 1932, to February, 1934) was he able to give it his undivided attention for more than a few days at a time. Besides Zelda and Scottie and a large house with servants to be attended to, there were the constant financial worries. Scribner's monthly advance was not sufficient to cover his expenses, and before long he was back again writing for the magazines. But with the novel absorbing most of his creative energy, the stories were harder to write than ever. He wasted hours on countless ideas that eventually fizzled out and managed to finish only six stories during this time. Although none of them was especially good, Ober managed to sell five. But only after Fitzgerald had revised them further at the request of magazine editors who were increasingly hard to please.

By June, 1932, after five months in the hospital, Zelda was well enough to be moved to "La Paix." Although she continued to require nursing, Fitzgerald refused to give up hope that she might eventually be cured. During the following winter he took time off from his novel to help her write a play for a local dramatic club, and he also provided

---

[*] Since *Tender Is the Night* is available in two different texts, the original 1934 version (which begins with Rosemary's point of view) and the 1952 version edited by Malcolm Cowley (in which Rosemary's section has been moved to a later position), it should be noted that all references to this novel are, unless otherwise specified, to the 1934 text.

some lyrics for a musical revue that was staged by neighborhood ama-
teurs. During the spring of 1933, however, Zelda's eccentricities grew
more pronounced and by summer her physicians had given up all hope
of her recovery. In January, 1934, while Fitzgerald was in the midst of
the delicate job of correcting and revising the galley proofs of *Tender
Is the Night,* she suffered a third collapse—the gravest so far—and again
had to be hospitalized.

Most of this time Fitzgerald himself had not been well. His habit of
working until he was exhausted, often for twenty-four hours or longer
at a stretch, fortified only by liquor, cigarettes, and black coffee, did not
help matters. After such a bout, he frequently spent several days in bed.
His nerves were bad, and he was becoming more and more of a hypochondriac. He was especially worried about his tubercular tendencies;
a protracted cold usually sent him packing to the hospital. His Ledger
during the year and a half that he devoted to writing *Tender Is the
Night* makes gloomy reading: "Servant trouble . . . political worries,
almost neurosis . . . drinking increased . . . arguments with Scottie . . .
quarrel with Hemingway . . . quarrel with Bunny Wilson . . . quarrel
with Gerald Murphy . . . breakdown of car . . . tight at Eddie Poe's . . .
sick again . . . first borrowing from mother . . . sick . . . "The Fire" [which
Zelda started accidentally, gutting the entire top floor of "La Paix"] . . .
Zelda weakens and goes to Hopkins . . . one servant and eating out."

In the midst of this confusion, *Tender Is the Night* slowly took form.
By August, 1932, the main outlines had been sketched, and, during
September and October, Fitzgerald blocked out the chapters and prepared summaries describing the main characters. At this time he also
made himself an elaborate work schedule on which he noted the number
of words he hoped to write—weekly, daily, even hourly—until the book
was finished. On this chart he faithfully recorded his progress each day
until, two weeks later, he had fallen so far behind that he gave it up.[1]

It was September, 1933, before the first draft was finished. He spent
the next four weeks polishing up the opening chapters, and, on October
eighteenth, after a visit to "La Paix," Max Perkins accepted *Tender Is
the Night* for publication. It was to appear first as a four-part serial in
Scribner's, beginning with the January, 1934, issue; the book version
would then be made up from the magazine galley proofs and be released
early in April. The first installment was to be set up immediately; the
other three, all of which needed further revision, were to be delivered
successively in November, December, and January. Besides his regular
royalties, Fitzgerald was to receive $10,000 for the serial rights, $4,000
in cash and $6,000 to be applied against his debt to Scribner's.[2]

After extended correspondence with Scribner's promotion department, he reluctantly agreed to "Tender Is the Night" as the title. Originally, it had been his own suggestion, but, after further thought, he had decided the average book buyer would think it too lyrical. Alternative choices were "The Drunkard's Holiday," "Dr. Diver's Holiday," "Dick and Nicole Diver," and simply "Richard Diver"—the one that he liked best, but that Scribner's felt was inappropriate.[3]

The second installment, consisting primarily of the flashback covering the Divers' earlier history, was delivered to Scribner's on schedule in November. But Fitzgerald still faced the difficult job of cutting his remaining manuscript of 80,000 words down to to two installments of around 30,000 each. The novel was to have been 100,000 words long, but his manuscript had run over by some 50,000. The obvious place to cut was in the second half, much of which was awkward and long-winded. In December, 1933, he took Zelda to Bermuda with the idea of spending a quiet month reworking the last two installments. Instead, he became ill and made little progress. When they returned to "La Paix" after Christmas, he was obliged to work night and day for the next week to get his already overdue third installment into publishable shape. "This was a hurried business," he told Perkins apologetically, "& I intend to do the polishing on the proof. . . . I'll probably have rewritten the whole thing by spring."[4]

But as things turned out, there was never time for him to rewrite it as he hoped. His plan had been to have the last installment completed early in January so that he could spend the next three or four weeks carefully correcting and revising the magazine proofs, which would then be set up in book form. Instead, by the end of January he found himself in the predicament of having to manage three different projects at once: smoothing up the last installment of his manuscript, trying to correct the galley proofs for the second and third magazine installments, and revising the page proofs that were being set up for the book from the text of the first magazine installment. In the midst of this confusion, Zelda collapsed for the third time. He was heartsick about the whole business. Couldn't Scribner's delay the book version until the magazine proofs were out of the way, so that he could give the book proofs the thorough, over-all revision he felt they needed? "I am already confused," he wrote Perkins, "by the multiplicity of irons I have in the fire." But April eleventh had already been set as the publication date. Scribner's did not want to forfeit the publicity resulting from the serialization; besides, Perkins was reluctant to delay again the novel he had postponed so often during the past nine years. As a result, *Tender Is the*

Night never received the final revision that its harassed author knew it should have had.[5]

He had the best of intentions. "Any attempt by an author to explain away a partial failure in a work is of course doomed to absurdity," he wrote Edmund Wilson before the hard-cover version appeared, "—yet I could wish that you, and others, had read the book version rather than the magazine version which in spots was hastily put together. The last half for example has a *much* more polished façade now. . . . I have driven the Scribner proof-readers half nuts but I think I've made it incomparably smoother."[6]

That this was wishful thinking can be readily seen by comparing the serial and hard-cover versions of *Tender Is the Night*. It was the history of *The Beautiful and Damned* all over again. Fitzgerald deleted some passages of inflated prose, put back several episodes that had been omitted from the serialized version because of the sex, and smoothed up some awkward sentences. But, as in his revision of the serial version of his earlier novel, he made only a very few stylistic changes. Most were in the first half of the book where they added little, since it was the later parts that needed the most attention. The opening chapters— salvaged from "The Boy Who Killed His Mother"—had already been reworked many times.

The novel that Scribner's published in book form on April eleventh contained obvious flaws which prevented many reviewers from discerning its more admirable qualities. No one was more uncomfortably aware of these shortcomings than Fitzgerald himself. The margins of his manuscript as well as his personal copy of the published text provide eloquent evidence of this dissatisfaction. "Isn't this a little querulous?" we find him noting opposite one passage in the manuscript. And elsewhere: "Remember to avoid Hemingway," and "This is a poor scene—rewrite entirely before general revision. Remember these two [Dick and Nicole] are all we have and if they get thin the interest dies. The above is thin and sordid, badly imagined and unfelt." "Tiresome stuff," he put at the top of another page—this time in his copy of the book. And on another: "You bog down the book (this is DULL) and never pick it up."[7]

"I did not manage, I think in retrospect, to give Dick the cohesion I aimed at," he later wrote in a letter to one of *Tender's* admirers. And to Max Perkins:[8]

It has become increasingly plain to me that the very excellent organization of a long book or the finest perceptions and judgment in time of revision do not go well with liquor. A short story can be written on a bottle, but for a novel you need the mental speed that enables you to keep the whole pattern in your head and ruthlessly sacrifice the side-shows as Ernest did in "A Farewell to Arms." If a mind is slowed up ever so little it lives in the individual part of a book rather than in a book as a whole; memory is dulled. I would give anything if I hadn't had to write part III of "Tender is the Night" entirely on stimulant. If I had one more crack at it cold sober I believe it might have made a great difference.

The clumsiest writing occurs in Chapters XI to XXII, which describe Dick Diver's feelings during the seven-year-long disintegration of his marriage. This was all part of that ill-fated third installment of the magazine version which Fitzgerald had taken along to Bermuda but on which he had been unable to work. It was also the part that was based most directly on Fitzgerald's personal experience, on his complicated feelings about the mentally unstable wife whom he could no longer treat as a normal human being. In writing this section, he abandoned both of the literary devices that had helped him to control his material in what he had written thus far: Rosemary Hoyt's point of view which he had adopted in Book I, and the third-person narration that he had used in describing Dick Diver's youth in the flashback section at the beginning of Book II. Now, in this third quarter of the story, he hoped to show the extent of Dick's moral disintegration, and his growing sense of guilt, by adopting Dick's point of view. But Fitzgerald was himself implicated in Dick's situation to such an extent that he was unable to deal with it objectively. Instead he lost the necessary aesthetic distance and plunged into a subjective account that at times becomes maudlin with self-pity.[9]

The difficulty was that at this stage Fitzgerald had gotten himself involved in telling two different stories which never quite tied together. The first was the one he had been planning for the past seven years—the tale of the man betrayed by the charm and beauty of American expatriate life in the south of France. The second was the quite different story of a husband hopelessly in love with a schizophrenic wife—a story inspired by Zelda's *Save Me the Waltz*.[10]

Looking back, it seems doubtful that Fitzgerald would ever have overcome the mental block preventing him from completing the first of these two stories, "The Boy Who Killed His Mother." But the stock market crash in the fall of 1929, combined with Zelda's collapse six months later, forced on him a painful realization of the price that this expatriate life had exacted from its inhabitants. This realization was further intensified by the appearance of Zelda's novel two years later. From these events there gradually emerged the idea of Dick Diver, the charming psychiatrist-expatriate whose history embodied both themes. In his charm and social grace Dick exemplified the best traits of that expatriate experience that, from 1919 until 1929, had inspired one of the most fruitful eras in the history of American art. Dick is the creator of the glamorous world he inhabits as well as its most poignant victim: the measure of its moral worth.

Once Fitzgerald had the outlines of Dick Diver's career firmly in mind, he was able to go back and make effective use of most of the material he had written for "The Boy Who Killed His Mother." What would happen to Dick when he discovered that the international café society to whose amusement he had devoted his creative energy and imagination was no longer worthy of his efforts? The story, as Fitzgerald originally planned it, would fall naturally into two parts. "We have . . . the hero treated from without and then entirely from within," he reminded himself in one of his preliminary notes. Dick's exterior virtues would be presented at the beginning from Francis Melarky's point of view. But because of all that he now represented, Dick would be given a more heroic role than had been intended for Seth Piper. And since Dick's subsequent moral disintegration was to be indicated by means of a series of extramarital entanglements, there was reason for replacing Francis, the handsome young film-cutter, with an eighteen-year-old starlet named Rosemary Hoyt.[11]

For Rosemary's external appearance, Fitzgerald now drew heavily on his memories of Lois Moran, the young Hollywood actress whom he met during his trip to California in 1927. Like Rosemary, Miss Moran had been taken abroad by her mother for her education, and had acted in several European films while she was still in her early teens. Through them she attracted the attention of an American producer and was offered a job in Hollywood. A striking blonde with more culture and refinement than the usual movie actress, she was famous before she was eighteen. Her relationship to Fitzgerald was not the erotic one that developed between Dick and Rosemary, however. Since 1927 she had seen very little of the Fitzgeralds; and soon after *Tender Is the Night* appeared she retired from the screen and married a government official who later became a prominent American airlines executive.[12]

Dick Diver shares with Fitzgerald's other heroes the role of the outsider. He is the poor boy who destroys himself by his quest for an impossible dream. But Dick differs from his predecessors—from Gatsby and Francis Melarky—in his qualities of mind and sensibility. His imagination is not only capable of creating the radiant world that Rosemary discovers at the beginning of the novel, but he has the insight to see through that world to its rotten core. Thus, he is more tragic than any of Fitzgerald's previous heroes. Fitzgerald wrote in another of his preliminary notes:[13]

> The novel should do this. Show a man who is a natural idealist, a spoiled priest, giving in for various causes to the ideas of the haute Burgeoise [sic], and in his rise to the top of the social world losing his idealism, his talent and turning to drink and dissipation. Background is one in which the liesure [sic] class is at their truly most brilliant & glamorous such as Murphys.

In another note, he said:[14]

> *The Drunkard's Holiday* will be a novel of our time showing the break up of a fine personality. Unlike *The Beautiful and Damned* the break-up will be caused not by flabbiness but really tragic forces such as the inner conflicts of the idealist and the compromises forced upon him by circumstances.

And of his hero, Dick Diver, he wrote:[15]

> The hero was born in 1891. He is a well-formed rather athletic and fine looking fellow. Also he is very intelligent, widely-read—in fact he has all the talents, including especially great personal charm. This is all planted at the beginning. He is a superman in possibilities, that is, he appears to be at first sight from a burgeoise point of view. However he lacks that tensile strength—none of the ruggedness of Brancusi, Leger, Picasso. For his external qualities use anything of Gerald [Murphy], Ernest [Hemingway], Ben Finny, Archie Mcliesh, Charley McArthur or myself. He looks, though, like me.
>   The faults—the weakness such as the social climbing, the drinking, the desperate clinging to one woman, finally the neurosis, only come out gradually.
>   We follow him from age 34 to age 39.

"*He has all the talents, including especially great personal charm.*" Of Dick Diver's many gifts, the one that, in Fitzgerald's opinion, led most directly to his downfall was his pursuit of that elusive quality called "charm." What more fitting subject was there for contemporary tragedy than this theme of the man of genius destroyed by charm? During Fitzgerald's own lifetime he had seen charm transformed from a simple Victorian virtue usually associated with flowers, women, and children to an important American industry. During the 1920's, especially, charm schools, charm manuals, charm magazines had proliferated at an alarming rate. Charm and "good taste" were gradually supplanting the mere possession of money as evidence of success and prestige. Nowhere was charm more admired than in the new professions of advertising and selling, about which Fitzgerald could find little to admire.

Ever since he had begun "The Boy Who Killed His Mother," Fitzgerald had been searching for some way of dramatizing his convictions about the tragic consequences of this excessive over-valuation of charm. He wrote an admirer in 1929:[16]

> About five years ago I became, unfortunately, interested in the insoluble problems of personal charm and have spent the intervening time on a novel that's going to interest nobody and probably alienate the remaining half dozen who are kind enough to be interested in my work. Unfortunately my sense of material is much superior to my mind or my talent and if I ever survive this damned thing I shall devote my life to musical comedy librettos . . .

One source for Fitzgerald's interest in the subject of charm was the fiction of Willa Cather, particularly *A Lost Lady*. In the letter to her that had accompanied his gift of a copy of *The Great Gatsby* in April, 1925, he praised the skill with which she had conveyed the charm of her heroine, Marian Forrester. In her reply Miss Cather pointed out that charm, like most other ideal qualities, is conveyed more effectively in fiction by the demonstration of its effect on other people, than by the author's attempting to describe it directly. Fitzgerald was so struck by this observation that he later quoted from it literally in one of the passages at the beginning of *Tender Is the Night* in which he analyzed Dick Diver's heroic charm:[17]

> To be included in Dick Diver's world for a while was a remarkable experience: people believed he made special reservations about them, recognizing the proud uniqueness of their destinies, buried under the compromises of how many years. He won everyone quickly with an exquisite consideration and a politeness that moved so fast and intuitively that *it could be examined only in its effect* [my italics].

Dick Diver, in other words, was conceived in heroic terms as nothing less than the original "Man of Distinction," the ubiquitous prototype of so many glossy advertisements for luxury goods, and the epitome of the American way of life. The son of a poor but respectable Episcopalian clergyman, Dick in his youth easily acquired all the badges of conventional middle-class success: a scholarship to Yale, a Rhodes Fellowship to Oxford, a medical degree at Johns Hopkins, and three years of post-doctoral study with the finest Viennese psychiatrists. He has all the stigmata of the man who is on the make. But, instead of continuing the medical career for which he has been trained, he decides to marry the daughter of a fabulously wealthy Chicago meat-packing family. Henceforth he will devote his imagination and energy, and his wife's fortune, to the creation and enjoyment of an expatriate existence of surpassing beauty and charm. "Watching his father's struggles in poor parishes had wedded a desire for money to an essentially unacquisitive nature." In his whole-hearted commitment to this ideal, Dick reflects the priestlike devotion of his father. But Dick is a "spoiled" priest. Renouncing the "grace" of his father's vocation, he has dedicated himself instead (as Fitzgerald ironically remarks) to the pursuit of a very different kind of "grace and adventure."[18]

Dick's dream is to create a life of surpassing beauty for Nicole and himself. It must include social relationships as well as the physical setting. How far he has succeeded we are shown at the beginning of the novel by the rapturous admiration for the Divers' way of life reflected in Rosemary's enchanted eyes. The mood is established from the very first sentence, with its evocation of the breath-taking beauty of the hushed Riviera summer. Gradually the Divers and their friends emerge as part of this beauty—their qualities of charm and taste underscored by contrast with the rowdier English and American tourists Rosemary encounters on the beach. "At that moment," Fitzgerald comments, "the Divers represented externally the exact furthermost evolution of a class." It is the dynamic American middle class, of course, possessed at last of enough money, leisure, and taste to gratify its most rarefied aesthetic desires—gratifying them, as we might expect, primarily in social terms.[19]

Before long, we discover with Rosemary that the charm of this existence is due primarily to Dick Diver's energy and imagination. To Rosemary, he is a paragon among men. "He is after all a sort of super-man," Fitzgerald would later tell an admirer who wanted to dramatize *Tender Is the Night,* "an approximation of the *hero* seen in overcivilized terms—taste is no substitute for vitality but in the book it has to do duty for it. It is one of the points on which he must never show weakness as Siegfried could never show physical fear."[20]

In this sense, it is not unfair to describe the first hundred pages or so of *Tender Is the Night* as one of the best guides ever written on the theory and practice of charm. Every aspect of Dick Diver's personality is examined from this point of view in meticulous detail. Take his voice, for instance:[21]

> His voice, with some faint Irish melody running through it, wooed the world, yet she felt the layer of hardness in him, of self-control and of self-discipline. . . . [It] promised that he would take care of her, and that a little later he would open up whole new worlds for her, unroll an endless succession of magnificent possibilities.

Or the complex art of arranging a day so that it assumes the formal beauty of a work of art:[22]

> The Divers' day was spaced like the day of the older civilizations to yield the utmost from the materials at hand, and to give all the transitions their full value. . . .

Or the executive skill that is the secret of Dick's famous parties:[23]

> The enthusiasm, the selflessness behind the whole performance ravished her, the technique of moving many varied types, each as immobile, as dependent on supplies of attention as an infantry battalion is dependent on rations, appeared so effortless that he still had pieces of his own most personal self for everyone.

Rosemary, responding naïvely to the "expensive simplicity" of the Divers' way of life, is "unaware of its complexity and its lack of innocence, unaware that . . . the simplicity of behavior also, the nursery-like peace and good-will, the emphasis on the simpler values, was part of a desperate bargain with the gods and had been attained through struggles she could not have guessed at." But Nicole, who has watched Dick marshal his energy time after time in preparation for one of his gala affairs, senses something of the cost that it entails.[24]

> [She] saw that one of his most characteristic moods was upon him, the excitement that swept everyone up into it and was inevitably followed by his own form of melancholy, which he never

displayed but at which she guessed. This excitement about things reached an intensity out of proportion to their importance, generating a really extraordinary virtuosity with people. Save among a few of the tough-minded and perennially suspicious, he had the power of arousing a fascinated and uncritical love. The reaction came when he realized the waste and extravagance involved.

Here Fitzgerald was writing about himself as well. Like Dick Diver, he could exercise great charm when he wished to. "In his personal relations," Arthur Mizener says in *The Far Side of Paradise,* "he created a sense of unguarded impulsiveness—perfectly genuine even when used consciously—which was hard to resist. . . . He created an air of interest in those he was with, when he chose to, which is rarely provided for anyone except by himself. He understood very well the mechanism of this effect."[25]

But it was obtained only through the most arduous exercise of will. When that will failed, his natural exuberance and intensity of feeling spilled over into violence and irresponsibility. "The luxuriance of your emotions under the strict discipline which you habitually impose on them," he wrote in one of his Notebook entries, "makes that tensity in you that is the secret of all charm—when you let that balance become disturbed, don't you just become another victim of self-indulgence?— breaking down the solid things around you and, moreover, making yourself terribly vulnerable?"[26]

Externally, Dick appears to Rosemary to be in perfect control of himself and the society he dominates. But what if he begins to doubt the absolute value of the career to which he has dedicated his talents? Not only is charm amoral, but its exercise requires the suspension of moral judgment. What is charm, after all, but the giving away of yourself in little pieces until finally there is nothing left of the individual you once were? "If you spend your life sparing people's feelings and feeding their vanity," Dick finally realizes, "you get so you can't distinguish what *should* be respected in them." Once his immaculate purpose is blunted, he is no longer able to function in his chosen social role. Nor can he any longer provide Nicole with the certitude she needs to hold her fragile mental world together. Instead, she turns elsewhere for support—to her long-time admirer, the amoral Tommy Barban. At the end, his integrity as a person destroyed, Dick has become superfluous.[27]

What is the source of Dick's eventual self-knowledge? Not surprisingly, the bases of his moral judgment of himself and the society he inhabits are those that served Nick Carraway in *The Great Gatsby.* Like

Nick, Dick Diver owes his capacity for judgment to the moral heritage represented by his father, and to his deep-seated apprehension of the certainty that he must die. Before the fact of death not only material possessions but even the social graces of charm and taste become irrelevant.

Dick's first judgment of himself occurs in Chapter XX, Book I, while he is stalking the streets of a shabby suburb of Paris hunting for Rosemary. Although she loves him and had previously offered to go to bed with him, he had refused her because he did not love her. But now, by committing adultery and betraying Nicole's love for him, he thinks that he can bring upon himself the damnation he believes he deserves for the greater sin of having married Nicole for her money. "He knew that what he was now doing marked a turning point in his life."[28]

> . . . Dick's necessity of behaving as he did was a projection of some submerged reality: he was compelled to walk there . . . just as another man once found it necessary to stand in front of a church in Ferrara [Canossa?], in sackcloth and ashes. Dick was paying some tribute to things unforgotten, unshriven, unexpurgated.

And, we might add, "unabsolved." His first mistake had been his renunciation of his father's vocation in order to play the priestly role of father-confessor to a crowd of rich, spoiled Americans. Like Nick Carraway, "Dick loved his father—again and again he referred judgments to what his father would probably have thought or done. . . . [H]is father had been sure of what he was . . . [believing] that nothing could be superior to 'good instincts,' honor, courtesy, courage." Dick's error was his placing the social values of taste and charm above the more fundamental moral instincts.[29]

It is no coincidence that the street down which Dick roams looking for Rosemary bears the ironic name, "Rue de Saintes Anges," nor that its dreary shop signs, "Déclaration de Decès," "Vêtements Ecclésiastiques," "Pompes Funèbres," all speak of death and the church. Instead of finding Rosemary, he encounters a sinister-looking American selling newspapers, who greets him familiarly and shows him a newspaper cartoon depicting "a stream of Americans pouring from the gangplank of a liner freighted with gold." This mysterious stranger shows up unexpectedly again at the end of the book in the episode where Dick is relinquishing his claims to Nicole and preparing to drop below the horizon of civilized society. On this occasion, the newspaper vendor again brings out his soiled cartoon clipping. "You think I'm not going to get part of that?" he asks Dick, pointing to the picture of the well-dressed Americans carrying their bags of gold. "Well, I am." It is not only gold he is talking about, but the people who possess and are possessed by it, like Dick and his friends. There is no doubt about whom this sinister figure was intended to represent. He is the Devil, the symbol of sin and death, like the vacant eyes of Dr. T.J. Eckleburg. Fitzgerald took the paragraph describing him *verbatim* from a 1927 *Post* story, "A Short Trip Home," in which his evil nature was made even more explicit.[30]

Fitzgerald intended that Dick should damn himself a second time by committing adultery with a woman in a hotel at Innsbruck (Chapter XVIII, Book II). Discouraged because Nicole's illness has not responded to treatment, Dick leaves her at the mental sanatorium and goes on a holiday to Munich and then to Austria. In Chapter XVII he encounters Tommy Barban and Tommy's friend, a wealthy American named Hannan. When Hannan hears that Dick is en route to Innsbruck, he offers him a lift. But Hannan is a loud, brassy person; besides, the prospect of riding in Hannan's limousine with the rest of his family and the governess does not appeal to Dick. Instead he goes on alone, and in the next chapter he persuades himself that a mysterious woman staying at his Innsbruck hotel is the dream girl whom he has been pursuing in his imagination for so long.

In the earliest version of this chapter, Dick plans to go to bed with her, only to learn afterwards to his dismay that she is the governess—actually, Hannan's mistress. Later, Fitzgerald deleted this assignation, but the atmosphere of self-disgust and irresponsibility persists. The death imagery is no less explicit than when Dick was tracking down Rosemary along the Rue des Saintes Anges. In the previous chapter Tommy Barban had shocked Dick by telling him the news that Abe North was dead, killed in a barroom brawl. The death theme is sounded again at the end of this chapter as Dick, grieving for Abe, watches a parade of World War I veterans march past carrying wreaths to the graves of their dead comrades-in-arms.[31]

In the next chapter—at the Innsbruck hotel—Dick's affair with his dream girl is abruptly cut off by the arrival of a cable from America announcing the death of his father. Comparing his own career with that of his priestly father, Dick realizes the depths to which he has brought himself and decides to attend the funeral. Kneeling at his father's grave not long afterwards, he says farewell not only to his father ("Good-by, my father—good-by, all my fathers") but to the moral heritage that he has so irresponsibly betrayed.[32]

The religious note occurs again at the end of the novel when Nicole finally asserts her independence by having a physical love affair with Tommy Barban. This time, Fitzgerald describes Nicole's preparations for her meeting with Tommy as though she were a pagan priestess readying herself for the rites of Venus. "She bathed and anointed herself and covered her body with a layer of powder," he says, ". . . put on the first ankle-length day dress that she had owned for many years, and crossed herself reverently with Chanel Sixteen."[33]

Soon afterwards, Dick Diver takes leave of the gay world of the summer Riviera that he had helped to create, but in whose values he no longer believes. As he departs, Fitzgerald says, Dick "raised his hand and with a papal cross . . . blessed the beach from the high terrace." A blasphemous gesture—as one critic has asserted? Is it not rather the sign of Dick's acknowledgment that he is damned?[34]

This, in brief, was the first of the two stories that Fitzgerald hoped to tell in *Tender Is the Night*. It was a restatement in more heroic terms of the theme he had unsuccessfully tried to develop in "The Boy Who Killed His Mother"—the tragedy of a man betrayed by charm. His new novel, as he now began to outline it, was to run to "a little over a hundred thousand words," and would consist of "fourteen chapters, each 7,500 words long." He would begin with the wonderful Riviera opening from "The Boy Who Killed His Mother," and follow this with a flashback describing Dick's previous history, including his courtship of Nicole. This would form about one-third of the book. Then, picking up the original narrative at the point where it had been interrupted by the flashback, he would devote the remaining two-thirds to Dick's moral decline, and the accompanying disintegration of his marriage. In the preliminary synopsis that Fitzgerald made at this time, he said:[35]

> The hero born in 1891 is a man like myself brought up in a family sunk from haute burgeoisie to petit burgeoisie, yet expensively educated. He has all the gifts, and goes through Yale almost succeeding but not quite but getting a Rhodes scholarship which he caps with a degree from Hopkins, & with a legacy goes abroad to study psychology in Zurich. At the age of 26 all seems bright.

But at this point Fitzgerald introduced a new element—the theme of the husband married to a mentally-unbalanced wife. It was not enough that Dick should ruin his career by marrying for money and succumbing to a life of ease and dissipation.

Then he falls in love with one of his patients who has a curious homicidal mania toward men caused by an event of her youth. Aside from this she is the legendary *promiscuous* woman. He "transfers" to himself & she falls in love with him, a love he returns.

After a year of non-active service in the war he returns and marries her & is madly in love with her & entirely consecrated to completing the cure. She is an aristocrat of half American, half European parentage, young, mysterious & lovely, *a new character*. He has cured her by pretending to a stability & belief in the current order he does not have, being in fact a communist—liberal—idealist, a moralist in revolt. But the years of living under patronage ect. & among the burgeoise have seriously spoiled him and he takes up the marriage as a man divided in himself. During the war he has taken to drink a little & it continues as secret drinking after his marriage. The difficulty of taking care of her is more than he has imagined and he goes more and more to pieces, always keeping up a wonderful face.

At the point when he is socially the most charming and inwardly corrupt he meets a young actress on the Rivierra who falls in love with him. With considerable difficulty he contains himself out of fear of all it would entail since his formal goodness is all that is holding his disintegration together. He knows too that he does not love her as he loved his wife. Nevertheless the effect of the repression is to throw him toward all women during his secret drinking when he has another life of his own which his wife does not suspect, or at least he thinks she doesn't. On one of his absences during which he is in Rome with the actress having a disappointing love affair too late he is beaten up by the police. He returns to find that instead of taking a rest cure she has committed a murder and in a revulsion of spirit he tries to conceal it and succeeds. It shows him however that the game is up and he will have to perform some violent & Byronic act to save her for he is losing his hold on her & himself.

He has known slightly for some time a very strong & magnetic man and now he deliberately brings them together. When he finds under circumstances of jealous agony that it has succeeded he departs knowing that he has cured her. He sends his neglected son into Soviet Russia to educate him and comes back to America to be a quack thus having accomplished both his burgeoise sentimental idea in the case of his wife and his ideals in the case of his son, & now being himself only a shell to which nothing matters but survival as long as possible with the old order.

At the beginning Fitzgerald seems to have experienced no major difficulties in the writing of the story outlined in this synopsis. One reason was that he was able to make such good use of the material from "The Boy Who Killed His Mother." It had to be reworked, of course. He had to establish from the beginning the heroic nature of Dick Diver's taste and charm. This he did by cleverly identifying him with the breath-taking beauty of the setting in which the reader and Rosemary first encounter him. Next, he developed the opposing theme of waste and dissipation—muted at first, but reaching a crashing crescendo at the end of Book I when Rosemary learns that Nicole is insane. This theme, in a minor key, is sounded briefly and casually during Rosemary's first encounter with the Divers, when Dick suddenly says ". . . It's not one of the worst times of the day." After this it is repeated again and again, each time with greater emphasis: in the sad little pilgrimage Rosemary makes with Dick and Nicole to the World War I military cemetery outside Paris; in Abe North's helpless fits of drinking; in the sudden shooting of the American on the railway platform at the Gare Saint Lazare; in the sinister newspaper vendor; finally, in the discovery of the body of the dead Negro that triggers Nicole's collapse and reveals to Rosemary the ugly secret hidden behind the polished façade Dick and Nicole present to the world.

None of these incidents in a minor key contribute much to the forward movement of the novel. But each serves an important thematic purpose, and as a whole they possess an emotional power that is cumulative in its effect. Fitzgerald was very much aware of this fact. When Max Perkins suggested, for example, that the scene of the shooting in the Gare Saint Lazare was confusing and unnecessary, and should be deleted, Fitzgerald objected on the following grounds:[36]

> It serves all sorts of subtle purposes and since I have decided that the plan of the book is best as originally conceived, the small paring away would be very little help and I think would do more harm than good.

"I have decided that the plan of the book is best as originally conceived." Instead of explaining Dick's failure, Fitzgerald was more interested in making the reader feel what it is like to fail as Dick has failed. In its complex arrangement of imagery, scenes, and episodes around a major and a minor theme, Fitzgerald's novel (in the first half, at any rate) resembles a musical composition more than a conventional narrative in prose.

Like the breath-taking opening chapter, the flashback describing Dick Diver's earlier history and the lyric episode of his wooing of Nicole were written easily and with marvelous effectiveness. But so far all of this was by way of introduction. The trouble started when Fitzgerald reached the subject of Dick's marriage midway in Book II. It continued all through the muddy middle chapters and ceased only with Dick's decision to separate from Nicole, which led to the final denouement.

One major difficulty was lack of space. According to Fitzgerald's discarded outline, the introductory material leading up to the Divers' married life together was to have comprised only a third of the story— approximately 35,000 words. Instead, the opening chapters and the flashback that followed ran to twice this amount—close to half of a novel that totaled only 130,000 words. One result of this imbalance was that Dick's *external* qualities received a great deal more emphasis than originally planned. Fitzgerald never succeeded in bringing the heroic protagonist treated from Rosemary's point of view into congruence with the pitiful husband who is treated from within throughout the middle chapters of the story. He was still too close to his own unhappy marriage to be able to treat it with detachment. Time and time again he lost himself in private remorse and self-pity. A good example of this is the passage in Chapter XI, Book II, where Dick and Nicole and Baby Warren are together around a table in a Swiss *Bierstube*. Dick, who has become tired of nursing the ill Nicole, begins to dream about a love affair with an imaginary woman. Suddenly he decides that this dream girl is actually one of the girls in the room—a girl sitting at a table nearby.[37]

> Behind him [Fitzgerald says] the girl had leaned forward into a smoke ring and was picking up something from the floor. Nicole's face, fitted into his own across the table—her beauty tentatively nesting and posing, flowed into his love, ever braced to protect it.

Even with different punctuation, it is not easy to follow the sense of this passage. But it is much more lucid than the maudlin version in which it first appeared (I have used italics to show the deleted parts as they appear in Fitzgerald's manuscript):[38]

> Behind him the girl had leaned forward into a smoke ring and was picking up something. Symbol of what? *What old lecher.* Nicole's face, loving and lovely, fitted into his own across the table—

tight, clean and complete, her beauty, delicately, *only* tentatively nesting and posing *always* flowed into his love, into him standing *with legs* with his feet apart braced to protect it—the idea of *all life* duty on a chart *came to* was in him *it the same moment* but he could not seem to freeze *offhand* into *it an immediate* the adjustment. This, thou I will and must continue to envelop *you; and I am* likewise I'm sick *of* with you. *Poke your head here, there and everywhere, your lovely head—how either its mine and I'm tired of it, or best how* But how could I find *looking everywhere,—how could I find* another such lovely lovely. I was only gone *given* one time and *I see met you there* I saw you at the moment when I was best *equipped to for blind with another* prepared for partial and permanent blinding.

From this touching earlier version we can see that Fitzgerald is trying to say that although Dick no longer loves the demented Nicole in a normal manner, nonetheless the memory of the love they knew continually comes between him and every other woman. It is especially poignant because we know it was true of Fitzgerald's feeling about Zelda. But it was an idea he found difficult to put into words.

Another example of his failure to tie up loose threads occurs in the episode at the Innsbruck hotel already mentioned, where Dick gets involved with the Hannan governess. When Fitzgerald decided to delete most of this episode (Book II, Chapter XVIII) from the final version, he forgot to go back one chapter and cut out the preliminary material about Hannan and the governess. The result is that after a careful introduction to Hannan and several references to the governess, neither is ever heard of again!

Fitzgerald was aware of the necessity for careful control over the many details of his complicated plot. On his preliminary work chart, in 1932, he had marked out the fourteen chapters to be written, noted the number of words for each, and drawn a graph showing the rising and falling action. As he finished the draft of each chapter, he put down the number of completed typed pages. But two-thirds of the way through he realized that not only was he writing much more than he had planned, but he had already strayed far afield from his original structure and so he abandoned the chart. Nor did he replace it with a new one. Later, he would regret that he had not followed an outline more carefully in the writing of this complex and confusing novel.[39]

Another mistake was his decision to make Dick Diver a psychiatrist. At the time psychiatry was a rich new field for the popular novelist. But despite Fitzgerald's interest in the technical aspects of Zelda's condition, and his many conversations with her physicians, he really did not know enough about psychiatry to treat it authoritatively. Most important of all, he did not understand how a psychiatrist's mind works.

Before the book was published he asked a specialist at Johns Hopkins to read over his typescript, and afterwards assured Max Perkins that this physician had said that not only was "all the medical stuff . . . accurate," but that *Tender Is the Night* "seems the only good thing ever written on psychiatry." But this is just not so. It is easy to excuse minor inaccuracies like Fitzgerald's misuse of "Cheyne-Stokes tendencies," "cervicle of the brain," and other technical terms. More difficult to overlook is his assumption that anyone with Dick's careful training would so cavalierly disregard well-established professional ethics and marry someone as ill as Nicole, with whom a doctor-patient relationship already existed. It is even more difficult to expect that someone with Dick's intelligence would commit himself to such a marriage, knowing that it was based on the patient's psychotic transference of her affections to her physician, and that it was destined to end with her cure. Dick afterwards is caught in a tragic dilemma: Shall he cure Nicole and lose her love, or destroy himself by dedicating himself to taking care of her? But the alternatives are so unlikely for a psychiatrist that, by getting caught in such a position, Dick loses heroic stature in our estimation. Besides, if Nicole's love is not a genuine, normal love, is the loss of it really so costly? Following her recovery, Nicole reverts to type and chooses instead the more fitting companionship of Tommy Barban. Dick's plight is merely a pathetic one.[40]

The truth is that Dick is not at all a convincing psychiatrist. He is too much like his creator. He is an artist—"an artist in people and in providing for their enjoyment," as Fitzgerald described him in a short synopsis that he provided for the *Scribner's Magazine* version. Dick's frustrated effort to finish the great book on which he has been working for so many years—his *opus magnum*—are not the struggles of the scholarly writer of a scientific treatise, but those of the frustrated author of *Tender Is the Night*. "Most of us have a favorite, a heroic time in our lives." For Dick, according to Fitzgerald, this time had not been during medical school, nor in the clinic (as it would be for the usual research scientist), but the lonely months that he spent writing the manuscript of his first book—a manuscript that, subsequently revised, was to serve as "the backbone of the book he published . . . in 1920" that was to make him famous and to establish his professional reputation.[41]

But once we have made our way through the blurred middle section of *Tender Is the Night,* we come in the final quarter to chapters that are written with the freshness and detachment of the brilliant opening section. Fitzgerald has given up trying to explain the obscure reasons for Dick's (and his own) unhappy marriage, and is no longer justifying himself against the attack of *Save Me the Waltz.* He has returned to his original theme of the man destroyed by charm. These concluding chapters reveal the ugly underside of that expatriate world whose shimmering surface so captivated Rosemary at the beginning. The irresponsibility and wasteful extravagance of this world are portrayed in a series of episodes in which Dick encounters a menagerie of representative specimens: the winsome, vicious Peruvian homosexual; Mary North, remarkably altered for the worse since Abe's death; the repellent Lady Caroline Sibley-Biers. When Mary and Lady Caroline finally get their just deserts and are jailed, Dick musters up his exhausted social talents long enough to charm the chief of police into freeing them. But it is a social role he no longer respects enough to maintain. By now his moral insight into himself and the world which he dominated for so long has reached the point where he is incapable of functioning successfully as a social being.

Perhaps, had there been more time, Fitzgerald could have reconciled the pathetic story of Dick's marriage to an insane woman with his original story of the man destroyed by charm. The more deeply committed he was to his material, and the closer it was to his immediate experience, the more he overwrote. He needed time to revise, as we can see by comparing passages from the early drafts of "The Boy Who Killed His Mother" with the heavily revised versions that were incorporated into *Tender Is the Night.* Take, for example, the episode in the second chapter of Book I, early in the story, where Rosemary becomes acquainted with Mrs. Abrams, the McKiscos, and the rest of their circle on the beach. The purpose of this encounter is to contrast, for Rosemary's benefit, the shoddy qualities of the former group with the finer-textured conduct of the Divers and their friends, whom Rosemary meets a few pages later. In Fitzgerald's first version he tried to convey this by directly describing the McKiscos and their circle, and Rosemary's feelings about them. The result was overblown expository prose, of which the following is only a short sample (Rosemary here is still Francis Melarky):[42]

Mr. McKiscoe spoke only in irritation at his wife's loquacity, but the rudeness annoyed Francis, and looking back at the beach where sat Mrs. Abrahams and her two young homosexuals, and thinking that he was already in a way part of this group, he got to his feet with a sudden nessessity to escape. These people—possibly excepting Mrs. Abrahams—had no value, not even a human value, unless one should meet them under circumstances different from any into which the course of their unadventurous lives was likely to throw them. It was all so unpleasant for they were second rate and sensitive enough to see it [in] each other but not intelligent enough to see it in themselves. They smelt of cheapness and pretension under an endless sheen of proud words used for purposes of concealment— words that had revenged themselves by having eventually no meaning to them at all.

After many revisions, Fitzgerald succeeded in transforming the chunky prose represented by this short quotation into the swift-paced conversation between Rosemary and the McKiscos that appears in the published text. After listening to the McKiscos' fatuous talk, what more do we need to be told about them? As for Rosemary, Fitzgerald summed up her feelings about the McKiscos, finally, with the simple comment that she left them and "swam back to the shore where she threw her peignoir over her shoulders." We can imagine for ourselves the expressive shrug that accompanied this gesture. Later, telling her mother about her adventures on the beach, and her meeting with the charming Divers and their friends, Rosemary laconically adds, "There were some other people, but they weren't nice." So, by breaking up his heavy-footed first-draft prose and inserting dialogue and images, Fitzgerald was able to convey his thought with force and economy. But such virtues of style had to be earned, and the price was painstaking revision.[43]

"Proud words used for purposes of concealment—words that had revenged themselves by eventually having no meaning at all." Albert McKisco and his friends were not the only people who used words in this shabby way. When Fitzgerald's imagination grew fatigued and could not objectify his emotions, he lapsed into the same bad habit. Several years later, after an evening with Nathanael West (whose fiction he greatly admired), Fitzgerald would wonder if West's longwindedness in conversation was not prompted by the same impulse that was responsible for his own tendency at times to overwrite. "I think when I am [long-winded] . . . I don't want to be liked or to teach or to interest," he wrote in his Notebook after their meeting. "That is my way of saying 'Don't like me—I want to go back into my dream.'" The problem he faced in *Tender Is the Night* was that of reshaping the material of his experience so that he could entertain as well as preach.[44]

"I have decided that the plan of the book is best as originally conceived," Fitzgerald had told Perkins in January, 1934, when the latter recommended omitting the episode of the shooting in the Gare Saint Lazare on the grounds that it might confuse the reader. Yet, four years later Fitzgerald was to be so dissatisfied with the "plan" of *Tender Is the Night* that he would try to get Perkins to bring out a new edition arranged in a different form. Instead of having it begin with Book I, which is told from Rosemary's point of view, he wanted it to start with the flashback chapters at the opening of Book II, in which he had described Dick Diver's prior history.

—[T]hat book is not dead [he wrote Perkins from Hollywood in December, 1938]. . . . Its great fault is that the *true* beginning— the young psychiatrist in Switzerland—is tucked away in the middle of the book. If pages 151–212 were taken from their present place and put at the start, the improvement in appeal would be enormous.

Whereupon he cut up his own personal copy, rearranged it in this fashion, glued it back together and marked it "This is the *final version* of the book as I would like it."[45]

Fourteen years later, in 1952, Scribner's published a new version of *Tender Is the Night* rearranged and edited by Malcolm Cowley according to this scheme. (It is likely that many readers today know the book only in this second version.) Mr. Cowley prefaced his edition with a thoughtful introduction that lists what he considers to be the advantages of this rearrangement. Nonetheless, there are strong reasons (historical as well as aesthetic) favoring *Tender Is the Night* in its original 1934 form.[46]

In the first place, the changes Fitzgerald told Perkins he wanted to make in December, 1938, were not based solely on artistic considerations. He was looking desperately for a way to get his name back into print again. His letter to Perkins was written almost immediately after he had been notified by Metro-Goldwyn-Mayer that his lucrative contract as a script writer would not be renewed. Not only was he still heavily in debt, but he had the idea for a new novel about the movie industry (*The Last Tycoon*) on which he was eager to start work. But now financial circumstances presented him with the unhappy choice of either striking out on his own as a free-lance script writer in Hollywood, or trying to win back his old popular audience. But it had been several years since he had sold a story to a big magazine. Did anyone still remember his name? Perhaps a new edition of *Tender,* with a different beginning, would get the critical notice he hoped for. If not, he had several other projects for Perkins' consideration. One was a new edition of *This Side of Paradise* for which Fitzgerald would write a humorous glossary explaining the out-of-date slang. Another was a one-volume triple-decker to consist of *Paradise, Gatsby,* and *Tender Is the Night.* A third was a new volume to consist entirely of his Phillippe and his Basil Duke Lee stories from 1928. There is no doubt that he had abandoned his critical judgment when he made this last suggestion. Not only had he opposed the idea when Perkins had suggested it several years before, but such a volume would have included four stories so poor that he had already stripped and scrapped them, as well as a fifth so bad no magazine editor would publish it.

Thus, Fitzgerald's proposal to reverse the first two sections of *Tender Is the Night,* when it has been examined in the context of the rest of his letter, does not appear to have been a detached aesthetic judgment. It is true that he had been dissatisfied with his novel ever since he had let it go to press. But nowhere among his various expressions of this dissatisfaction, prior to the economic crisis he faced in December, 1938, is there a hint that he was unhappy over the book's structure, or that he thought a different beginning would help matters. As late as 1936, in his correspondence with Bennett Cerf about a possible Modern Library reprint, he had expressly disavowed any desire to change the novel's form.[47]

The truth is that to do justice to the tragedy of Dick's marriage, Fitzgerald would have had to replan and rewrite most of *Tender Is the Night.* The rearrangement he advocated in 1938 did little to overcome his main artistic problems. On the other hand, it did serious damage to the other story about the effects of charm over which he had brooded for so many years. Living in a society where charm is still regarded as a moral value, we have missed the devastating analysis of that society that is the book's most enduring achievement. To date, most of the criticism directed toward *Tender Is the Night* has been mistakenly preoccupied with its failure or success as a story of marriage.

"I am interested in the individual only in his rel[ation] to society," Fitzgerald wrote in his copy of Joyce's *Dubliners.* "We have wandered in imaginary loneliness through imaginary woods for a hundred years— too long." This is perhaps a better description of his aspirations than his achievement. But it offers penetrating insight into the nature of his art. He had begun as a full-fledged romantic. "The Romantic Egotist," his first ambitious work, was a prime example of that "imaginary loneliness" that had dominated so much of the fiction of the previous hundred years. Even *The Great Gatsby*, as we know from its history, had begun as a fragment of autobiography. But in both novels, successive revisions had carried him from introspection to that broader vision of the relationship of man to society that is the hallmark of Fitzgerald's most enduring work.[48]

With *Tender Is the Night* he took another step forward artistically. Here from the beginning he had attempted to treat the individual's relation to society objectively by structuring it as tragedy. The tragic power of charm had been the book's main theme ever since he had first conceived of it in the Murphys' garden at Antibes back in 1925. This initial conception had provided him with a functional structure as well as an organizing point of view. Both dominate the first half of the story, and it is here that his original intention is most fully realized. This is the strongest argument for retaining *Tender Is the Night* in its 1934 form, rather than the later Cowley rearrangement. The latter subordinates the tragic theme of charm, as we see it first established through Rosemary's eyes; it emphasizes instead the weaker, more autobiographical aspects, where Fitzgerald was still wandering with his hero "in imaginary loneliness through imaginary woods." Throughout his career, the measure of his achievement as an artist would be the degree to which he could make use of and at the same time transcend personal experience.

XIII
The "Crack-Up" Essays and the Last of the Stories:
1934-1937

The reviews of *Tender Is the Night* were generally unfavorable, and its sale of only 15,000 copies during 1934 was not nearly enough to cover Fitzgerald's debt to Scribner's. "What worries *me* is the possibility of being condemned to go back to *The Saturday Evening Post* grind at the exact moment when the book is finished," he had written Max Perkins back in 1933 while the novel was still taking shape. The subsequent months of cutting and polishing had left him "in the black hole of Calcutta, mentally exhausted, physically exhausted, emotionally exhausted and, perhaps, morally exhausted," he later wrote Harold Ober. But no sooner were the last page proofs of *Tender* in the mail than he was obliged to go back to his commercial work again.[1]

This time, besides his magazine stories, he tried several other ways of earning money:[2]

> In actual work since I finished the last proof of the novel in the middle of March, eight months ago [he wrote Perkins in November], I have written and sold three stories for the *Post*, written another which was refused, written two and a half stories for the *Redbook*, rewritten three articles of Zelda's for *Esquire* and one original for them to get emergency money, collaborated on a 10,000 word treatment of "Tender Is the Night" which was no go, written an 8,000 word story for Gracie Allen, which was also no go, and made about five false starts on stories which went from 1000 to 5,000 words, and a preface to the Modern Library edition of "The Great Gatsby."

Convinced by the poor sales of *Tender* that his private life was not a lucrative source of material for popular fiction, he now turned elsewhere for subject matter. His first project was a series of magazine stories about a ninth-century French warrior named Philippe, Count of Villefranche. There were to be eleven stories in all, carrying Philippe from youth through a triumphant old age. Each would be a self-contained unit, but the series as a whole would illustrate the emergence of France as a unified nation under Philippe's leadership. Fitzgerald hoped to sell the series to the *Post*, and eventually to collect them in a volume to be called *The Castle*.[3]

The project had a special appeal in that it would allow its author to forget his many disappointments while he lost himself in medieval French history. The first in the series, "The Darkest Hour," was written in April, 1934, while Fitzgerald was still waiting to see how critics and the public would respond to *Tender Is the Night*. When not only *The Saturday Evening Post* but several other leading magazines turned this story down, however, his initial enthusiasm for Philippe evaporated. Meanwhile, Harold Ober had gone ahead and arranged for *Redbook* to buy the entire series of eleven for $1,750 per story. In view of their author's slipping popular reputation, this was not an unreasonable price. But Fitzgerald was furious that Ober would accept anything less than the $3,000 he had been getting for his stories. Even though Edwin Balmer, fiction editor of *Redbook*, promptly ran "The Darkest Hour" in the October issue, Fitzgerald refused to write any more Philippe stories and spent the summer of 1934 instead on what he hoped would be more lucrative projects.

These included the scripts for several radio shows as well as two movie scenarios: one based on *Tender Is the Night;* the other, a comedy for George Burns and Gracie Allen. No one bought them, however, and after a wasted summer, Fitzgerald went back reluctantly to Philippe. But, discouraged by *Redbook's* low price, he decided he could afford to work only ten days on each story—including research as well as writing. The results were so slipshod that after buying three, Balmer hastily called the whole deal off. Two of these eventually appeared in *Redbook*, but the third was so bad that Balmer never published it.

Meanwhile, Fitzgerald's reputation was slipping in the editorial offices of the other big magazines. So long as the myth persisted that he was a featured *Saturday Evening Post* writer, Ober had been able to sell the stories rejected by the *Post* at high prices to such rivals as *McCall's*, *Collier's*, and *Liberty*. But once the truth leaked out, Fitzgerald's stock dropped sharply with these competitors, too. By 1937 the only magazine that was regularly publishing his fiction was the newly established *Esquire*. Arnold Gingrich, *Esquire's* talented editor, had long been one of Fitzgerald's admirers, and was eager to publish anything by Fitzgerald he could get. But he could not afford to pay more than $200 or $300 for a story—less than a tenth of Fitzgerald's regular price.

All during this time there had not been a new collection of Fitzgerald's short stories since *All the Sad Young Men,* which had appeared in 1926. Perkins had hoped to bring out a new volume to coincide with the publication of *Tender Is the Night.* But Fitzgerald insisted that the stories to be included should first be revised; then he had gotten involved in so many other projects during 1934 that the collection was repeatedly postponed. "My plan was to do my regular work in the daytime and do [i.e., revise] one story every night," he explained to Perkins in November, "but as it works out, after a good day's work I am so exhausted that I drag out the work on a story to two hours when it should be done in one and go to bed so tired and wrought up, toss around sleepless, and am good for nothing next morning except dictating letters, signing checks, . . . ect. [sic]"[4]

Consequently *Taps at Reveille,* Fitzgerald's fourth and last collection of short stories, did not appear until the spring of 1935, a year after *Tender Is the Night.* By then, the latter had been forgotten, and this new volume sold fewer than three thousand copies. It contained an unusually generous selection of eighteen stories—more than twice as many as his previous volumes. Among them were some of his finest pieces: "Babylon Revisited," "Crazy Sunday," "Family in the Wind," "A Short Trip Home," "Last of the Belles," and the best of the Basil Duke Lee and Josephine Perry stories. But none of these better stories had been written more recently than 1932. The rest were little more than clever potboilers. Even so, they were considerably better than the tired stories he was writing in 1935 and 1936. By now the intricate mechanism that had turned out a $3,000 story regularly every six weeks for so many years had finally broken down. Nor did there seem much likelihood that it could be set running again.

But Fitzgerald was unwilling to admit that this was the case. Throughout 1935 and most of 1936 he continued to try to regain his dwindling commercial market. After the Count Philippe fiasco with *Redbook,* he struggled to get two other fictional series started. The first was a string of stories about doctors and nurses, with a hospital setting. When these petered out he started a series about a thirteen-year-old girl and her widowed father, based on Scottie and himself. Like the hospital stories, these got off to a good start and then lost vitality. Ober was able to get rid of the poorer ones by changing the names of the father and daughter and selling them to some second-string magazines. "Lo, the Poor Peacock," the last of the group, was so bad, however, that the *Pictorial Review*, which bought it, never published it.[5]

In his restless quest for new material to stimulate his jaded imagination, Fitzgerald now went to the extreme of paying good money for the right to make use of other people's experiences. He persuaded one of his hospital nurses to sell him the rights to her life story; and another time he bought the reminiscences of a daredevil stunt driver whom he met on an auto trip in North Carolina. There was nothing wrong with this practice, of course, except that Fitzgerald was the kind of writer who wrote best about his own feelings and emotions. In 1935, during a visit to Tryon, North Carolina, he was inspired to write a short story based on the life of Mrs. Nora Flynn, one of the famous Langhorne girls, and the sister of Lady Astor and Mrs. Charles Dana Gibson. Mrs. Flynn's history contained enough romantic material for a shelf full of novels. But Fitzgerald's account, "The Intimate Strangers," which was published in the June, 1935, *McCall's*, was one of his poorest stories. It ignored practically everything he had ever learned about story writing. Instead of selecting and building up a few crucial episodes, he crammed a mass of factual details into one flat, monotonous narrative.[6]

Finally, when he could no longer find inspiring subject matter in the lives of his friends and acquaintances, he began writing stories without knowing exactly what he was writing about. That is the most charitable explanation for a story as bad as "The Passionate Eskimo," which *Liberty* bought for $1,500 and featured in its June 8, 1935, issue. Fitzgerald started out by describing some Eskimos on exhibit at the Chicago World's Fair, then he lost the thread of his plot and consequently his reader's attention. What Kenneth Littauer of *Collier's* said in a letter to Harold Ober rejecting another Fitzgerald story, "Offside Play," applies to most of the other magazine stories he was writing at this time:[7]

> There is a great deal of good stuff in this story but the action is altogether too complicated. Unless we are mistaken the whole thing needs to be simplified and very sharply focused. For instance, the introduction of a co-ed wife for Van Kamp [the hero] is a piece of strongarm work that ought to make a master of subtleties like Fitzgerald blush for shame. . . .

"It isn't particularly likely that I'll write a great many more stories about young love," Fitzgerald wrote Littauer, by way of an explanation:[8]

I was tagged with that by my first writings up to 1925. Since then I have written stories about young love. They have been done with increasing difficulty and increasing insincerity. I would either be a miracle man or a hack if I could go on turning out an identical product for three decades.

I know that's what's expected of me, but in that direction the well is pretty dry. . . . You see, I not only announced the birth of my young illusions in *This Side of Paradise* but pretty much the death of them in some of my later *Post* stories like "Babylon Revisited." Lorimer seemed to understand this in a way. Nevertheless, an overwhelming number of editors continue to associate me with an absorbing interest in young girls—an interest that at my age would probably land me behind the bars.

I have a daughter. She is very smart; she is very pretty; she is very popular. Her problems seem to me to be utterly dull and her point of view completely uninteresting. In other words, she is exactly what I was once accused of being—callow. Moreover she belongs to a very overstimulated and not really adventurous generation—a generation that has been told the price of everything as well as its value. I once tried to write about her. I couldn't.

With these words, Fitzgerald bid a belated farewell to the lucrative flapper-formula magazine story with which he had so long been associated in the public mind, and which had served him so well. No longer able to believe in it, he could no longer write it. As he admitted wryly about this time in a note at the end of the manuscript of "Day Off from Love," a silly flapper story he was unable to finish: "The trouble is of course that I forgot the real idea."[9]

In every way, the three years that elapsed between the publication of *Tender Is the Night* and Fitzgerald's departure for Hollywood in the summer of 1937 were the saddest years of his life. Throughout this period, Zelda continued to be confined to a mental institution. Several times she had tried to commit suicide, and hope for her recovery had dimmed. Early in 1934, Fitzgerald and Scottie moved from "La Paix" to 1307 Park Avenue, Baltimore; a year later they moved again to an even more modest address in a nearby apartment hotel. To make matters worse, Fitzgerald's drinking had now progressed to the point where he could no longer control himself in public. Occasionally he drank himself helpless, and his nights were beginning to be haunted by attacks of delirium tremens. More and more, Scottie was left in the care of understanding friends like the Obers, the Perkinses, and the Turnbulls. Luckily, they had children of her age and were able to give her the home life her father wanted for her but could himself no longer provide.

Yet, the most remarkable thing of all was that during this same time he was writing some of the finest prose of his career. During the fall of 1935 and the following winter, he wrote the three "Crack-Up" essays that were published first in *Esquire* and later republished in *The Crack-Up*, the posthumous volume of Fitzgerald's miscellaneous writing that Edmund Wilson edited in 1945. These three autobiographical essays were followed in 1936 by four more: "Author's House," "Afternoon of an Author," "An Author's Mother," and "Early Success." Together with three earlier autobiographical essays and sketches, "Outside the Cabinet Maker's" (1928), "My Lost City" (1932), "Sleeping and Waking" (1934), and two later ones, "Financing Finnegan" (1937) and "The Lost Decade" (1939), they comprise the best portrait we have of Fitzgerald. Collected, these twelve pieces would form a volume of distinguished prose worthy of being placed on the same shelf with *The Great Gatsby*, *Tender Is the Night*, *The Last Tycoon*, and the dozen or so of his finest stories.[10]

Of these sketches, the three so-called "Crack-Up" essays ("The Crack-Up," "Handle With Care," and "Pasting It Together") are the most personal. They were the first serious writing since *Tender Is the Night* in which Fitzgerald had tried to come to terms with his private experience. Now, after two years, he was finally able to examine his recent past and his present situation with detachment and clarity.

These essays had not been conceived as a unit. The first, "The Crack-Up," was written by Fitzgerald in October, 1935, in the little North Carolina mountain town of Tryon. One day during the previous February he had gotten into his car alone and, forsaking the wintry cold of Baltimore, had headed south in search of a change of scenery. It was the first vacation since his ill-fated trip to Bermuda with Zelda more than a year earlier. Since then he had experienced a great many disappointments, and the job he had just finished, correcting the galley proofs of *Taps at Reveille*, had left him physically and creatively exhausted. So, when he encountered the first balmy harbingers of spring at Hendersonville, North Carolina, in the foothills of the Blue Ridge Mountains, he took a room at a hotel, stopped drinking, caught up on his sleep, and spent several leisurely weeks exploring the budding countryside. Nearby, in the higher country, he discovered the resort town of Tryon—at first sight a straggling row of shops and homes hidden in the pines alongside the tracks of the Southern Railroad. But nestled in the surrounding hills he found an attractive community of comfortable homes and farms, fine inns and hotels, and miles of trails for hiking and riding.

Although it was frequented mainly by retired Northerners, Tryon was not so crowded as nearby Asheville, nor was it as fashionable a spa as Southern Pines and Aiken. But it enjoyed an unusually mild climate; and despite its lack of style, it was the seasonal home of a number of well-known people including William Gillette, Mrs. Calvin Coolidge, Nora and Lefty Flynn, Charles and Mary Beard, and Margaret Culkin Banning, the popular author and a native Minnesotan like Fitzgerald.

Following his return to Baltimore in March, Fitzgerald came down with a severe case of flu that put him in Johns Hopkins hospital. X-rays indicated that he was also suffering from a flare-up of his long-dormant tuberculosis. He was finally released from the hospital in May with a warning from his physician that if he didn't rest and take care of himself he would be dead within the year. Arrangements were made for Scottie to spend the summer with friends, and to enter a New England boarding school in the fall. Zelda was moved from the mental hospital where she had been staying in New York State to a similar institution in the mountains between Asheville and Tryon. And Fitzgerald spent the better part of his next two years in North Carolina, dividing his time between Asheville (where he stayed when he visited Zelda) and Tryon.[11]

In the latter town he usually put up at Oak Hall, a comfortable, barn-like hotel perched on a rise overlooking the main street. Most of the summer of 1935 he spent in bed, occasionally going out at noon to Misseldine's, the local drug store, for his meals. Here he was often seen consuming the soft drinks and candy bars that had become for him a substitute for alcohol. (Some years later a physician would diagnose this abnormal craving for sweets as hyperinsulinism, a disease that he believed to be one of the reasons for Fitzgerald's heavy drinking.) In the evening, when he felt up to it, he would visit the Bannings or Flynns. He badly needed new friends and a change of scenery.[12]

Living alone leaves so many loopholes for brooding [he wrote Mrs. Turnbull, in Baltimore] and when I do face the whole tragedy of Zelda it is simply a day lost. I think I feel it more now than at any time since its inception. She seems so helpless and pitiful. Liquor used to help put it out of my mind and it was one of the many services my old friend Barleycorn did me. However he has outlived his usefulness in that as well as all other regards.

Gradually, with rest and pleasant company, he recovered his health as well as his old objectivity. "Living alone in a very small town," he would afterwards say, "did more to restore my nervous strength than any other thing."[13]

It was at Tryon, in October, 1935, at a time when life looked bleakest, that he wrote the first of his "Crack-Up" pieces—a halting, still quite tentative effort to analyze the reasons for his present state of mind. The secret of his art, won only after the painful act of self-discovery, had been his skill in writing about himself with objective detachment. Following the example of Keats, his favorite poet, he had learned how to cultivate a negative capability toward himself and his experience—believing that (as he said at the beginning of "The Crack-Up"):[14]

> —the test of a first-rate intelligence is the ability to hold two opposed ideas in the mind at the same time, and still retain the ability to function. . . . I must hold in balance the sense of the futility of effort and the sense of the necessity to struggle; the conviction of the inevitability of failure and still the determination to "succeed"—and, more than these, the contradiction between the dead hand of the past and the high intentions of the future. If I could do this through the common ills—domestic, professional and personal—then the ego would continue as an arrow shot from nothingness to nothingness with such force that only gravity would bring it to earth at last.
>
> For seventeen years, with a year of deliberate loafing and resting out in the center—things went on like that, with a new chore only a nice prospect for the next day. I was living hard, too, but: "Up to forty-nine it'll be all right," I said. "I can count on that. For a man who's lived as I have, that's all you could ask."
>
> —And then, ten years this side of forty-nine, I suddenly realized that I had prematurely cracked. . . .
>
> I began to realize that for two years my life had been a drawing on resources that I did not possess, that I had been mortgaging myself physically and spiritually up to the hilt. . . . I realized that in those two years, in order to preserve something—an inner hush maybe, maybe not—I had weaned myself from all the things I used to love. . . . I saw that even my love for those closest to me was become only an attempt to love, that my casual relations—with an editor, a tobacco seller, the child of a friend, were only what I remembered I *should* do, from other days. . . .
>
> All rather inhuman and undernourished, isn't it? Well, that, children, is the true sign of cracking up.

His conversational tone could neither disguise the fact that "The Crack-Up" was essentially a confessional essay, nor that its author was engaged in an act of self-absolution. It closed appropriately with a verse from St. Matthew—one of the saddest verses in the Bible: "Ye are the salt of the earth But if the salt hath lost its savour, wherewith shall it be salted?"

Arnold Gingrich was delighted to have it for *Esquire* and asked for more. Fitzgerald, who had returned to his apartment in Baltimore, replied by writing two more essays that covered pretty much the same ground as the first, but with more humor and detachment. The mere act of spreading his gloom out on paper where he could look at it had been a good thing. In the second piece, "Handle With Care," he reviewed the major disappointments of his life, from his failure to become a campus leader at Princeton to his recent mistakes in the writing of *Tender Is the Night*. In "Pasting It Together," he tried to develop a practical working philosophy for the immediate future. Now that he had purged himself of some of his bitterness, he was ready to indulge in some hard, serious thinking—"a measure that no one ever adopts voluntarily," he ruefully admitted. ". . . God, was it difficult! The moving about of great secret trunks . . ."[15]

> I only wanted absolute quiet to think out why I had developed a sad attitude toward sadness, a melancholy attitude toward melancholy and a tragic attitude toward tragedy—*why I had become identified with the objects of my horror and compassion* . . . Identification such as this spells the death of accomplishment.

His inability to isolate his own feelings from those of his hero had been the reason for the failure of *Tender Is the Night;* yet when he tried to write magazine stories about the experiences of other people, the results were equally disappointing at the other extreme—wooden and contrived. Without his double vision, he had nothing to write about. "When Wordsworth decided that 'there had passed away a glory from the earth,' he felt no compulsion to pass away with it, and the Fiery Particle Keats never ceased his struggle against t.b. nor in his last moments relinquished his hope of being among the English poets."

The only way open to Fitzgerald was to make[16]

> a clean break . . . something you cannot come back from; that is irretrievable because it makes the past cease to exist. So, since I

could no longer fulfill the obligations that life had set for me or that I had set for myself, why not slay the empty shell who had been posturing at it for four years? I must continue to be a writer because that was my only way of life, but I would cease any attempts to be a person—to be kind, just or generous. . . . There was to be no more giving of myself—all giving was to be outlawed henceforth under a new name, and that name was Waste. . . .

In the last of these essays, "Pasting It Together," Fitzgerald made a valiant attempt to reform: henceforth he would dedicate himself only to his art.

I have now at last become a writer only. . . . Let the good people function as such. . . . A writer need have no such ideals unless he makes them for himself, and this one has quit. The old dream of becoming an entire man in the Goethe-Byron-Shaw tradition, with an opulent American touch, a sort of combination of J.P. Morgan, Topham Beauclerk and St. Francis of Assisi, has been relegated to the junk heap of the shoulder pads worn for one day on the Princeton freshman football field and the overseas cap never worn overseas.

It sounded convincing until he took a sharp look at himself in this new guise and collapsed into ironic laughter. "I felt like the beady-eyed men I used to see on the commuting train from Great Neck fifteen years back —men who didn't care whether the world tumbled into chaos tomorrow if it spared their houses." Forsake his moral responsibilities to other people? "Make the past cease to exist?" What would there be left for him to write about?[17]

Like his best stories and essays, these "Crack-Up" pieces were moral rather than literal autobiography—a kind of do-it-yourself therapy for the spirit. In them he absolved himself, one by one, of his various sins— sins of omission as well as commission. More significant is the fact that through this act of confession he was able to release his long-clogged creative powers. For, with these "Crack-Up" essays, Fitzgerald commenced the last and most mature period of his career.

In these essays, too, we can watch his progress from despair and self-pity to a confident detachment marked by the recovery of his sense of humor. For the first time in many months he no longer saw himself as the victim of a tragic destiny, but as a slightly absurd and very human being. Henceforth, when he wrote about himself it would be the comic aspects of his predicament that he would describe. The results were such amusing and beautifully written essays as "Financing Finnegan" and "The Lost Decade," as well as the series he wrote for *Esquire* about Pat Hobby, the hard-drinking Hollywood script writer. Because he no longer regarded himself as a tragic hero, he was able to use certain aspects of his life imaginatively in the fabrication of the most detached and genuinely tragic of all his novels—*The Last Tycoon*. In this respect, the writing of the "Crack-Up" series was a liberating act for Fitzgerald, a necessary step in his development as a novelist of wider scope and finer sensibility.

But in 1936, most of his friends did not see the "Crack-Up" essays in this light. When they were printed in the company of *Esquire's* glossy haberdashery advertisements, both Max Perkins and Harold Ober were apprehensive that their appearance would further damage Fitzgerald's already battered reputation with the bigger magazines. And Hemingway, who had already lectured Fitzgerald on the faults of *Tender Is the Night,* decided that since his old friend was now wearing his heart on his sleeve, anyone was free to take pot shots at it. ("There are always those," Fitzgerald had written in "Handle With Care," "to whom all self revelation is contemptible.") Four months after the last of the "Crack-Up" pieces, Hemingway publicly wrote off Fitzgerald in the pages of *Esquire* in one of his best-known short stories, "The Snows of Kilimanjaro."[18]

The rich were dull and they drank too much, or they played too much backgammon. They were dull and they were repetitious. He remembered poor —— —— [here, in the *Esquire* version of this story, "Scott Fitzgerald" appeared] and his romantic awe of them and how he had started a story once that began "The very rich are different from you and me." And how some one had said to ——, "Yes, they have more money." But that was not humorous to ——. He thought they were a special glamorous race and when he found they weren't it wrecked him just as much as any other thing that wrecked him.

He [i.e., Hemingway's hero in the story] had been contemptuous of those who wrecked. You did not have to like it because you understood it. He could beat anything, he thought, because no thing could hurt him if he did not care.

When Fitzgerald protested, Hemingway agreed to omit his name from subsequent reprintings of the story. But quite apart from this connection, "The Snows of Kilimanjaro" shares several other things with the "Crack-Up" essays (from which, most likely, it partially derives). Both works, published so closely together, were landmarks in the literary history of the 1930's. In them, two of the most talented writers of the era publicly disavowed their former way of life and, crying *mea culpa*, denounced the excesses of the recent Boom Years. Lamenting the waste and irresponsibility of his wild years in Paris, Hemingway's hero in "The Snows" decides to devote himself henceforth exclusively to the practice of his art. True, he dies soon after this decision. But there is no doubt about the seriousness of his resolution. The value of his dedication is symbolized by the legend of the leopard who tried unsuccessfully to climb to the peak of the sacred mountain, Kilimanjaro. Though it froze to death before it achieved its goal, its carcass is permanently preserved in ice at the summit, and can be seen to this day by viewers watching from below—an eternal symbol of the immortality of art.[19]

Fitzgerald, in the last of his "Crack-Up" essays, had argued himself around to a similar position: "I have now at last become a writer only." But it was a pose which—unlike Hemingway—he could not sustain for very long. As we have seen, he had too sharp a sense of his own limitations, and he collapsed at the end into mocking laughter. He was too human not to recognize his own comic vulnerability. This quality, especially, distinguished his fiction from Hemingway's. Both writers wrote primarily out of their own personal experience. But at his best Fitzgerald achieved a quality of "double vision" that let him dramatize that experience objectively without sacrificing humor and compassion.

It was a virtue that had eluded him during the writing of portions of *Tender Is the Night;* but with the "Crack-Up" essays it had finally returned. Probably the most striking proof of this new objectivity is the fact that no sooner had he finished the last of these poignant essays than he blithely approached the editor of *The Saturday Evening Post*, suggesting that he undertake a longer series in a similar vein for his old readers of the *Post!* Although he had lived entirely in these essays every moment that he was writing them, as soon as they were out of his system, he saw them as so much marketable material. Later, he would speak of them wryly as his "gloom articles." And at the end of his life, when he was dying, he coolly noted on the margin of the manuscript of *The Last Tycoon*, "thoughts from Crack-Up," as a reminder to introduce some of the gloomier passages from the essays into the episode where Monroe Stahr realizes that he, too, is soon to die.[20]

The *Post* turned down his proposal. But Fitzgerald went ahead anyway and wrote four more autobiographical essays in a lighter vein, all but one of which appeared eventually in *Esquire*. The first two, "Author's House" and "Afternoon of An Author," discussed his professional problems as a writer. The other two were in a more nostalgic vein. "An Author's Mother" was a bittersweet portrait of Molly McQuillan Fitzgerald, who was dying at the time, and for whom her unruly only son had at last developed a compassionate understanding. "Early Success," first published in the short-lived *American Cavalcade*, described in rippling prose the events of 1919 and 1920 that had culminated in the appearance of *This Side of Paradise*. All seven of these essays were so different in quality from the tired magazine stories he had been turning out that it seems incredible that they were written by the same person. While he could no longer conjure up the slick romances he had once contrived with such facility, he could diagnose his faults with ruthless humor and detachment:[21]

> The problem was a magazine story that had become so thin in the middle that it was about to blow away. The plot was like climbing endless stairs, he had no element of surprise in reserve, and the characters who started out so bravely day-before-yesterday couldn't have qualified for a newspaper serial. . . . He went through the manuscript underlining good phrases in red crayon and after tucking these into a file slowly tore up the rest of the story and dropped it into the wastebasket. Then he walked the room and smoked, occasionally talking to himself. . . . "The perfect neurotic," he said, regarding himself in the mirror. "By-product of an idea, slag of a dream."

"I don't know whether those articles of mine in *Esquire*—that crack-up series—represented a real nervous breakdown," he afterwards told a friend who had written him a letter of sympathy after reading them. "In retrospect it seems more a spiritual 'change of life'—and a most unwilling one—it was a protest against a new set of conditions which I would have to face and a protest of my mind at having to make the psychological adjustments which would suit this new set of circumstances. . . . The sensitive cannot make themselves overnight into specimens of the 'tough-minded'—the great ally is time, though I know that is a pretty old saw."[22]

A "new set of circumstances" was merely Fitzgerald's way of referring to the job as a Hollywood screen writer that now loomed ahead as the only way out of his financial predicament. What other choice remained? He had tried the radio without success, and his commercial reputation had dropped to the point where he was being published only by *Esquire*. "For over 3 years the creative side of me has been dead as hell," he admitted frankly to his cousin Ceci; while to Perkins he reported "my chief failure is my inability to see a workable future." By the summer of 1936, his debts to Scribner's, to his insurance company, and to Perkins, Ober, and other friends, amounted to over forty thousand dollars.[23]

Nonetheless, every instinct warned him against taking a job in Hollywood. "I hate the place with a sincere hatred," he had written Ober in 1935. And in the second of his "Crack-Up" pieces, several months later, he had described his great fear that:

> the novel, which at my maturity was the strongest and supplest medium for conveying thought and emotion from one human being to another, was becoming subordinated to a mechanical and communal art that, whether in the hands of the Hollywood merchants or Russian idealists, was capable of reflecting only the tritest thought, the most obvious emotion. It was an art in which words were subordinate to images, where personality was worn down to the inevitable low gear of collaboration. As long past as 1930, I had a hunch that the talkies would make even the best selling novelist as archaic as silent pictures. People still read, . . . but there was a rankling indignity, that to me had become almost an obsession, in seeing the power of the written word subordinated to another power, a more glittering, a grosser power. . . .

"Never any luck with movies," he reminded himself not long after this in "Afternoon of An Author." "Stick to your last, boy."[24]

But his name was still gilt-edged in Hollywood. "You rate out here as a highbrow writer but you rate as a thoroughbred writer and not a talkie hack . . . and therefore people look up to you," a friend had recently written him from the movie colony. Besides, he was determined not to cut his exorbitant living expenses so long as it meant sacrificing either Zelda's or Scottie's welfare, even though they accounted for most of his overhead. "Such stray ideas as sending my daughter to a public school, putting my wife in a public insane asylum, have been proposed to me by intimate friends," he wrote Max Perkins, "but it would break something in me that would shatter the very delicate pencil-end of a point of view."[25]

So, when one of the studios invited him to come out during the summer of 1936, he seriously considered accepting—only to have to call it off at the last minute because of a swimming pool accident that wrenched his shoulder and put him in a cast for several months. His mother's death in September provided him with a small legacy, and as soon as he was able he tried his hand again at some magazine stories. But Ober could not sell any of them. Consequently, when Ober reported the following spring that Metro-Goldwyn-Mayer was asking for his services, Fitzgerald had no alternative but to accept. Ober had arranged for M-G-M to pay him one thousand dollars a week for six months, beginning in July. If all went well—that is, if Fitzgerald stayed sober and tended to his business—the contract was to be extended in January, 1938, for a year at $1,250 a week. Of this sum, Fitzgerald was to receive four hundred dollars weekly in cash and the remainder was to be retained by Ober to cover his agent's fee and to be applied against Fitzgerald's debts.[26]

In June, just before setting out for California, Fitzgerald wrote as his farewell to Perkins and Ober a short story, "Financing Finnegan," that was not only one of the funniest pieces he had ever written, but an appropriate climax to his "Crack-Up" years. Finnegan was an exaggerated portrait of Fitzgerald himself, an author whose

> career had started brilliantly and if it had not kept up to its first exalted level, at least it started brilliantly all over again every few years. He was the perennial man of promise in American letters— what he could actually do with words was astounding, they glowed and coruscated—he wrote sentences, paragraphs, chapters that were masterpieces of fine weaving and spinning. It was only when I met some poor devil of a screen writer who had been trying to make a logical story out of one of his books that I realized he had his enemies.
> "It's all beautiful when you read it," this man said disgustedly, "but when you write it down plain it's like a week in the nut-house."[27]

The story was obviously written with Ober and Perkins in mind, and the comic tone beautifully sustained throughout. Poor Finnegan is the despair of both his editor and his literary agent, but they have so much cash invested in him that they dare not disown him, no matter what he does next. Yet no matter how irresponsible his behavior, his irrepressible charm and talent continually assert themselves. In a sense, "Financing Finnegan" was Fitzgerald's rueful apology to his old friends, just as his concluding sentences were an affectionate promise of better things to come. Much as Fitzgerald hated to go to Hollywood, he intended to do his best. "The movies are interested in him—if they can get a good long look at him first," he said at the end, "and I have every reason to think that he will come through. He'd better."[28]

XIV
Hollywood Script Writer

Fitzgerald reported for work at Metro-Goldwyn-Mayer's Culver City lot on July 7, 1937, the memories of his two previous Hollywood visits painfully fresh in his mind. On the Southern Pacific's *Argonaut* coming west he had reviewed the history of both those ventures in a long letter to Scottie. The 1927 assignment writing "Lipstick" for United Artists had miscarried because of his own carelessness. "I had been loafing for six months for the first time in my life and was confident to the point of conciet. . . . Total result—a great time and no work." But the 1932 job for M-G-M on "Red-Headed Woman" had failed for a different reason. He had foolishly let himself be teamed up with a collaborator—a studio hack with whom he fought over every scene. Instead of going to Irving Thalberg, M-G-M's vice-president in charge of production, and insisting that he work on his script alone, he had quarreled with the rest of the staff, and finally quit in disgust. As a result, he was credited with the bad script as well as blamed for having run out on his job.[1]

But this time things would be different. "I want to profit by these two experiences—" he wrote Scottie. "I must be very tactful but keep my hand on the wheel from the start—find out the key man among the bosses and the most malleable among the collaborators—then fight the rest tooth & nail until, in fact or in effect, I'm alone on the picture. That's the only way I can do my best work. Given a break I can make them double this contract in less [than] two years."

His first job was the relatively easy one of polishing up the script of

"A Yank at Oxford," soon to be filmed in England with Robert Taylor in the title role. He contributed several new scenes, made some changes in the rest of the dialogue, and then devoted the rest of July to reading over the scripts of some recent M-G-M hits and having them shown in the studio theater. In August, he was given his first major assignment, the preparation of a "treatment" of Erich Maria Remarque's recent novel, *Three Comrades*. In a treatment, the writer was expected to reduce to straightforward expository narrative the main story line that he felt should be followed in making the film. Metro was notorious for its practice (introduced by Thalberg) of hiring several different writers to prepare independent treatments for the same film. Afterwards, at a series of conferences, they would all get together with the film's producer, and the best parts (presumably) of each treatment would be salvaged. Then a team of writers (not necessarily the ones who had written the treatments) would be ordered to weave this material into a final script. Suspecting that some such system was being used for *Three Comrades*, Fitzgerald begged Joe Mankiewicz, the producer, to let him go ahead on his own and turn his treatment into a full-dress script. He felt, quite rightly, that the expository form of the treatment would not do justice to his ideas, and that only a script of his own, complete with dialogue and detailed descriptions of the settings, could convey adequately the kind of film he had in mind.[2]

But Mankiewicz, after reading Fitzgerald's preliminary treatment and listening to him, ordered him instead to collaborate on the final script with a veteran M-G-M author, E.E. Paramore, Jr. Paramore and Fitzgerald had known each other back in New York in 1921. Paramore also knew a great deal more than Fitzgerald about the technical problems of film making. They differed radically in their views as to how the script should be written, however, and soon were quarreling over every scene. Nonetheless, Fitzgerald restrained himself as best he could until January, when his contract was extended for twelve months at the new figure of $1,250 per week. Then he blew up, flew off angrily for a holiday with Zelda in Florida, and sent Mankiewicz a bitter letter accusing him and Paramore of having wrecked the film. "To say I am disillusioned is putting it mildly. . . . I think you now have a flop on your hands."[3]

Instead, the Mankiewicz-Paramore production of *Three Comrades* was a great success. Margaret Sullavan, in the feminine lead, won the New York Film Critics' Award as the best actress of the year. And Frank Nugent, in his New York *Times* review, praised the picture especially for its outstanding literary qualities, rating it "obviously one of 1938's ten best" films.[4]

On his copy of the final script, Fitzgerald noted "37 pages mine, about ⅛, but all shadows and rhythm removed." He also preserved the treatment he himself had originally written for Mankiewicz. Comparing these, we can see how radically his views of how *Three Comrades* should be filmed differed from the version that was actually made. Fitzgerald wanted to emphasize the novel's mood of feverish gaiety mixed with cynical despair, that expressed so well the attitude of German youth during the sad decade following World War I. To convey this on the screen, he wanted to write scenes of serious social and political significance, leavened with others of broad comic satire. Instead, Mankiewicz and Paramore preferred to center the story dramatically around the friendship of the "three comrades," played by three well-known stars: Robert Taylor, Jimmie Stewart, and Robert Young. Fitzgerald's treatment was original and unconventional, but it would have required an unusually talented director to turn it into a good film. The Mankiewicz-Paramore version was a much more predictable box-office success in every way.[5]

Fitzgerald's next assignment was the preparation of a script, "Infidelity," for Joan Crawford. After his initial treatment had been approved, he went to work on the shooting script with energy and enthusiasm, only to have the whole project dropped because of unexpected censorship difficulties. His next job was "The Women," based on Clare Boothe Luce's recent Broadway play. Here he was teamed up with his old friend Donald Ogden Stewart, whom he had first known back in St. Paul in 1919. Stewart, then a young businessman with literary inclinations, had been living down the street when Fitzgerald returned from New York that summer to write *This Side of Paradise;* and the two men had spent many an evening together discussing Fitzgerald's novel. Later, Stewart had written several humorous books and then gravitated to Hollywood, where he was now established as a successful writer of sophisticated film comedies. He and his new wife, the widow of Lincoln Steffens, were also among the film colony's most outspoken leftwing radicals. Knowing of Fitzgerald's interest in Marxism, Stewart now did his best to involve his old friend in the activities of the Hollywood Popular Front.

Although Fitzgerald had played host to local Communists back in Baltimore, he had gradually become disillusioned and was no longer willing to give them his support. Besides, he had to conserve his remaining energy. "It will interest you to know that I've given up politics," he had written his cousin Ceci in 1936, before coming West. "For two years I've gone half haywire trying to reconcile my double alleigence [sic] to the class I am part of, and the Great Change I believe in. . . . I have become disgusted with the party leadership and have only health enough for my literary work, so I'm on the sidelines. It had become a strain making speeches at 'Leagues Against Imperialistic Wars. . . .' "[6]

Fitzgerald's work on "The Women" did not amount to much more than polishing Donald Ogden Stewart's already excellent script. But in the autumn of 1938 he received a much more responsible assignment, helping to convert a recent best-selling biography of Madame Curie into a film. So far, he had not had a screen credit since *Three Comrades*. His contract was due to expire in January, and if he wanted M-G-M to extend it for another year, this would be his last chance to prove what he could do. "On the next two weeks during which I finish the first part of 'Madame Curie' depends whether or not my contract will be renewed," he wrote Scottie in the late autumn. "So naturally I am working like hell." But he was not at his best under pressure. He pushed himself too hard, tensed up, and began quarreling with the wrong people. "I disagreed with everybody about how to do [it]," he explained to Scottie several weeks later, "and they're trying it another way." When his contract ran out early in January, it was not renewed.[7]

Yet, despite many disappointments, his eighteen months on the Metro-Goldwyn-Mayer lot had not been entirely fruitless. He had paid off a considerable portion of his indebtedness. He had learned a lot about the movie industry and was already beginning to think about using it as the subject of his next novel. And he had slowed up on his drinking. Now there was only an occasional spree. When he drank, it was usually because of some disappointment—either at the studio, or after a visit to Zelda, who continued to show little sign of improvement. Once, also, he made a nuisance of himself during a meeting with Ginevra King, whom he had not seen for twenty years.

He had also fallen in love. Sheilah Graham was a stranger like himself, a pretty English girl who had come out to Hollywood as a reporter for a national news syndicate. Petite, fair, well-scrubbed, and with regular, classic features, she did not realize how much she resembled the other girls—Zelda Sayre, Lois Moran, Ginevra King—to whom Fitzgerald had been attracted. He met her soon after his arrival in Hollywood in the summer of 1937 and before long they were head over heels in love. Miss Graham's story of their friendship, *Beloved Infidel*, is a fascinating and moving document. But she knew very little about his previous history, or the professional reasons why he had come to

Hollywood. Therefore, to attain its full value, her account of their months together must be put back into the context of his entire career. It must also be supplemented by Fitzgerald's own record, as we can reconstruct it from his manuscripts and his notes, and his letters to Ober, Perkins, and other friends.

During the latter part of 1938, while he was still working for Metro, he began to talk more and more openly with Miss Graham about his idea of writing a novel about the movie industry, to be based on the life of Irving Thalberg, the M-G-M production chief who had died suddenly in 1936, when he was only thirty-six years old. For the time being, his project had to be kept a secret. Financially, Fitzgerald was in no position to start work on it; indeed, one of his reasons for wanting his contract renewed was so that he could get clear of debt and put aside enough money during 1939 to work full-time on the novel. But when M-G-M let him go in January, 1939, he decided he would try to get by as a free-lance script writer. A local movie agent had promised to find work for him at a fifteen-hundred-a-week salary. It was Fitzgerald's hope that he could alternate lucrative short-term assignments in the studios with periods of rest, during which he could work on *The Last Tycoon*.

Things did not turn out as he had hoped. Free-lancing proved to be much more strenuous than he had bargained for. He had to be ready to go to work with little advance notice; and once on the job, there was little of the loafing enjoyed by the regular employees. Although the pay was high, the jobs usually did not last very long. Worst of all, they were the kind of jobs he disliked—helping a hack straighten out a snarled-up scene, or tinkering with someone else's script.

His first assignment, with Selznick-International, was repolishing the already highly polished script of *Gone With the Wind*. To date, it had been refurbished by more than a dozen other writers, and there was little for him to do. "Do you know in that 'Gone With the Wind' job I was absolutely forbidden to use any words except those of Margaret Mitchell," he wrote Perkins, "that is, when new phrases had to be invented one had to thumb through [it] as if it were Scripture and check out phrases of her's which would cover the situation."[8]

At the end of this job, although he was ill, he unwisely let his agent talk him into taking a ten-week assignment with Walter Wanger, at that time an independent producer, who was getting ready to film "Winter Carnival." For this story of college life, Wanger, who had attended Dartmouth, planned to shoot most of the background footage in New Hampshire during the Dartmouth Winter Carnival (the weekend of February eleventh and twelfth, 1939). It was Wanger's desire that Fitzgerald should go along to benefit from a fresh exposure to American college life. (As though Fitzgerald had not already written the classic treatment of the subject in *This Side of Paradise*!) But Fitzgerald was in no shape to make the trip. Not only was he downcast by his recent weeks of free-lance movie work, but, according to Sheilah Graham, his latent tuberculosis had flared up again and he was running a temperature of 102 degrees. Under such circumstances, the worst thing he could possibly do was to go abruptly from sunny Southern California to icy New Hampshire. But he needed the money as well as the continued confidence and goodwill of his Hollywood agent too badly to refuse.[9]

Also assigned to the script was a young writer named Budd Schulberg, the son of the production head of Paramount studio—one of Wanger's former bosses. Schulberg himself was only two years out of Dartmouth. Unaware of Fitzgerald's past history as a drinker, he innocently offered his companion a glass of champagne on the plane trip East—thereby launching Fitzgerald on a spree of epic proportions. From champagne he quickly went on to straight gin, disgracing himself and the rest of the party before a welcoming committee of Dartmouth professors. After Wanger fired him, Fitzgerald proceeded to New York City where, several days later, he turned up in a hospital ward, drunk and seriously ill from pneumonia.

This was the famous expedition that later provided Budd Schulberg with the material for his popular novel, *The Disenchanted*. Although Mr. Schulberg insists that Manley Halliday, his hero, was not intended to be a literal portrait of Fitzgerald, the two continue to be identified with one another. One reason for this is that, until the recent appearance of Sheilah Graham's *Beloved Infidel*, the Schulberg novel, published in 1950, was the only detailed account in print of Fitzgerald's last years. How much Mr. Schulberg actually depended on the Dartmouth trip with Fitzgerald for *The Disenchanted* can be seen from the much earlier account of that trip he wrote in 1941 in the *New Republic*. His decision to turn this brief encounter with Fitzgerald into a full-length novel was prompted in large measure by his meeting with Arthur Mizener a half-dozen years later. At the time Mr. Mizener was at work on his biography of Fitzgerald, *The Far Side of Paradise*. For various reasons, Mr. Mizener was obliged to deal with Fitzgerald's last years in Hollywood in discreet generalities. However, since he had access to the Fitzgerald papers and other additional information, he was able to furnish Schulberg with material that had been omitted from his biography. Out of his conversations with Mr. Mizener, his own brief memories of Fitzgerald, and his fertile imagination, Schulberg constructed *The Disenchanted*. Appearing as it did within a few weeks of *The Far Side of Paradise*, it was assumed to be the private history that Mr. Mizener had not told. This intimate association between the two books and their respective authors was further emphasized by Mr. Schulberg's formal dedication of *The Disenchanted* to Mr. and Mrs. Mizener, as well as by the laudatory review of the Mizener biography that he generously wrote for the front page of the Sunday book section of the New York *Times*.

The Disenchanted, however, is not a distinguished novel. Artistically, it comes nowhere near Schulberg's brilliant *What Makes Sammy Run?* which, except for *The Last Tycoon*, is probably the best novel that has been written about Hollywood. Nor is *The Disenchanted* a faithful portrait of Fitzgerald. Schulberg not only did not know Fitzgerald very well, but what little he saw of him was under the most unfavorable circumstances. Manley Halliday is Schulberg's idea of what the Fitzgerald he hardly knew must have been like. He was interested in him primarily as a symbol. The one thing that Fitzgerald was most desperately trying to be at this particular time was a responsible writer. Yet this is a fact that continually eludes the author of *The Disenchanted*. After devoting several hundred pages to his hero's drunken escapades, Schulberg suddenly tells his reader at the end of the book that, all during these goings on, Manley Halliday has been writing his greatest novel. But no place in the story has there been any evidence that Halliday has been writing, or that he knows how to write, or that Schulberg himself understands the connection (if any) between alcohol and creativity. After all, anyone can get drunk and make an ass of himself—and that is what Halliday does for most of the story. What makes Fitzgerald's last years in Hollywood of interest is not his drinking, but the fact that he was trying to write the finest novel of his career—and almost succeeded.[10]

Sheilah Graham, who accompanied Schulberg and Fitzgerald on their ill-fated plane trip East, gives a more faithful account of that adventure in *Beloved Infidel*. But even she was not in a position to know about all the pressures that led to Fitzgerald's outburst of drinking in the spring of 1939. It was his way of protesting against conditions he was no longer able to accept. After almost two years in Hollywood, he no longer had any illusions left about his talents as a screenwriter. Except for the debts that he had paid off, he had little else to be proud of. He had lost his magazine public, wrecked his lucrative arrangement at

Metro-Goldwyn-Mayer, and now after two months on his own, was fed up with free-lancing. What he wanted more than anything else was to get at his new novel. "Conditions in the industry somehow propose the paradox: 'We brought you here for your individuality but while you're here we insist that you do everything to conceal it,'" he wrote Max Perkins after returning from Dartmouth. ". . . I think it would be morally destructive to continue here any longer on the factory worker's basis."[11]

In one sense, his Dartmouth behavior was only a repetition of the similar gesture he had made in 1919 when, quitting his copy writer's job in a New York advertising agency, he went on a three-day drunk and then borrowed the money for a railroad ticket home to St. Paul, where he wrote *This Side of Paradise*. In both cases, he had compromised as long as he could. It was no easier for Fitzgerald at twenty-two to fly in the face of middle-class conventions, give up his girl and his job, and go back home to write his novel, than it was for the conscientious father and husband of twenty years later to thumb his nose at the tycoons of Hollywood. In both cases, large amounts of liquor supplied the necessary courage.

Besides, Fitzgerald was ill—how ill we can guess from a letter he sent Mrs. Frank Case in May, 1939, after his return from Dartmouth.[12]

> The situation goes back several months. . . . Very much against my will, I was persuaded to take a job to which I felt spiritually inadequate because I needed a rest from pictures and because my health was growing steadily worse. I was going to sleep every night with a gradually increasing dose of chloral—three teaspoonfulls—and two pills of nembutol every night and 48 drops of Digitalin to keep the heart working to the next day. Eventually one begins to feel like a character out of the "Wizard of Oz." Work becomes meaningless and effort a matter of the medicine closet. To the last job, I brought a great deal of individual enthusiasm, but by the end of the last week I was doing it on gin and to a person of my constitution the end of that is fairly plain.
>
> I am sorry though it was so very plain . . .

In March he worked for M-G-M several weeks on a film called "Air Raid." But he was still in bad shape physically, and at the end of this assignment—and after a bitter fight with Miss Graham—he took Zelda to Cuba for a two-week vacation; but it ended disastrously for him in the alcoholic ward of Bellevue Hospital in New York. This time his physician told him in no uncertain terms that, if he continued in this way, he would be dead within the year.

On his return, Miss Graham took him back and rented a cottage for him on the Edward Everett Horton estate in Encino, a small town in the San Fernando valley near Hollywood. Here he spent the summer and autumn in bed, blocking out his novel and trying to sell an occasional story. During June and July, his movie agent lined up several jobs for him, but he was too ill to take them. Then in September, when he felt up to taking one, the offers mysteriously dried up. He became convinced that he was being blackballed because of his Dartmouth behavior. In any event, he was unable to find movie work until the following February, 1940.[13]

Meanwhile, he had been trying to write some marketable commercial stories. In June he had sent Ober a feeler, cautiously inquiring whether there was any hope that the popular magazines were still interested in him. Ober replied reassuringly that a really good "Fitzgerald" story in the old, familiar vein was always worth at least $2,500. Encouraged by this, he tried to hammer together something light and amusing, but it was a hopeless task. His first attempt was so long-winded that Ober sent it back with instructions to chop it in half. Even then the story was promptly turned down by *Collier's* and *The Saturday Evening Post*. By now, Fitzgerald was unable to pay his rent. CANT YOU ARRANGE A FEW HUNDRED ADVANCE FROM A MAGAZINE SO I CAN EAT TODAY AND TOMORROW, he wired Ober desperately on July 14. When Ober refused and sent back the rejected story, Fitzgerald angrily demanded to know what was wrong now. Poor Ober was obliged to forward the comments of one well-known editor, who claimed "it was so garbled in the telling you can't see the story for the words."[14]

To this Fitzgerald replied with a proud, pathetic letter formally severing all further relations with the friend and adviser who had handled his business affairs so skillfully for the past twenty years.[15]

You now have plenty of authors who produce correctly and conduct their affairs in a business-like manner. On the contrary, I have a neurosis about anyone's uncertainty about my ability that has been a principal handicap in the picture business. And secondly, the semi-crippled state into which I seem to get myself sometimes (almost like the hero of my story 'Financing Finnegan') fills me, in the long nights, with a resentment toward the absurd present which is not fair to you or to the past. Everything I have ever done or written is *me*, and who doesn't choose to accept the whole cannot but see the wisdom of a parting. One doesn't change at 42 though one can grow more tired, and even more acquiescent—and I am very close to knowing how you feel about it all: I realize there is little place in this tortured world for any exhibition of shattered nerves or anything that illness makes people do.

He was now so hard up for money that he had to borrow against his dilapidated 1932 Ford to pay Edward Everett Horton the rent. There was still his old stand-by, *Esquire*. But when he wrote Arnold Gingrich, he found that he still owed him an unwritten story for which he had accepted an advance two years before! Hastily clearing up this debt, he persuaded Gingrich to let him undertake a series of stories for *Esquire* about a broken-down Hollywood script writer named Pat Hobby. Between September, 1939, and March, 1940, he ground out seventeen of these stories, widely varying in quality, for an average price of $300. During these six months, they were his sole source of income.[16]

Meanwhile, he was also busy digesting his notes about the movie industry. Although *Collier's* so far had sent back all of his stories, Kenneth Littauer, the fiction editor, had expressed genuine interest as soon as he heard that Fitzgerald was at work on a novel. He even said that if the first few chapters looked good, he might be able to advance enough money against the serial rights so that Fitzgerald could finish it. So far, however, Fitzgerald felt he had nothing ready to show Littauer. "Four months of sickness completely stripped me," he wrote him in September, "and until your telegram came I had counted on a build-up of many months' work before I could *consider* beginning the novel."[17]

But Littauer appeared ready to advance $15,000 if Fitzgerald could send him an acceptable 15,000-word opening. This, however, seemed physically out of the question. Would *Collier's* accept a smaller number of words, if they looked good enough? Taking time off from his Pat Hobby stories, Fitzgerald worked feverishly during October and November, and finally completed a 6,000-word first chapter. But the effort left him trembling and exhausted. "I think it's literally about fifty-fifty whether he'll want it or not," he wrote Max Perkins (who also received a copy), while he was nervously waiting for *Collier's* decision. ". . . Of course, if he will back me it will be a life saver, but I am by no means sure that I will ever be a popular writer again." FIRST SIX THOUSAND PRETTY CRYPTIC THEREFORE DISAPPOINTING, Littauer wired back on November twenty-eighth. But Perkins, guessing what those 6,000 words had cost Fitzgerald, eased the blow with a telegram that reached Encino

that same afternoon. A BEAUTIFUL START STIRRING AND NEW. WIRING $250.
WILL SEND $1000 BY JANUARY.[18]

December, 1939, and January, 1940, were one prolonged nightmare
for Fitzgerald. He was behind in the rent, drinking again, no longer
caring about anything or anybody. After an especially ugly fight, Miss
Graham broke with him for what she then thought was for good and all.
When she told him, before leaving, that if he kept on he would surely
kill himself, he turned his back and said, "I want to die."[19]

But in spite of the drinking and the quarrels, he continued to grind
out Pat Hobby stories. By January, poor Gingrich had more than a year's
advance supply tucked away in his *Esquire* files! When he cried
"enough," Fitzgerald rummaged around in his desk, and mailed Gingrich everything else that he had on hand, including a sodden, sentimental poem he had written to Sheilah Graham entitled "Beloved Infidel." When Gingrich replied that he did not want to run more than
one story by the same author per issue, Fitzgerald suggested that he
buy the stuff anyway and publish them as by "Paul Elgin" or "John
Darcy."[20]

> I'm awfully tired of being Scott Fitzgerald anyhow, as there
> doesn't seem to be so much money in it, and I'd like to find out if
> people read me just because I am Scott Fitzgerald or, what is more
> likely, don't read me for the same reason. . . . If the idea interests you
> I might invent a fictitious personality for Mr. Darcy. My ambition
> would be to get a fan letter from my own daughter.

Gingrich promptly returned the inept story, "Dearly Beloved," that accompanied this pathetic letter. But he did take another almost as bad,
"On an Ocean Wave," which he printed as the work of "Paul Elgin."[21]

In spite of Fitzgerald's treatment of her, Miss Graham realized that
he was going through a bad time, and at the end of January they were
together again. Several days later his financial crisis was temporarily
eased when Lester Cowan, an independent producer, bought the film
rights to "Babylon Revisited" for $800. Soon afterwards Columbia Pic-
tures, which was interested in the Cowan venture, agreed to pay Fitzgerald $2,500 for a film script based on the story (with a $2,500 bonus
if the script was accepted). In April, Miss Graham rented a flat for him
in Hollywood at 1403 Laurel Avenue, in the same building where she
had her apartment. He had stopped drinking, but was in bed most of the
time now and needed her to look after him. It was "the smallest apart-

ment . . . that will permit me not to *look poor*," he wrote Scottie, "which I can't afford to do in Hollywood."[22]

The summer of 1940 was devoted to the script of "Cosmopolitan," as "Babylon Revisited" had now been named, but Columbia could not be satisfied and it was not accepted. Then, at the end of August, he got a job at Twentieth Century-Fox working on "Brooklyn Bridge." Although his contract was only for several weeks, there was a possibility that it might be extended indefinitely. In that case he might even be able to put enough money aside so that he could finish the first draft of his half-written novel. He had been writing it with care, and the completed first draft might be good enough to get the advance that he needed in order to revise it. It was a slender hope, but the best that he had. As soon as he had signed up with Twentieth Century-Fox he sat down and made himself a work schedule:[23]

> A September 1st Schedule at the end of my 44th Year   1940
> Sept 1st—2nd Sure job
> Sept 22—Oct 20 Possible job (to save $2000)
> Three days planning novel
> Write on it to Dec 1st possibly *finishing* 1st draft. . . .
> *Not* another story—no more stories.

No more stories! "Brooklyn Bridge" was shelved before long, but Fitzgerald was kept on so that he could work on a screen adaptation of Emlyn Williams' play, *The Light of Heart*. This, too, was scrapped a few days later. But Fitzgerald, whose contract still had several weeks left to run, found himself in the pleasant position of being paid with nothing to do, and went promptly back to the novel. His plan was to keep at it "as long as my illgotten gains hold out," he wrote his Hollywood agent on November fifth. "When I finish one more chapter, probably Wednesday or Thursday," he wrote again on the twenty-sixth, "I'm going to add up my finances and figure how long I can continue as a free agent, and then I'll come to you and talk over possibilities for the future." Next day he wrote Arnold Gingrich that he was well past the mid-point of his first draft and hoped to have it finished by February.[24]

He no longer had any illusions left about his abilities as a screenwriter. "I just couldn't make the grade as a hack," he wrote Max Perkins, "—that, like everything else, requires a certain practised excellence." But *The Last Tycoon* was something else again. "I think my novel is good," he wrote Edmund Wilson on November twenty-fifth. "I've written it with difficulty. It is completely upstream in mood and will get a certain amount of abuse but is first hand and I am trying a little harder than I ever have to be exact and honest emotionally. I honestly hoped someone else would write it but nobody seems to be going to." It was slow work, though—a page a day. "But a good page," according to John O'Hara, who visited him in November and heard him read parts of it aloud.[25]

On the twenty-eighth, however, Fitzgerald had a severe heart attack and was ordered back to bed for a long rest. "I'm still in bed but managing to write and feeling a good deal better," he told Scottie on December seventh. "It was a regular heart attack this time and I will simply have to take better care of myself." On the thirteenth, he wrote Perkins that, in spite of his being bedridden, the novel was progressing, "—in fact progresses fast. I'm not going to stop now till I finish a first draft which will be some time after the 15th of January. However, let's pretend that it doesn't exist until it's closer to completion. We don't want it to become —'a legend before it is written,' which is what I believe Wheelock [John Hall Wheelock of Scribner's editorial staff] said about 'Tender Is the Night.' Meanwhile you will send me back the chapters I sent you as they are all invalid now, must be completely rewritten, etc. The essential idea is the same and is still, as far as I can hope, a secret. . . . This is the first day off I have taken for many months. . . ."[26]

The very next day, December fourteenth, he set himself a new schedule of one thousand words a day. By writing this much seven days a week, he figured that his first draft should be finished four weeks later, on January eleventh. Thereafter, he stuck steadily to this routine. There was no time for any more letters to Perkins, and only one for Scottie. "I am still in bed," he wrote, "—this time the result of twenty-five years of cigarettes. You have got two beautiful bad examples for parents. Just do everything we didn't do and you will be perfectly safe." On the twenty-second, he had a second attack while escorting Miss Graham to the opening of a new film, and he died two days later in her living room from another attack, a few minutes after two o'clock in the afternoon.[27]

XV

The
Last Tycoon:
The Hollywood
Theme

Hollywood, like other successful institutions, has never lacked for enemies. Since Fitzgerald's death, he has often been cited as proof of the movie industry's profligate waste of talent. According to one story, the screen adaptation of "Babylon Revisited" that Fitzgerald made for Lester Cowan in 1940 was actually one of the finest scripts ever written in Hollywood. Several years later, the story goes, when Cowan hired a famous author to revise it, the latter returned it to Cowan unchanged, saying, "This is the most perfect motion-picture script I have ever read." Whereupon Cowan reportedly replied, "You're absolutely right. I'll pay you two thousand a week to stay out here and keep me from changing one word of it."[1]

The truth is that Fitzgerald's screen adaptation of "Babylon Revisited" was not especially good. In his attempt to stretch an excellent magazine story into a ninety-minute film, he cheapened and padded it almost beyond recognition. To the story of Charles Wales's touching effort to regain custody of his small daughter, he added a sentimental love story between Wales and a hospital nurse, as well as a gangster subplot that brought the film to a close with a slapstick cops-and-robbers chase across Paris. In the process, the tender father-daughter relationship of the original story, and the memorable mood of *temps perdu*, were both virtually obliterated.[2]

None of Fitzgerald's movie scripts, from his 1927 scenario for "Lipstick" and his 1934 adaptation of *Tender Is the Night* through the work of his Hollywood years, is distinguished, or of more than routine interest.

Like most of his magazine stories, his scripts suffered from overplotting. Plots, of course, had always been his chief weakness and this was an especially severe handicap for a would-be movie writer. Given a good, clear story line, a skillful director can flesh out the rest of the picture with the technical resources at his command—actors, camera, sets, etc. Somerset Maugham's stories make exceptionally good films because he almost invariably spins a good yarn.

But Maugham lies at the far end of the spectrum from a writer like Fitzgerald. In the latter's best work, plot has been reduced to a minimum. For the most part, Fitzgerald drew on the mythology of folklore. His best novels and stories retell the familiar legends of youth's coming of age, the grail quest, the noble fool, the self-made man. Here the narrative pattern was simple, direct, and free of artifice. He had little or no talent for the well-made yarn. His art lay rather in the skill with which he used dialogue, imagery, dramatic situations, and atmosphere to revitalize the old myths and give them present-day relevance. No wonder he could not convert "Babylon Revisited" into a successful movie. Every effort Hollywood has so far made to transfer his fiction to the screen has failed because his art is so circumscribed by its exclusively *literary* qualities. To express his fictions through the camera, a director would have to invent cinematographic conventions to convey the ideas and feelings that Fitzgerald expresses through the quite different medium of prose.

Thus, it was almost inevitable that Fitzgerald should fail in Hollywood. He lacked those rational habits of mind so essential for the technician who is fated to work in a large, collaborative industry. In a big picture studio such as Metro-Goldwyn-Mayer's during the 1930's, decisions were reached and policies formulated only after much preliminary planning. That is why a device like the "treatment" played such an important role in determining the choice of a potential film. But a treatment represented exactly that kind of rational approach to experience that Fitzgerald had never mastered. When M-G-M's editorial department expressed interest in his proposal for making a film based on his Basil Duke Lee *Saturday Evening Post* stories, the first thing he was asked to produce was a treatment outlining the kind of a film he had in mind. Instead, Fitzgerald submitted a long letter explaining why he disliked treatments—"one of those bastard forms, neither summary or short story, which I am unable to write." As a result, M-G-M promptly lost interest.[3]

Another reason for his failure in Hollywood was that he instinctively realized that there was little place for the writer in the movies. The script writer, like the actor, the cameraman, the set designer, is only one of the many technical elements that go into the making of a successful film. Every work of art, whatever the medium, is finally the end product of one single, unifying imagination. And in movie making (even more, perhaps, than in the legitimate theater) the only individual who is so functionally situated that he can exercise this responsibility is the director.

Fitzgerald, who had always been fascinated by the movies, had sensed this back in 1924, long before he knew very much about the industry from the inside. At that time, he had unsuccessfully tried to persuade George Horace Lorimer to let him write an article on the subject for *The Saturday Evening Post*, tentatively titled "Why Only Ten Percent of Movies Succeed." Only the outline exists, but the point about the director's role was very clear. "Complexity of the Movie Situation Should be a Director's business," he noted at the top of his proposed essay. "Experiments with authors are failures [,] with commercial dominance are failures [,] with 'star' dominance are failures. . . . The cry for better pictures means more intelligent directors and not more highbrow stories. They [the directors] do not realize that "Do and Dare" by Horatio Alger done with *new symbols*, new *conventions* would require more *intelligence* than a diluted version of Joseph Conrad's *The Rover*. . . . The movie people are too lenient on their directors. It is the director not the censor or the poor exhibitor or the star who is absolutely responsible." "This idea developed, tentative solution, examples, etc.," he explained, would form the proposed essay. "Incidentally," he assured Lorimer in a postscript, "I have no desire to be a movie director."[4]

It was not a new or original insight. About this time Pudovkin, the Russian producer and critic, was saying much the same thing in his classic series of lectures, *On Film Technique*. But so long as Fitzgerald viewed movie making in this way it was difficult for him to respect his role as a script writer, no matter how much he was paid for his scripts. When he did occasionally forget the screen writer's lowly function and decided to take his scripts seriously, as in the *Three Comrades* job, he reverted to his role as a responsible novelist and then fought tooth and nail for that autonomy which any creative artist must exercise over his medium. No wonder he had trouble with an expert like Joe Mankiewicz![5]

But even though script writing as a career offered little challenge to him, he had always been fascinated by the motion-picture industry as literary subject matter. As far back as 1920, so he said, he had tried unsuccessfully to persuade D.W. Griffith that the craft of movie making itself was a wonderful subject for a picture. According to Fitzgerald, Griffith had laughed at him, but the success of *Merton of the Movies* not long afterwards proved Fitzgerald right.[6]

For a long time he had been especially fascinated by the career of Irving Thalberg, the boy genius who more than any other single individual was responsible for Metro-Goldwyn-Mayer's top position among the movie studios. Where a lesser novelist, down on his luck in Hollywood, might easily have made his own plight the subject of his novel, Fitzgerald turned instead to the more heroic legend of Thalberg, the great organizing genius who, more than anyone else, was responsible for the transformation of a cheap form of entertainment into a billion-dollar, mass-production industry that for a time shaped the tastes and values of movie-goers throughout the world.

Few movie-goers were aware of the magnitude of Thalberg's contribution, however, when he died in 1936, only thirty-seven years old. Although, as chief of M-G-M production, he had been responsible for the filming of hundreds of box-office hits, he had never once permitted his name to appear on a film. The son of a Brooklyn lace merchant, he had been a frail, sickly child. An attack of rheumatic fever disrupted his schooling and weakened his heart. But he also possessed ceaseless drive and energy. At seventeen, after a night-school business course, he got his first job as a stenographer in the New York office of Universal Pictures. Here his talents caught the eye of the president, Carl Laemmle, Sr., who made him his private secretary. From then on Thalberg's rise was breathtaking. Before he was twenty he was running Universal's Hollywood studio. Several years later he left Universal to run the studios of the L.B. Mayer Company. In 1924 when Loew's, the giant theater chain, combined the Metro, Goldwyn, and Mayer Studios, Thalberg, aged twenty-five, was made vice-president in charge of all M-G-M production.

Under Thalberg's leadership, M-G-M rapidly forged ahead to become the biggest, richest, and best-known movie studio in the world. His success was not due to any single talent, but rather to a unique combination of talents: a thorough understanding of the technical side of picture making, an uncanny ability to anticipate popular taste, and a gift for working creatively with people. There were other producers who were greater artists. Thalberg's genius lay in his superb executive ability. He was the first producer to put the manufacture of high-quality films on a production-line basis, and yet retain their individual integrity. As head of M-G-M production he set a production schedule of one "A" quality film a week—and met this schedule week after week with a string of successful films. From his early silent film hits ("Ben Hur," "The Big

Parade," "The Hunchback of Notre Dame") to such later trail-blazing successes as "Marie Antoinette" and "A Midsummer Night's Dream," he steadily turned out pictures that set standards for the entire industry. The success of his "Broadway Melody" taught Hollywood that it could create original musical shows rivaling Broadway's best. Thalberg's production of sophisticated modern comedies like "The Guardsman" and "Dinner at Eight" surpassed even the original New York stage productions in elegance and polish. Through films he made it possible for millions to enjoy expensive productions of plays and musicals that hitherto had been accessible only to a lucky few.

As chief of M-G-M's studio, Thalberg insisted on the same independence for his artists that he himself asserted—although this involved him in a constant battle with the New York office, interested primarily in profits. He was willing to lose money on occasional experimental films which might pioneer new conventions that, in time, might lead to box-office hits. Such experiments attracted the loyalty of the many talented foreign artists who preferred M-G-M and Thalberg over any other Hollywood studio. Intelligent, shrewd, sensitive, dedicated, Thalberg did more than any other individual to make Hollywood, for a time, one of the most glamorous cities of the world. But there was a price: insomnia, neurosis, and finally death from exhaustion. Since his death, Thalberg has emerged as one of Hollywood's most authentic heroes. "Modest in demeanor, somewhat reserved, and vastly considerate of the talents and opinions of his subordinates in whom he inspired uncommon loyalty and devotion . . . Thalberg was," according to the *Dictionary of American Biography*, "the shining example of the motion picture executive." Bosley Crowther's history of Metro-Goldwyn-Mayer, *The Lion's Share*, is one long paean of praise to Thalberg's memory. He was, Crowther says, "the grand fulfillment of professional Hollywood's sublime ideal . . . the symbol of its worth."[7]

Very little of all this, however, was evident to Fitzgerald while Thalberg was alive. It was only after his death in 1936, and after Fitzgerald himself had gone to work for M-G-M, that he began to appreciate Thalberg's greatness. The two met back in 1927, when Fitzgerald was writing for United Artists on "Lipstick," but they had known each other only socially. On his second visit in 1931 to work for M-G-M on "Red-Headed Woman," however, he had reported first to Thalberg. But that venture, like the first, had ended badly. Fitzgerald resented having to team up with one of Thalberg's regular M-G-M writers; and since Thalberg was supposed to have invented the practice of writers working in teams, this visit did not increase Fitzgerald's admiration.

Just how much Fitzgerald's feelings about Thalberg in 1932 were tempered by dislike we can see in the short story, "Crazy Sunday," that he wrote soon after his return from Hollywood. Here, the hero, Miles Calman, is an easily recognizable portrait of Thalberg. In depicting Calman, Fitzgerald drew upon a number of well-known stories about Thalberg as well as upon his own personal impressions. Like Thalberg, Calman is "the only American-born director with both an interesting temperament and an artistic conscience . . . the only director on the lot who did not work under a supervisor and was responsible to the money men alone. . . . [H]e had never made a cheap picture though he had sometimes paid heavily for the luxury of making experimental flops." And like Thalberg, who had recently married Norma Shearer, Calman is married to a beautiful actress named Stella Walker. Calman's mother lives with her son, just as Mrs. Thalberg lived with her son and Miss Shearer.

In "Crazy Sunday," the action is narrated by a young writer from the East named Joel Coles. Like Fitzgerald, Joel is a recent arrival who is still learning about screen writing. At first, he violently dislikes Miles Calman, whom he considers responsible for the lowly position of the studio script writer. Thus, when Joel is invited to a Sunday cocktail party at the Calman residence, he brusquely tells the doting Mrs. Calman that he is personally "against" everything her son stands for. Calman himself, on his first appearance, cuts a sorry spectacle with his silly remarks about his various psychiatrists and his neuroses. Like Thalberg, Calman is a nervous hypochondriac who has a violent prejudice against alcoholics. "Meshed in an industry," Fitzgerald says, "he had paid with his ruined nerves for having no resilience, no healthy cynicism, no refuge —only a pitiful and precarious escape."

On the other hand, Joel is swept off his feet at his first meeting with Calman's wife, the lovely Stella Walker. And since Stella seems to be miserable in her marriage, Joel obligingly fills in as her escort. They are alone together not long after this first party when a telegram arrives announcing that Calman has been killed in an airplane crash. Now, stripped of her husband's Pygmalion-like presence, Stella reverts to type before Joel's astonished eyes. She is seen as nothing more than a tramp whom Calman had taken from the streets and made into his greatest production. At this point, "Crazy Sunday" fails as a work of fiction for readers who find it impossible to reconcile the charming Stella Walker of the first part of the story with the brassy nymphomaniac she has become at the end. Nor is there much consistency between the pathetic Miles Calman to whom we were first introduced and the heroic producer whose death leaves Joel so profoundly moved. Nonetheless, it is clear that in "Crazy Sunday" Fitzgerald was trying to develop in Miles Calman an imaginative figure of heroic proportions whose abilities, in the long run, far outshone his obvious shortcomings. "Everything he touched he did something magical to . . . ," Joel realizes in the last paragraph of the story. "He even brought that little gamin alive and made her a sort of masterpiece . . . What a hell of a hole he leaves in this damn wilderness."[8]

This was Fitzgerald's opinion in 1932, when Thalberg was at the height of his power. How big that hole was actually to become, Fitzgerald himself would not fully realize until he returned to the M-G-M lot five years later in 1937. Without Thalberg, according to Bosley Crowther's history of Metro-Goldwyn-Mayer,

> . . . the studio [had] lost its savor. . . . It became a mere mass-producing combine, a huge motion picture dispensing machine. . . . The sense of an inspirational influence, a *genius domus,* the studio had had while he was there, even under the unit system, was gone. There was little or no sense of closeness or creative participation with [L.B.] Mayer who was now the supreme administrator. The air that emanated was one of remote authority.

Or, as Fitzgerald's old friend, Charlie MacArthur, put it somewhat more succinctly: working at Culver City after Thalberg's death was like "going to the automat."[9]

When, in the fall of 1936, Fitzgerald learned of Thalberg's death, his first emotion had been one of relief. "Thalberg's final collapse," he wrote a friend, "is the death of an enemy for me, though I liked the guy enormously. . . . I think . . . that he killed the idea of either Hopkins or Frederick March doing 'Tender Is the Night.'" But whatever resentment he had felt toward Thalberg living soon evaporated after he had spent eighteen months on the M-G-M lot that no longer had Thalberg to guide its destiny. For, as Crowther documents again and again in his history of Metro-Goldwyn-Mayer, neither M-G-M nor the industry at large was able to find a successor to fill his place. Thalberg's death marked the ultimate triumph of the commercialism that for so many years he had successfully held at bay. The battle between the idealists still loyal to Thalberg and the cohorts of the New York financiers was still raging on the M-G-M lot when Fitzgerald arrived a year later. But the end was already in sight. It was this epic conflict, symbolized by the heroic figure of the dead producer, that Fitzgerald intended to portray in the most ambitious of all his books, *The Last Tycoon*.[10]

The earliest evidence that Fitzgerald had been thinking of writing a new novel occurs in a letter to Perkins dated October 16, 1936, in which he said he had one "planned, or rather I should say conceived," that would make a book "certainly as long as Tender Is the Night" and would take at least two years to write. He was too broke at the moment even to think of starting work on it, however. "I certainly have this one more novel [in me]," he wrote, "but it may have to remain among the unwritten books of this world."[11]

Since this letter was written soon after news reached him about Thalberg's death, one wonders if the book he mentions was to have been based on Thalberg's career. The first mention of *The Last Tycoon* does not occur until December, 1938, over two years later, again in a letter to Max Perkins. By then, according to Sheilah Graham, Fitzgerald had already accumulated a large collection of notes for his novel, though he had not yet begun to write it. Knowing what we do about Fitzgerald's methods of working, it seems quite possible that the idea for *The Last Tycoon* had been taking shape gradually in Fitzgerald's mind for several years.[12]

As part of his preliminary planning during 1937 and 1938, he not only took copious notes about the more technical aspects of M-G-M's complex operations, but he read everything that he could lay his hands on relating to Thalberg, including an excellent article on the M-G-M organization that had been published in a 1933 issue of *Fortune*, as well as an article on movie making written by Thalberg himself and published in *The Saturday Evening Post* that same year. "Thalberg has always fascinated me," Fitzgerald wrote Kenneth Littauer in 1939, in a letter outlining his plans for *The Last Tycoon:*[13]

His peculiar charm, his extraordinary good looks, his bountiful success, the tragic end of his great adventure. The events I have built around him are fiction, but all of them are things which might very well have happened, and I am pretty sure that I saw deep enough into the character of the man so that his reactions are authentically what they would have been in life. So much so that he may be recognized—but it will be also recognized that *no single fact is actually true*. . . . This is a novel not even faintly of the propaganda type. Indeed Thalberg's opinions were entirely different from mine in (this has been in my mind for three years) because he is one of the many respects that I will not go into. I've long chosen him for a hero

266   F. Scott Fitzgerald

half-dozen men I have known who were built on the grand scale. . . .
Certainly if Ziegfeld could be made into an epic figure, then what
about Thalberg who was literally everything that Ziegfeld wasn't?

Among Fitzgerald's notes was the draft of a letter he intended to send
his good friend Norma Shearer when *The Last Tycoon* was finished, asking her permission to make use of some of the incidents from her husband's life. Although he had not known Thalberg well, Fitzgerald wrote,
the impression he had made had been "very dazzling." And Monroe
Stahr, the hero of his novel, had been inspired primarily by that impression, "though I have put in some things drawn from other men, and,
inevitably, much of myself. I invented a tragic story and Irving's life
was, of course, not tragic except his struggle against ill-health because
no one has ever written a tragedy about Hollywood. *A Star is Born* was
a pathetic and often beautiful story, but not a tragedy and doomed and
heroic things do happen here."[14]

But, although Fitzgerald saw the heroic aspects of Thalberg's career,
he did not intend to gloss over Monroe Stahr's very real limitations as a
human being. Stahr shares Thalberg's hypochondria, his ruthlessness
and his impatience with mediocrity, his inability to relax, and his rather
middle-class artistic taste. "Stahr left certain harm behind him just as he
left good behind him," Fitzgerald reminded himself in one of his many
notes.[15]

Primarily, it was Thalberg's superb managerial abilities that held
Fitzgerald's fascinated attention: Thalberg—the head of a huge collaborative enterprise; the artful juggler of budgets, casting lists, shooting
schedules; the skilled supervisor of unit producers, directors, assistant
directors, actors, cameramen, cutters, script writers, and craftsmen and
technicians of every kind. Where was there a more striking illustration
of the union of native managerial talent and modern mass-production
techniques for the production of a unique work of art? From boyhood,
Fitzgerald had always admired successful executives, from tycoons like
James J. Hill and Grandfather McQuillan, and the politicos on the
Princeton campus, to talented social impresarios and party-givers like
Gerald Murphy.

It was not mere managerial talent alone that he admired, but the
ability to use that talent in the creation of something of genuine aesthetic
value—a magnanimous gesture, a heroic image, one of the Murphys'
memorable Riviera parties, a colorful Broadway show, or a first-rate motion picture. Back in 1926, Fitzgerald had unsuccessfully tried to persuade Ring Lardner to write "the real history of an American [theatrical]

manager—say Ziegfeld." But after he became acquainted with Thalberg, Ziegfeld's achievements paled by comparison.[16]

Thus, it was important that Monroe Stahr's executive capabilities should be firmly established from the very beginning of the novel. In one of his notes for an episode in the first chapter, Fitzgerald said:[17]

> This will be based on a conversation that I had with Thalberg the first time I was alone with him in 1927, the day that he said a thing about railroads. As near as I can remember what he said was this:
>
> We sat in the old commissary at Metro and he said, "Scottie, supposing there's got to be a road through a mountain and . . . there seem to be a half dozen possible roads . . . each one of which, so far as you can determine, is as good as the other. Now suppose you happen to be the top man, there's a point where you don't exercise the faculty of judgment in the ordinary way, but simply the faculty of arbitrary decision. You say, 'Well, I think we will put the road there,' and you trace it with your finger and you know in your secret heart, and no one else knows, that you have no reason for putting the road there rather than in several other different courses, but you're the only person that knows that you don't know why you're doing it and you've got to stick to that and you've got to pretend that you know and that you did it for specific reasons, even though you're utterly assailed by doubts at times as to the wisdom of your decision, because all these other possible decisions keep echoing in your ear. But when you're planning a new enterprise on a grand scale, the people under you mustn't ever know or guess that you're in doubt, because they've all got to have something to look up to and they mustn't ever dream that you're in doubt about any decision. These things keep occuring."
>
> At that point, some other people came into the commissary and sat down, and the first thing I knew there was a group of four and the intimacy of the conversation was broken, but I was very much impressed by the shrewdness of what he said—something more than shrewdness—by the largeness of what he thought and how he reached it by the age of twenty-six, which he was then.

Gradually, as Monroe Stahr's image took shape in Fitzgerald's imagination, his resemblance to the historical Thalberg decreased, and he assumed a personality that was both more individualized and more representative. Fitzgerald began to think of him as embodying the virtues of the ideal executive, much as he had once conceived of Dick Diver as possessing heroic qualities of social leadership and charm. Turning from the facts of Thalberg's career, Fitzgerald investigated afresh the lives of several other well-known political and military leaders from the past. He read Philip Guedalla's biography of the Duke of Wellington, as well as A.H. Burne's study of three Civil War generals, *Lee, Grant and Sherman,* and J.A. Froude's *Julius Caesar.* In the last of these, the Victorian Froude portrayed the noblest Roman of them all as a nineteenth-century English liberal who fought in the name of the people against a corrupt, tyrannical, aristocratic senate that eventually betrayed and murdered him. Froude's Caesar was a skillful leader of men who possessed great executive abilities, and who, because of his insight into human nature, was able to direct the most diverse talents, welding them into a loyal, purposeful organization. Undoubtedly this interpretation of Caesar had a discernible influence on Fitzgerald's conception of Stahr. John O'Hara, visiting his old friend for the last time not long before Fitzgerald's death, was somewhat nonplused to find Fitzgerald constantly steering the conversation back to the exploits of Julius Caesar. He was further disconcerted when, at his departure, Fitzgerald insisted on lending him his old battered copy of Froude's book, so that O'Hara could read up on the subject.[18]

Besides Stahr's affinities with Caesar, Fitzgerald also planned to emphasize certain parallels between his hero and two potent American political executives: Abraham Lincoln and Andrew Jackson. Jackson was intended to illustrate the ruthless, autocratic elements in Stahr's personality. Old Hickory was the first strong American president, and Stahr was a general waging war on a dozen fronts at once—against lazy subordinates, jealous associates, penny-pinching financiers, power-hungry labor unions. In his single-minded struggle to maintain independent authority over his organization, Stahr—like any other general—found it necessary at times to permit himself a minor moral infraction for the sake of a larger good. Stahr's ruthlessness in this respect is brought out at the beginning of the story by his attitude toward Manny Schwartz, the worn-out producer whom he brutally snubs because he has lost his usefulness. Significantly, Schwartz soon afterwards commits suicide on the steps of "The Hermitage," Andrew Jackson's homestead near Nashville. But even Manny Schwartz perceives Stahr's heroic qualities. Before he kills himself he takes the trouble to send Stahr a message warning him of his many enemies, and praising him as "the best of them all."[19]

Further on in the novel, Fitzgerald planned to bring out Stahr's affinities with the somewhat different, and more compassionate, figure of Abraham Lincoln. Stahr was also to be an expert political strategist, an artist in human relationships. Instead of removing his enemies, for instance, Stahr follows Lincoln's practice and keeps them where he can watch what they are doing. Like Lincoln, he knows how to use the element of play as a means of getting things done. At one stage in Fitzgerald's planning, he intended to have Stahr meet his death in front of the capitol in Washington. When Fitzgerald himself died, he was still not certain how he was going to work out the full implications of the Lincoln-Jackson association that he had so far indicated only in crude terms.[20]

Fitzgerald also went out of his way to make Monroe Stahr's origins more lowly and impoverished than Thalberg's had been, in order to link his hero more firmly with the Lincolnesque myth of rags-to-riches success that he had already examined in *The Great Gatsby*. Here it is significant to recall that practically all of the manuscript of *The Last Tycoon* was written after the outbreak of the European War in September, 1939, and that Fitzgerald's beloved France and her allies were fighting for a cause Fitzgerald believed to be America's and his own. Back in 1928, in a newspaper interview foreseeing that crisis, he said that the nation's survival lay "in the birth of a hero who will be of age when America's testing comes." Such a leader, he believed, would probably emerge "out of the immigrant class in the guise of an East Side newsboy." Stahr, the poor tailor's son from the Bronx, derives from that Horatio Alger myth of success in which Fitzgerald still firmly believed.[21]

But just as Monroe Stahr is a more complex and tragic symbol of that myth than the pathetic Gatsby had been, so Fitzgerald's view of his native country had changed drastically from that which he recorded in *The Great Gatsby* in the early 1920's. After the disillusioning expatriate years abroad, Fitzgerald no longer believed the United States to be that corrupted earthly paradise whose lost innocence he had hymned in the final sentences of *The Great Gatsby*. Instead, as the war clouds gathered, he saw both Stahr and the nation he represented as symbolizing the best values of the West. In one of the random notes lying between the pages of his *Last Tycoon* manuscript he said:[22]

I look out at it and I think it is the most beautiful history in the world. It is the history of me and my people. And if I came here yesterday like Sheilah I should still think so. It is the history of all aspiration—not just the American dream but the human dream and if I came at the end of it that too is a place in the line of pioneers.

Stahr was intended to exemplify the ideal qualities of the successful American business executive. His business is that of applying native production-line techniques to the mass production of unique works of art, at the rate of one each week. He is *par excellence* that most indigenous of all our achievements, the American business manager. The nature and extent of his managerial talents are best seen in Chapters II and III, in which we are shown one of Stahr's typical business days. Both chapters deserve thoughtful study by any aspiring junior executive. Here we see Stahr confronting and solving one major problem in human relations after another; tactfully but effectively removing a director who has failed to manage his movie crew; reviving the jaded spirits of a team of script writers; persuading a group of hard-nosed New York financiers that the artistic prestige to be gained from an unconventional film will more than make up for its probable financial losses; smoothing the jangled nerves of a spoiled, neurotic actress who, for better or worse, is still a valuable piece of studio property that must be kept in condition; restoring the shattered self-confidence of a cameraman whose services are irreplaceable; winning the confidence of a high-priced British novelist, who cannot get through his head just what picture making is all about.

Stahr's success in this role is due to two particular gifts—his articulateness, and the interest in people as individuals that allows him, despite his own aesthetic limitations, to work effectively with creative artists. Both are superbly brought out in one of the best scenes in the book in which Stahr explains to George Boxley, the British novelist, how movie making differs from other kinds of creative activity. Stahr does so merely by telling Boxley a story consisting of a series of dramatic actions. When Boxley's interest is inevitably aroused, Stahr suddenly stops, and reminds him that all he had been doing is "making pictures." Not only has Stahr made his point, but Fitzgerald has demonstrated his hero's genius for communicating with temperaments radically different from his own. The episode itself consists entirely of dialogue and images, and reads so smoothly that it seems to be nothing more than a literal transcription of something Fitzgerald had once observed. But it is more than this. Although some of the inspiration came from a conference that he had once witnessed at which Aldous Huxley was present, Fitzgerald also built the episode from his memories of many other such conferences, all of them carefully reported in his notebooks. As an author, Fitzgerald resented the script writer's menial position in the studio as vehemently as George Boxley did. But he did not let this resentment color his treatment of Monroe Stahr's very different view of the script writer's responsibilities. And, at the end, Boxley is brought around to a grudging admiration of Stahr's managerial genius. Stahr also is an artist, Boxley acknowledges, but he[23] was an artist only, as Mr. Lincoln was a general, perforce and as a layman. . . . He had been reading Lord Charnwood and he recognized that Stahr like Lincoln was a leader carrying on a long war on many fronts; almost single-handed he had moved pictures sharply forward through a decade . . .

So far, the significance of Fitzgerald's portrait of Stahr as a heroic businessman has been overlooked by *The Last Tycoon's* admirers. Yet Monroe Stahr is one of the best renderings we have had in our literature of that most typical of all American figures. Traditionally, the businessman in literature has been portrayed almost solely as the object of scorn and ridicule. From Trimalchio and Pantaloon, Volpone and Monsieur Jourdain, Bouvard and Pécuchet, to Père Grandet, and the Buddenbrooks and Forsytes, the business mentality has almost never been regarded as admirable. Even in the United States, that most businesslike of civilizations, the businessman has been portrayed more often as a Babbitt than a man of creative talent. Professor E.E. Cassady, after an exhaustive study of the dozens of American novels dealing with the subject, notes that the businessman has never been presented in our literature as "a large-minded, generous, disinterested, heroic character."[24]

Henry James, with his characteristic insight, recognized the businessman as our civilization's most representative figure. But, lacking any practical contact with business itself, James was forced to admit (after several unsuccessful attempts to portray him in his fiction) that "before the American businessman I was absolutely and irremediably helpless." In more recent years, many other writers—Frank Norris, Theodore Dreiser, Edith Wharton, Sinclair Lewis, among them—have tried to come to terms with him in their work. But even they were content, for the most part, to describe him outside business hours. We see the businessman boring his wife, ruining his children's lives, stumbling on the social ladder. But we rarely see him in the office where whatever ability and imagination he possesses would be most tellingly demonstrated. What sets *The Last Tycoon* apart from other novels about the businessman (with the exception, perhaps, of Howells' *The Rise of Silas Lapham*) is that Fitzgerald conceived of Monroe Stahr as a doomed and heroic figure whose heroism and whose doom were both the consequences of his success as a man of business. Stahr, in short, is the self-made man whose destruction is brought about by the business organization that his talents and imagination have created. His studio has become so large and complex that he can no longer control its destiny. Instead, he is caught between the divisive forces that are fighting for domination.

On the one hand there are the New York financiers and theater owners who provide the capital for Stahr's films. Interested only in profits, they see motion pictures solely as commodities to be made as cheaply and sold as dearly as possible. In the novel, forces representing these interests are scheming to replace Stahr by his more subservient and less competent rival, Pat Brady.[25]

On the other hand, Stahr finds himself confronted by the ever growing threat of the labor unions. Here the danger is that his own artists will collectively force him to abandon the artistic standards he has hitherto defended against such odds. As a producer, Stahr knows that no picture can be better artistically than the director. Therefore the director must command absolute loyalty from his subordinates. This is the price for a first-rate product in any collaborative enterprise. Stahr insists on his sole right to dictate the artistic standards for the studio, but in exchange he shares his success generously with his artists.

But all this, he fears, is threatened by the growing power of the labor unions. They will insist on substituting watered-down, abstract, professional standards of competency for those that Stahr has created by himself. Moreover, the unions will divert his workers' attention from quality films to extraneous political, social, and economic considerations. This is implied by the figure of Brimmer, the Communist labor organizer who appears briefly in Chapter VI. The one thing both the unions and the New York moneymen share is their suspicion of Stahr's preoccupation with the artistic considerations of his job. This is a mystery neither is able to comprehend. Yet Stahr's battle is a hopeless one. In the past, he has been able to command his employees' loyalties by his personal friendship, but now the studio has become too large. Inevitably, his artists are beginning to look to one another for that respect and understanding they once received from Stahr. Ill, tired out by years of hard work, he no longer has the energy to resist the opposing forces closing in on him.

Although he is a doomed figure, it is wrong to say, as one commentator has, that Stahr therefore is "completely anomalous in the twentieth century." In a sense he *is* representative of the old-fashioned paternalistic employer. But as the head of a flourishing organization, Stahr surely has a more permanent significance. Every organization begins as the shadow of a man; but if it succeeds, it becomes an independent institution with an existence all its own. Then, like every other organism, it is responsible for its own survival. And in that struggle for survival no other organism, not even the individual who created it, becomes as important as itself. Stahr's predicament is thus a very familiar one. He is the individual locked in a struggle with the organization he has created, but which he no longer has the power to control. His plight is peculiarly relevant to our own super-organized society. Stahr, the tired businessman, grimly clinging to his job until he dies of a heart attack (or is carried away stubbornly sitting at his desk, like a recent president of Montgomery Ward)—is he really an outmoded hero? Fitzgerald's title, *The Last Tycoon,* was surely chosen for its ironic overtones. The *last?* How many other imaginative organizers—capitalistic, socialistic, communistic, or whatever their label—are destined to repeat Stahr's tragic destiny?[26]

It is also ironic that Wylie White, the disillusioned screen writer who, of all the other characters in the book most resembles Fitzgerald, should be the person who understands Stahr best, and sees his tragic flaw. Stahr's strength, and his weakness, is that he cares too much. Herein lies his nobility and his pathos, his triumph and his doom. Instead of quitting while he is ahead, cutting his losses, and accepting the girl who loves him and wants to take care of him, Stahr insists on remaining at the helm of his sinking ship. Wylie White, like Fitzgerald, was "a free-lancer . . . [who] had failed from lack of caring." "But here," Wylie realizes, as he witnesses Stahr's tragedy, "here was Stahr to care for all of them."[27]

Finally, quite apart from Stahr's role as the representative American business manager, Fitzgerald also thought of him as a moral symbol for the Hollywood film community itself—that glittering Babylon he had once described as "one of the most romantic cities in the world." Although Hollywood had defeated Fitzgerald as surely as it had destroyed Irving Thalberg, it continued nonetheless to fascinate him. Through the idea of Monroe Stahr, he hoped to be able to come to terms with his own ambiguous feelings about the screen colony.[28]

He hoped to do this by telling Stahr's story from the point of view of someone as morally involved as Fitzgerald was with the problem of Hollywood. For this narrator he chose Cecilia Brady, the college-age daughter of Pat Brady, Stahr's bitterest enemy as well as his closest associate. Unlike both her father and Stahr, Cecilia has enjoyed the so-called "advantages." Born and bred a stone's throw from Sunset Boulevard, she is herself as much a Hollywood production as one of Stahr's "A" pictures. But she has also had the benefits of an exclusive Eastern girls' college. There, looking back on Hollywood from the greener perspective of a secluded New England campus, she has seen it in all its stark and pretentious ugliness. Although she can no longer accept the movie colony at its own inflated value, neither can she write it off as easily as her supercilious Eastern classmates. It is, after all, the most vital part of herself, and if Cecilia is ever to know herself, she must begin by understanding the culture that produced her.

In this sense, Cecilia Brady's desire to understand Monroe Stahr is the result of her need to comprehend Hollywood as a moral idea. How desperate that necessity was we can guess from the fact that in one version of *The Last Tycoon*, Fitzgerald planned to have Cecilia tell Stahr's tragedy while she herself was dying of tuberculosis. In this version Stahr was to have been murdered.

Was there actually any moral justification for Hollywood, anyway? Nathanael West, a talented Hollywood writer whose work Fitzgerald admired, had asked this question in *The Day of the Locust* in 1939, and replied with an unqualified negative. The Hollywood he described in that novel had been a nightmare so horrible that only the distortions of surrealism were able to do his hatred of it justice. West's Hollywood is a moral waste land not unlike the waste land of Dr. T.J. Eckelburg—but West's hatred burned more intensely than Fitzgerald's. At the end of *The Day of the Locust*, West destroyed Hollywood in a righteous, Old Testament holocaust of smoke and flame.

Much as Fitzgerald admired this novel, he could not accept West's over-simplified solution to the problem. *The Day of the Locust* was "literature," he said, but "the underworld of literature." It was concerned only with partial truths. To a novelist like West, or Wylie White, or George Boxley, or even Fitzgerald himself, Hollywood might indeed seem like a nightmare world. But what were good writers like these doing wasting their time in Hollywood? For those who were morally involved in the community, what help was the literary hatred of an acknowledged outsider? To someone like Cecilia Brady, the judgments of the Wests and Boxleys were, at best, irrelevant. Wasn't there some positive value to justify the movie community's existence and hence, her own? In the story of Monroe Stahr she found that vindication—Stahr, "who almost single-handed . . . had moved pictures sharply forward . . . to the point where an "A" production was wider and richer than that of the stage."[29]

"At certain points," Fitzgerald says in another note for the novel, "one man appropriates to himself the total significance of a time or place." For Cecilia, Stahr was such a man. "You can take Hollywood for granted," she tells the reader on the first page of her story, ". . . or you can dismiss it with the contempt we reserve for what we don't understand. It can be understood, too, but dimly and in flashes. Not half a dozen men have ever been able to keep the whole equation in their heads. Perhaps the closest a woman can come to the set-up is to try to understand one of these men."[30]

Was there no *better* way to get at the meaning of Hollywood? By an odd coincidence, another investigation also got under way in January, 1939—the same month that Fitzgerald was fired from his Metro-Gold-wyn-Mayer job and began to make serious plans for writing *The Last Tycoon.* This second project was nothing less than a full-dress sociologi-cal analysis of the movie community by a team of expert social scientists, backed by a quarter of a million dollars of Carnegie and Rockefeller foundation money. It was inaugurated with all the ballyhoo of one of the picture industry's own "A" productions. Among its distinguished sponsors were such well-known scholars as Margaret Mead and Gregory Bateson, with Walter Wanger himself serving as the representative of the industry's highest echelons.

For the next two years a team consisting of two sociologists, an econo-mist, a statistician, and various foreign language translators, industrial engineers, personnel experts, management consultants, and their as-sistants, thumped and prodded the recumbent form of the ailing movie industry. They read everything that had been written about the subject, recorded hundreds of interviews, and prepared, distributed, tabulated, and analyzed some forty-two hundred questionnaires. The results were summarized in a book by Leo Rosten, *Hollywood: The Movie Makers, The Movie Colony,* which was published in 1941, the same year that Fitzgerald's unfinished *The Last Tycoon* posthumously appeared.[31]

The Rosten volume was in every way the most comprehensive and authoritative study that had thus far been made of the movie industry. Yet its 368 pages of text, plus an additional 78 pages of charts and ap-pendices, did little more than confirm the diagnosis of Hollywood's ills that Fitzgerald had reached in less than one hundred pages of memo-rable prose. Central to both works was the idea that the key figure in Hollywood was the director (or the producer, when he also exercised the responsibility for the direction of a film). The future of the movie industry depended on the creative ability and freedom that these men brought to the making of pictures. Once they had been provided with the money and other resources (human and mechanical) necessary for a film, they should be allowed to exercise total authority, just as they should be expected to take full responsibility for the results. This is the same conclusion Bosley Crowther arrives at in his history of M-G-M, *The Lion's Share.* It was also the conclusion Fitzgerald had reached back in 1924 in "Why Only Ten Percent of the Movies Succeed," and it is the central theme of *The Last Tycoon*. Yet the film industry's failure to recognize this fact after Thalberg's death was the primary reason for its subsequent decline. World War II, when gas rationing temporarily provided the studios with a large captive audience, only postponed the inevitable day of reckoning. Television, instead of being responsible for Hollywood's downfall, merely administered the final *coup de grâce*.

Thus, *The Last Tycoon*—in spite of its fragmentary state—continues to be the most profound analysis we have had in fiction of the motion-picture industry. And writing this novel, under severe physical and emotional handicaps, constitutes Fitzgerald's most heroic act. Where the Carnegie and Rockefeller Foundation scholars were treated with every courtesy, Fitzgerald was obliged to pursue his writing secretly, convinced that if news of his novel got about, he would be blackballed by the major studios. When he found out that Max Perkins had innocently told Charles Scribner of his plans, he wrote Perkins desperately, denying everything:[32]

> He [i.e., Mr. Scribner] seemed under the full conviction that the novel was about Hollywood and I am in terror that this misinformation may have been disseminated to the literary columns. If I ever gave such an impression it is entirely false: I said that the novel was about some things that had happened to me in the last two years. It is distinctly *not* about Hollywood (and if it were it is the last impression that I would want to get about).

So Fitzgerald struggled on alone in his doomed attempt to finish *The Last Tycoon*.

XVI
The
Last Tycoon:
The Tragic
Form

Even though there is some likelihood that Fitzgerald may have been planning a novel about Irving Thalberg as early as the fall of 1936, almost three years were to elapse before he decided on its actual form. As late as March, 1939, we find him writing Harold Ober that he is still undecided which of "several plans" to adopt. But several weeks later, during a visit to New York, he talked the project over with Max Perkins. Encouraged by Perkins' enthusiasm, he hired a typist as soon as he got back to California and settled down to serious work.[1]

His first step was to make a rough outline so that, as he explained to Perkins, "unlike *Tender,* I may be able to put it aside for a month and pick it up at the exact spot factually and emotionally where I left off." Next he blocked out the chapters, breaking each down into the various minor episodes. He then devoted the rest of the summer to classifying and organizing the notes he had been collecting for so many months, dictating new ones where necessary. He was still sensitive about what he had come to regard as the many mistakes of *Tender Is the Night.* Indeed, *Tender* had become for him a haunting example of what not to do, while *The Great Gatsby* represented the standard he wanted to surpass. In a typical note he reminded himself:

> *Tender* is less interesting toward the climax because of the absence of conversation. The eye flies for it and skips essential stuff for they don't want their characters resolved in dissection and analysis, but like me in action that results from the previous. All the more reason for *emotional* planning.

This new novel, he told Kenneth Littauer, was, unlike *Tender Is the Night*, "not the story of deterioration—it is not depressing and not morbid in spite of the tragic ending. If one book could ever be 'like' another, I should say it is more 'like' *The Great Gatsby* than any other of my books." The same refrain occurs in a letter to Gerald Murphy, where he said that his new novel was "as detached from me as Gatsby"; while to Perkins he insisted, "people will *buy* my new book and I hope I shan't again make the many mistakes of *Tender*."[2]

Thus, in planning *The Last Tycoon*, he rejected the expository or "philosophical" form of *Tender Is the Night* (as he had once described it) and *The Beautiful and Damned*, and adopted instead the more dramatic and more economical design of *The Great Gatsby*, so much better suited to his talent. According to this preliminary outline, *The Last Tycoon* was not only to have been the same length as *Gatsby*, but was to have had the same number of chapters—nine. Structurally, these chapters were to have been organized about what he described in that outline as *Gatsby's* "five act structure." As in *Gatsby*, the events in *Tycoon* were to be presented from the point of view of a first-person narrator. And the action was to develop by means of a series of short, carefully designed dramatic episodes. In further deference to *Gatsby*, Fitzgerald even went so far as to draw up a list of the novel's major characters, setting opposite each one the name of a corresponding character from *The Last Tycoon*. This did not mean that he was consciously modeling the characters in *Tycoon* upon those in the earlier novel. Rather, the list seems to have reminded him that he must keep the relationships between his leading characters as taut and clear-cut as those in *Gatsby*, not letting them diffuse as he had in *Tender Is the Night*. One of the notable things about *The Great Gatsby* is the economy with which a handful of characters convey the values of a wide cross-section of society. In planning the ending of *The Last Tycoon*, he also harked back to the method of its predecessor. In another preliminary note, he said:[3]

> The epilogue can model itself quite fairly on the last part of Gatsby. We can go back to Cecilia as a narrator and have her tell it with the emphasis on herself so that what she reveals about what happened . . . seems to be revealed as if she was now a little weary of the story, and [had] told all she knew about it, and was returning to her own affairs. In it she might discuss whom she married and try to find an equivalent of that nice point in Gatsby where the narrator erases the dirty word that the boy has scrawled in chalk against the doorstep. . . . and I think I'll do my own method of ending probably

on a high note about Stahr but that will solve itself in the writing. And toward the end I'll tend to go into a certain cadenced prose.

His outline called for a book of 51,000 words, made up of nine chapters, each chapter to be composed of several short episodes of about 2,500 words. Of this he completed five and a half chapters at the time of his death. These were edited by Edmund Wilson and published posthumously in 1941. It is unfair, of course, to judge the novel Fitzgerald hoped to write either by his tentative outline or the fragment he left behind. At his death, a great many problems still remained that would "solve themselves" only "in the writing." For instance, the point at which his manuscript broke off was, according to his outline, the mid-point of the novel. Therefore it should have run to around 25,000 words or so; instead it was some 45,000 words long. At this rate, the completed first draft would have been almost twice as long as he contemplated. Undoubtedly, some of it might have been cut during subsequent revision. Even so, it seems likely that *The Last Tycoon* would have turned out to be a much longer novel than he planned.

At the end of Fitzgerald's outline was a revealing sentence which Edmund Wilson deleted when he reproduced the outline in his edition of *The Last Tycoon.* Here, Fitzgerald had said that he was writing his novel for two people—"Scottie at 17" and "Edmund Wilson at 45—It must please them both." Those portions of the story that dealt with Stahr's career in pictures, his theories of film making and the management of his studio, were written with Wilson especially in mind. Wilson, too, was interested in the cinema as an art form as well as an entertainment medium. After reading "Crazy Sunday" back in 1932, he had written Fitzgerald enthusiastically, "your story in the Mercury was swell —wish you would do something more about Hollywood, which everybody who knows everything about it is either scared or bribed not to tell about or have convinced themselves is all right."[4]

Because of his fear of being black-listed if word got out that he was writing about Hollywood, Fitzgerald had been obliged to keep the subject of his new book a secret from his old friend. But Wilson knew he was at work on a big project of some kind. "I hope it's about Hollywood," he wrote Fitzgerald only a few weeks before the latter's death.[5]

I've just read practically all the novels ever written on the subject and none of them really does much with it. They all either deal with the fringes or the extras, etc., or just treat Hollywood as an episode in somebody's life. I suppose they are all really scared to go to the mat with the industry itself.

At this particular moment, Wilson himself was finishing a book about Hollywood called *The Boys in the Back Room*. In a series of essays devoted to the literary work of nine well-known authors who were associated in some way with California (O'Hara, Steinbeck, Cain, etc.), he had argued that they had all been damaged by the West Coast—either by the movie industry or the enervating climate. But when Wilson read the manuscript of *The Last Tycoon* some time later he was obliged to modify this theory. His old friend had been a dramatic exception. In Hollywood Fitzgerald, at any rate, had found his greatest theme. By this time *The Boys in the Back Room* was in galley proofs; Wilson could only mention Fitzgerald's unpublished novel in a hasty postscript. There, however, he claimed that *The Last Tycoon* was the finest novel that had been written about the movie community. In 1948, in another survey of the fiction written about Hollywood, Franklin Walker also reached the same conclusion. Nothing has been published since then to alter these judgments.[6]

Where the story of Stahr, the moving-picture tycoon, was written with Wilson in mind, the story of Stahr's love affair with the exotic Kathleen (or Thalia, as she is called in some drafts) was written for those teen-age readers of popular fiction represented by Fitzgerald's own eighteen-year-old daughter. If *The Last Tycoon* could please the critic whose opinions Fitzgerald respected most, as well as the mass audience of Scottie's generation, then Fitzgerald would have reached that literary goal toward which he had been struggling for so many years. He would have written a novel that combined the wide popular appeal of *This Side of Paradise* with the artistry of *The Great Gatsby*: a modern classic. More than ever before, he was consciously aware of what he was trying to do. He had set his sights on a goal that was well within the range of his talent, and there is good reason to believe that, had he lived, he would have attained it.

At the time of his death, however, Fitzgerald had not yet succeeded in bringing the episodes treating Stahr's love affair with Kathleen into as sharp a focus as those dealing with Stahr's career as a film producer. The full implications of that love affair were still not clear in Fitzgerald's own mind. Initially, Kathleen was to have represented one of the several values—love, peace of mind, companionship—that Stahr forfeited by his single-minded devotion to his career. Kathleen is willing to break off her engagement to another man in order to give Stahr the care and affection he needs. Had he been willing to quite his job and go off with her, he would probably have escaped his fate. But he cannot make such a choice. "He has had everything in life," Fitzgerald says in another of his notes, "except the privilege of giving himself unselfishly to another human being."[7]

Such was the role that Fitzgerald outlined for Kathleen in his original plan. But as the writing progressed, Stahr's emotional involvement with her assumed larger proportions. One reason for this may have been a purely practical one. After Fitzgerald learned that *Collier's* might be willing to advance the money to finish the novel, he may have decided to stress the sex interest more than he had first intended. Not only this, but Kathleen was a character with romantic possibilities that were still to be exploited. She was, as Fitzgerald had written Littauer, "the most glamorous and sympathetic of my heroines."[8]

Thus, there was always the danger that Stahr's affair with Kathleen would get out of control and spoil the original plan. Before he died, Fitzgerald had become aware of this. He still intended that Stahr should break off with her before it was too late. "As some point," he reminded himself, "something happens (invent some small detail of interest) which gives Stahr the idea: After all, this is not what I intended. I didn't intend to marry the girl. It's against the logic of my life." Stahr becomes so passionately involved with Kathleen, however, that one wonders how Fitzgerald would have resolved this dilemma, had he lived.[9]

At the time of his death, it seems unlikely that he yet knew the answer. Kathleen was modeled on Sheilah Graham; and Fitzgerald's feelings about her were in as confused a state as Stahr's toward Kathleen. Miss Graham had broken off her engagement to the Marquis of Donegal in order to be with Fitzgerald. But their romance was doomed from the start. So far as he was concerned, Zelda's unwillingness to give him a divorce automatically prevented him from remarrying. No matter what his own wishes were, he felt that his chief responsibilities were to her and Scottie. Besides, he was still in debt, ill, and haunted by a foreboding that he had not long to live.

Had Miss Graham been a harder and more ruthless person, she might have saved herself a great deal of heartbreak. But, to her everlasting credit, she was not. Indeed, she needed Fitzgerald as much as he needed her. She was not the expatriate aristocrat she pretended to be. She was a poor girl from the London streets who had made her way up the slippery English social ladder entirely on her own. Fitzgerald was the first American to whom she felt she could divulge the facts about her tawdry past. She did so with trepidation, and to her astonishment, this only increased his respect for her. Had she been better acquainted with his fiction, this would not have come as such a surprise. In one short story after another, Fitzgerald had celebrated the triumph of the poor but beautiful and talented shopgirl who outsmarts the wealthy debutantes and wins the rich, handsome hero. That Miss Graham, single-handedly, had defeated the whole English social system only made him love and admire her the more!

They were cut from the same cloth. Even at the height of his success, when he had been accepted by the most exclusive circles, Fitzgerald still continued to think of himself as an outsider, the boy from the wrong end of Summit Avenue. Strip him of his money, and he was sure that he would drop out of sight as quickly as Dick Diver had dropped from view at the end of *Tender Is the Night*. Because Sheilah and he were so much alike, they could keep no secrets from each other. Before long, she knew him at his worst as well as his best. As the writing of his novel progressed, demanding all the energy and discipline that he could muster, there were many times at the end of a long day's work when all that he had left of himself for her was a fragile, empty husk.

The excitement and mystery of their first months together is reflected in Stahr's lyric meetings with Kathleen in the first two chapters of *The Last Tycoon*. Most of this material was blocked out, and much of it first written, during the autumn of 1939. After *Collier's* rejected it Fitzgerald was obliged to put it aside for several months. Meanwhile, the bleak, despondent winter of 1939–1940 intervened, culminating in his break-up with Miss Graham. When she eventually returned, it was on a different basis. Their initial infatuation was replaced with a deeper, more mature knowledge of their mutual need for one another. During the ten months that remained to them, Fitzgerald stopped drinking and worked steadily at his occasional movie jobs and on his novel.

Thus, during the course of the story, his attitude toward Sheilah Graham changed, just as Stahr's changed toward Kathleen. What the consequences were to be we cannot know. As a result, however, the Kathleen of the last three chapters of the book is not always consistent with the girl we meet at the beginning. Fitzgerald's comments about her in his preliminary notes, and the personality he actually created, do not always agree. Stahr, for instance, was to have thrown her over because she was "poor, unfortunate and tagged with a middle-class exterior, which doesn't fit in with the grandeur Stahr demands of life." Yet in the story Kathleen has acquired an even more glamorous background than Miss Graham's. Instead of being merely engaged to a marquis, Kathleen is the mistress of a king. Another contradiction is her language, which alternates between the extremes of high-toned speech and a slovenly vernacular slang. The physical love scenes between Stahr and Kathleen are also much more intense than Fitzgerald planned them to be. Both Miss Graham and his typist were of the same opinion when he read them aloud. Stahr's relationship to Kathleen, in short, was so uncrystallized that Fitzgerald still had considerable revising ahead.[10]

Like Kathleen, Cecilia Brady, the narrator, also changed a great deal during the course of the writing. At first, Fitzgerald thought of her as exemplifying the things about Scottie's generation that he disliked—a generation that had "been told the price of everything as well as its value." At one point he even wondered if she were not too unattractive to function effectively as his narrator. "I must not alienate the reader from her at the beginning," he reminded himself, "but must give the feeling that 'Well, I don't like this girl much, but I am going to stick around and see what she has to say because she let drop a few things that make me think that given the right circumstances she might have been worthwhile."[11]

But as he got to know Cecilia better, he began to take the same sympathetic interest in her that he had taken in Nick Carraway; as they grew in Fitzgerald's imagination, he endowed them both with his affection. Like Nick, Cecilia too has a moral stake in the community. During the course of her story, Monroe Stahr literally becomes for her a "star." In his first plan, Fitzgerald had planned to have Stahr seduce her. But as the writing progressed, this idea was abandoned. Instead Stahr becomes a substitute father, taking the place of her own disreputable father, who is plotting Stahr's destruction. Gradually, Cecilia's feelings toward Stahr became those that Fitzgerald hoped his own daughter would have some day toward himself and his own work. He had seen relatively little of Scottie during the last few years—years in which she had been changing from a girl into a woman. Often, when they had been together, he had been at his worst. "I think when you read this book, which will encompass the time when you knew me as an adult," he wrote her late in 1939, "you will understand how intensively I knew your world. . . . I am not a great man, but sometimes I think the impersonal and objective quality of my talent and the sacrifices of it, in pieces, to preserve its essential value, has some sort of epic grandeur."[12]

Little is gained from listing the obvious flaws in a novel still so far from completion. *The Last Tycoon* can be enjoyed for the many episodic scenes that come off brilliantly. It can also be admired for the tragic idea embodied in the character of Monroe Stahr. Despite the structural similarities to *The Great Gatsby, The Last Tycoon* is more successful as a formal tragedy. This is because Stahr has an identity of his own independent of his relationship to Cecilia, the narrator, whereas Gatsby exists only because of Nick Carraway's tragic sensibility. Stahr is also a more tragic figure than Dick Diver in *Tender Is the Night,* since Dick is rarely heroic except externally, in the effect he has on other people. Stahr is, in short, Fitzgerald's most fully rounded tragic hero, seen "simultaneously from within and without." But the result was not "the pathetic story" that, years before, Paul Rosenfeld had predicted— "the legend of a moon which never rose." Instead, the nobility of Stahr's dream for the film industry and the magnitude of his own achievement far outweigh the pathos of his death.[18]

To see this, we need only compare *The Last Tycoon* with *The Great Gatsby* and *Tender Is the Night.* Even in its fragmentary condition, the unfinished first draft of *The Last Tycoon* is a much more accomplished piece of writing than the early drafts that survive from these two earlier novels. The best scenes have a coolness of tone, a controlled detachment, a precision of language, a rippling spontaneity, unlike anything he had written before. Such craftsmanship could only result from the most rigorous self-criticism. The manuscript of *The Last Tycoon* bristles with notes and comments that show how carefully he was scrutinizing his work, even at this early stage. "Dramatize and make clear," he reminded himself. "No good, think out." "Not very good." "Not too hot." "Time lapses not good." "No drawing together [referring to a scene between Stahr and Kathleen]." "Must be brighter. Has become stilted with rewriting." "Stress Negro's effect on Stahr." "Don't look, rewrite from passion and mood." "What is missing is passion and imagination." "ACTION IS CHARACTER."

"This character must not develop into merely a piece of character analysis," Fitzgerald says of Stahr at one point. "Each statement that I make about him must contain at the end of every hundred words some pointed anecdote or story to keep it alive. I want to have as much drama throughout as old Laemmle on the telephone." He made preparatory notes for almost every one of his episodes, and each episode was intended to play a specific functional role in the development of the story. (The thirty episodes are listed by number on the outline Edmund Wilson included in his edition of the novel.) Episode Ten, for example, a short scene at the end of Chapter III where Stahr lunches with other studio executives at the commissary, was designed to clarify Stahr's relationship with his business associates and to emphasize their lack of sympathy for his progressive theories about picture making. As part of his homework for this brief scene, Fitzgerald filled one of his small notebooks with eight pages of data describing M-G-M's organizational structure and its business and financial procedures. Each one of Stahr's luncheon companions in this scene was a thinly disguised portrait of an actual studio official.[14]

The best evidence we have of the remarkable aesthetic distance Fitzgerald had succeeded in putting between his novel and his own personal history is to be found in the scenes between Stahr and the studio script writers. They include some of the funniest Fitzgerald had ever written. Like Thalberg, Stahr is credited with having invented the system of having several different writers simultaneously working on the same script. It would have been easy for Fitzgerald to have sided with the writers and attacked Stahr for a procedure that had caused him so much grief. But Fitzgerald no longer had any illusions about the fatuity of trying to defend the writer in a medium where the director must necessarily be supreme. "Explain his attitude toward authors and how it was like Bernard Shaw's in *Plays: Pleasant and Unpleasant,*" he reminds himself in one of his notes about Stahr. "That is, he liked them but to some extent saw them as a necessary evil. How thereafter he developed the process of having one author working behind another, practically his own invention."[15]

Like all Fitzgerald's heroes, Stahr was an aspect of himself. But he also has certain virtues Fitzgerald admired but did not possess. Where Nick Carraway exhibited tolerance and a sense of responsibility toward his fellow man, and Dick Diver possessed heroic charm and taste, Stahr is remarkable for his rational habits of thought and his ability to get along with people. One wonders, though, how long Fitzgerald would have been able to maintain his cool detachment toward his hero. By the time he reached the end of the fifth chapter—the last he was to finish—both he and Stahr were close to death. Here and in the fragment of chapter six that followed, Fitzgerald found it impossible not to identify his feelings with those of his sick and exhausted hero. "He was due to die very soon now," Stahr's physician says to himself at the last examination.[16]

Within six months one could say definitely. What was the use of developing the cardiograms? You couldn't persuade a man like Stahr to stop and lie down and look at the sky for six months. He would much rather die. He said differently, but what it added up to was the definite urge toward total exhaustion that he had run into before. Fatigue was a drug as well as a poison, and Stahr apparently had derived some rare almost physical pleasure from working light-headed with weariness. It was a perversion of the life force he had seen before, but he had almost stopped trying to interfere with it.

If there were ever a time when Fitzgerald deserved to be excused for losing his detachment and slopping over into the turgid banalities of *Tender Is the Night*, it was now. Instead, confronted with the twin dooms of both Stahr and himself, he clung to his double vision as never before, and continued to write faultless prose as long as he could keep his pencil moving. One of the most perfect scenes is the last—Episode Seventeen—in Chapter VI. What saved it from the mistakes of the past was its crisp dramatic structure and Cecilia Brady's controlling point of view. "Stahr is about to die and is sick unto death without knowing it," one of the preliminary notes for this scene reads. The heroics of the earlier chapters are over. Now we see Stahr at his worst, "white and nervous and troubled . . . so transparent that you could almost watch the alcohol mingle with the poison of his exhaustion." He has been drinking and the combination of liquor and worn-out nerves makes an explosive mixture. Before long he begins to quarrel with a husky young Communist union organizer named Brimmer, whom Cecilia has brought along at Stahr's insistence to discuss the studio's labor troubles. When Stahr blindly strikes out at him with his fist, Brimmer easily knocks him flat on his back.

"Is this *all*," the embarrassed Brimmer asks Cecilia incredulously. "This frail sick person holding up the whole thing?"

Yes, this *is* all. Stahr's imperfections, like Fitzgerald's, emphasized the magnitude of his accomplishments.[17]

XVII
The Tragic
Sense of Life

Most of the accounts of Fitzgerald's death that appeared in the nation's press during Christmas week of 1940, if they ventured an assessment of his literary reputation, fell back on the old clichés about the Jazz Age "laureate" that he had been tagged with at the start of his career. *Time* magazine patronizingly pointed out that "in his social outlook Fitzgerald never got beyond the somewhat sophomoric conversation on socialism that closes *This Side of Paradise*," and that his fiction portrayed "a generation that was at best pathetic, at worst self-pathetic." Cruelest of all was the attack Westbrook Pegler launched against his memory the day after Christmas in his newspaper column. Overlooking Fitzgerald's fiction, which he apparently had not read for many years, Pegler attacked Fitzgerald personally as a horrible example of just about everything Pegler disliked. (Several days later Pegler received the coveted Pulitzer prize in journalism for newspaper writing "that redounded to the credit of the profession.")[1]

The reason for much of this critical myopia was that during Fitzgerald's lifetime most of the professional critics and commentators had been so blinded by the glitter of his early success that they had failed to recognize the more solid achievement of his later work. In 1950, when Alfred Kazin set about collecting into one volume the best criticism that had so far been written about Fitzgerald, he found little worth preserving that had appeared during Fitzgerald's lifetime except the 1923 essay by Paul Rosenfeld and a few book reviews.[2]

For this neglect academic scholars and teachers of English were as much to blame as the professional critics and pundits. Take the case of V.L. Parrington's *Main Currents in American Thought,* probably the textbook history of American letters most widely used on university campuses during the 1930's and 1940's. Professor Parrington wrote off Fitzgerald impatiently as "a bad boy who loves to smash things; a bright boy who loves to say smart things. . . . Precocious, ignorant—a short candle already burnt out." Professor Harlan Hatcher, in *Creating the Modern Novel* (1935), ended his unflattering account of Fitzgerald's career with the comment that "there was a minus value to Fitzgerald's work. When it ceased to be news the novels [sic!] were stale because they lacked the permanent searching of the soul that makes one generation read another's novels." Carl Van Doren's popular history, *The American Novel: 1789–1930,* published the year Fitzgerald died, acknowledged the superior quality of *The Great Gatsby,* but then dismissed it briefly in a phrase as "a short, realistic novel about a romantic bootlegger."[3]

Throughout the decade following Fitzgerald's death, the authors of college English texts, whenever they could find room for a discussion of Fitzgerald's work, continued to repeat the tired myth of the boy genius whose promise was snuffed out in 1929 along with the Golden Boom. In *Shapers of American Fiction* (1947) Professor George Snell felt obliged to limit his comments on Fitzgerald to *The Great Gatsby* and its predecessors because after 1925, he explained, Fitzgerald's "genius burned out like a meteor." In 1948 Professor Alexander Cowie brought out a bulky, encyclopedic history, *The Rise of The American Novel,* which had space for a brief treatment of only one of Fitzgerald's books —*This Side of Paradise.* Even worse was the case of Professor Joseph Warren Beach's *American Fiction* (1941), one of the few really outstanding surveys of recent American writing to appear during the decade. Professor Beach not only omitted Fitzgerald's novels from his discussion altogether, but failed to include any of them in the long list of "best American novels" recommended for the guidance of his readers.[4]

But if the English professors were mistaken in dismissing Fitzgerald from serious consideration as an author, the professional historians also judged him superficially. Professors Henry Steele Commager and Samuel Eliot Morison in *The Growth of the American Republic,* probably the most widely used college textbook in American History, ended a moving chronicle of the vicissitudes of the Great Depression with the dramatic but inaccurate statement that at its close "Fitzgerald had appropriately committed suicide." On the contrary, he died of a heart attack, as all the newspaper accounts faithfully reported—died, as Malcolm Cowley has said, "not like a strayed reveler but like a partner of the elder J.P. Morgan, working too hard until his heart gave out." Another frequently repeated story had it that when he died all of his books were out of print. Touching, but untrue. Scribner's 1940 catalogue lists nine titles, and seven are listed for 1941.[5]

As a kind of compensation for the treatment he received from most academicians and professional book reviewers during his lifetime, Fitzgerald had the satisfaction of knowing that his work was admired by a small but select group of contemporary writers whom we now acknowledge to be among the most notable of the period—Gertrude Stein, T.S. Eliot, Ring Lardner, Ernest Hemingway, Edmund Wilson, John Dos Passos, H.L. Mencken, Thomas Wolfe, Thornton Wilder, Nathanael West, John O'Hara. Eliot's opinion that *The Great Gatsby* was the first advance in the American novel since James is well known. Less known is Thomas Hardy's statement, made shortly before his death, that Fitzgerald was one of the few younger American writers whose work he followed with any interest. Since then, Fitzgerald has been one of the most conspicuous influences on the new generation of novelists since World War II. Like Faulkner's, his imprint is recognizable in the fiction of William Styron. And Salinger's alter ego, Buddy Glass, has said that *The Great Gatsby* served as his childhood *Tom Sawyer*.[6]

Most of the credit for the dramatic shift in Fitzgerald's reputation since his death belongs to a handful of American critics, among them the best of our age. The reappraisal began with Edmund Wilson's 1941 edition of *The Last Tycoon*, which included a discerning introductory essay. Four years later Wilson followed this with his New Directions edition of the *Crack-Up* volume. In 1945 New Directions also brought out a new edition of *The Great Gatsby* with an introduction by Lionel Trilling. In 1950 Arthur Mizener's biography, *The Far Side of Paradise*, appeared, followed a year later by the Kazin volume of critical essays. In 1951 Malcolm Cowley brought out a rearrangement of the text of *Tender Is the Night* which incorporated Fitzgerald's suggested changes. Two years later Cowley collected into one volume twenty-eight of Fitzgerald's short stories and in 1958, Mizener edited *Afternoon of an Author,* a volume of Fitzgerald's hitherto uncollected stories and essays. By now the "revival" was in full swing. Since then, a new book about him has appeared almost every year.

Outside the United States the revival has occurred more slowly.

During Fitzgerald's lifetime his magazine stories were often reprinted in England or translated for European magazines. But, as at home, it was the flimsiest ones that usually received the widest magazine circulation. Today, however, his best novels and stories have been translated into every major language and his reputation is as high in London and Paris as in New York—perhaps higher. The most recent volume of his work to appear, *Afternoon of an Author,* is really a collection of left-over material. Yet, dazzled by "the marvelous tender comeliness" of its prose, a reviewer for the staid London *Times Literary Supplement* has said of it: "There is not a dead sentence among any of the essays in this volume, not a sentence when Fitzgerald's magic fails to work." So widespread is the interest in Fitzgerald's fiction in England today that a uniform, multi-volume, collected edition of his work—something that still does not exist in this country—is currently being brought out in London under the distinguished editorship of J.B. Priestley.[7]

But although Fitzgerald's reputation among serious writers is now well assured, he continues to be regarded with suspicion by many professors of English. The case of the chairman of the English Department at Princeton, who went to his grave insisting that Fitzgerald was not capable of writing *The Great Gatsby,* is only an extreme example of the suspicion he generates. Granted that Fitzgerald could write like an angel, they argue, the trouble is that he couldn't "think."

The charge is not a new one. Writing about his friend back in 1923 in *The Bookman,* Edmund Wilson complained that Fitzgerald had "been given imagination without intellectual control of it. He has been given a desire for beauty without an aesthetic ideal; and he has been given a gift of expression without ideas to express." Since then this charge has often been repeated, not least by such admirers as Messrs. Mizener, Kazin, and Cowley. When they praise him it is for reasons other than his quality of mind. The charge that he had nothing significant to say was leveled against him with particular force by the late Professor Perry Miller of Harvard, an authority on seventeenth-century American Calvinism. Commenting on the Fitzgerald revival in *The Nation* some years ago, Professor Miller found the whole business "baffling." Fitzgerald's fiction, in his opinion, dealt with only "a limited, even silly, segment of American experience," and Fitzgerald's manner of treating it was "cheap, tawdry and histrionic."[8]

A "novel of ideas" like *Gulliver's Travels* or *The Magic Mountain* is, of course, as far removed as can be from *The Great Gatsby* and *Tender*

Is the Night. Fitzgerald would have experienced great difficulty under-standing the point of view of the narrator in Gide's *The Counterfeiters* who says: "Ideas . . . interest me more than men—interest me more than anything." An intellectual shower bath like Aldous Huxley's *Point Counter Point* left Fitzgerald unmoved. "A very poor novel, what I've read of it," he wrote on the title page of his copy.[9]

Like many other intelligent people who got little out of the college classroom, Fitzgerald was always uncomfortable in the midst of ab-stract discourse. From childhood, reality had existed for him at the emotional rather than the conceptual level of experience. Intellectuals are correct in suspecting him of harboring an instinctive distrust of rational modes of thought. Lacking these habits of mind, he tended in later life to be unnecessarily modest about his own intellectual attain-ments. Although he read widely and collected a respectable library, he rated himself "way below average" on most topics outside the craft of writing. He admired and envied people like Edmund Wilson and Irving Thalberg, who combined analytical habits of thought with artistic sensi-bility. Among the notes for *The Last Tycoon* is a reminder to be sure to stress Monroe Stahr's rationality—a trait, he ruefully noted, he himself did not possess.[10]

But the absence of recognizable problems and issues in his fiction does not mean that Fitzgerald could not deal with human themes of profound and lasting significance. Yet, because they are buried so expertly beneath the surface sparkle of his style, they can be easily overlooked. But the fact that the ideas are not neatly packaged and labeled in Fitzgerald's fiction does not make them nonexistent or less important. As Edmund Wilson wrote in *The Triple Thinkers*, in 1938:[11]

> People who have everything clear in their minds, who are not capable of identifying themselves imaginatively with, who do not actually embody in themselves, contrary emotions and points of view, do not write novels or plays at all—do not, at any rate, write good ones. And—given genius—the more violent the contraries, the greater the works of art.

Intellectually, Fitzgerald's greatest contribution was his discovery of the tragic ambiguities imbedded in ordinary, everyday American bourgeois experience. I say "bourgeois" rather than "middle-class" to emphasize the urban, business-centered aspects of our civilization that he knew best. The distinction is an important one. When he began writing almost a half-century ago, the American middle class was still dominated for the most part by the values of small-town, rural society. The great resurge of interest in Fitzgerald's work is undoubtedly due in part to the fact that the urban values and problems which he describes are more representative of society today than when his work first appeared.

It is a mistake to say—as many still do—that Fitzgerald was a spokesman for the very rich. He was interested in the rich only in their relationship to the middle class, and he wrote about them invariably from a middle-class point of view. If his writings are preoccupied with money, this is because money is a preoccupation of the middle class. People with inherited wealth usually interest themselves in other things.

To identify this particular urban element of American middle-class society, John Dos Passos has coined the useful term "The 42nd Parallel." By this Dos Passos meant much more than just that geographic line running roughly across the map from New York and Philadelphia, through Pittsburgh, Cleveland, Chicago, to Denver and San Francisco. He meant also a common fund of values and attitudes. Along this line are concentrated most of our cities, people, wealth, business, and industry. The 42nd Parallel is the dynamic mainstream of American civilization. Its standards are the familiar ones of prestige, money, success, popularity, and material well-being. The central tenet of its faith is the belief that anyone can rise in the world and become rich, successful, and happy, if he only works hard enough, uses his wits, and is self-reliant. Indeed, it is his moral duty to do so. Its hero is the self-made man.

Every notable American novelist of the past fifty years has been obliged to come to terms in some manner with the 42nd Parallel. Each has responded in his own way. Dos Passos himself gave us a brilliant, impressionistic account of its superficial characteristics in his trilogy, *U.S.A.*, but he rarely penetrated beneath its surface. Ernest Hemingway, who grew up along the 42nd Parallel in the middle-class Chicago suburb of Oak Park, literally ran away from it when he was seventeen years old, and never returned. His fiction celebrates, instead, the very different virtues of the older, Latin civilizations, notably those of Spain, Italy, and Cuba. Sinclair Lewis, another Midwesterner like Fitzgerald and Hemingway, responded to the challenge of the 42nd Parallel by laughing at it—occasionally with the corrosive satire of *Babbitt*, more often in later years with the gentle ridicule of *Dodsworth*. William Faulkner, observing this aspect of our civilization from the more remote vantage point of rural Mississippi, saw it primarily as a menace to the older Southern agrarian order he cherished, and hated it. Although Faulkner does not hesitate to criticize his own world, it is never by the standards of the 42nd Parallel.

In his best work, Fitzgerald saw the 42nd Parallel as a tragic experience. He sought to understand as well as describe it, to sympathize as well as judge. Thus, in his work, it became a stage for heroic action and tragic destinies, and he penetrated more deeply into its meaning than any other novelist of his generation.

As a young man, no James J. Hill or Philip McQuillan believed more passionately in the American dream—the dream of the 42nd Parallel. But with Fitzgerald's early success came a more profound understanding of the native experience. From the naïve romanticism of *This Side of Paradise* and the somewhat more complex irony of *The Beautiful and Damned,* he moved toward the freer and more comprehensive form of tragedy. It was a big step forward, intellectually as well as artistically. An awareness of the absurdities and paradoxes of life is a more useful point of view for the novelist than a passionate idealism. The double vision of irony releases wit and humor and saves the disillusioned author from the pitfalls of a shallow cynicism. At its best, irony can produce a masterpiece like *Candide* or *Gulliver's Travels.* But it cannot create great human dramas because it cannot generate significant actions or evoke more than a narrow range of emotions. Who ever acted from motives of irony? Prior to *The Great Gatsby,* little of importance transpired in Fitzgerald's stories because nothing seemed to matter very much. At this stage he needed to be reminded, as Rilke once reminded another young writer, that irony is "only one of the many means of grasping life."[12]

If you feel you are getting too familiar with it [i.e., irony], if you fear this growing intimacy with it, then turn to great and serious objects, before which it becomes small and helpless. Seek the depths of things; thither irony never descends. . . . Under the influence of serious things either it will fall from you . . . or else it will strengthen into a stern instrument and take its place in the series of tools with which you have to cultivate your art.

Out of his ambiguous involvement with the 42nd Parallel, Fitzgerald created in *The Great Gatsby* his first compelling work of fiction. In 1924 he was still too deeply committed to the values of American middle-class business society to disavow them entirely. Without them he would never have fulfilled his childhood dreams. But the momentum that had carried him so far, so fast, brought him finally to the other side of

Paradise. It was this new, unexplored suburb of the 42nd Parallel whose moral geography he charted in his most significant work.

At first, Fitzgerald celebrated the 42nd Parallel's unique moral values: its belief in individual responsibility, its romantic idealism and its heightened sensitivity to the promises of life. But later he also recognized its limitations: its shabby aesthetic standards, its habit of confusing social and moral values, its deadening materialism. Because he was so profoundly involved in the moral life of this society, his judgment of it was tempered by sympathy as well as understanding. And unlike the other novelists of his generation, he saw that involvement as a tragic experience. All three of his major heroes—Jay Gatsby, Dick Diver, Monroe Stahr—are heroes of the 42nd Parallel.

This alone constitutes a notable advance in American letters. The tragic view of life, depending as it does on the belief that man is capable of heroic action, was never more out of fashion than during Fitzgerald's lifetime. What would most of his Jazz Age friends have thought if they had known he would someday write a heroic tragedy about—of all things—the American businessman? Sinclair Lewis's *Babbitt* was supposed to have taken care of that. So far as tragedy was concerned, the prevailing view was that the hero's day was over. Men were believed to be the pathetic victims of forces beyond their control—specifically the economic, biological, and psychological forces asscciated with Marx, Darwin, and Freud. This was the view promulgated over and over during the 1920's in the novels of Dreiser and the plays of O'Neill and their followers. At the end of the decade Professor Joseph Wood Krutch even wrote a book to explain why heroic tragedy could no longer be written. "If the plays and novels of today deal with little people and less mighty emotions," he argued, "it is not because we have become interested in commonplace souls, but because we have come, willy-nilly, to see the soul of man as commonplace and its emotions as mean."[13]

Whatever Fitzgerald's intellectual limitations, he was at least unwilling to accept this philosophy. The view of human nature that finally released the full force of his creative energies, beginning with *The Great Gatsby*, was the more traditional one that saw man as capable of fulfilling a tragic destiny. "I can't give you the particular view of life that I have (which as you know is a tragic one) without dulling your enthusiasm," we find him later writing to his fourteen-year-old daughter in 1936. "But . . . I feel that it is your duty to accept the sadness, the tragedy of the world we live in, with a certain *esprit*." Or, as he wrote her several years later:[14]

Once one is caught up into the material world, not one person in ten thousand finds the time to form literary taste, to examine the validity of philosophic concepts for himself or to form what, for lack of a better phrase, I might call the wise and tragic sense of life. . . .

By this I mean the thing that lies behind all great careers, from Shakespeare's to Abraham Lincoln's, and as far back as there are books to read—the sense that life is essentially a cheat and its conditions are those of defeat, and that the redeeming things are not "happiness and pleasure" but the deeper satisfactions that come out of the struggle. Having learned this in theory from the lives and conclusions of great men, you can get a hell of a lot more enjoyment out of whatever bright things come your way.

This tragic awareness did more than anything else to release the full potential of Fitzgerald's genius. It provided him with a formal means for the imaginative ordering of his experience, so that he could treat it with understanding as well as detachment. Artistically, however, it was a long step from a sense of the tragic complexities that emerged in him about 1923 to the embodiment of that sense in a viable work of art. As a novelist he had yet to create a hero who was indeed tragic, who could command the reader's admiration as well as his compassion. To this pursuit, from about 1923 onward, he devoted the rest of his life.

We can watch him struggling in this direction in the surviving drafts that we have of *The Great Gatsby*. But because the book has two half-heroes—Nick the thinker and Gatsby the doer—instead of a single tragic hero, its artistic power is divided and diffused and it fails as formal tragedy. *Tender Is the Night* was also intended to be tragedy and Dick Diver possessed the attributes of a truly tragic hero: a keen intellect and a fine sensibility. He was to be the modern middle-class American raised to heroic stature and then destroyed by an excess of virtue, by his fatal gift of charm. But Fitzgerald could not maintain the necessary aesthetic distance, and halfway through, Dick lost his heroic attributes. As a result this novel also fails to sustain the tragic vision.

In the fragmentary *Last Tycoon*, Fitzgerald most fully realized his desire to write a modern tragedy that would fit the traditional design. Monroe Stahr is the classic hero who compels our respect and admiration as neither Gatsby nor Dick Diver could. Stahr is one of the archetypal heroes of American society—the self-made man doomed to fulfill his tragic destiny as a successful man of affairs. In the process Stahr defines both the possibilities and the tragic shortcomings of his legendary dream.

Over the years, the tragic sense of life emerged to provide Fitzgerald with a moral vantage point from which he could reconcile the contradictions inherent in his experience. In these contradictions he found the subject matter of his greatest fiction. Humor, wit, irony, imagery, rhythm —all these literary resources were released for him to a degree that they never were in his other work. The tragic sense not only provided him with subject matter, but it also helped him overcome another difficulty—the old nemesis of plot. In tragedy, the plot rarely varies, and the fatal sequence of events stays pretty much the same.

The sources of this tragic vision were deeply rooted in his childhood. We do not have to involve ourselves with the prickly question of Fitzgerald's "Catholicism" to recognize the formative role that his religious training played in shaping his moral judgements. He ceased thinking like a Catholic but it was harder to stop feeling like one. The questions he raises in his fiction are frequently religious: the meaning of death, of God, of good and evil, of individual responsibility. Lacking the disciplined mind of the philosopher, he worked out his answers in his fiction.[15]

Another source of his tragic vision was his sense of the past. In his Notebook he says of one of his characters:

> He had one of those minds, so incomprehensible to the literary man, which are illiterate not through insensibility but through the fact that the past and the future are with them contemporary with the present, having no special value or pathos of their own.

Such a person, he believed, was incapable of fulfilling his moral potential as an individual. The past, for Fitzgerald, was a corridor echoing with unfulfilled dreams and neglected responsibilities; his fiction was the means whereby he could atone for his misdeeds and earn a belated absolution. "Again and again in my books," he told John O'Hara, "I have tried to imagize my regret that I have never been as good as I intended to be."[16]

This belief that an awareness of the qualitative difference between time-present and time-past serves as a source of moral insight was one that Fitzgerald shared with a number of older American writers—Hawthorne, Melville, Mark Twain, Henry James, and Willa Cather—as well as with contemporaries like Hemingway and Faulkner. It is perhaps the most distinctive characteristic of our native literary tradition. Like Hemingway, Fitzgerald especially admired Mark Twain's *Adventures of Huckleberry Finn*. In reply to a request from Cyril Clemens for a statement commemorating the centenary of Twain's birth in 1935, Fitzgerald wrote:[17]

> Huckleberry Finn took the first journey back. He was the first to look *back* at the perspective of the West. His eyes were the first eyes that looked at us objectively that were not eyes from overseas. There were mountains at the frontier but he wanted more than mountains to look at with his restless eyes—he wanted to find out about men and how they lived together. And because he turned back we have him forever.

Where Hemingway's famous eulogy of *Huck Finn* in *The Green Hills of Africa* was concerned mainly with its literary technique, Fitzgerald admired *Huck* instead for what it said about "men and how they lived together." This was also the point of his note in his copy of *Dubliners,* that he was "interested in the individual only in his relation to society." In his novels and stories Fitzgerald's heroes are destroyed because they attempt to fulfill themselves through their social relationships. They cannot distinguish between social virtues like popularity, charm, and success, and the more lasting moral values.[18]

It comes as something of a surprise to find that an author whose fiction is so notable for its brilliant settings—Paris, Hollywood, the Riviera—took so little interest in places apart from their human aspects. Places held little interest for him until they acquired associations through personal relationships. "France is a bore and a disappointment," he wrote Shane Leslie in 1920, during his first trip to Europe, "chiefly because we know no one here." Yet in *Tender Is the Night,* France provides him with some of his most iridescent settings. In another letter to Mrs. Bayard Turnbull he says, "I hear it is beautiful here, but without people all places are the same to me." At the time he was staying at a fine hotel in one of the most beautiful parts of western North Carolina. But he knew no one there; and to feel at ease with people he needed to commit himself wholly to an established group. "It always strikes me as very strange when I find new people in the world," he once wrote Mabel Dodge Luhan, "because I always crystallize any immediate group in which I move as being an all-sufficient, all-exclusive cross-section of the world at the time I know it."[19]

It was this primary interest in the drama of human relationships that prompted one of Fitzgerald's oddest and most discerning literary judgments. Comparing himself with Hemingway and Tom Wolfe in a 1934 letter to Max Perkins, who was literary godfather to all three, he identified them with Wordsworth, the poet of "The Prelude" and "The Excursion" rather than, as one might have expected, with the Keats of the great odes.[20]

What family resemblance there is between we three as writers is the attempt that crops up in our fiction from time to time to capture the exact feel of a moment in time and space, exemplified by people rather than by things—that is, an attempt at what Wordsworth was trying to do rather than what Keats did with such magnificent ease, an attempt at a mature memory of a deep experience.

Like Dick Diver, Fitzgerald "cared only about people; he was scarcely conscious of places except for their weather, until they were invested with color by tangible events." Thus he differed from Hemingway who believed that "unless you have geography, background, you have nothing." One of the first things that Hemingway had noticed about him when they met in 1925 was Fitzgerald's lack of interest in nature and places for their own sake. Anyone who has tried unsuccessfully to find the physical settings described in Fitzgerald's fiction—the elusive Long Island of Gatsby's parties, Dick Diver's beloved Riviera, or the Paris of "Babylon Revisited"—knows that he was more accurate at describing moral than physical geography. His settings are true to the extent that they are harmonious with the people who inhabit them. The test of his art is: Does it convince us that, had we been there at the time, it would have seemed that way to us too?[21]

Occasionally the glamor that surrounds his stories is more convincing than the people he is describing. This raises the question of where the source of the values was that he was depicting—in the object that embodied them, or in himself? For many years he believed that the values he described in his stories were objective facts. It was only after he went out to Metro-Goldwyn-Mayer in 1937 that he began to realize that the world whose charm and glamor he had believed in for so long was only an imaginative projection of himself. Less than a year after his arrival on the M-G-M lot we find him writing Gerald Murphy about his work:[22]

To me it is a new phase, or, rather, a development of something that began long ago in my writing—to try to dig up the relevant, the essential, and especially the dramatic and glamorous from whatever life is around. I used to think that my sensory impression of the world came from outside. I used to actually believe that it was as objective as blue skies or a piece of music. Now I know that it was within, and emphatically cherish what little is left.

For the writer preoccupied with the creation of new values, the most appropriate literary form is that of tragedy. Tragedy creates a value by showing us a hero who believes in it intensely—so intensely that he may even be destroyed by this belief. Tragedy convinces us of the truth of a value not by demonstrating it objectively, but by convincing us of what it feels like to believe in it as the tragic hero believes.

"Show me a hero," one of the later passages in Fitzgerald's Notebooks goes, "and I will write you a tragedy." In general, though, he felt that the American ethos had not been especially hospitable to the writing of serious tragedy. "There has never been an American tragedy," he told a newspaper reporter in 1928. "There have only been great failures. That is why the story of Aaron Burr—let alone that of Jefferson Davis—opens up things that we who accept the United States as an established unit hardly dare think about."[23]

It had not always been that way in American writing. Yet even the occasional exceptions—*Daisy Miller, The Portrait of a Lady, My Ántonia*—implied somehow that tragedy was not a masculine kind of American experience. In another Notebook passage he observed:[24]

Fifty years ago we Americans substituted melodrama for tragedy, violence for dignity under suffering. That became a quality that only women were supposed to exhibit in life or fiction—so much so that there are few novels or biographies in which the American male, tangled in an irreconcilable series of contradictions, is considered anything but an unresourceful and cowardly weakwad.

Fitzgerald was not the first American tragic writer. But he was certainly one of the first of the post-World War I generation of novelists to write about contemporary experience in tragic terms. Faulkner's *Absolom! Absolom!* in 1936 and Hemingway's *For Whom the Bell Tolls* in 1939 are proof that others were rediscovering the tragic tradition. But *The Great Gatsby* was published in 1925. Moreover, of all the writers of the period, Fitzgerald addressed himself most directly to the central tragic theme of American experience during the years between the two World Wars. Both decades, the Booming Twenties and the Great Depression of the Thirties, confused money, or the lack of it, with moral well-being. From *Gatsby* to *The Last Tycoon*, the morality of money is Fitzgerald's major theme.

Thus, despite the jibes of the scholars and pundits, Fitzgerald's reputation may ultimately rest as solidly upon his intellectual achievement as upon his inimitable prose style. To have made the American myth of success the basis for high tragedy; to have transformed the self-made man into a tragic hero; to have exposed the moral limitations of such established social values as charm, popularity and good taste; and to have reaffirmed the moral value of the individual imagination while at the same time revealing its tragic limitations—all this would appear to have been an intellectual achievement of the highest order. Fitzgerald's fiction is a solid rock upon which the writers who came afterward have already begun to build.

Notes

The following abbreviations are used in the notes:

AOA   *Afternoon of an Author,* Princeton University Press, Princeton, 1957; Charles Scribner's Sons, New York, 1958.

ASYM   *All the Sad Young Men,* Charles Scribner's Sons, New York, 1926

B & D   *The Beautiful and Damned,* Charles Scribner's Sons, New York, 1922

CU   *The Crack-Up,* edited by Edmund Wilson, New Directions, 1945

EH   Ernest Hemingway

EW   Edmund Wilson

F & P   *Flappers and Philosophers,* Charles Scribner's Sons, New York, 1920

FFL   Frances Fitzgerald Lanahan ("Scottie")

FSF   F. Scott Fitzgerald

FSOP   *The Far Side of Paradise,* Arthur Mizener, Houghton, Mifflin Co., Boston, 1951

Gatsby   *The Great Gatsby,* Charles Scribner's Sons, New York, 1925

HDP   Henry Dan Piper

HO   Harold Ober

JPB   John Peale Bishop

LT   *The Last Tycoon,* Charles Scribner's Sons, New York, 1941

MP   Maxwell Perkins

NLM   *Nassau Literary Magazine,* Princeton University

OF   Files of Harold Ober Associates, Inc., New York, now deposited in Princeton University

PF   Fitzgerald Papers, Firestone Library, Princeton
          University
PULC   *Princeton University Library Chronicle*
SEP   *The Saturday Evening Post*
SF   Files of Charles Scribner's Sons, Inc., New York
SMTW   *Save Me the Waltz,* Zelda Fitzgerald, Charles
          Scribner's Sons, New York, 1932. (Because of
          its greater accessibility I have cited the Lon-
          don, 1953, edition, which has a different pagi-
          nation.)
SSC   *The Stories of F. Scott Fitzgerald,* edited by Mal-
          colm Cowley, Charles Scribner's Sons, New
          York, 1951
TAR   *Taps at Reveille,* Charles Scribner's Sons, New
          York, 1935
TITN   *Tender Is the Night,* Charles Scribner's Sons,
          New York, 1934
TJA   *Tales of the Jazz Age,* Charles Scribner's Sons,
          New York, 1922
TLS   London *Times Literary Supplement*
TSOP   *This Side of Paradise,* Charles Scribner's Sons,
          New York, 1920
ZSF   Zelda Sayre Fitzgerald

The three main sources of Fitzgerald papers are:

PF   The Fitzgerald Papers in the Firestone Library at
          Princeton, comprising letters, literary manu-
          scripts, documents, and correspondence. Since
          I used these papers, certain of them, mainly
          scrapbooks which include some manuscript
          material, have been removed by Mrs. Lana-
          han. For a description of this collection see
          Arthur Mizener, "The F. Scott Fitzgerald Pa-
          pers," *PULC* 12:4, 190–95 (Summer, 1951).
SF   Files of Charles Scribner's Sons, New York, com-
          prising letters from Fitzgerald and copies of
          letters to him from Maxwell Perkins and other
          members of the firm.
OF   Files of Harold Ober Associates, New York, com-
          prising a file of Fitzgerald's letters to Mr.
          Ober and other members of the firm of Paul
          Reynolds, with which Mr. Ober was associ-
          ated until 1929, as well as with Mr. Ober and
          members of the Ober firm, copies of letters to
          Fitzgerald, and some of his manuscripts. These
          are now deposited at Princeton.
A recent listing of Fitzgerald's manuscripts in the major
American libraries will be found in *American Literary*

Manuscripts, ed. J.W. Jones, H.D. Piper, *et al.*, Austin, Texas, 1961.
For a check list of Fitzgerald's published works see H.D. Piper, "F. Scott Fitzgerald: A Check-List" *PULC* 12:4, 196–208 (Summer, 1951), supplemented by H.D. Piper, "Scott Fitzgerald's Prep School Writings," *PULC* 17:1, 1–2 (Autumn, 1955). For a check list of Zelda Fitzgerald's published writings see H.D. Piper, "Zelda Sayre Fitzgerald: A Check-List" *PULC* 12:4, 209–10 (Summer, 1951).

FOREWORD

1. EW, "Sheilah Graham and Scott Fitzgerald," *The New Yorker*, January 24, 1959, 107–116; FSF to Robert Bridges, n.d. (*ca.* May, 1922) SF.

   In quoting from Fitzgerald's unpublished manuscripts and correspondence, I have transcribed all misspellings, errors in punctuation, inconsistencies in capitalization, as faithfully as possible. As a result I occasionally differ with versions published elsewhere. Sometimes these discrepancies can be accounted for by the difficulty of reading Fitzgerald's handwriting. Fitzgerald's editors and biographers have not always been completely accurate in the matter of transcription. For further discussion of this problem see Matthew Bruccoli's review (*American Literature*, 36:1, 99–100. March, 1964) of *The Letters of F. Scott Fitzgerald* edited by Andrew Turnbull (Charles Scribner's Sons, New York 1963).

2. Gilbert Seldes, "Uneasy Chameleons," *SEP*, January 1, 1927. Throughout this book it has been the practice to cite all references only at the end of the appropriate paragraph. The order in which the references are cited corresponds to the order in which they appear in the paragraph. However, when an indented quotation concludes a paragraph, the superscript identification appears immediately before the quotation.

3. *AOA*, 185; Scrapbook, PF.

4. To MP, n.d. (*ca.* June 1, 1925), SF.

I

1. "Reade, Substitute Right Half," St. Paul Academy *Now and Then* 2:3, 10–11 (February, 1910), reprinted in *PULC* 17:1,11–13 (Autumn, 1955). See also HDP, "Scott Fitzgerald's Prep School Writings," same issue of *PULC*, 1–10.

2. Philip W. Fitzpatrick to HDP, January 15, 1945; EH to FSF, May 28, 1934, PF.

3. Ms. of "The Romantic Egoist," 6, PF; "Author's House," *AOA*, 184.

4. W.S. Maugham, *The Summing Up* (W. Heinemann, Ltd., London, 1938), 55–56; Harold Nicolson, *Byron: The Last Journey* (Constable and Co., London, 1934), 39; "Author's House," *AOA*, 185.

5. General C.C. Andrews, ed., *History of St. Paul, Minn.* (D. Mason & Co., Syracuse, New York, 1890), Part II, 174. (See also the portrait of P.F. McQuillan, Part I, 372.) J. Fletcher Williams, *A History of the City of St. Paul and the County of Ramsey, Minn.* (St. Paul, Coll.

of Minnesota Historical Society, 1876), Vol. 4, 43, has a photograph of the "McQuillan Block."

6. Undated newspaper clipping in Scrapbook, PF.

7. Clipping from Baltimore *Sun*, February 12, 1890, Scrapbook, PF. Interesting information about the McQuillan and the James J. Hill families will be found in *Some Letters of Monsignor James E. Caillet and August N. Chemidlin 1868–1899*, ed. by Clara Hill Lindley (St. Paul, privately printed, 1922), 93–94, 113 (Fitzgerald's annotated copy is at Princeton); "The Cruise of the Rolling Junk," *Motor* (New York), March, 1924.

8. Lorena McQuillan to FSF, n.d. (*ca.* 1937–38) PF; E. Fitzgerald of Keenglas, "Knights of Kerry," *Cornhill Magazine* 151, 719–32 (June, 1935); see also various clippings about the Maryland Fitzgeralds in FSF's scrapbooks (including Towson, Maryland, newspaper clipping for March 3, 1933), PF.

9. To Mrs. C.A. Taylor, August 14, 1940; see also to HO, received June 3, 1926, PF. In an unpublished piece, "Variety in American Education," PF, FSF says that his father attended Georgetown, his grandfather John Scott, attended St. John's College, Annapolis, and the latter's father attended Washington College, Maryland. Other Maryland relatives, he adds, attended William and Mary College and the University of Virginia.

10. Michael Mok, "The Other Side of Paradise," New York *Post*, September 25, 1936; Ledger, *passim*, PF.

11. Ledger and manuscript Chapter I of "The Romantic Egotist," PF.

12. C.N.B. Wheeler to HDP, February 13 and March 22, 1945; FSF to John O'Hara, July 18, 1933, PF.

13. Ledger, 1896–1911, PF.

14. Mrs. Herbert Lewis to HDP, May 7, 1946; C.N.B. Wheeler to HDP, February 13, 1945.

15. To "Morton" August 9, 1939, PF;

to MP, n.d. (*ca.* Christmas, 1933), SF. See also "An Author's Mother," *Esquire,* September, 1936.

16. Michael Mok, "The Other Side of Paradise," New York *Post,* September 25, 1936; see also "The Death of My Father," *PULC* 12.4, 187–89 (Summer, 1951); an unpublished manuscript draft of "Early Success," which differs from the published essay, PF; HDP, "FSF and the Image of His Father" in the *PULC* issue cited here; also C.N.B. Wheeler to HDP, March 22, 1945; and J. de Q. Briggs to HDP, April 2, 1945; and Ledger, 1906, PF.

17. Two undated letters from FSF to Mrs. Fitzgerald (*ca.* 1917 and 1930) mention his father's literary interests, PF. See also *CU*, 174; "Author's House," *AOP*, 183–189; and Chapter I of "The Romantic Egotist" manuscript, PF.

18. Victor Weybright, *Spangled Banner: The Story of Francis Scott Key* (Farrar & Rinehart, New York, 1935) *passim.* "End of Hate," *Collier's* 105:9 (June 22, 1940); interview, *New York World,* April 3, 1927, 12; first manuscript chapter, "The Romantic Egotist," PF.

20. To his mother from Camp Chatham, Orillia, Ontario, July 18, 1907, PF; to his father, July 15, 1907, and Mr. Fitzgerald to his son, July 30, 1907, PF. See also *St. Nicholas Magazine* 37:12, 1147 (October, 1910).

21. *NLM* 71:1 (April, 1915).

22. *PULC* 12:4, 187–89 (Summer, 1951).

23. *Gatsby,* 1–3.

24. *TITN,* 262–67, 175–76; FSF, "The Death of My Father," *PULC* 12:4, 187–89 (Summer, 1951).

25. C.N.B. Wheeler to HDP, February 13, 1945, and March 22, 1945; "What I Think and Feel at Twenty-Five," *American Magazine* 94:16 (September, 1922); Ledger, January, 1909, PF.

26. Ledger, *passim* PF.

27. He mentions this experience both

in his Ledger and in Chapter I of "The Romantic Egotist" (five manuscript chapters of which are at Princeton); see Chapter VI of the present book for further discussion of the relation of Fitzgerald's short story "Absolution" to his own childhood and to *The Great Gatsby*.

28. Ledger and manuscript "Thoughtbook," PF.

29. C.N.B. Wheeler to HDP, February 13, and March 22, 1945; Philip W. Fitzpatrick to HDP, January 15, 1945; and Ledger, PF.

30. "Author's House," *AOA*, 183–189; TSOP, 227, 229, 331; *B&D*, 188–89.

31. "Who's Who—and Why," *AOA*, 83–86.

32. "Forging Ahead," *AOA*, 34.

II

1. *Newman School, Lakewood, New Jersey*, Philadelphia, Pennsylvania, n.d., a catalog with a historical introduction. Fitzgerald's copy of his *Newman School Alumni Directory* (May, 1930) shows that he sometimes used the surnames of Newman boys for characters in his stories, PF.

2. Ledger, 1911–1912, PF; "What I Think and Feel at Twenty-Five," *American Magazine* 94:16 (September, 1922).

3. "Author's House," *AOA*, 185

4. Roy McCardell, New York *Morning Telegraph*, November 12, 1922. See manuscript copies of "The Captured Shadow" and clippings of his Newman School activities in his scrapbooks, PF. See also "The Captured Shadow," *SEP* 201:26, 12 (December 29, 1928).

5. To Miss Magoffin, February 17, 1912, PF; his poem seems never to have been published.

6. See clippings of the Newman-Kingsley game, Scrapbooks, PF.

7. Ledger, PF; see H. D. Piper, "Scott Fitzgerald's Prep-School Writings," *PULC* 17:1, 1–10 (Autumn, 1955).

8. *American Magazine* 94:16 (September, 1922).

9. A copy of this play, apparently in Miss Magoffin's handwriting, a playbill, and some photos of the cast, are at Princeton.

10. Mrs. Herbert Lewis to HDP, May 7, 1946.

11. Scrapbook, PF.

12. Edmund Wilson to FSF, August 28, 1915, PF.

13. Scrapbook, PF.

14. John Biggs to HDP in conversation.

15. "Princeton," *College Humor* 13:1, 28 (December 1927); I am indebted to Professor Frank Macdonald of Princeton for the story about Jesse Lynch Williams; Fitzgerald's copy of Williams' volume of stories, *Princeton Stories*, is among his books at Princeton. Many passages are underlined and Fitzgerald undoubtedly was influenced by it in some of his own later stories about college life.

16. Professors Frank Macdonald and Gordon H. Gerould of Princeton to HDP in conversation.

17. Charles Donahoe to FSF, January 6, 1916, and to HDP, May 13, 1947.

18. To FFL, April 12, 1940; see scrapbooks for reviews and correspondence from theatrical agents and producers, PF.

19. Charles Donahoe to FSF, May 31, 1916, PF. The 1916 Triangle show, "Safety First" was written by John Biggs and J.F. Bohnenfalk, but Fitzgerald was invited to write the lyrics and acted the role of a young girl in the production.

20. To FFL October 8, 1937, PF; Ginevra King Pirie to HDP, May 12, 1946. See clippings on Ginevra King in scrapbooks, PF.

21. *TSOP*, 49.

22. *TSOP*, 131; *AOP*, 78.

23. On pre-World War I Princeton, see Christian Gauss *PULC* 5:2, 41–50 (February, 1944), and article by Edmund Wilson in the same issue; introduction by Edmund Wilson to T.K. Whipple, *Study Out the Land* (University of California, Berkeley, 1943); and FSF, "Princeton," *College Humor* 13:1, 28 (December, 1927), reprinted in *AOP*, 70–82.

24. To FFL, June 12, 1940, PF.

25. Miscellaneous manuscript notes for *LT*, PF; *CU*, 297.

26. *Ibid*, 76.

27. *Nassau Herald: Class of 1917*, Princeton University.

28. *Ibid*, 100; *AOP*, 84; *CU*, 246.

29. Although FSF wrote in an early unpublished draft of his essay "Early Success" that his commission was dated on his twenty-first birthday, the commission is actually dated October 26, 1917, PF.

30. H.D. Piper, *PULC* 17:1, 1–10 (Autumn, 1955).

31. *CU*, 180; To "Morton," August 9, 1939, PF.

32. "Thoughtbook" PF.

33. St. Paul Academy *Now and Then*, 2:3:10 (February, 1910) and 2:4, 9 (March, 1910).

34. These words are misspelled in the manuscript of "The Romantic Egotist" and *TSOP*, PF.

35. *TJA*, ix

36. Clipping of this *Daily Princetonian* review in FSF's album, PF; also see letter to MP, n.d. (*ca.* August, 1922), commenting on it, SF; *CU*, 303.

37. *CU*, 297.

38. *CU*, 305.

39. *NLM* 72:241 (January, 1917).

40. *NLM* 73:55 (May, 1917); T. S. Eliot, *Selected Essays* (New York, Harcourt, Brace & Co., 1932), 124–25.

41. *TSOP*, 73–75.

42. *CU*, 161.

43. *Gatsby*, 184–5.

44. H. L. Mencken to FSF, June 13, 1919, PF; see scrapbooks for other critics' comments on his Princeton stories, as well as comments on FSF's work by editors of other college magazines, PF.

III

1. Fay to FSF, October 10, 1917; EW to FSF, December 3, 1917; JPB to FSF, October 2, 1917; Fay to FSF, August 22, 1917, PF.

2. Telegram, Fay to FSF, August 8 (?), 1917; Fay to FSF, August 22, 1917, PF; on the Red Cross Mission see H.P. Davison, *The American Red Cross in the Great War* (New York, MacMillan, 1920) 268; William Hard, *Raymond Robins' Own Story* (New York, Harper, 1920) 10; Hermann Hagedorn, *The Magnate: William Boyce Thompson and His Time* (New York, Reynal and Hitchcock, 1935) 181–89, 207; Shane Leslie, *Dublin Review* 167: 286–93 (October–December, 1920).

3. Fay to FSF, October 4 and 10, 1917, PF.

4. *American Magazine* 94:16 (September, 1922).

5. Fay to FSF, October 10, 1917; Leslie to FSF, November 26, 1917, January 1, 1918, February 28, 1918, April 20, 1918, May 11, 1918, July 17, 1918, PF; Leslie to Charles Scribner, May 6, 1918, SF.

6. Ledger, PF.

7. See Chapter XI for further treatment of ZSF.

8. Ledger, PF.

9. "Ten Years in the Advertising Business," *Princeton Alumni Weekly* 29:9; 585 (February 22, 1929); T.A. Boyd, *St. Paul Daily News*, August 28, 1921; "Editors," *Smart Set*, to FSF, June 3, 1919; MP to FSF, September 16, 1919, PF.

10. A.B. Maurice, "Authors and Best Sellers," *World's Work* 42; 185–99

(June, 1921); Malcolm Cowley, "Profile of Maxwell Perkins," *The New Yorker* 2; 32–36 (April 1, 1944); Heywood Broun, New York *Tribune*, April 2 and 11, 1920; Charles Scribner to Shane Leslie, December 29, 1920, SF; see *Bookman* monthly tabulation of best sellers, Summer, 1920 to Spring, 1921.

11. John O'Hara, *New Republic* 104:9, 311 (March 3, 1941); Katharine Brush, "The Time of my Life," *Ladies' Home Journal* 57:1; 55–56 (January, 1940), book title: *This Is On Me* (New York, Farrar & Rinehart, 1940); A.P. Hackett, *Fifty Years of Best Sellers* (New York, R.R. Bowker Co., 1945), 41.

12. To MP, April 23, 1938, SF.

13. W.Y. Tindall, *Forces in Modern British Literature* (New York, A.A. Knopf, Inc., 1947), 176–77; Van Wyck Brooks, *The Confident Years* (New York, Dutton, 1952), 493; Susanne Howe, *Wilhelm Meister and His English Kinsmen* (New York, Columbia University Press, 1930), *passim;* Justin O'Brien, *The Novel of Adolescence in France* (New York, Columbia University Press, 1937); Aldous Huxley, *Crome Yellow* (London, Chatto & Windus, 1921), 26.

14. *The Education of Henry Adams* (Boston, Houghton Mifflin Co., 1918) ix; to MP, September 4, 1919, SF.

15. Frances Newman, *Letters* (New York, Liveright, 1929) 40; Fay to FSF, October 4 and 10, 1917, PF.

16. T.K. Whipple, *NLM* 79:5; 294–96 (December 1913); EW, *NLM* 70: 7; 533–34; Henry James, "The New Novel," *Notes on Novelists* (New York, Charles Scribner's Sons, 1914); Edith Wharton, *The Writing of Fiction* (New York, Charles Scribner's Sons, 1925) 163; K.F. Gerould, "British Novelists Limited," *Yale Review* 7; 161–85 (October, 1917); M.R. Proctor, *The English University Novel* (Berke-ley, University of California, 1957) 154.

17. Cyril Connolly, *Enemies of Promise* (Boston, Little, Brown & Co., 1939), 39.

18. Fay—FSF correspondence, February 19, 1915 to December 9, 1919, PF; Ledger, PF.

19. On Fay see newspaper obituary, Scrapbook, PF; anonymous introduction to Sigourney C.W. Fay's posthumously published book of sermons, *The Blood of the Lamb and Other Essays* (New York, Encyclopedia Press 1922); Shane Leslie, *Dublin Review* 167, 286–93 (October–December 1920); J.T. Ellis, *Life of James Cardinal Gibbons* (Milwaukee, Bruce Publishing Co., 1952), II, 266. On Leslie see Shane Leslie, *American Wonderland* (London, M. Joseph, Ltd., 1936), 65–69; Fitzgerald's review of Leslie's novel, *The Oppidan*, New York *Tribune*, May 14, 1922, IV, 7; Stephen Gwynn, *The Letters and Friendships of Sir Cecil Spring Rice* (Boston, Houghton Mifflin Co., 1929), II, 420.

20. Shane Leslie, "Some Memories of Scott Fitzgerald," *TLS* (October 31, 1958), 632, which differs in some details from his manuscript account of this friendship, PF.

21. Mrs. Winthrop Chanler, *Autumn in the Valley* (Boston, Little, Brown, & Co., 1936), 78, 80, 83, 124; FSF to Mrs. Bayard Turnbull, Sept. 26, 1933; Henry Adams, *Letters 1892–1918*, edited by W.C. Ford (New York, Houghton Mifflin Co., 1938) 630; H.D. Cater, *Henry Adams and His Friends* (Boston, Houghton Mifflin Co., 1947) cv; R.P. Blackmur, "Henry Adams: Three Late Moments," *Kenyon Review* 2:24 (Winter, 1940); to MP, September 4, 1919, SF; according to Douglas Cater, Fay's article, "The Genesis of the Super-Germans," which was published in the *Dublin Review* in

April, 1918, was "practically all written by Adams."

22. ZSF to HDP in conversation; FSF to C.E. Delbos, January 13, 1919 (misdated 1918), PF; FSF, "A Short Autobiography," *The New Yorker* 5:14,22 (May 25, 1929).

23. Leslie to FSF, January 23, 1919 and August 6, 1920, PF.

24. To EW, January 10, 1918, PF.

25. To Charles Donahoe, n.d. (postmarked October 14, 1918) PF. See five manuscript chapters of "The Romantic Egotist" at Princeton.

26. T.A. Boyd, St. Paul *Daily News*, August 28, 1921.

27. EW to FSF, October 7, 1917; discarded manuscript "Preface" to *TSOP*, PF.

28. Charles Donahoe to FSF, n.d. (postmarked February 15, 1918) and October 27, 1918 PF; JPB to FSF n.d. (*ca.* February 1918) and March 18, 1918, PF.

29. Chapter I, manuscript of "The Romantic Egotist," 26–27, PF.

30. *TSOP*, 12–17.

31. Owen Johnson, *Stover at Yale* (New York, Frederick A. Stokes Co., 1911), 257–58; according to Robert McAlmon, in *Being Geniuses Together* (London, Secker & Warburg, 1938), 279–80, Johnson claimed that the Jazz Age actually began with the appearance of his novel, *The Salamander* in 1914; but a comparison of this work

with *TSOP* underscores the originality of the latter novel.

32. H.G. Wells, *The New Machiavelli* (New York, Duffield & Co., 1910), 210.

33. Letters from various girls to FSF, *ca.* 1916–1917, PF.

34. Alexis de Tocqueville, *Democracy in America* (New York, Oxford, 1947), 44; Van Wyck Brooks, *The Wine of the Puritans* (New York, M. Kennerly Co., 1909), 28, 47.

35. Randolph Bourne quoted in Alfred Kazin, *On Native Grounds* (New York, Reynal & Hitchcock, 1941), 184.

36. Mrs. Frank Learned, *The Etiquette of New York Today* (New York, F.A. Stokes Co., 1906), 284–6.

37. F.O. Matthiessen, *The Notebooks of Henry James* (New York, Oxford University Press., 1947), 52; *CU*, 26–27.

38. EW, *Bookman* 55:1:20–25 (March 1922; republished in *The Literary Spotlight*, ed. John Farrar, New York: George H. Doran Co., 1924; Thomas Sancton "The New York Myth," *New Republic* 107; 112–14 (July 27, 1942).

39. This sentence from the manuscript of Fitzgerald's essay, "Early Success" (PF), does not appear in the version published in *American Cavalcade*, October, 1937, and later reprinted in *CU*, 85–90.

IV

1. To MP, September 18, 1919, SF; MP to FSF, September 23, 1919, SF.

2. To Robert Bridges, October 3 and October 20, 1919, SF; Bridges to FSF, October 17 and October 30, 1917, PF; Bridges to FSF, September 22, 1917, refusing "My First Love," and June 19, 1919, refusing "Young Irony" from *TSOP*; "The Cut-Glass Bowl" and "The Four Fists" are in *F&P*.

3. To Ludlow Fowler, n.d. (post-

marked November 10, 1919), PF.

4. To. P.R. Reynolds, October 28, November 1, and November 14, 1919, OF; F.L. Allen, *Paul Revere Reynolds* (New York, privately printed, 1944).

5. "The Ice Palace" is reprinted in *F&P* and *SSC*.

6. To HO, December 30, 1919 and January 8, 1920 (misdated 1919) OF; the sheet of instructions that Fitzgerald used for "Bernice Bobs Her Hair" is at Princeton.

7. To Ludlow Fowler, January 1, 1920 (misdated 1919) and n.d. (postmarked February 4, 1920) PF; to MP, n.d. (*ca.* January, 1920), SF.

8. To MP, n.d. (*ca.* January–February 1920) SF; to MP, November 10, 1920, SF; see note on "Camel's Back" in table of contents, *TJA.*

9. "The Offshore Pirate" and "The Jelly-Bean" are in *F&P*; the latter story was omitted from *SSC*, but deserves to be brought back into print.

10. To HO, June 2, 1920, OF.

11. To HO, February 11, 1920, OF; to MP, February 3, 1920, SF; Fitzgerald's papers include his record of most of the payments he received for his fiction, PF.

12. F.L. Allen, *Only Yesterday* (New York, Harper, 1931) 51; "Echoes of the Jazz Age," *CU*, 13.

13. *TJA,* 68.

14. President Hibben to FSF, May 27, 1920, PF; to Hibben, June 3, 1920, Hibben Papers, Princeton Library; to MP, n.d. (*ca.* December, 1921), SF.

15. Wire to Zelda, February 4, 1920, in Zelda's scrapbook, PF; Montgomery, Alabama, *Advertiser,* March 20, 1920.

16. To HO, July 17, 1920, OF.

17. To MP, September 18, 1919 SF; to HO, February 5, 1922 (misdated 1921) OF; see also to MP, February 6, 1922 and n.d. (*ca.* February 10, 1922), SF.

18. F.L. Mott, *History of American Magazines* (1885–1905), v. 4 (Cambridge, Massachusetts: Harvard University Press, 1957), 671–711; J.P. Wood, *Magazines in the United States, Their Social and*

Economic Influence (New York, Ronald Press, 1949), 145–52; John Tebbel, *George Horace Lorimer and The Saturday Evening Post* (New York, Doubleday & Co., 1948) *passim.*

19. Lloyd Morris, *Postscript to Yesterday* (New York, Random House, 1947), 272.

20. Robert Elias, *Theodore Dreiser* (New York, A.A. Knopf, 1948), 141.

21. *CU,* 87–88.

22. FSF's *Post* stories were published in *SEP* from February to June, 1920; the first obvious imitation of his style appears in an August issue, and by September the magazine's cover girl is wearing a one-piece bathing suit; the October advertisements begin to feature dancing in the illustrations and the use of cosmetics in advertisements; and by November the cover girl has bobbed her hair.

23. *F&P,* 3.

24. Katharine Brush, "The Time of My Life," *Ladies' Home Journal* 51:1, 55–56 (January, 1940), published in book form as *This is on Me* (New York, Farrar & Rinehart, 1940).

25. To HO, November 11, 1923, OF; "Gretchen's Forty Winks," "The Sensible Thing," and "The Baby Party" are in *ASYM* and the last two are also in *SSC.*

26. To HO, February 5, 1922, OF.

27. J.P. Wood, *Magazines in the United States, Their Social and Economic Influence* (New York, Ronald Press, 1949), 151–152.

28. FSF, review of Booth Tarkington's *Gentle Julia, St. Paul Daily News,* May 7, 1922.

29. *CU,* 322.

V

1. To MP, September 18, 1919, SF; To Robert Bridges, October 25, 1919, SF (FSF's second title was apparently suggested by W.N.P.

Barbellion's book, *The Journal of a Disappointed Man* (New York, George H. Doran Co., November, 1919), which had just been published with an introduction by H.G. Wells. At the time it was believed that Wells had written the book, although it was later revealed that the author was another Englishman named Bruce Frederic Cummings).

2. To HO, n.d. (ca. December, 1919) OF; Bridges to FSF, November 1, 1919, SF.

3. To MP n.d. (ca. December, 1919) SF; to HO, January 8, 1920 (misdated 1919) and February 3, 1920, OF.

4. To MP, n.d. (ca. February, 1920) SF.

5. To HO, n.d. (ca. December, 1919) OF.

6. To HO, July 17 and 26, 1920, OF; to MP, July 7, 1920, SF.

7. To Charles Scribner, August 12, 1920, SF.

8. To MP, December 31, 1920, SF.

9. Ledger; "The Rubber Check," SEP, August 6, 1932.

10. To MP, November 10, 1920; see also to MP, February 13, March 30 and April 21, 1921, SF; and to HO, January 13, April 22 and August 10, 1921, OF.

11. St. Paul Daily News, August 28, 1921.

12. To MP, August 25, 1921, SF.

13. To HO, November 29, 1921, OF; CU, 255-56; to MP, October 20, 1921, SF.

14. G.J. Nathan to Zelda, July 28 and August 16, 1920, PF; H.L. Mencken to FSF, September 9, 1920, PF; Zelda to Ludlow Fowler, n.d. (postmarked August 10, 1920), PF; G.J. Nathan, Intimate Notebooks (New York, A.A. Knopf, 1932), 57, 105-07.

15. Samuel Butler, Note-books (New York, E.P. Dutton, 1907). FSF's copy at Princeton is dated by him "April 17, 1917," but his comment, "The most interesting human document ever written," is dated September 19, 1919.

16. CU, 87.

17. TSOP, 224.

18. Sherwood Anderson's Memoirs (New York, Harcourt, Brace & Co., 1942) 333-37; B.F. Wilson, "F. Scott Fitzgerald," Smart Set, April, 1924, 33 (see also TFSP, 333, for details of FSF's meeting with Dreiser); to MP, n.d. (ca. December 20, 1924) SF.

19. To MP, February 3, 1920, SF; Mencken to FSF, October 7, 1920, PF; Charles G. Norris to FSF, November 15, 1920, PF; Bookman 54:3,253-4 (November, 1921).

20. HDP, "Frank Norris and Scott Fitzgerald," Huntington Library Quarterly 19:4,393-400 (August, 1956).

21. Bookman 55:1,20-25 (March 1922) reprinted in The Literary Spotlight ed. by J. Farrar (New York, George H. Doran Co., 1924), 125-134.

22. B&D, 414, 416; on FSF's manuscript of B&D, the earlier title, "The Beautiful Lady Without Mercy" has been crossed out, and his title page contains a stanza from Keat's "La Belle Dame Sans Merci," that is omitted from the book title page; see Metropolitan, March, 1922, for the final paragraph of the B&D serial version quoted here.

23. To Shane Leslie, September 17, 1920, PF; to JPB, n.d. (ca. March 1922) PF; see also Bishop's review of B&D, Vanity Fair 16:8, 8-9 (October 1921), and MP to John Biggs, March 4, 1941, SF.

24. To FFL, June 14, 1940, PF; B&D, 211-12.

25. William Troy, Accent 6,56 (1945), reprinted in Fitzgerald: The Man and His Work ed. by Alfred Kazin (New York, World Publishing Co., 1951), 188.

26. B&D, 412.

27. Charles Jackson, The Lost Weekend (New York, Farrar & Rinehart, 1944), 149.

28. To HO, n.d. (ca. November 1921) and December 27, 1921, OF; to MP, January 9, 1922, SF; G.J. Nathan, The Theatre, The Drama,

The Girls (New York, A.A. Knopf, 1921), 16 (also 72); see also Nathan to FSF, February 14 and August 31, 1922, PF.

29. EW to FSF, May 26, 1922, PF; to MP, n.d. (*ca.* July 1922) SF.
30. To HO, March 2, 1922, OF.
31. *Bookman* 58:1, 57–58 (September 1923).
32. *Bookman* 55:1,20 (March, 1922),

reprinted in *The Literary Spotlight,* ed. by J. Farrar, New York, George H. Doran Co., 1924; see also *Vanity Fair,* 19:3, 24–25.

33. Perkins' comment is on FSF's letter to him, n.d. (*ca.* January, 1923) SF.
34. Maxwell Geismar, *Last of the Provincials* (Boston, Houghton Mifflin, Co., 1947), 312.

VI

1. To MP, May 26, 1921, and n.d. (*ca.* March, 1922), SF.
2. To MP, n.d. (*ca.* June, 1922) and n.d. (*ca.* June, 1922), SF.
3. *SSC,* 144–145.
4. *SSC,* 156, 158.
5. To HO, December 12, 1922 ("Winter Dreams" is here entitled "Recklessness") OF; to HO, November 12, 1923, OF; to MP. n.d. (*ca.* November, 1923), SF.
6. To "Ceci," n.d. (*ca.* Autumn, 1922), PF.
7. "How to Live on $36,000 a Year," *SEP,* April 5, 1924; "How to Live on Practically Nothing a Year," *SEP,* September 20, 1924; "Wait Till You Have Children of Your Own," *Woman's Home Companion,* 51:13 (July, 1924); Burton Rascoe, *We Were Interrupted* (New York, Doubleday, 1947), 168.
8. To MP, October 27, 1924, SF; F has misspelled Fontaine Fox and Donald Brian.
9. To MP, n.d. (*ca.* April, 1924), SF.
10. To MP, June 18, 1924, SF; to John Jamieson, April 15, 1934, PF; see also Vernon MacKenzie, editor, *These Stories Went to Market* (New York, R.M. McBride Co., 1935), xviii.
11. *SSC,* 163, 169–171.
12. *SSC,* 171.
13. *SSC,* 163.
14. *Gatsby,* 118.
15. First chapter of "The Romantic Egotist" manuscript, 14, PF; Vernon MacKenzie, editor, *These Stories Went to Market* (New

York, R.M. McBride Co., 1935), xviii; Ledger for 1907, PF.
16. To Ludlow Fowler, n.d. (*ca.* August, 1924), PF.
17. The passage quoted here from the pencil manuscript of *Gatsby* follows immediately after the final sentence of Chapter I of the published text, PF.
18. This deleted passage occurs in Chapter I of the pencil draft of the *Gatsby* manuscript, at a place corresponding to line 19, page 25 of the published text, PF.
19. The deleted comparison of Gatsby's car to a hearse occurs in the pencil version, *Gatsby* manuscript, at a point corresponding to line 6, page 77, of the published text; another reference to a hearse occurs on page 82 of the published text; MP to FSF, April 7, 1924, PF; *Gatsby,* 77, 215.
20. The deleted reference to Dr. Eckleburg's eyes occurs at a point in the pencil version of the manuscript corresponding to line 3, page 28 of the published text; *Gatsby,* 30.
21. *Gatsby,* 207, 197 (although Wolfshiem's name has been corrected to "Wolfsheim" in the most recent edition of the novel, I have kept Fitzgerald's original spelling of it throughout).
22. *Gatsby,* 213, 192.
23. *TSOP,* 303.
24. *Gatsby,* 2.
25. *CU,* 270, 271; JPB to FSF, n.d. (*ca.* January, 1925) PF; *CU,* 310.

VII

1. MP to FSF, November 18 and 20, 1924, SF; J.H. Wheelock, editor *Editor to Author: The Letters of Maxwell E. Perkins* (New York, Charles Scribner's Sons, 1950) 38–40; MP to Ring Lardner, November 29, 1924, SF.
2. To MP, n.d. (*ca.* Dec. 20, 1924) SF.
3. *Gatsby*, 202.
4. *Gatsby*, 212.
5. *Time,* December 11, 1944, 84.
6. MP to FSF, August 8, 1924, PF.
7. Ring Lardner to FSF, August 8, 1925, PF.
8. The histories of E.M. Fuller and Co., of Edward Fuller, and of his business associates, can be traced through the New York *Times Annual Index,* 1920–28 and the annual index, 1922–24, of the *Commercial and Financial Chronicle;* for Fuller's flying exploits see New York *Times,* July 11, 1921, 11:3.
9. Feature article on Charles Stoneham, New York *Times,* September 9, 1923, VIII:2:1; see also Gene Fowler, *The Great Mouthpiece: A Life Story of William J. Fallon* (New York, Blue Ribbon Books, 1931), 326–340.
10. Stanley Walker, *The Night Club Era* (New York, Fred A. Stokes Co., 1933), 10; Lloyd Morris, *Postscript to Yesterday* (New York, Random House, 1947), 75.
11. *Gatsby,* 161; pencil draft of *Gatsby* manuscript, 206, PF.
12. To HDP in conversation, February 6, 1950.
13. To JPB, n.d. (*ca.* Summer, 1925) PF.
14. Lord Raglan, *The Hero: A Study in Tradition, Myth and Drama* (New York, Vintage, 1956), 174–75; see also Arnold Toynbee, *A Study of History* (Oxford University Press, 1934) III, 259.
15. B.B. Bruestle, "*The Fool of Nature*" in the English Drama of Our Day (Philadelphia, University of Pennsylvania, 1932), 14–19; Jessie L. Weston, *From Ritual to Romance* (Cambridge University Press, 1920), 28.
16. New York *Herald Tribune,* March 4, 1923.
17. *Gatsby,* 179.
18. "Sir Richard Whittington," *Dictionary of National Biography;* Rev. Samuel Lysons, *The Model Merchant* (London, Hamilton, Adams, & Co., 1860); *The History of Sir Richard Whittington* by "T.H.", edited with an introduction by H.B. Wheatley, F.A.A. (London, for the Villon Society, 1885); see also Louis B. Wright, *Middle Class Culture in Elizabethan England* (Chapel Hill, North Carolina, University of North Carolina Press, 1938), 1–3, 616–617; on Paul Bunyan, Daniel F. Hoffman, *Paul Bunyan: Last of the Frontier Demi-Gods* (Philadelphia, University of Pennsylvania Press, 1952).
19. F.C. Watkins, *New England Quarterly,* 27:2, 249–52 (June 1954); pencil manuscript of *Gatsby,* Chapter III, PF.
20. *AOA,* 35.

VIII

1. To MP, n.d. (*ca.* July, 1922), SF; *Gatsby,* Modern Library Edition (New York, Random House, 1934).
2. New York *World,* April 3, 1927, magazine section 12.
3. *TFSP,* 162–3; *SMTW,* 109–29;

Zelda Fitzgerald to HDP, March 13, 1947; Andrew Turnbull; *F. Scott Fitzgerald* (New York, Charles Scribner's Sons, 1962), gives the French flyer's name as "Edouard Josanne."

4. Ledger, 1924, PF.
5. To MP, n.d. (*ca.* August 20, 1924) SF.
6. To HO, September 20, 1924, OF; *CU*, 264–65, 267–69; to MP, October 27, 1924, SF.
7. *Dial*, August, 1925; Edith Wharton to FSF, July 2, 1925, PF; see also her letter to FSF, July 8, 1925, PF, and *CU*, 309.
8. EW, "Imaginary Conversations: F. Scott Fitzgerald and Van Wyck Brooks," *New Republic* 38, 248–53 (1924), reprinted in his *Discordant Encounters* (New York, A. & C. Boni, 1926), 35–60.
9. The lists of FSF's favorite novels are among his miscellaneous papers at Princeton; Henry James, *The American Scene* (New York, Charles Scribner's Sons, 1907), 99–102, 311–12, 333.
10. H. James, *The American*, New York Edition, v. ii, (New York, Charles Scribner's Sons, 1907), vi–vii; reprinted in R. P. Blackmur, editor, *The Art of the Novel*, (New York, Charles Scribner's Sons, 1934).
11. F. W. Dupee, *Henry James* (New York, Sloane Associates, 1951), 281.
12. To President John Grier Hibben, June 3, 1920, Hibben Papers, Princeton University.
13. *TFSP*, footnote 6, 336; FSF's review of Thomas Boyd's *Through the Wheat*, New York *Evening Post*, May 26, 1923.
14. *Gatsby*, Modern Library Edition (New York, 1934); Baltimore *Sun*, May 3, 1925; CU, 270; to MP, n.d. (*ca.* July 15, 1928) SF.
15. Joseph Conrad, *Lord Jim* (New York, Doubleday, Page & Co., 1927), 76; also see FSF's comments on Conrad's use of first-person narrator in *LT*, 134.
16. R. W. Stallman, *Twentieth Century Literature* 1:5, 12 (1955); the description of the refreshments at Gatsby's party (*Gatsby*, 48) echoes a well-known stanza from Keats's *The Eve of St. Agnes;* the description of the light falling on the floor in Gatsby's music room (*Gatsby,* 115) is indebted to Keat's *An Ode to a Nightingale.*
17. On Conrad's early development see J.D. Gordan, *Joseph Conrad: The Making of a Novelist* (Cambridge, Massachusetts, Harvard University Press, 1941).
18. Joseph Conrad, *Lord Jim* (New York, Doubleday, Page & Co., 1927), 21; *Gatsby,* 57.
19. *Lord Jim,* 21–22; *Gatsby,* 134.
20. FSF quotes the last line of *My Ántonia* on the last page of his 1940 unpublished essay, "My Generation," PF.
21. Willa Cather, *My Ántonia* (Boston, Houghton Mifflin Co., 1918) 364; FSF also mentions *My Ántonia* in his review of Booth Tarkington's *Gentle Julia*, St. Paul *Daily News* 23:68 (May 7, 1922).
22. *Dial*, 16:79–80 (January, 1924); *A Lost Lady* (New York, A.A. Knopf, 1923), 102, 42; *Gatsby,* 8; see Willa Cather to FSF, April 28, 1925, acknowledging a letter to her from FSF in which he apparently speaks of having borrowed a passage from *A Lost Lady* for *Gatsby*, PF.
23. New York *Evening Post* 3:143 (October 28, 1922); *International Book Review* 1:4, 35–6 (March 1923); on the Anderson novel see New York *Herald*, 9:5 (March 4, 1923).
24. St. Paul *Daily News*, September 25, 1921; New York *Evening Post* 3:715 (May 26, 1923).
25. *International Book Review* 1:4, 35–6 (March, 1923).
27. Katherine Brush, *Ladies Home Journal* 57:1, 55 (January, 1940), reprinted in *This Is on Me*, (New York, Farrar & Rinehart, 1940).
27. All the versions of the *Gatsby* manuscripts mentioned here are at Princeton.
28. Pencil manuscript, *Gatsby*, 21, PF.
29. *AOA*, 132.
30. Pencil manuscript, *Gatsby,* 9.
31. *Gatsby*, 43.
32. *CU*, 69, 322.

33. Pencil manuscript, *Gatsby*, Chapter III, PF.
34. *Gatsby*, 58.
35. To MP, n.d. (*ca.* December 1, 1924), SF (where FSF calls Chapter V his "favorite" chapter).
36. To MP, (*ca.* August 15, 1924) SF, and Ludlow Fowler, n.d. (*ca.* August 1924), PF; to MP, September 10, 1924, and *ca.* November 7, 1924, SF.
37. To MP, n.d. (*ca.* December 20, 1924), SF; to HO, n.d. (*ca.* February 18, 1925) OF; to MP n.d. (*ca.* April 10, 1925), SF.
38. To MP, n.d. (*ca.* December 1, 1924), SF.

39. *Gatsby* manuscript, galley 48, PF.
40. *Gatsby*, 134.
41. *CU*, 271.
42. *Gatsby*, 182.
43. *Gatsby*, 194.
44. The deleted passage came just before "when the blue smoke . . ." *Gatsby*, line 8, page 213.
45. *Gatsby*, 211–12, 212–13.
46. Chapter II, "The Romantic Egoist" manuscript, 19, PF.
47. *CU*, 67.
48. To MP, n.d. (*ca.* December 20, 1924), n.d. (*ca.* February 18, 1925), and April 10, 1925, SF.

IX

1. To HO, September 20, 1924, OF.
2. To HO, n.d. (*ca.* March 15, 1925); see also to HO, January 21, 1925, OF.
3. To Ludlow Fowler, n.d. (*ca.* March–April 1925); see also to Ludlow Fowler, n.d. (*ca.* August 1925) and November 6, 1925, PF; and to HO, April 1, April 25, and October 14, 1925, OF.
4. *SSC*, 177.
5. *SSC*, 178.
6. *SSC*, 179–80, 205.
7. MP to FSF, April 21, 1922, SF.
8. See FSF's copy of H.L. Mencken, *Prejudices: Second Series* (New York, A.A. Knopf, 1920), 66–74, PF.
9. J.N. Wheeler to Paul R. Reynolds, December 16, 1924, OF. See also Ray Long to Reynolds, December 4, 1924, and FSF to HO, January 9, 1925, OF; FSF to MP, October 27, 1924 and January 24, 1925, SF.
10. MP to FSF, April 20, 1925, SF; W. Collins Sons, Ltd., to Curtis Brown, Ltd., June 15, 1925, SF; MP to FSF, October 6, 1925, SF.
11. To MP, n.d. (*ca.* April 24, 1925), SF.
12. To HO, March 10, 1926, OF; to MP, February 20, 1926, SF.
13. See contract with *Liberty*, June 5,

1926, and related correspondence, PF.
14. To MP, n.d. (*ca.* June 1926); Zelda to MP, n.d. (*ca.* November, 1926) SF.
15. To MP, n.d. (*ca.* August, 1926) SF; J.W. Considine to FSF, December 30, 1926, PF.
16. Considine to FSF, January 4, 1927 and April 23, 1927, PF; HO to Paul R. Reynolds, April 27, 1927, OF; the manuscript of "Lipstick" is at Princeton.
17. John Biggs, Jr., to HDP, conversation, June 22, 1945. "Ellerslie" is now the site of a duPont Company pigment factory and the residence has been converted into an office building.
18. MP to Ring Lardner, October 20, 1927, SF; see also MP to Lardner, October 11, and Lardner to MP, October 13, 1927, SF; and FSF's correspondence with Parker, Fowler, Wilder, etc., for 1927, PF; Joseph Hergesheimer to HDP, conversation, July 11, 1951.
19. Michael Fisher, former neighbor of FSF at "Ellerslie," to HDP, conversation, May 24, 1950.
20. To MP, n.d. (*ca.* March 1, 1929) SF.
21. *SSC*, 270.

22. *AOA*, 164.

23. To HO, November 11, 1930, OF; "Babylon Revisited," *SSC*, 385–402.

24. To MP, n.d., (*ca.* Aug. 20, 1931) SF; to HO, October 29 and November 6, 1931 (the contract was for six weeks work at $1,200 plus travel expenses, and Fitzgerald was recommended for the job by Katharine Brush).

25. To FFL, n.d. (*ca.* July 4, 1937), PF.

26. To Alfred Dashiell, n.d. (*ca.* October 2, 1932) SF; to MP, telegram, November 30, 1931, SF.

27. To MP, March 24 and March 25, 1932, and September 29, 1933, SF; HO to FSF, February 25, 1932, OF; "Crazy Sunday," *SSC*, 403–418.

28. *SSC*, 431.

29. To HO, January 2, 1931, OF; HO to FSF, January 6, 1932, OF.

30. To HO, received May 13, 1930; OF; see also HO to FSF, August 30, 1933, and F. L. Mott, *A History of American Magazines* (Cambridge, Mass., Harvard University Press, 1957), IV, 671–717, on Lorimer's relinquishment of his editorship of the *SEP*.

31. *AOA*, 131–132.

32. Unpublished manuscript outline of "I Take Hard Cases," PF.

33. HO to FSF, May 19 and June 11, 1931, OF.

34. Manuscript "Instructions to my Literary Executor," PF.

35. A more exact total depends upon how you classify semi-autobiographical pieces like "Financing Finnegan" and "Outside the Cabinet Makers"; see list of F's stories to be reprinted, or to be scrapped, in Red Ledger (*ca.* 1938–1939), PF.

36. *AOA*, 137–41 (HO's note on the manuscript of this piece says "declined by seven magazines," PF).

37. Five Basil stories are republished in *TAR*, 1–132; three others are in *AOA*, 15–69; the last, "That Kind of Party," has been published in *PULC*, 4:12, 169–80 (Summer, 1951).

38. Three Josephine stories are in *TAR*, 133–200; the other two are "A Snobbish Story," *SEP*, November 29, 1930, and "Emotional Bankruptcy," *SEP*, August 15, 1931.

39. *SSC*, 304; "The Love Boat," *SEP*, October 8, 1927; "The Rough Crossing," *SSC*, 254–270; "A New Leaf," *SEP*, July 4, 1931; "Two Wrongs," *SSC*, 304.

40. "The Bowl," *SEP*, January 21, 1928.

41. "The Rubber Check," *SEP*, August 6, 1932; "Six of One," *Redbook*, February 1932.

42. "Wait Till You Have Children of Your Own," *Woman's Home Companion*, July, 1924; "A Freeze Out,' *SEP*, December 19, 1931; "Six of One," *Redbook*, February, 1932.

43. "The Swimmers," *SEP*, October 19, 1929.

X

1. Zelda to MP, n.d. (*ca.* November 15, 1924), SF; FSF to MP, n.d. (*ca.* December 20, 1924), SF.

2. To MP, May 1, 1925, SF; *CU*, 272.

3. Ledger, August, 1925, PF; to MP, August 28, 1925, SF; to JPB, September 21, 1925, PF.

4. To Paul R. Reynolds, September 2, 1925, OF; to MP, n.d. (*ca.* October 1925) SF; to HO, October 14, 1925, OF.

5. To MP, n.d. (*ca.* December 27, 1925) SF; to HO, n.d. (*ca.* May, 1926) OF; *Liberty* contract with FSF, June 5, 1926, PF.

6. MP to Ring Lardner, October 20, 1927, SF; FSF to MP, n.d. (*ca.* February 18, 1928), SF.

7. To MP, n.d. (*ca.* July 1, 1928) and n.d. (*ca.* July 21, 1928), SF.

8. Ledger, summer and fall, 1928, PF.

9. To MP, n.d. (*ca.* November 1,

1928), and n.d. (ca. November 10, 1928), SF.

10. MP to FSF, November 13, 1928; PF; Ledger, winter, 1928–29, PF; FSF to MP, n.d. (ca. March 1, 1929) SF.

11. MP to Ring Lardner, June 20, 1929, SF; FSF to MP, n.d. (ca. June, 1929) and September 1, 1929, SF; Ledger, summer, 1929, PF.

12. MP to FSF, November 30, 1929, PF.

13. To MP, n.d. (ca. November 15, 1929), SF; to HO, March 14, 1930, OF; to MP, n.d. (ca. May, 1930), SF.

14. To MP, n.d. (ca. May, 1930), SF; to HO, May 13, 1930, OF.

15. Thornton Wilder to HDP, May 14, 1947; Allen Tate to HDP, conversation, February 6, 1950; FSF to HO, November 11, 1930, OF; to MP, n.d. (ca. January 1931), SF.

16. To MP, n.d. (ca. January 1, 1931) SF; to "Ceci," February 23, 1931, PF.

17. To MP, n.d. (ca. December–January, 1931–1932), SF.

18. MP to FSF, April 7, 1927 and June 2, 1927, PF.

19. Malcolm Cowley, introduction to TITN (New York, 1951) iv; the manuscript of "The Boy Who Killed His Mother" is at Princeton; on FSF's failure to make an outline for this novel, see his letter to MP, May 29, 1939, PF.

20. Ledger, December, 1924; HDP, "note," Interim (Seattle, Washington), 4:1 and 2, 3–5 (1954); in TITN Francis and his mother are now Dick Diver and Baby Warren, Dick's sister-in-law.

21. To MP, August 28, 1925 and n.d. (ca. February 8, 1926), SF; Genevieve Forbes, "The Direst Murder in the History of Chicago," Liberty, June 28, 1924, same issue as FSF's story, "The Sensible Thing;" Ring Lardner to FSF, June 5, 1924, PF.

22. To MP, n.d. (ca. February 8, 1926), SF.

23. To MP, n.d. (ca. June, 1929), SF; the new opening of the novel is in manuscript, PF.

24. Lewis Jacobs, Rise of the American Film (New York, Harcourt, Brace & Co., 1939), 379–80.

25. Jacobs, loc. cit.; see TFSP for a different interpretation, 213.

26. To MP, n.d. (ca. January 15, 1932), SF.

27. Zelda to MP, n.d. (ca. March 12, 1932), SF; FSF to MP, March 16, March 28, and ca. May 14, 1932, SF; MP to Zelda, May 16, 1932, SF, accepting SMTW for publication; FSF to "Dick," September 29, 1932, describing Zelda's unsuccessful attempts at revision, PF; SMTW was published by Scribner's in October, 1932.

XI

1. "Eulogy on the Flapper," Metropolitan 55:5, 38 (June, 1922); for a complete list of Zelda's published writings see HDP, "Zelda Sayre Fitzgerald: A Checklist," PULC 12:4:209–10 (Summer, 1951).

2. SMTW, 11 (because of its greater accessibility, I have cited the Grey Walls Press, London, 1953, edition of SMTW throughout).

3. Zelda's scrapbook, PF; FSF to Mrs. Sayre, September 9, 1928, PF; on John Tyler Morgan see Dictionary of American Biography (New York, Charles Scribner's Sons), 1928–1936; on Judge Sayre, see Who's Who, 1928–29; on the Machen family, Lamb's Biographical Dictionary of the U.S., edited J.H. Brown (Boston, J. H. Lamb Co., 1903) and G. Glenn Clift, Governors of Kentucky, 1792–1942 (Cynthiana, Kentucky, Hobson Press, 1942).

4. *SMTW*, 41–2.
5. *Ibid.*, 15, 133, 129, 150.
6. *Ibid.*, 151–153.
7. *Ibid.*, 136–7, 149.
8. *Ibid.*, 190–91; on Madame Egorova see Gerald Murphy to FSF, September 19, 1925, PF; also S. Hurok, *S. Hurok Presents* (New York, Hermitage House, 1953), 71–2.
9. *SMTW*, 164, 190–1.
10. *Ibid.*, 250.

11. *Ibid.*, 167, 251.
12. *Ibid.*, 268, 194–5.
13. *Ibid.*, 265; New York *Times, March* 12, 1948, 33.
14. *Ibid.*, 75, 270.
15. *Ibid.*, 157–8, 160–2, 191.
16. *Ibid.*, 185.
17. To HDP, conversation, March 14, 1947.
18. *SMTW*, 155, 222, 179–80.
19. *Ibid.*, 247–49.

XII

1. Ledger, August, 1932, PF ("the novel plotted and planned, nevermore to be permanently interrupted"); the chart is among the *TITN* papers at Princeton.
2. To MP, September, 25, and October 11, 1933, SF; MP to FSF, October 18, 1933, PF.
3. To Alfred Dashiell, October 29, 1933, SF; MP to FSF, November 6, 1933, SF.
4. To MP, Christmas, 1933; SF; see also to MP, November 13, 1933, SF.
5. To MP, January 13, 1934, SF.
6. *CU*, 278; *TITN* was serialized in *Scribner's Monthly*, January–April, 1934.
7. *TITN* manuscript, 177, 255, 386–90. See F's copy of *TITN*, 362, 369, PF.
8. To Mrs. E.S. Jarrett, February 17, 1938, PF; to MP, March 11, 1935, SF.
9. Chapters XXII and XXIII, which should be exempted from this criticism of the second half of Book II, had been revised many times, and were originally intended as the opening chapter of "The Boy Who Killed His Mother."
10. In 1938 Fitzgerald told Sheilah Graham that *TITN* should have been two separate books, Sheilah Graham and Gerold Frank, *Beloved Infidel* (New York, Henry Holt & Co., 1959), 240.
11. Manuscript notes, *TITN*, PF.
12. Dorothy Spensley, "No Convent Belle," *Photoplay* 32:3, 70; also see clippings on Lois Moran in FSF's scrapbooks, PF.
13. Notes to *TITN*, PF; see also *FSOP*, 307–8.
14. *Ibid.;* see also *FSOP*, 309.
15. *Ibid.;* see also *FSOP*, 309–310.
16. To Betty Markell, September 16, 1929, PF.
17. Willa Cather to FSF, April 28, 1925, PF, unfortunately Miss Cather's will prohibits direct quotation from her letters; *TITN*, 35.
18. *TITN*, 263, 175.
19. *Ibid.*, 27.
20. To Mrs. E.S. Jarrett, February 17, 1938, PF.
21. *TITN*, 24, 20.
22. *Ibid.*, 26.
23. *Ibid.*, 102.
24. *Ibid.*, 26–27, 35.
25. *FSOP*, xii.
26. *CU*, 209.
27. *TITN*, 233.
28. *Ibid.*, 119. (Ferrara here is probably confused with the neighboring city of Canossa, scene of Henry IV's humiliating penance before Pope Gregory in 1077.)
29. *TITN*, 265–266.
30. *Ibid.*, 119–21, 399; "A Short Trip Home," *TAR*, 323–48.
31. *Ibid.*, Book II, Chapters XVII and XVIII.
32. *Ibid.*, 260–7.
33. *Ibid.*, 375.
34. *Ibid.*, 406; F.J. Hoffman, *The Twenties* (New York, Viking Press, 1955), 374.

35. *TITN* manuscript, PF. See *FSOP*, 308–9.
36. To MP, January 18, 1934, SF.
37. *TITN*, 231.
38. *TITN* manuscript, Chapter XI, 445–61 (pencil version), PF.
39. The chart is among the *TITN* papers, PF.
40. To MP, Christmas, 1933, SF; I am indebted to Thoburn Snyder, M.D., of Philadelphia for his analysis of the medical aspects of *TITN* which I have made use of here.
41. See FSF's synopsis at the beginning of the second installment of *TITN*, *Scribners'* February, 1934; *TITN*, 152.

42. *TITN* manuscript, PF.
43. *TITN*, 13, 16.
44. Typed note in FSF's Notebooks, omitted from *CU* version.
45. To MP, January 18, 1934 and December 24, 1938, SF; see FSF's copy of *TITN*, PF.
46. Revised version of *TITN*, edited by Malcolm Cowley, (New York, Charles Scribner's Sons, 1952), and included with *Gatsby* and *LT* in *FSF: Three Novels* (Charles Scribner's Sons, 1953).
47. To Bennett Cerf, August 13, 1936, PF.
48. FSF's copy of James Joyce's *Dubliners*, PF.

XIII

1. To MP, September 29, 1933; SF; to HO, December 8, 1934, OF; *Editor to Author: The Letters of Maxwell E. Perkins* (New York, Charles Scribner's Sons, 1950), 95.
2. To MP, November 8, 1934, SF.
3. Three Philippe stories were published in the October, 1934, and June and August, 1935, issues of *Redbook;* the fourth was published posthumously in the November, 1941 issue. For FSF's intentions about them see his manuscript, "General Plan," PF; HO to FSF, December 5, 1934, PF; and FSF's letters to HO, May 29, 1939, OF, and to Neal Begley, March 26, 1940, PF.
4. To MP, November 8, 1934, SF.
5. HO to FSF, June 2, 1939, OF.
6. Data obtained from Dick York, April 24, 1936, about his stunt auto driving, among FSF's miscellaneous notes, PF; FSF to a Mrs. Kennedy, July 29, 1939, PF; Mrs. Nora Flynn in conversation with HDP, February 10, 1947.
7. Littauer's comments are quoted in HO to FSF, February 15, 1938, PF.
8. Draft of letter to K. Littauer, n.d. (*ca.* July 25, 1939) PF.
9. Typescript of unfinished "Day Off From Love," PF.

10. The "Crack-Up" essays appeared in the February, March, and April, 1936, issues of *Esquire* and were reprinted in *CU;* "Author's House" is in the July, 1936, *Esquire* and *AOA;* "Afternoon of an Author" in the August, 1936, *Esquire* and *AOA;* "An Author's Mother" in the September, 1936, *Esquire;* "Early Success" in *American Cavalcade,* October, 1937, and in *AOA* (a somewhat different earlier ms version is at Princeton); "Outside the Cabinet Maker's" is in December, 1928, *Century* and *AOA;* "My Lost City" was first published in *CU;* "Sleeping and Waking" is in the December, 1934, *Esquire* and *CU;* "Financing Finnegan" in the January, 1938, *Esquire* and *SSC;* "The Lost Decade" in the December, 1939, *Esquire* and *SSC.*
11. Ledger, 1935, PF; to Ceci, May 10 and June 11, 1935, PF;
12. To Mrs. Bayard Turnbull, n.d. (*ca.* June 1935) PF; Sheilah Graham and Gerold Frank, *Beloved Infidel* (New York, Holt & Co., 1958), 273.
13. To Mrs. Bayard Turnbull, n.d. (*ca.* June, 1935) PF; to Roger Garis, February 22, 1938, PF.
14. *CU,* 69–73.
15. *Ibid.,* 78, 80–81.

16. *Ibid.*, 81–84.
17. *Ibid.*, 82.
18. Ernest Hemingway, "The Snows of Kilimanjaro," *Esquire*, August, 1936; for FSF's friends' reactions to the "Crack-Up" series see MP to John Biggs, March 23, 1941, PF; FSF to Marie Hamm, October 25, 1936, PF; Hamilton Basso to EW, October 14, 1944, PF.
19. On FSF's reaction to "The Snows" see Mizener, *FSOP*, 270–71 and FSF to Beatrice Dance, n.d. (*ca.* autumn, 1936), PF.
20. *LT* ms., PF.
21. Graeme Lorimer of *SEP*, to HO, March 10, 1936, OF; *AOA*, 178–9.
22. To a Mrs. Feley, July 20, 1939, PF; on his later feelings about the

"Crack-Up" essays see also the early manuscript version of "Early Success," PF.
23. To Ceci, n.d. (*ca.* July 5, 1937) PF, to MP, n.d. (*ca.* February, 1937, SF.
24. To HO, January 10, 1935 (1936?), OF; *CU*, 78; *AOA*, 178.
25. Charles Warren to FSF, October 12, 1934; to MP, October 16, 1936, SF.
26. Telegram, HO to FSF, August 13, 1936, PF; *CU*, 280; contract with M-G-M dated August 21, 1937, PF; FSF to HO, n.d. (*ca.* June, 1937) specifying way in which salary is to be allocated, OF.
27. *SSC*, 449.
28. *SSC*, 455.

XIV

1. To FFL, n.d. (*ca.* July 5, 1937) PF.
2. To Joseph Mankiewicz, September 4, 1937, PF; see also to Ted Paramore, October 24, 1937, PF.
3. To Mankiewicz, January 20, 1938; see also to Mankiewicz, January 17, 1938, and Paramore to FSF (telegram), January 25, 1938, all PF.
4. New York *Times*, June 3, 1938, page 17, and January 3, 1939, page 18.
5. FSF's comment appears on his copy of the final script of *Three Comrades*, dated February 1, 1938; see also his unfinished script dated September 1, 1937, and a second script by him and Paramore dated January 6, 1938, all PF.
6. To Ceci, n.d. (*ca.* August 1934) PF.
7. To FFL n.d. (autumn, 1938) and n.d. (*ca.* January 1939), PF.
8. To MP, February 25, 1939, SF.
9. Sheilah Graham and Gerold Frank, *Beloved Infidel* (New York, Henry Holt & Co., 1958), 269; George O'Connell, Dartmouth News Bureau, to HDP, June 16, 1958; FSF to Berg, Dozier, Dozier & Allen, February 23, 1940, PF.

10. Budd Schulberg, "Fitzgerald in Hollywood," *New Republic*, March 3, 1941, in which he erroneously puts the Dartmouth Winter Carnival in November; Schulberg, *The Disenchanted* (New York, Random House, 1950); Schulberg review of Arthur Mizener, *The Far Side of Paradise*, New York *Times*, January 28, 1951.
11. To MP, February 25, 1939, SF.
12. To Mrs. Frank Case, May 3, 1939, PF.
13. Edward Everett Horton to HDP in conversation, April 29, 1949; FSF's only movie assignment between April, 1939 and February, 1940 was a week's work at M-G-M on "Raffles."
14. To HO, July 19, 1939, OF, and HO to FSF, July 18, 1939, PF; see also HO to FSF, June 2 and 30, 1939, PF; and see FSF to HO, May 29 and July 7, 1939, PF; and FSF to MP, July 19, 1939, PF.
15. To HO, July 19, 1939, PF.
16. Arnold Gingrich, to FSF, July 24, 1939 (see also Gingrich to FSF, September 14, 1938 and February 1, 1939) PF.

17. To Kenneth Littauer, September 29, 1939, PF; see also to MP, October 20, 1939, SF.
18. Littauer (telegram) to FSF, November 28, 1939 and MP (telegram) to FSF, November 28, 1939, PF; see also Littauer to FSF, October 10, October 19, and November 2, 1939 (all PF) and FSF to MP, November 20, 1939, SF.
19. *Beloved Infidel*, 301.
20. To Arnold Gingrich, February 7, 1940; PF; see also to Gingrich, July 15, 1940, PF.
21. *Esquire*, February, 1941.
22. To FFL, June 12, 1940, PF; see *Beloved Infidel*, 309; to MP, February 21 and May 20, 1940, SF; manuscript draft of "Cosmopoli-

tan" (here called "Honoria") dated May 29, 1940, revised draft, dated August 12, 1940, and letters to Lester Cowan, May 28 to August 16, 1940, PF.
23. Notes for *LT*, PF.
24. To Bill Dozier, November 5 and November 26, 1940, PF; to Arnold Gingrich, November 27, 1940, PF.
25. To MP, May 20, 1940, SF; to EW, November 25, 1940, PF; John O'Hara, "Certain Aspects," *New Republic*, March 3, 1941.
26. To FFL, December 7, 1940, PF; to MP, December 13, 1940, SF.
27. Schedule dated December 14, 1940 in notes for *LT*, PF; to FFL, n.d. (*ca*. December 20, 1940), PF; *Beloved Infidel*, 330.

XV

1. Bennett Cerf, "Tradewinds," *The Saturday Review of Literature*, August 16, 1947.
2. Ms. of the film script, "Cosmopolitan," PF (an early draft is titled "Honoria").
3. To Eddie Knopf, October 26, 1938, PF.
4. Outline of article, "Why Only Ten Percent of the Movies Succeed," submitted to *SEP* by HO with covering letter dated March 18, 1924, OF.
5. V.I. Pudovkin, *On Film Technique* (London, V. Gollancz, 1930), 73.
6. To HO, n.d. (*ca*. February 1936) OF.
7. *Dictionary of American Biography*, *Supplement II* (New York, Charles Scribner's Sons, 1958), 657; Bosley Crowther, *The Lion's Share* (New York, Dutton, 1952), 74 and *passim;* on Thalberg, also see *Time* 27:12, 72 (September 21, 1936), and Allene Talmey, *Doug and Mary and Others* (New York, Macy-Masius, 1927), 165–70.
8. *SSC*, 403, 409, 416, 418.
9. Crowther, *op. cit.*, 239.
10. To C. O. Kalman, September 19, 1936, quoted in *TFSP*, 348; on

Thalberg's attitude toward FSF's movie adaptation of *TITN* see Samuel Marx to FSF, April 24, 1934, OF; on FSF's feelings about Thalberg after his death, see Sheilah Graham and Gerold Frank, *Beloved Infidel* (New York, Henry Holt, 1958), 214–215.
11. To MP, October 16, 1936, SF.
12. To MP, December 24, 1938, PF; Graham and Frank, *Beloved Infidel*, 214.
13. Irving Thalberg and Hugh Weir, "Why Motion Pictures Cost So Much," *SEP*, November 4, 1933, 10; *Fortune* 6:6, 50 (December 1932); FSF to Kenneth Littauer, September 29, 1939, PF.
14. Manuscript draft of letter from FSF to Norma Shearer, PF.
15. Manuscript notes for *LT*, PF.
16. To MP, n.d. (*ca*. May 1926) SF; on FSF's intentions regarding Stahr see long letter from Sheilah Graham to EW, June 11, 1941, PF.
17. *LT*, 134-135.
18. FSF's papers contain numerous lists of books which he read during his Hollywood years (1937-40), among them: Philip Guedalla, *Wellington* (New York, Harper & Bros., 1931);

A.H. Burne, *Lee, Grant and Sherman* (New York, Charles Scribner's Sons, 1939); J.H. Froude's *Caesar: A Study* (New York, Charles Scribner's Sons, 1879). On FSF and Caesar see John O'Hara, *New Republic*, March 3, 1941. Lord Charnwood's *Lincoln* is mentioned in *LT*, 106; the *Lincoln* by John Hay mentioned in one of FSF's reading lists at this time was probably *Lincoln and the Civil War in the Letters and Diaries of John Hay*, selected by Tyler Dennett, (New York, Dodd, Mead, 1939). On Lincoln's executive abilities see J.G. Randall, *Lincoln the President* (New York, Dodd, Mead, 1945) I, 372; II, 229, 247–248, 255, 268.

19. *LT*, 16.
20. *Ibid*, 48–49.
21. New York *World*, interview, April 3, 1927, 12 (magazine).
22. Typed notes for *LT*, PF.
23. *LT*, 30-32, 106; FSF's notes for the scene on pp. 30–32 are in his notebook, PF (Boxley, the novelist, is based on Aldous Huxley according to these notes).
24. E.J. Cassady, "The Business Man in the American Novel," unpublished dissertation, Berkeley, Calif., 1939, 261; on the business man as a literary figure see Miriam Beard, *A History of the Business Man* (New York: Macmillan, 1938) *pas-*

sim; on the American businessman in literature see John Chamberlain, "The Business Man in American Fiction," *Fortune* 35:5,134 November, 1948), an essay which ignores *LT*.

25. Henry James, Preface to *The Reverberator, A Passionate Pilgrim and Other Tales* (New York, Charles Scribner's Sons, 1908) xvii, reprinted in Henry James, *The Art of the Novel*, edited by R.P. Blackmur (New York, Charles Scribner's Sons, 1934); Cassady, *op. cit.*, 183.

26. Eugene Ziller, "The Tycoon as Hero and Myth in American Literature: Cowperwood and Gatsby," unpublished Columbia University M.A. dissertation, February, 1949, 161; *TFSP*, 99.

27. *LT*, 42.
28. To HO, February 8, 1936, regarding request from L.G. Braun of the Paris Opera Ballet corps, for a scenario for a ballet, OF.
29. FSF's comment on West is on a scrap of paper among his notes for *LT*, PF; *LT*, 106.
30. Manuscript notes for *LT;* PF; *LT*, 3.
31. L.C. Rosten, *Hollywood: The Movie Colony, The Movie Makers* (New York, Harcourt, Brace, 1941).
32. To MP, May 22, 1939, PF.

XVI

1. To HO, March 2, 1939, OF; to MP, May 29, 1939, PF; also see Sheilah Graham and Gerold Frank, *Beloved Infidel* (New York, Henry Holt, 1958), 277-8.
2. To MP, May 22, 1939 (the second letter to Perkins is dated May 20, 1940), PF; notes to *LT*, PF; *LT*, 141; to Gerald Murphy, September 14, 1940, PF; see also FSF to Kenneth Littauer, July 18, 1939, in which FSF emphasizes that *LT* will not be like *TITN*, PF.
3. To JPB, April 7, 1934, PF; *LT*, 142-3; notes for *LT*, PF.

4. *LT* outline, among notes, PF; EW to FSF, November 7, 1932, PF.
5. EW to FSF, November 1, 1940, PF.
6. EW, *The Boys In the Back Room: Notes on California Novelists* (San Francisco, Colt Press, 1941); Franklin Walker, "Hollywood in Fiction," *Pacific Spectator* 2:127–33 (Spring, 1948)
7. *LT*, 139.
8. *Ibid.*
9. Note for Chapter VII, *LT*, PF.
10. *LT*, 140; Notes for Episide 14, PF.
11. To Kenneth Littauer, July 25, 1939, PF; Notes for Episode 13, *LT*, PF.

12. To FFL, October 31, 1939, PF.
13. *CU*, 322
14. The notebook is with F's notes and manuscript drafts for *LT*, PF.

15. Notes, Episode 8, *LT*, PF; *LT*, 57–8.
16. *LT*, 108
17. *LT*, 126–7, 118.

XVII

1. *Time*, January 27, 1941, Westbrook Pegler, New York *World Telegram*, December 26, 1940.
2. Alfred Kazin, *F. Scott Fitzgerald: The Man and His Work* (New York, World Publishing Co., 1951).
3. Vernon L. Parrington, *Main Currents in American Thought* (New York, Harcourt, Brace, & Co., 1930), III, 386; Harlan Hatcher, *Creating the Modern American Novel* (New York, Farrar & Rinehart, 1935), 72; Carl Van Doren, *The American Novel* (New York, Macmillan, 1940), 326.
4. G.D. Snell, *Shapers of American Fiction: 1798–1947* (New York, Dutton, 1947), 158; Alexander Cowie, *The Rise of the American Novel* (New York, American Book Co., 1948), 747; Joseph Warren Beach, *American Fiction* (New York, Macmillan, 1941).
5. H.S. Commager and S.E. Morison, *Growth of the American Republic*, 3rd. edition, revised and enlarged (New York, Oxford, 1942), II, 568; Alfred Kazin, *F. Scott Fitzgerald: The Man and His Work* (New York, World Publishing Co., 1951); Scribner's 1940 Catalogue; *Publisher's Trade List Annual* for 1940, 1941 (The Scribner 1941 Catalogue listed seven of FSF's works); *TFSP*, 299.
6. *CU*, 310 (see also T.S. Eliot to John Hall Wheelock, October 31, 1933, SF); O'Hara to HDP, conversation, February 26, 1950; HDP, "Fitzgerald, Mark Twain and Thomas Hardy," *Fitzgerald Newsletter* #8 (Winter, 1960); Buddy Glass, the narrator in J.D. Salinger's story "Zooey" makes this remark, and I have indentified Buddy with the author, *The New Yorker*, May

4, 1957; on Styron's debt to FSF see Richard Forester, "An Orgy of Commerce," *Critique*, 3:3,59–70 (Summer, 1960).
7. *TLS*, January 24, 1958, 41; on the Bodley Head edition of FSF's works see *TLS*, October 17, 1958, 592, and November 27, 1959, 695.
8. The Wilson essay was reprinted in *The Literary Spotlight*, edited by John Farrar (New York, George H. Doran Co., 1924), 125–34; Alfred Kazin, *On Native Grounds* (New York, Reynal & Hitchcock, 1942), 77 (quoting EW) and 179; Glenway Wescott, *CU*, 329; Malcolm Cowley, *SSC* xvi; *TFSP*, 103; Perry Miller, *Nation* 173:17, 356–57 (October 27, 1951); for similar criticisms of FSF's thought see L. and M. Gurko *College English* 5, 372–76 (April 1949) and A.J. Lubell *South Atlantic Quarterly* 54, 96–106 (January, 1955).
9. A. Gide, *The Counterfeiters* (New York, Knopf, 1927), 175; FSF's copy of *Point Counterpoint* is at Princeton.
10. On FSF's views regarding his own intellectual abilities see his letter to Ernest Boyd, n.d. (*ca.* 1922) PF ("I have so little general culture that my opinions wouldn't be of the slightest value"), and his unpublished manuscript, "How I would Grade My Knowledge at 40," PF; notes for *LT*, PF.
11. EW, *The Triple Thinkers*, revised edition (New York, Harcourt, Brace, & Co., 1948), 178.
12. Rainer Maria Rilke, *Letters to a Young Poet* (New York, W.W. Norton & Co., 1934), 17.
13. J.W. Krutch, *The Modern Temper* (New York, Harcourt, Brace & Co., 1929), 119.

14. To FFL, November 17, 1936; *CU*, 306.

15. A short, pioneer examination of FSF's Catholicism is H.W. Hausermann, "Fitzgerald's Religious Sense," *Modern Fiction Studies* 2, 81–82 (1956).

16. *CU*, 199–200; to John O'Hara, July 25, 1936, PF.

17. Carbon of statement on Mark Twain prepared for Cyril Clemens, PF; see HDP, "Fitzgerald, Mark Twain and Thomas Hardy," *Fitzgerald Newsletter* #8 (Winter, 1960).

18. Ernest Hemingway, *The Green Hills of Africa* (New York, Charles Scribner's Sons., 1935) 22; FSF's copy of Joyce's *Dubliners* is at Princeton.

19. To Shane Leslie, May 24, 1921; to Mrs Bayard Turnbull, n.d. (*ca.* June, 1935); to Mabel Dodge Luhan, May 10, 1934–all PF.

20. To MP, July 30, 1934, PF; on certain aspects of FSF's debt to Keats see R.L. Schoenwald, "F. Scott Fitzgerald as John Keats," *Boston University Studies* in English 3:1, 12–21 (Spring, 1957).

21. *TITN*, 288; Carlos Baker, *Hemingway: The Writer as Artist* (Princeton University Press, 1952), 49; Hemingway to FSF, July 1 (1925?), PF.

22. To Gerald Murphy, March 11, 1938, PF.

23. *CU*, 122; New York *World*, April 3, 1927, 12 (magazine).

24. *CU*, 208.

Index

Switzerland, 169, 183
Swope, Herbert, 102

Tales of the Jazz Age, 77–79, 97, 98
Talmadge, Constance, 161, 162
Taney, Roger Brooke, 6
Taps at Reveille, 231, 234
Tarkington, Booth, 15, 18, 24, 36, 48, 173
"Tarquin of Cheapside," 30
Tate, Allen, 183
Taylor, "Ceci," 102, 183, 242, 248
Taylor, Deems, 102
Taylor, Robert, 246, 247
Teapot Dome scandal, 96, 99
Tender Is the Night, 8, 11, 12, 158, 172, 174, 175, 178, 184, 190, 191, 192, 204, 205–28, 229, 230, 231, 237, 239, 240, 258, 264, 277, 278, 282, 284, 286, 289, 290–91, 295, 297
Thackeray, W. M., 132
Thalberg, Irving, 167, 245, 246, 249, 261–68, 269, 273, 277, 285, 291
This Side of Paradise, 14, 23, 24, 25, 27, 28, 30, 34, 36, 37–63, 64, 68, 76, 79, 83, 84, 86, 89, 91, 93, 110, 111, 122, 125, 131, 136–37, 193, 227, 233, 241, 247, 252, 287, 288, 293
Thompson, Colonel William Boyce, 38
"Thoughtbook," 29, 30, 53, 58, 83
Three Comrades (Remarque), 246–47, 260
Time (magazine), 287
Tocqueville, Alexis de, 59
Tolstoy, Leo, 25, 47
Train, Arthur, 173
Trilling, Lionel, 289
Troy, William, 93
Truex, Ernest, 95
Tryon, North Carolina, 232, 234–35, 236
Turnbull, Mrs. Bayard, 235, 297
Twain, Mark, 35, 296–97
Twentieth-Century Fox, 256
"Two for a Cent," 80
"Two Wrongs," 174–75

United Artists, 161, 245, 282
Universal Pictures, 261

Vanderbilt, Cornelius, 181
Vanderbilt, Gertrude, 115
Van Doren, Carl, 288
Van Dyke, Henry, 24
Van Vechten, Carl, 163
"Variety," 65
Vegetable, The, 76, 87, 94–99, 100, 103, 124

Walker, Franklin, 280
Walker, Jimmy, 120
Walker, Stanley, 118
Walpole, Hugh, 43, 50, 102
Wanger, Walter, 249–50, 275
Warner, H. B., 17
Warner Brothers, 160
Warren, Robert Penn, 69, 132, 183
Wells, H. G., 43, 48, 50, 51, 58, 82–83, 84
West, Nathanael, 225, 274, 289
Westport, Connecticut, 84, 87
Wharton, Edith, 45, 61, 127, 129, 135, 271
Wheeler, C. N. B., 14
Wheelock, John Hall, 257
White Bear Lake, 19
Whitman, Walt, 25
Whipple, T. K., 24, 44–45
Whittington, Sir Richard, 123
"Why Only Ten Percent of Movies Succeed," 260, 275
Wilde, Oscar, 24, 47, 87
Wilder, Thornton, 163, 183, 289
Williams, Blanche Colton, 80
Williams, Emlyn, 256
Williams, Jesse Lynch, 22
Wilmington ("Ellerslie"), Delaware, 162–63, 180
Wilson, Edmund, Jr., 20, 24, 25, 27, 37, 45, 48, 51, 62, 77, 80, 83, 86, 87, 95, 97–98, 111, 127, 130, 172, 206, 208, 234, 256, 279–80, 289, 290, 291
Wilson, Woodrow, 24, 38, 60
"Winter Carnival," 249
"Winter Dreams," 79, 80, 101, 102